Home–School Relations

SECOND EDITION

Home–School Relations

Working Successfully with Parents and Families

Glenn Olsen
University of North Dakota

Mary Lou Fuller
University of North Dakota, Emeritus

Boston   New York   San Francisco
Mexico City   Montreal   Toronto   London   Madrid   Munich   Paris
Hong Kong   Singapore   Tokyo   Cape Town   Sydney

Series Editor: *Traci Mueller*
Editorial Assistant: *Erica Tromblay*
Senior Marketing Manager: *Elizabeth Fogarty*
Editorial-Production Service: *Omegatype Typography, Inc.*
Composition Buyer: *Linda Cox*
Manufacturing Buyer: *Andrew Turso*
Cover Administrator: *Kristina Mose-Libon*
Electronic Composition: *Omegatype Typography, Inc.*

For related titles and support material, visit our online catalog at www.ablongman.com.

Between the time Website information is gathered and then published, it is not unusual for some sites to have closed. Also, the transcription of URLs can result in typographical errors. The publisher would appreciate notification where these occur so that they may be corrected in subsequent editions.

Library of Congress Cataloging-in-Publication Data

Home–school relations : working successfully with parents and families / [edited by] Glenn Olsen, Mary Lou Fuller.—[2nd ed.].
    p. cm.
  Includes bibliographical references and index.
  ISBN 0-205-36772-0
    1. Home and school—United States—Case studies. 2. Parent–teacher relationships—United States—Case studies. 3. Early childhood education—Parent participation—United States—Case studies. 4. Special education—Parent participation—United States—Case studies. I. Olsen, Glenn W. (Glenn William) II. Fuller, Mary Lou.

LC225.3 .H65 2003
371.19'2—dc21

                    2002026144

Printed in the United States of America

10   9   8   7   6   5   4   3   2   1   07   06   05   04   03   02

To my wife, Barbara Hager-Olsen;
our three daughters, Sarah, Ann, and Becca;
and my parents, Helen May and Kermit Olsen.
My parents provided the early inspiration to continue learning
and to pursue teaching and writing.

—Glenn Olsen

To my parents, husband, children, and grandchildren
for all of the lessons they have taught me, the love they have given,
and the joy they have provided. Thank you.

—Mary Lou Fuller

CONTENTS

Foreword   xv

Preface   xvii

About the Authors   xxi

1 An Introduction to Families   1
Mary Lou Fuller and Glenn Olsen

Defining "Family" and Determining Family Responsibilities   3

Families, Their Children, and Teachers   4

Changing World, Changing Families   4

Home–School Relations in the Past   5

Looking at Families   6

Parent Involvement   10

References   11

2 Families and Their Functions— Past and Present   12
Mary Lou Fuller and Carol Marxen

The Evolution of the Family   13

Contemporary U.S. Families   22

Patterns of Marriage, Divorce, and Remarriage   25

Functional Families   32

Dysfunctional Families   34

Summary   35

Recommended Activities   35

Additional Resources   36

References   42

3 Diversity among Families   44
Ivan E. Watts and Sandra Winn Tutwiler

The Changing Family   45

Family Structure   46

Alternative Family Structures   47

Ethnic and Cultural Diversity   49

African American Families   51

Asian American Families   54

Latino Families   56

Native American Families   57

Religious Diversity   59

Summary   60

Recommended Activities   61

Additional Resources   61

References   69

4   Parents' Perspectives on Parenting   71
Karen W. Zimmerman

Becoming a Parent   72

Parenting Styles   74

Parenting Behaviors in Diverse Family Structures   76

Single-Parent Families   79

Divorced Noncustodial Fathers and Mothers   81

Stepparent Families   82

Rewards and Satisfactions of Parenthood   85

Summary   86

Recommended Activities   87

Additional Resources   87

References   89

5   Teachers and Parenting   92
Judith B. MacDonald

Teaching and Parenting   94

Teachers' Perspectives on Parents   96

Parents' Perspectives on Teachers and Schools   102

Summary   107

Recommended Activities   107

Additional Resources   108

References   110

6 Parent–Teacher Communication: Who's Talking?   111

Sara Fritzell Hanhan

Building a Coequal Relationship   113

Barriers to Two-Way Communication   114

Aids to Two-Way Communication   117

Initial Communication   118

Regular Communication   119

Written Communication   120

Parent–Teacher Conferences   122

Communication with Parents of Middle School Students   124

Other Ways of Communicating on a Regular Basis   127

Communication on Special Occasions   128

Summary   131

Recommended Activities   131

Additional Resources   132

References   133

7 Parent Involvement in Education   134

Soo-Yin Lim

Defining Parent Involvement   135

The Benefits of Parent Involvement: What Research Has to Say   136

Six Types of Parent Involvement   137

Foundations of Facilitating a Meaningful Parent Involvement   150

Recommended Activities   154

Additional Resources   154

References   157

8 Families and Their Children with Disabilities   159
AmySue Reilly

Historical Perspective   161

Number of Children Receiving Special Educational Services   163

Federal Special Education Laws and Legislation   163

Family Systems   167

Summary   174

Additional Resources   174

References   178

9 Family-Involvement Models   182

Family Involvement in Special Education   183
Mary McLean and Margaret Shaeffer

A Family Systems Conceptual Framework   184

Family-Centered Intervention   185

Family-Involvement Models in Early Childhood Education   189
Soo-Yin Lim

Head Start   189

Early Head Start   191

Title I/Even Start   192

National Association for the Education
of Young Children (NAEYC)   192

Minnesota Early Childhood Family Education (ECFE)   193

AVANCE   195

Parent and Child Education (PACE)   195

Summary   196

Family-Involvement Models in Elementary Education   196
Marci Glessner

Teachers Involve Parents in Schoolwork (TIPS)   197

MegaSkills   198

Center for the Improvement of Child Caring (CICC)   198

National Network of Partnership Schools   199

School Development Program (SDP)   200

Summary   200

Family-Involvement Models in Middle Schools   201
J. Howard Johnston and Aimee Fogelman

The Outcomes of Involvement   201

Impediments to Family Involvement   203

A Model for Family Involvement   206

Contextual Considerations   210

Engaging Culturally Diverse Parents   210

The Model in Operation   211

Supporting Parent Involvement and Securing Assistance
for the School   213

What Advice Can We Give Parents?   214

Summary   215

Recommended Activities   215

Additional Resources   216

References   218

10 Education Law and Parental Rights   220

Gloria Jean Thomas

History of the Legal Relationship between Parents
and Schools   221

State Constitutions and Education   223

State Legislatures and Education   224

State and Federal Courts and Education   225

Summary   247

Recommended Activities   247

Additional Resources   248

References   248

11 Family Violence   250

Tara Lea Muhlhauser and Douglas D. Knowlton

Child Abuse and Neglect   253

Domestic Violence   260

Recommendations for Action   265

Recommended Activities   268

Additional Resources   269

References   271

12 Poverty   273

Mary Lou Fuller

What Is Poverty?   274

Myths about Poverty   276

The Effects of Poverty   277

Schools and Families of Poverty   279

Working with Low-Income Families   282

Suggestions for Working with Low-Income Parents   282

Summary   285

Recommended Activities   286

Additional Resources   286

References   289

13 Fatherhood, Society, and School   290

Charles B. Hennon, Glenn Olsen, and Glen Palm

Basic Premises   292

Fatherhood in Context   294

Conduct of Fathering   297

Understanding Fathering   301

Fathering and School Achievement   302

Benefits of Involving Fathers in Schools   304

Society-Level Interventions   306

Community-Level Interventions   307

Parent Education   309

Fathers' Involvement with Schools   309

Family-Level Interventions   312

Summary   314

Recommended Activities   315

Notes   316

Additional Resources   316

References   320

14 School Choices in Education   324
Joe Nathan

Four Features of School Choice Programs   325

Rationale   326

Brief Historical Background   326

Vouchers   327

Home-Schooling   329

Magnet Schools   330

Schools within Schools   331

New Small Schools   333

The Charter School Movement   335

Post-Secondary Options   338

Sharing Facilities   338

Summary   339

Recommended Activities   339

Additional Resources   340

References   341

15 School Violence and Bullying   342
John H. Hoover, Mary Beth Noll, and Glenn Olsen

School Violence   343

Bullying and Violence   344

Basic Bullying Information   345

Adjustment Problems Associated with Bullying   347

Family Interaction Patterns Affecting the Bullying
and Victimization of Children   348

Social Cognitive Schemes: A Way for Educators to Understand
the Role of Families in Bullying and Victimization   349

Home–School Relations and Bullying: What Educators
and Future Educators Should Know   351

Summary   356

Recommended Activities   357

Additional Resources   358

References   360

Index   363

FOREWORD

Home–School Relations: Working Successfully with Parents and Families is a thoughtful guide to more productive relationships between parents and teachers, homes and schools. It begins with the premise that parents are their children's first and most important teachers, and further, that the dispositions, language, values, and cultural understandings that help guide children and young people are learned most fully within families (and, importantly, this book makes the conception of families inclusive of the many child-nurturing arrangements that exist).

While those in schools often say that they value active parent participation, parents are not always treated as full partners. They typically don't learn enough about what their children will be learning in school, how their children's growth as learners will be assured, what special efforts will be made to support their children if they begin to struggle academically or socially or how they, as parents, can be most helpful to their children's academic learning beyond school. They need all of this information if they are to be the full partners they want to be.

Sometimes, the messages that come to parents about the foregoing are not in their languages. At other times, those in schools suggest times for meetings that are in conflict with other family-related commitments. Moreover, when parent conferences occur, they are scheduled most often for a short time period, the teachers do most of the talking, the child is most often absent. It is an exchange teachers in most schools don't look forward to with great enthusiasm. And parents don't often come expecting to learn very much. Such conditions need to change. If the schools do not actively acknowledge and encourage a strong partnership role for parents, children's education will be limited, not as intense, as full, as it needs to be.

How does a productive partnership get constructed? What do teachers need to know to be a part of the construction? This book provides a useful map—an inspiring guide—that grows out of a set of solid commitments to parents as well as to the preparation of teachers able to extend themselves on behalf of parents. I suggest "able to" because I understand that the desire to involve parents is insufficient. Knowledge of how to proceed, the realities of family life across cultures, and skills are also needed. This book provides that kind of assistance.

The editors and contributors to *Home–School Relations* are people with experience as classroom teachers, parents, and teacher educators. They use that experience well, providing numerous examples of productive home–school interchange. It is important to note that little attention has been placed on home–school relations in teacher education programs, in part because there hasn't been much credible literature. This book fills a large share of that void. It helps change the landscape, placing before us a vision of what is possible when teachers and parents work closely together. I am pleased the editors and contributors are sharing their work with the educational community and with parents.

Vito Perrone
Harvard Graduate School of Education

PREFACE

In order to be effective as educators, we must understand the families from which our students come and the opportunity and encouragement they receive to develop the skills necessary in creating positive working relationships. This book examines the nature of the contemporary family—what it looks like, how it functions, and its relationship to the schools. This includes the important related topics of diversity (cultural, racial, religious, sexual orientation) and the effects of income on families. To understand a family you must understand diversity. This book also includes topics that have been neglected by other work in the field, such as fathers' roles, school choices, poverty, and parents' perspectives of schools, in order to help educators better understand the complexities of home–school relations.

In addition to providing the reader with an understanding of what families look like and how they function, this book is highly practical. It provides descriptions of successful parent-involvement programs, has an excellent chapter dealing with communication skills and activities (newsletters, conferences, etc.), and provides the reader with much-needed information about family violence. Also, with the incorporation of students with special needs into the classroom, many teachers find they have not been prepared to work with the parents of these students. This text will be very useful to these teachers. Other chapters help educators understand the important and neglected areas of the legal and policy aspects of home–school relations, school violence and bullying, and school choices.

Students

The organization of this book is based on the principles of good learning. First and foremost, the learners are actively involved in their own learning. Objectives are presented at the beginning of each chapter, allowing an overview of the material; there are also exercises throughout each chapter to help the readers reflect on the material they have read. Finally, there are lists of resources at the end of each chapter that allow students to further pursue any of the topics that were addressed in the chapter.

Faculty

College faculty have many demands on their time; this text has been designed to be as helpful to the teacher as possible. At the end of most chapters there are suggestions for activities designed to help make the class interactive, reflective, and stimulating.

This text employs the Internet as a teaching tool and provides World Wide Web addresses to help students get started. There are also lists of articles, books, and videos that can be used as class resources for assignments or as resources for students' pursuit of their personal interests.

Important Features

Diversity

A chapter is devoted to diversity (cultural/racial, economic, religious, as well as family structure). Diversity is not only addressed in this single chapter, but is also woven throughout the book. This is of particular importance because most pre-service teachers come from white, middle-class backgrounds. Most have had little meaningful interaction with families that differ from theirs.

Poverty

There is a chapter on the effects of poverty on the family. No other book that we reviewed looks at this important topic, even though the statistics are surprising: 16 percent of all children live below the poverty line, and of those, 21 percent are children six and under. Economic status has a tremendous effect on the academic performance of children, yet this subject is often ignored.

Voice of the Parent

Generally the voices of parents are missing from books of this nature. This book not only includes parents' perspectives on parenting, but also their feelings about their relationships with the schools and educators.

Families of Children with Special Needs

Students with special needs were at one time the exclusive domain of special education programs. However, with the widespread movement of classroom inclusion, teachers must have an understanding of working with the parents of children with special needs.

Fathers' Roles

Fathers are generally only footnotes in educational literature. It is important to understand the father and his role if we are to understand the family in totality.

School Choices

Parents have more educational choices now than in the past. Some families choose to send their children to private schools or to unique programs within the public schools. Many school choice options are examined.

Bullying and School Violence

Teasing and bullying are frequently discussed in connection with school violence. These topics have become important issues within the school environment. These authors also give suggestions for ways to stem bullying and school violence.

We hope that you will find this book to be thorough, thought-provoking, current, and practical. We designed this book because we grew frustrated with the limited available material, particularly on some topics. We are very happy with the results, and hope you will be too. Please feel free to contact us if you have questions or comments about the book. We would love to hear about your successes so we can pass them on to other teachers.

Glenn Olsen, Ph.D.
Professor
Teaching & Learning Dept.
University of North Dakota
Grand Forks, North Dakota 58202-7189
Phone: 701-777-3145
Email: *glenn_olsen@mail.und.nodak.edu*

Mary Lou Fuller, Ph.D.
Professor Emeritus
Chester Fritz Distinguished Professor
Rose Isabel Kelly Endowed Chair
1548 N. Sunset Blvd.
Safford, Arizona 85546
Phone: 928-348-4865
Email: *mary_fuller@und.nodak.edu*

Acknowledgments

We would like to thank a number of people who helped us compile this book. Librarian Owen Williams, University of Minnesota, Crookston, was a tremendous help in finding critical information. The fifteen young artists who did the drawings on the first page of every chapter made the book more personal. Thank you to Suzanne St. Michell who came through for us at the last minute to help with proofing and typing. We also want to thank Phyllis LeDosquet and Marci Glessner, University of North Dakota, for their assistance with this manuscript. A special thanks to the University of North Dakota writing group, including Libbey Rankin, who helped motivate me to start and finish this project. Finally, we would like to thank the reviewers of this edition: Linda Cundiff, University of Tennessee at Chattanooga; Dr. Kay Halverson, Florida Gulf Coast University; and Maria Elena Halverson, University of Alaska–Fairbanks.

ABOUT THE AUTHORS

Editors

Mary Lou Fuller is a Professor Emeritus and a Chester Fritz Distinguished Professor in the Department of Teaching and Learning in the College of Education and Human Development at the University of North Dakota. She is currently an adjunct professor at Northern Arizona University–Thatcher. She has been a school psychologist and a classroom teacher in the primary grades and for Head Start. She has co-authored two books, *The Adult Learner on Campus* and *Teaching Hispanic Children*, written many chapters for other books, and written over thirty articles. Her areas of research include the family, multicultural education, the adult learner, and home–school relations.

Glenn Olsen is a professor in the Department of Teaching and Learning at the University of North Dakota. His Ph.D. is from the University of Wisconsin–Madison. He has taught at community and technical colleges in Minnesota and Wisconsin. He has coauthored one book, *Teasing and Harassment: The Frames and Scripts Approach for Teachers and Parents*, and has edited another book. He is president elect of the North Dakota Association for the Education of Young Children. In addition to the two books, he has published over twenty articles during his twenty-three years in higher education. His research interests include teasing, bullying, and school violence, multicultural education, fathering, and leadership. Dr. Olsen gives state and local presentations on bullying and school violence. Dr. Olsen is on his local school board and has three teenage daughters ranging in age from 15–18.

Contributing Authors

Aimee L. Fogelman is currently a doctoral student in the Department of Secondary Education at the University of South Florida. Her research explores the improvement of the home–school connection, global child advocacy, and literacy learning in multiple contexts.

Marci Glessner is a faculty member in the Department of Teaching and Learning at the University of North Dakota where she teaches graduate and undergraduate classes in literacy. She has taught in elementary classrooms, as well as provided workshops for teachers, administrators, and parents in North Dakota and Minnesota. Her research interests include emergent readers and writers, but are mostly related to working with her three young children Sophie, Lucy, and John.

Sara Fritzell Hanhan is an associate professor of early childhood education and associate provost at the University of North Dakota. She has been teaching undergraduate and graduate courses, including courses in home–school relations, since 1980. In addition to advocating for a strong presence of parent voices in schools, she is interested in ways of documenting the work that teachers, children, and families do in those schools. She is on the board of the National Association for the Education of Young Children (NAEYC). Her most stable interest, however, is her family, which includes a new grandson, Anders.

Charles B. Hennon is a professor in the Department of Family Studies and Social Work and is the director of the Family and Child Studies Center at Miami University, Oxford, Ohio. Previously, Dr. Hennon was a professor of child and family studies at the University of Wisconsin–Madison. His areas of specialization include rural families, the allocation of resources to various family roles, and family stress and its effective management. He is the founding editor of the *Journal of Family and Economic Issues,* has edited or authored five books, and has written over fifty journal articles and book chapters.

John H. Hoover is a professor of special education at St. Cloud State University, Minnesota. His academic interests are mental retardation, child-on-child aggression (including teasing, bullying, and school violence), and secondary education for students with disabilities. He has written more than fifty articles or book chapters and gives national presentations on bullying and school violence. He is married to Elizabeth Weber Hoover and has three children, Amelia, Ray, and Donny.

J. Howard Johnston is a professor of secondary education at the University of South Florida. Until 1990, he served as professor of curriculum and instruction at the University of Cincinnati, where he has also served as dean of the Graduate School of Education and acting dean of the College of Education. Dr. Johnston is a well-established author, lecturer, and researcher. He has written over 100 works on middle-level education and has presented over 500 invited papers and lectures in the United States, Canada, the Caribbean, Europe, and Asia. Two of his most recent books, *The New American Family and the School* (1990) and *Teaching Disadvantaged, At-Risk Youth* (1992), reflect his interest in the changing nature of the American population and the need to structure schools for success.

Douglas D. Knowlton is currently the vice chancellor for academic affairs at the University of Minnesota, Crookston. He previously held a position as an associate professor in the special education program in the Teaching and Learning Department at the University of North Dakota. He is a licensed clinical psychologist and was in private practice at the Family Institute in Grand Forks, North Dakota.

Soo-Yin Lim is an assistant professor in the Early Childhood Education Department at the University of Minnesota, Crookston. She has been at that institution for over fifteen years, and prior to full-time teaching was the director of the University of Minnesota, Crookston, Child Development Center. She has been active in local and state early childhood education associations. Her current research interests include the use of technology and student learning in teacher education and international early childhood education issues.

Judith B. MacDonald is an associate professor in the Department for Curriculum and Instruction at Montclair State University. Her research interests have focused on the reciprocal effects of being a teacher and a parent. She has recently studied the effects of motherhood on prospective teachers.

Carol Marxen is an associate professor of education at the University of Minnesota–Morris. She is active as a teacher, researcher, and writer. She has written numerous articles and book chapters. She is currently serving on a national multicultural board for the American Association of Teacher Education. Her primary area of expertise is early childhood education.

Mary McLean is currently professor and chair of the Graduate Department of Exceptional Education at the University of Wisconsin–Milwaukee. Before moving to Milwaukee, Dr. McLean directed programs in early childhood special education at Auburn University and the University of North Dakota. She is the former president of the division for early childhood of the Council for Exceptional Children.

Tara Lea Muhlhauser is the assistant dean at the University of North Dakota School of Law and the former director of the Children and Family Services Training Center at the University of North Dakota. She is currently an adjunct member in the Department of Social Work and the School of Law. She is a licensed social worker and attorney, specializing in child welfare, family law, children's rights, and family violence issues.

Joe Nathan directs the Center for School Change at the University of Minnesota's Humphrey Institute of Public Affairs. A former inner-city public school teacher and administrator, he has won awards for his work from student, family, and professional groups. He has written four books, and since 1989, has written a weekly column published by four major daily newspapers in Minnesota. He also has written guest columns for *USA Today, Wall Street Journal, Atlanta Constitution, Detroit News,* and the *Philadelphia Inquirer.* Twenty-two state legislatures and eight congressional committees have invited him to testify. He is married to an urban public school teacher, and has been a PTA president. Nathan's three children have all attended urban public schools.

Mary Beth Noll is currently the chairperson of the Special Education Department at St. Cloud State University, Minnesota. Her primary interest is in working with the families of students with emotional and behavioral disorders. Dr. Noll holds bachelor's, master's, and doctoral degrees from the University of Kansas at Lawrence. Dr. Noll worked for over twelve years as a behavior support specialist and teacher of behaviorally disordered children in the Shawnee Mission Kansas public schools.

Glen Palm is a professor of child and family studies at St. Cloud State University, Minnesota, where he teaches courses in child development and parent education. He also coordinates the parent education program at SCSU. He is a parent educator in the St. Cloud early childhood family education program where he has taught parent education classes for fathers for twelve years. Dr. Palm was co-editor of the book, *Working with Fathers: Methods and Perspectives,* and writes a regular column for Family Information Services on working with fathers. He is also the father of three children ages 9–18.

AmySue Reilly is an assistant professor at Auburn University. She received her Ph.D. from the University of New Mexico. Dr. Reilly is codirector of Project AIM (Auburn Intervention Model), an early intervention program for very young children and their families. Currently, she is the project director of a U.S. Department of Education project that helps prepare professionals to work in the field of early childhood special education.

Margaret (Peggy) Shaeffer is an associate professor in the Department of Teaching and Learning at the University of North Dakota and also serves as the director of teacher education. Prior to joining the faculty at the University of North Dakota, she was on the faculty at the University of Wyoming in Laramie. She has worked with young children with disabilities and their families in Minnesota and Wyoming public and private schools. She teaches graduate-level classes in early childhood special education and her research interests are in the development of interdisciplinary programs for the preparation of professionals in early intervention.

Gloria Jean Thomas is an adjunct professor of educational leadership and a member of the graduate faculty at Idaho State University in Pocatello. She teaches public school and higher education administration courses. Her Ph.D. is from Brigham Young University, where she specialized in school law. She has had many articles published on school law, the principalship, and rural schools, and is the lead author of *The Law and Teacher Employment*.

Sandra Winn Tutwiler is a professor and the Education Department chair at Washburn University in Topeka, Kansas. She previously taught at Hamline University in St. Paul, Minnesota. She has also been a teacher and a counselor in elementary school, middle school, high school, and community college settings. Her research interests include school and family relations and the impact of education experiences on the quality of life for African American girls and women. She is currently working on an anthology of mothering experiences among women of color.

Ivan E. Watts is currently an assistant professor in educational foundations, leadership, and technology at Auburn University, Alabama. He received an Ed.D. in Educational Foundations from the University of Cincinnati in 1998, and has a M.S. in Policy Studies from the State University of New York at Buffalo. His bachelor's degree is from Ohio State University in criminal justice. Dr. Watts teaches courses at Auburn University in the areas of cultural foundations, sociology of education, and philosophy of education. His scholarly interests include youth/school violence in the context of structural violence and desegregation. He is coauthor of the chapter "Desegregation" in *Knowledge and Power in the Global Economy*.

Karen W. Zimmerman is a professor in the Human Development, Family Living, and Community Educational Services Department at the University of Wisconsin–Stout. She received her Ph.D. in family environment and family and consumer sciences education from Iowa State University. She teaches courses in child development, parent education, family life issues, and family and consumer education curriculum evaluation. She is the graduate program director in home economics.

Home–School Relations

1

An Introduction to Families

MARY LOU FULLER

Professor Emeritus
University of North Dakota

GLENN OLSEN

University of North Dakota

This chapter provides the background information to help you realize the benefits of understanding families—how you, your students, and your students' families will benefit, and how you will become a more effective educator. More specifically, this chapter will help you consider:

- The purpose and behaviors of families
- The need for families to protect their children
- The need to socialize children into the familial culture
- The teacher's role
- Home–school relations of the past
- The changing family

The job of an educator is much more complicated today than it was in the past. Not only must educators understand the issues traditionally embodied in the subject matter of home–school relations, but they also must view families in a sociological and educational framework in order to understand how they function. Only by doing so can teachers work with students' families in the most effective manner.

As always, teachers must conduct parent–teacher conferences and understand various parent involvement models—pre-school, elementary, middle school, as well as models for parents of students with special needs. Now, however, we also must know about changes in contemporary families and their effect on the ways that families function. We must understand how families are influenced by cultural backgrounds, financial resources (or lack thereof), and the changing roles of parents. Students may be from homes headed by single parents, foster parents, grandparents, or gay/lesbian parents; the family may practice a nontraditional religion or speak a language other than English in the home; the family may be "intact" or "blended." The variation in family types seems innumerable. The greater responsibilities that come with a more diverse group of families make it imperative that teachers go beyond classroom walls to understand the relationship between families and schools.

Teachers must also be aware of ways in which education can be influential in supporting families. This involves understanding and using public policy, advocacy, and the laws that pertain to the issues involving families and schools. Without this knowledge, teachers can react only to the needs of individual students and their families, when it would be of more benefit to provide broad support for a greater number of families.

Defining "Family" and Determining Family Responsibilities

The U.S. Bureau of the Census (2000) defines a family as two or more persons related by birth, marriage, or adoption who reside in the same household. This is a legal definition, relying solely on relationships determined by blood or contract. In contrast, the sociological definition of families considers the way that families function. Though not a sociologist, a second-grader developed a sociological definition when he observed, "A family is people who live together who help and love each other."

The second-grader took the important step of focusing on what families do as opposed to how they look. Families, for example, do two important things for children: protect them from a range of harmful influences, and prepare them to function within their cultures (that is, society). Whether we look at pre-Colombian Mayan families in Central America, Chinese families of the Ming Dynasty, contemporary Buddhist families of Thailand, or middle-class families in Houston, the primary purpose of these families was and is the same—to protect and prepare their children. What makes these families different is the everyday conditions they face and the manner in which they accomplish these similar goals.

Protecting Children from Danger

The nature of danger differs over time and with location. While prehistoric Aleutian parents feared saber-toothed tigers and parents of Dickens's industrialized England were concerned about their children working long hours in unhealthy environments, contemporary U.S. parents worry about their children's exposure to sex and violence in the media and on the Internet. Furthermore, parents in all times and places were, and remain, concerned about their children's health, nutrition, and safety. Again, what has changed is not the function of the family, but rather the nature of the dangers and the character of the society in which parents must prepare their children to live.

While families in the past worked hard to ensure their children's health and physical survival, contemporary parents can generally expect their children to survive and grow to maturity. Today parents often include in their concerns their children's emotional health.

Preparing Children for Society

How did you learn the proper way to act in a place of worship, in a museum, at a party, or at a family reunion? Although there usually is no formal instruction in these areas, most people know exactly what is expected of them, and behave accordingly. As children, we learned these skills through parental guidance and through observing members of our families and others as they interacted in various societal settings. Anthropologists refer to this learning as *enculturation*—the process by which a family and/or society prepares children to behave appropriately and appreciate their cultural values and traditions. Enculturation ensures that people in a given society understand and can interact appropriately with others within their society.

Families, Their Children, and Teachers

Stated simply, families strive to provide safe, nurturing environments in which children can learn to function in society. When most families lived in isolated rural areas, this socialization occurred predominantly under parental supervision. As the family was much more an isolated unit, these parents also played the roles of teachers, doctors, psychologists, and spiritual leaders for their children. Families continued to protect and nurture children as society became more industrialized and complex; however, this increasing complexity meant that parents found it more difficult to be totally responsible for all of their children's needs. Teachers, physicians, ministers, social workers, and institutions such as schools, public health services, churches, synagogues, community social services, and others began to play greater roles in the upbringing of children. Although schools assumed more of the educational responsibilities, families continued to be the first and most important teachers of children, because it is through families that children learn how to live in their worlds.

Teachers now have some responsibilities that have historically been within the parents' domain. Teachers have taken on the responsibility of educating because it requires skill and knowledge beyond that which can be reasonably expected of lay people in contemporary society. Even if parents have the skill and knowledge needed to handle these responsibilities, they may not have the time to provide a formal education for their children. The result is that educators' skills and knowledge complement and overlap those of the family.

If teachers' professional efforts are to complement those of parents, they need to have a better understanding of families and how they function. Henderson's research (1987) provides the rationale for this need: First, because educators' efforts at school correspond with those of the parents in the students' homes, educators need to know about their students' families to be maximally effective. Second, by understanding those responsible for children at home, educators can work with parents to help children to be safe and move comfortably into society. And third, this understanding will help to produce better teachers.

Changing World, Changing Families

Schools are changing, families are changing, and society as a whole is changing. It hasn't been that long since you started communicating with others using email or your cellular phone. You probably use a computer rather than a typewriter, a microwave instead of a stove, watch movies on your VCR or DVD player rather than in a theater, and withdraw money from an ATM or use a debit card instead of writing a check.

Schools have also changed. There are computers in the classroom. Children make use of the Internet and interactive television. Changes have also occurred in the cafeteria, which now includes salad bars and specialty foods. Yet, in spite of these changes, schools are still often viewed as fixed and unchanging institutions. The cardboard replica of the red, one-room schoolhouse with a bell tower—which is often found on classroom bulletin boards in September—is as much like the schools of today as a No. 2 pencil is like a word processor.

Schools also reflect the changes in the demographics of our society, changes including, but not limited to, the structure of the family, available economic resources and what those resources will (and will not) purchase. All of these changes—technological, societal, demographic—are reflected in the demands placed on families. Although families have always been under a certain amount of pressure, the nature of this stress seems to have changed and, in the process, increased significantly. Evidence of the changes can be seen with increased incidences of divorce, single-parenting, remarriage, blended families, adoption of children of other races, gay/lesbian families, mothers who never marry, the new sets of grandparents and other extended family members created by remarriage, and interracial marriages. The list could go on for pages.

Reflection...

Consider your immediate and extended family. How many different types of families are present? Make a list and ask your parents, or someone from their generation, how many of those particular family styles were present a generation or two ago.

Home–School Relations in the Past

As educators, our relationship with parents has an interesting history that parallels the economic history of this country. Although public schools were initially legislated in Massachusetts in the seventeenth century, it was many years before most parents saw public schools as a realistic opportunity for their children. At that time the economy was agrarian and the population rural; parents in these rural areas had a tremendous influence on the schools, the teachers, the teaching that took place, and even on how teachers could and could not behave outside of the classroom.

Initially rural schools outnumbered urban schools and were governed by a school board made up of men from the community. As the United States became more industrialized in the mid-1880s, a mass migration from rural to urban areas occurred. As the size of communities increased, the influence of the individual parent on the school decreased. School board members, generally prominent business men, were not people most parents knew or could easily access. At the same time, school districts increased in size and the boards came to rely more heavily on school administrators responsible for the day-to-day operation of the schools. Put simply, the power shifted from the parents (generally fathers) to male administrators and board members.

The role of parents shifted from that of being actively involved in running the school to that of guests of the school: They were invited to school for specific events and to confer about problems. Furthermore, whereas earlier it had been primarily fathers who dealt with schools and educational issues, the relationship between home and school gradually changed until the responsibility of dealing with schools rested with mothers. Dealings with the school became "women's work," and because the status of women was low at this time, mothers had little input and even less power in the education of their children.

During the 1950s–1970s, the parental role remained that of little influence, and mothers continued to be the parent most likely to interact with the school. Parents' group meetings, parent–teacher conferences, and so forth, were generally held in the afternoon, thus making it difficult for working fathers to attend. For practical purposes, fathers were seen as not needing to be actively involved with the day-to-day care and education of their children.

There were serious problems with this arrangement. Contrary to popular belief, a large number of mothers were part of the work force. These mothers were most often from ethnically/racially-diverse groups and/or low-income families. Because these women were not able to attend afternoon meetings, parent involvement in the schools became primarily an activity of white, middle-class women. This made a loud and clear statement about how minorities and the poor were valued by the schools during this time period.

The U.S. economy has changed dramatically since the 1970s. Presently, it takes two salaries to provide an equivalent spendable income that a single wage-earner could make in 1970 (Sherman, 1994). Consequently, in order to maintain a middle-class standard of living today, most mothers of school children are a part of the work force. As a result, even middle-class mothers are generally not available during school hours. The unavailability of parents from all economic and ethnic/racial segments of society during the school day demands a rethinking of both how to involve parents in the schools and what the nature of that involvement might be.

At the same time, many parents want to be more actively involved in their children's education, as opposed to being merely recipients of test scores and grades. This desire is complicated by the amount of time (or lack of time) parents can devote to the schools. These issues and more will be discussed in detail in the following chapters.

Looking at Families

Because children bring their family experiences with them to school, educators must understand families in order to best understand the children. Most books on home–

school relations focus on skills (parent–teacher conferences, parent-involvement programs, etc.), which are certainly important issues; indeed, they are covered in depth in this book. However, we feel strongly that knowledge and understanding of the family are prerequisites to truly meaningful relationships between the school and the home.

To assist you in acquiring the skills to meet this goal, we will examine four factors influencing families and focus on their impact (see Figure 1.1).

1. The spendable income available to a family
2. The ethnic, racial, and cultural background of the family
3. The structure of the family
4. Individual familial differences

Changing Income Levels of Families

Income, more than any other single factor, determines the quality of life for most families. An alarming 21 percent of the children in this country live in poverty. The result of poverty, as Fuller points out in Chapter 12, can be devastating to families and can make learning more difficult for the child.

The experiences that low-income families share with those from middle-class families are minimal. This is important to acknowledge because educators tend to come from middle-class homes (Webb & Sherman, 1989) and, therefore, have sensibilities and experiences that are very different from those of impoverished students. These middle-class sensibilities and experiences often restrict the understanding of poverty.

Although educators are generally caring, intelligent people who want the best for students, the disparity of life experiences between middle-class and poor families—a disparity that differs in both quality and quantity—is not often recognized. As a result, educators often hold stereotypes of low-income people that impede their abilities to work effectively with students from low-income families. Although educators want to meet the needs of all children, their understanding of poverty is often inadequate to accomplish the task.

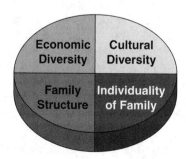

FIGURE 1.1   Factors to Consider When Examining Home–School Relations

The Changing Demographics
of Ethnicity/Culture/Race

The families of children in the public schools exhibit greater diversity than ever before, while teachers and pre-service teachers are still largely white, middle-class, and female (Fuller, 1994).

Approximately 31 percent of public school students are children of color. In fact, children of color make up the majority of school children in some states. Currently, 58 percent of school children in California are members of under-represented groups, and by 2020 these groups are expected to exceed the white mainstream population in schools (Wise & Gollnick, 1996). These children live in a range of ethnic, cultural, racial, familial, and economic milieus that are frequently different from those in which educators lived as children.

The ethnic/racial diversity of families has changed for a variety of reasons: Higher birthrates for people of color and changes in immigration patterns are two of the primary reasons for change. While early immigrants were generally from northern Europe or Canada (between 1951 and 1960, 67 percent of our immigrants came from Europe or Canada, 25 percent from Mexico or Latin America, and only 6 percent from Asia), in 1998, 34 percent of immigrants came from Asia, 44 percent were from Mexico and Latin America, and only 15 percent were from Europe and Canada (U.S. Census Bureau, 2001). This results in a change in the traditionally northern European appearance of many of our students and their families. More importantly, it also means that in addition to cultural diversity, non-Judeo-Christian religions, such as Islam, Buddhism, and Hinduism, are also adding to the richness and variety of our classrooms. Watts and Tutwiler discuss ethnicity, culture, and race in more depth in Chapter 3.

Understanding Diversity in Families

First, educators must understand their own cultural behaviors, values, traditions and family backgrounds. It is difficult to see how our backgrounds differ from others if we can't identify the characteristics of our own experiences. Without this conscious awareness of our own cultural and familial backgrounds our perceptions of students' families may be as limited as our individual histories and may cause us to make ethnocentric judgments about other families. At least, these judgments will hinder communication; at most, they will cause irreparable harm to the working relationships we are attempting to establish with our students and their families. It is only through understanding the needs and expectations of diverse groups that we are able to tailor our efforts in a manner appropriate to our students' families' needs.

It is important to remember that within all cultures (as well as socioeconomic groups, family structures, etc.) there is great diversity, and this diversity is as great within a given culture as it is among groups. This means that to appreciate families from a specific culture, a variety of factors must be considered.

Traditional and Assimilation.   One of these factors is the degree of assimilation exhibited by children and their families. Assimilation indicates the degree to which a family moves from one or more cultures to another—usually from the birth culture into the mainstream culture. For example, the more assimilated Native American children are the greater the move from the traditional culture toward that of the dominate culture. Even if families are closer to being members of the mainstream society than their traditional culture, knowledge about their traditional culture is important because it will help educators better understand the background influences on the student and their family's behaviors and attitudes.

Because there is great diversity within cultures (socioeconomic groups, family structures, etc.) it is impossible to describe families in their entirety; it is similarly impossible to produce a single generalization describing all the people in a culture. Descriptions exit about cultures and the people who participate in them that are over generalizations. These constitute *stereotypes*. Stereotypes are harmful because they deny that variability exists within a culture and its people and, in so doing, limit what the observer can see and expect of the people observed.

One way stereotyping causes problems for both teachers and their students' families results from the fact that only a single description exists, and it is forced to apply to all circumstances. In other words, simple explanations are offered for what are complex cultural phenomena. When teachers use stereotypes, they over-look the complexity of factors that influence behavior and thus cannot recognize patterns in their students' actions. This means behaviors not fitting the stereotype will appear haphazard and uninterpretable. When this happens teachers find it difficult to understand families of cultures that differ from theirs.

Changing Family Structure

Throughout history there has been a multiplicity of family styles: married, single parents (widow/widower), polygamous, polyandrous, stepfamilies, and so on. In contemporary western society it is not new configurations of the family that society is experiencing but changes in the number of certain configurations. For example, single-parent households headed by women are not new; however, the number of such families has almost doubled since 1970 (Ahlburg & De Vita, 1992). In 1970, 45 percent of families had children, while in 1995, only 35 percent had children. These figures are of particular importance because they help teachers understand the changes that are occurring in the families of their students.

Another change in the family is the increasing age of first-time parents. In 1994, men were approximately 27 years and women 25 when they married for the first time. This is an increase of more than four years for both men and women over the 1950 data (U.S. Bureau of the Census, 1995). This means that, among the many other changes, schools will be dealing with an older parent population than in the past.

Among these many familial changes is the role of fathers—more and more men are actively involved in parenting than at any other time since the industrialization of society in the western world. Divorce has also created different roles for fathers. Non-custodial fathers may well want to continue to be involved in their children's education. In addition, there are a growing number of fathers who are now awarded custody. These are generally new relationships for most educators. Hennen, Olsen, and Palm discuss fathers in more detail in Chapter 13.

Individuality of Families

Every family is different. Each brings a unique history and attributes that affect their experience as a family, and all families have their successes and failures. Some families are more functional and some more dysfunctional than others. Fuller and Marxen will discuss families in more detail in Chapter 2. There are families with children who have special needs, which Reilly discusses in Chapter 8, and all educators—whether they are teaching children with special needs or not—need to understand the families of these children. Inclusion of children with special needs is all around us. In our classrooms today, we have students who not long ago would have been segregated into "special" classes, but who are now mainstreamed into the traditional classroom. School buildings and transportation have been modified to allow students with disabilities to become a more integral part of the schools. This means we must also rethink our relationship with the parents of students with special needs to ensure they are a more integral part of the educational system.

We must also be informed about the nightmare of violence experienced by numerous children and their families. Knowledge and skills for dealing with the aftermath of violence are imperative before we can be effective advocates for the abused. Muhlhauser and Knowlton will discuss the issues relating to violence in Chapter 11.

Parent Involvement

Hanhan, in Chapter 6, discusses the history of home–school relations to help give us a historical perspective. Currently, parent involvement is designed to return parents to the school. Parents must be team members in the education of their children. Educators are experts in their field—children and the education of children—and parents are the experts on their children. However, because past experiences have given either parents or teachers disproportionate power in the relationship, both now have to learn to work as a team. This starts with a basic understanding of families and their view of parenting responsibilities, as well as educators' views of these responsibilities. Zimmerman (Chapter 4), MacDonald (Chapter 5), and Soo-Yin Lim (Chapter 7) discuss parents, schools, and teachers and their interrelationship.

Understanding families is the initial step in working with the families of students. The next step must be to involve parents in their children's education. There are a variety of good parent-involvement models to consider: early childhood, elementary, middle-school, and special education (Chapter 9). In addition, it is helpful to understand the experiences of parents who have decided to remove their family and children from the traditional school experience. Therefore,

Nathan (Chapter 14) discusses the history and rationale of the continued growth in numbers of parents choosing alternative educational programs for their children.

Teachers have a responsibility to be knowledgeable about legal issues concerning home-schooling, and to inform parents of their legal rights and obligations. Thomas, in Chapter 10, analyzes the laws and responsibilities surrounding parents and their rights. We as educators are sometimes ill informed about advocacy and public policy, and this makes it difficult to make systemic changes in home–school relations. We must be knowledgeable if we are to be effective. Hoover, Noll, and Olsen (Chapter 15) discuss school violence and bullying as a major education issue.

This book has been written to meet the needs of early childhood, elementary, middle school, and special education teachers. It will allow them to better understand and work with the contemporary family.

This book evolved out of a desire to better prepare teachers to work with families and to better serve students. We (Olsen and Fuller) teach in the area of home–school relations, as well as write and conduct research in this important discipline. We have used a variety of different books with our classes and were impressed by the quality of most, but we had a different vision—a vision that teachers would develop an in-depth understanding of families. With this goal in mind, we spent considerable time deciding what should be included in this book. We then invited people with special expertise in these areas to contribute. We wrote this book for our students, you, your students, and their families.

REFERENCES

Ahlburg, D. A., & De Vita, C. (1992). New realities of the American family. *Population Bulletin, 47*(2).

Fuller, M. L. (1994). The monocultural graduate in a multicultural environment: A challenge to teacher education. *Journal of Teacher Education, 43*(4), 269–278.

Henderson, A. (1987). *The evidence continues to grow.* Columbia, MD: National Committee for Citizens in Education.

O'Hare, W. P. (1996). A new look at poverty. *Population Bulletin, 51*(2).

Sherman, A. (1994). *Wasting America's future: The children's defense fund report on the cost of child poverty.* Boston, MA: Beacon Press.

U.S. Bureau of the Census. (1995, September). Household and family characteristics. *Current Population Series,* P20–483.

U.S. Bureau of the Census. (2000). Poverty in the United States (*Current Population Series P60–185*). Washington, DC: U.S. Government Printing Office.

U.S. Census Bureau. (2001). *Statistical Abstract of the United States 2001: The National Data Book.* Washington, DC: U.S. Government Printing Office.

Webb, R. B., & Sherman, R. R. (1989). *Schooling and society* (2nd ed.). New York: Macmillan Publishing Company.

Wise, A. E., & Gollnick, D. M. (1996). America in demographic denial. (National Council for Accreditation of Teacher Education). *Quality Education, 5*(2).

2 Families and Their Functions— Past and Present

MARY LOU FULLER
University of North Dakota

CAROL MARXEN
The University of Minnesota–Morris

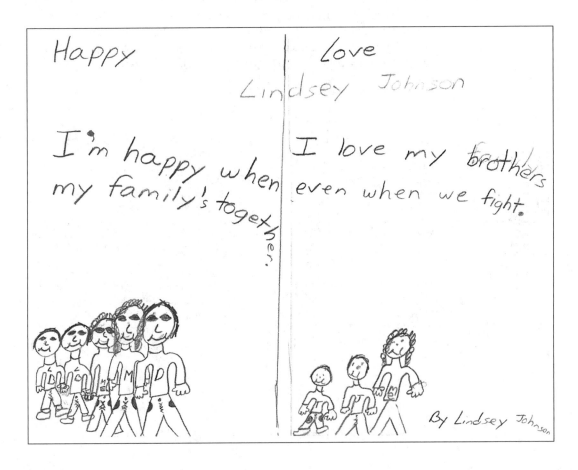

Happy

Love

Lindsey Johnson

I'm happy when my family's together.

I love my brothers even when we fight.

By Lindsey Johnson

In order for educators to provide the best learning environment for students, they must understand the families from which the students come. The majority of families do not fit the stereotype of the "all-American family." This chapter will introduce you to contemporary families. The purpose of this chapter is to help you:

- Trace the history of the family
- Identify the structures and needs of the contemporary family
- Compare historical and contemporary families
- Describe a functional and a dysfunctional family

This chapter provides the background information needed to help you understand families and consequently become a more effective teacher. More specifically, the chapter will help you: (1) take a historical perspective in viewing families of the past and the issues affecting them, (2) develop a perspective on how families look today, and (3) examine the characteristics of functional and dysfunctional families. In other words, reading and understanding the material in this chapter will provide you with a basic understanding of families and how and why they operate as they do. Because we are all fascinated by learning about ourselves and others, this chapter should be personally enlightening as well as informative.

The Evolution of the Family

Why Take a Historical Perspective?

Although the structure of families is changing, our stereotype of families is not. Although observations tell us differently, our perception of the all-American family is still an intact family with children, father employed outside the home, and mother staying at home. The reality is that this family currently accounts for less than 4 percent of U.S. families, and this percentage is declining (Johnson, 1990). Is this decline (which some perceive as a breakdown in family values) the cause of societal ills such as poverty, crime, drug abuse, and school failure? Or are the societal ills the cause of family problems? In other words, does a stronger family unit create a more stable economic, social, and political environment? Or does a growing, supportive, and prosperous economic, social, and political environment increase family stability? Looking at families from earlier times can help us consider these questions.

Skolnick (1991) encourages us to view families from other eras the way we would view families from different cultures. The comparison is appropriate because families at each point in history have their own sets of family values and family functions, which developed in response to the social, political, and economic environments of the time. They used those values and functions to do the same things contemporary families do: to protect their children and to prepare those children to take their places in society. Families have always struggled (as contemporary families do) with problems resulting from political, economic, and societal forces, so it is quite reasonable to look at earlier families in the same way as we look at present-day families. Indeed, doing so offers insights into how families develop their practices and values. Adopting a historical perspective may do more than document changes in families; it may offer insights concerning future trends. In particular, we will look at a range of historical families seeking to discover how they protected their children from threats to their well-being and how they prepared their children to be members of the societies in which they lived.

Early History

Prehistorical Families.   Conditions faced by primitive societies dictated that families work together for survival; constant effort was needed to protect everyone—especially children—from starvation, exposure to the elements, and disease. Practicality dictated that families sharing specific customs and beliefs band together for mutual security; these groups were called *clans. Tribes* were multiple clans living in the same vicinity and sharing the same culture. Tribes were better able than clans to protect their members against enemy tribes and to ensure that everyone had sufficient food to eat. Individuals who were disabled were cared for according to tribal custom. Children observed their parents, other adults, and members of their tribe and emulated what they saw. They learned from those responsible for them and, in so doing, became enculturated (socialized) into their culture. Because the continuation of the tribe was dependent on children carrying traditions from one generation to the next, a measure of how much children were valued is found in the fact that they were taught traditions, rules, and customs (Berger, 1995).

As cultures learned to meet basic survival needs more effectively (e.g., as food supplies became more reliable through domestication of animals and the cultivation of crops), the threats to the family changed. In particular, new problems of social organization emerged both within and among populations. Internally, individuals became more dependent on others outside their families, and externally, groups of people needed to learn how to deal with other groups. In a word, society became more complex, and children needed to learn much more if they were to become productive adults.

Greek and Roman Period Families.   We may speculate that this was the time when the task of educating children first became sufficiently complex. Moving education out of the realm of parental responsibility might allow parents to better protect their children while ensuring that their children learned what they needed to take their places in society as they reached adulthood. More specifically, Plato (427–347 B.C.), Aristotle (384–323 B.C.), Cicero (106–43 B.C.), and Polybius (204–122 B.C.) were Greek and Roman philosophers who believed that educating parents and children was important for the benefit of the state. However, their interest was reserved only to boys born to wealthy families. Boys needed to learn about governing, military strategy, managing commerce, and so forth—all activities expected of those who would lead their cultures.

Such a view represented little departure from earlier times. Families were still responsible for protecting their children, and because formal education was reserved for boys from families of nobility, girls still learned domestic skills at home. Boys from less prosperous families continued to learn within the family environment the skills and knowledge they needed to assume their roles in society. Although there were laws and customs allowing infanticide and the sale of children, Greek and Roman civilizations were generally supportive of families and children (Berger, 1995).

Family life and the role of children as members of family units changed considerably after the decline of the Roman Empire. Deterioration of the fabric of society meant that some threats which had been dealt with by large groups of people (e.g., defense of the community) again became the responsibility of families and family groups during the Middle Ages (400–1400). Simple survival reemerged as the primary goal for many individuals, and so children came to be viewed as property. In addition, the harshness and brevity of life meant that children were expected to become adults at a very young age and there was no time for education. Indeed, family life for the children of peasants was a constant struggle to simply satisfy the basic needs of food, clothing, and shelter. Only those few children born to noble families were educated. In addition, they were also prepared to be responsible for the property and the traditions they would inherit.

European Medieval Families.
Life was difficult for children during the Middle Ages, and harshness became a predominant focus of parenting behaviors. Families from both noble and peasant classes treated their children as miniature adults. Families had no appreciation of the developmental processes of childhood. The church of the time had an extraordinary influence on governmental matters, family life in general, and child-rearing practices.

The church taught that children were naturally evil, had to be told what to do, needed to be corrected constantly, and had to be punished harshly so that they could function well in society as adults. The term "beat the devil out of the child" came into existence because of this belief. It was very common for parents of all classes to emotionally neglect their young children or abandon them to a wet nurse, monastery, or nunnery. In other words, economic difficulties of the time and the church's view of children during Medieval times meant harsh treatment of children and little support for family life. Children generally were not well protected, and even though the boys of the wealthy were educated (as proposed by the Greeks and Romans), this experience was often a perversion of a healthy educational experience. We can be certain, however, that children learned how to behave as adults by watching and emulating the society surrounding them.

Renaissance and Reformation Families.
The Renaissance (1300–1400) and Reformation (1500–1600) periods that followed saw increased concern about freedom

for common people. This concern, accompanied by increased social organization that relieved some of the threats to families, and the important idea that a person is an individual rather than only a part of a group, made social classes less significant than during the Middle Ages. Individuality and freedom were extended to children and their schooling and better ensured that children were educated. The belief that children were pure and good was promoted in contradiction to the idea of original sin that the church had advocated during the Middle Ages.

Martin Luther (1482–1546), the father of the Reformation, proposed revolutionary child-rearing practices. He advocated that parents educate their children and teach them morals and the catechism. He maintained that families were the most important educators for children, that education was appropriate for both girls and boys, and that both genders would become better adults if they were educated.

Luther's ideas, followed by Johannes Gutenberg's invention of the printing press in 1439, meant that a few families would have access to books and could educate their children. In Europe, there were also more schools for the families who could afford them. However, school was still reserved for the sons of nobility, and education for the common person was not to come until much later.

The Age of Reason

The Age of Reason (1600–1700), also called the Period of Enlightenment, was an era of notable intellectual activity. Numerous religious leaders, philosophers, and educators introduced ideas about the way children learn and how families could best educate them. Comenius (1592–1670), a bishop, teacher, and writer, believed that all children were basically good; and Locke (1632–1704), an English philosopher, promoted the idea that children's minds are like "clean slates" on which parents and teachers could write what students were to learn.

While Comenius and Locke promoted education for maintaining a democracy, the philosopher Rousseau (1712–1778) took a social view of children. In his book *Emile,* he advocated a child's world that would be free from society's arrogant and unnatural ways. He introduced the concept of the whole child and promoted the idea that children needed a flexible, free atmosphere in which to mature according to their own natural timetables. Pestalozzi (1746–1827), a Swiss educator, was influenced by Rousseau. He expanded on Rousseau's belief of allowing a child's development to occur naturally by encouraging the child to learn basic skills. In addition, he believed that mothers from all socioeconomic classes should teach practical skills to their children at home, stressing the development of the whole child. Thus, the notion that families need to prepare their children for adulthood grew and included the important precepts that children are individuals that need to develop in a broad range of areas. Notice, though, that the family was still the central feature in the child's education.

Froebel (1782–1852) was a German educator who became known as the "father of kindergarten." He studied with Pestalozzi and eventually started a school for young children that promoted learning through play. Children's play, however, was guided by a trained teacher who planned activities that encouraged learning. Once again, a specially trained teacher relieved the family of some responsibilities for their children gaining the skills and knowledge they needed as adults.

Thinkers during the Age of Reason emphasized the worth and the dignity of humans and agreed with Francis Bacon's belief that "knowledge is power." In spite of the progress that was made toward valuing all individuals (including children), the Industrial Revolution changed how children were treated—in undesirable ways.

The Industrial Revolution

From the Age of Reason to the Age of Darkness—the Industrial Revolution was a period of child exploitation. The advent of the Industrial Revolution in the 1700s and 1800s brought social and political crises in France and England. During the Industrial Revolution, the economic condition was so desperate that families could no longer protect their children adequately; indeed, children became a liability to their families. Children from poor families, many as young as ten years of age, commonly worked ten- to fourteen-hour days in factories as cheap laborers.

This was not true for all children. Berger (1995) contends that "families tended to fit into three categories: the wealthy, who allowed others to rear their offspring and who exhibited indifference to children; the emerging middle classes, who wanted to guide, direct, and mold their children in specific patterns; and the poor and poverty stricken, who lacked the means to have much semblance of family life" (p. 44). Despite social class differences, children were still expected to act like adults from a very young age.

The political and economic structure of Europe during the Industrial Revolution changed how society viewed children and families. Concomitantly, colonies in the new world were developing their own political, economic, and social environment.

Colonial North American Family

While many city children were slaving in factories and living on the streets in the 1700s and 1800s, other children were helping on family-owned farms and businesses. Though economic life was a struggle, many colonial families were self-sufficient and so able to protect their children. In addition, they socialized them through secular and religious education—including opportunities for recreation (Seward, 1978).

It is important to realize that these families did not do this all on their own. Coontz (1995) reminds us that the government provided resources not available to families in Europe. "Prairie farmers and other pioneer families owed their existence to massive federal land grants, government-funded military mobilization that disposed [of] hundreds of Indian societies and confiscated large portions of Mexico, and state-sponsored economic investment in new lands, many of which were sold to settlers or spectators at prices far below the cost to the public treasury of acquiring them" (p. K6). During the 1700s, political and religious conflict, a growing economy, and free land allowed young families and individuals to move out on their own. The result was the emergence of an independent family structure (Skolnick, 1991). But what about the children? Although children were viewed as important and necessary for the family economy in the new world, child rearing in Puritan families remained as it was in Europe, strict and humiliating. Children were perceived as corrupt and it was the parent's responsibility to break their wills to rid them of their basic evil natures. Physical punishment was common and legitimate in this patriarchal society for wives as well as children (Skolnick, 1991), and obedience to the father was strictly observed.

Despite the romantic image of the family of this period, many children died in early childhood, and a person's life expectancy was less than fifty years. A significant number of women died in childbirth and, because of women's high death rate, "only a third of the marriages lasted more than ten years" (Skolnick, 1991, p. 25). Widowers remarried quickly because of necessity, and, consequently, there were few single-parent homes and numerous blended families (stepfamilies) during Colonial times. Black families were brought from Africa and did not have the advantages that were enjoyed by the new colonists. Because members were frequently separated from one another, the structure of black families varied significantly from the rest of society. We continue to feel the effects of the devastation of the black family today (Berger, 1995).

American Industrialization and the Family

From the 1850s to the 1920s, there was a dramatic shift away from the Puritan ideas of Colonial America. The country became more industrialized, urbanized, and prosperous. There was growth in manufacturing, with immigrants providing cheap labor for factories; gold was found in California; western lands were opened; and prosperous agricultural crops provided a surplus of food.

By 1920, the work week was shortened from six days to five, and the middle class had become larger. The working class profited, too; the strong economy and political climate allowed them many luxuries previously available only to the wealthy. Because of the country's affluence, society altered its beliefs about the duties of the family, the role of its members, and the image of the child.

A change in the function of the family appeared in rural areas. Increased agricultural productivity meant farm families began to raise cash crops rather than providing solely for their immediate needs, and families began to rely on the money they received to buy goods produced by others. At the same time, larger and more prosperous farms were possible because mechanization reduced the number of laborers needed. The need for fewer farm workers, in turn, began a migration from rural to urban areas.

Skolnick (1991) reminds us that there is a "remarkable parallel between economic expansiveness and the expansion of 'personal life'—a concern with inner experience…and psychological development across the stages of life" (p. 42).

Thus, economic growth was accompanied by an increase in the popularity of the writings of Locke, Rousseau, Pestalozzi, and Froebel, and childhood came to be viewed as a stage of development, with children being recognized as inherently good. Freud's psychoanalytic theory became popular and John Watson's behaviorist theory strongly influenced child rearing (Skolnick, 1991). In 1912, the government created the Children's Bureau to address concerns of undernourished, neglected, and abused children.

These changing attitudes toward children prompted further changes in the family unit. Relationships became more loving between husband and wife and between parent and child. Family members' roles were specific: fathers worked for financial security and mothers took care of the home and children. Middle- and upper-class mothers had servants to help take care of their children.

There was, however, a new middle-class working woman who challenged traditional gender roles, brought about the suffrage movement, and eventually, in 1920, earned women the right to vote. More women went to college as well.

The emergence of mandatory, free public schools was another major social change during the mid-1800s. Although schools assisted families with the education of their children in the past (that is, families still maintained the major responsibility for children's education), the government now took over primary responsibility for formal education with the advent of public schools. The government believed that females were not able to properly teach their children to become effective citizens for a democratic society, especially women of immigrant families. Thus Horace Mann's Common School was created for the purpose of Americanizing all citizens (Keniston, 1977). Families were still responsible for protecting children and educating them for adulthood, but much responsibility for the latter was now formally in the hands of the government.

World War I and the Great Depression brought many new ideas to a halt as mere survival became a daily struggle. As in the past, the functioning of the family and the roles of its members changed in response to economic and societal exigencies of the time.

The Great Depression and World War II

The political and economic impact of the Great Depression and World War II dramatically affected the functioning of the family. When men lost their jobs because of the Depression, they also lost their roles as family providers. They were further devastated as women joined the workforce and families moved in together to share resources and reduce expenses. The pattern of women working and families sharing housing continued through World War II as husbands and fathers became part of the military. In extreme cases, families were simply torn apart and children were often taken care of by their grandparents.

Educators saw the importance of education for young children, and child-care centers were created because of a need for them. The government, through the Works Progress Administration (WPA), came to the aid of families by funding nursery schools using unemployed teachers. From 1941 to 1946, the Lantham Act War

Nurseries were supported by the government to provide child care for children whose parents were part of the war effort. The most famous of these nurseries were the Kaiser Child Care Centers, which provided twenty-four-hour day care for working mothers during the war. The centers were closed when the war ended and the mothers gave up their jobs and returned to their homes (Gordon & Browne, 1993). Indeed, women working outside the home were viewed as wartime sacrifices, with men assuming the breadwinner role when they returned home from military service. It appeared that traditional gender-specific roles had been reestablished.

Reflection...

Imagine yourself living during the time of the Depression. What would your life be like? How would the Depression affect your family? Compare a family of the Depression era with a contemporary family.

1950s to 1970s

Americans experienced the greatest economic boom in history from the 1950s through the 1970s. Many sociologists believe that, because of the strong economic and political climate during the 1950s, societies in general and families more specifically were secure and solid (Coontz, 1995; Skolnick, 1991). The nuclear family of the 1950s was thought to be the "main source of childhood socialization and center of all personal happiness" (Coontz, 1995, p. K7) and completely independent from all outside sources.

Like the farm family of the 1920s, the idea of a completely self-reliant family is a myth. Government assistance programs of the 1950s helped veterans (primarily middle-class white men) obtain college educations and buy homes. In other words, it gave them a head start. Unfortunately, these programs did not assist people of color; ethnic groups; or single, divorced, and working mothers. The fact is, 30 percent of families lived in poverty during this supposedly "golden" period (Coontz, 1995). Moreover, women lost much of the independence they had gained before and during World War II.

At the same time, middle-class women were having more children and were tied to their suburban homes. Child-rearing practices of the 1950s were influenced by child development experts such as Erik Erikson, Arnold Gesell, and Benjamin Spock, whose messages were that children have individual differences that need to be nurtured and that each child proceeds through developmental stages at a rate that cannot be rushed. What each child needs, they argued, is not the stress that comes with being rushed through development, but love that comes with being recognized as unique and valued members of the family.

The 1960s and 1970s were times of social and political revolt. The children of the 1950s were raised to be independent, critical, and creative rather than obedient (Skolnick, 1991), and when they entered colleges and universities (which they did in record numbers), they questioned and criticized "all institutions—family, education, religion, economics, and government" (Berger, 1995, p. 68). They witnessed a society which ignored poverty and sanctioned racial injustice, and they accepted neither (Skolnick, 1991). The Vietnam War also served to tear the country apart with protests against U.S. involvement—protests that frequently caused strife and strained family relationships. The lack of a unified effort in favor of the war meant family conflicts were magnified.

Economic and political upheaval again caused the family's structure and function to change. More women went back to work, either as single mothers or to supplement the family income, making child care an important issue. Jean Piaget, a Swiss psychologist, gained in popularity at this time. He proposed a theory of cognitive development in children and expressed concern for their intellectual development, in particular the intellectual development of young children. On reading Piaget and his followers, parents were eager to help their children develop cognitively rather than simply letting nature take its course.

At the same time, the government began its War on Poverty with hopes of providing children from low socioeconomic families educational, medical, and mental health services. Head Start, a preschool program that included parent involvement, provided disadvantaged children the opportunity to get a head start before entering school. Because of Head Start's success, other programs for young children expanded rapidly. An important feature of Head Start is that in addition to having trained teachers work with children, parents are also involved and taught to work with their children.

In summary, families have had and will continue to have two responsibilities toward their children: They need to protect children from threats to their well-being, and they need to educate them so they can be productive members of the societies within which they live when they reach adulthood. What has changed has been the cultural matrix within which families function, a matrix to which families are bound by particular circumstances and events, and to which they react (Demos, 1996). Skolnick (1991) summarizes the relationship between families and society more generally by noting that "families are responsive to historical and cultural predicaments, and each such response invites new predicaments" (p. 48).

Changes have been both positive and negative. When they were positive, society grew in ways that made it easier for families to both protect and educate their children. This was the case, for example, in Greece and Rome, where social organization reduced the effort parents had to take to protect their children. It was also true of the Renaissance and Reformation periods when societal threats were reduced and the first recognition was made that children were individuals to be valued as such. And finally, after the Civil War and during the post–World War II period, the combination of economic prosperity and support from the government allowed families to expend more energy educating their children for adulthood.

Periods when families were most frustrated in addressing their responsibilities toward children were the Middle Ages and the Industrial Revolution, when economic deprivation threatened adults so severely that they were unable to look after their children. These were also times when society failed to recognize that being a child was different than being an adult, and that the proper maturation experiences for children did not include being treated like miniature adults.

Contemporary U.S. Families

We turn now to families in the United States at the close of the twentieth century and the ways in which they address the two tasks of protecting children and preparing them for adulthood. In doing so, we must consider the varieties of families commonly found in our contemporary society.

Most people think of children when they think of families. Yet only 24 percent of all families have minor children in their homes. Moreover, there is considerable diversity within that 24 percent (Field & Casper, 2001). In addition to intact families (both biological parents and minor children), there are households headed by single-parents, cohabiting couples, and gay parents; there are blended families and families headed by grandparents rearing minor children, in addition to numerous other structures. To make matters even more complex, there is great diversity within each of these family structures.

It is true that the structure of families has changed since the end of World War II and continues to change. Non-families (primarily single men and women) have become more prevalent than in the past perhaps because society has become more accepting of individuals who choose not to marry or who postpone marriage. Another area of change involves the increase in the number of other families (single-parent families, grandparent-headed families, foster homes, gay/lesbian families, etc.)—structures that in the past would not have been seen as "real" families (Field & Casper, 2001).

Although the number of married couples without children does not appear to have appreciably changed, the reason for their status has. Currently, couples may delay parenting for a variety of reasons (careers, etc.) or they may choose not to have children. In 1970 it was assumed that all married couples that could, would have children—infertility was a greater medical problem in 1970 than it is today. Although there are reasons for remaining childless that are shared by both groups, the couples may plan to have children in the future and are only temporarily childless or they may have already reared their children and they are no longer part of the immediate household.[1]

The big difference between families in 1970 and families in 2000 is the number of married couples with children. The advent of reliable, inexpensive birth control means that adults can put off child birth until they have established themselves; consequently, families are smaller and women are older than their mothers were when they had children (Field & Casper, 2001).

---

[1]Field and Casper used Census bureau data that generally does not count adult children (18 and over) as part of a household.

The number of single-parent families has also increased; indeed, it has doubled since 1970, due to divorce and the number of children born to unmarried mothers (up from 5 percent of all births in 1960 to 27 percent in 1989). In addition, the remarriage rate following divorce has grown, increasing significantly the number of blended families (Ahlburg & De Vita, 1992). Finally, because the baby boomers are largely moving out of the child-rearing years, there has been a decrease in the number of married couples with children.

As an educator who shares responsibilities with families for educating children, you must be well informed about the range and nature of family structures in your classroom. Though there are many different familial structures and they are all equally important, we will focus primarily on three groups: single unmarried mothers, single divorced mothers, and blended families. These three were selected because they are more apt to be misunderstood than the intact (traditional) family.

Single-Parent Families

Currently, half of all children will spend at least part of their lives in single-parent homes, and the mother will most likely be the custodial parent (Coontz, 1995; Johnson, 1990). These children will be in your classroom, and you must be knowledgeable about them so you can effectively meet their needs. The two largest categories of children of single-parent families are families headed by an unmarried mother and single-parent homes created by divorce. Single-parent homes account for a large number of families and, unfortunately, single-parent households are perhaps the most stereotyped of all family structures.

Unmarried Mothers

Thirty-one percent of all children are born to unmarried mothers. Unfortunately, there is a lot of confusion as to just what that figure means. The public's perception of this population is one of unmarried teens living on welfare. The reality is that there are two very different populations within this group—teenagers and women 20 and older. Contrary to the public's perception, women 20 and older is the larger of the two groups, accounting for 54 percent of the births to unmarried mothers (Usdansky, 1996).

Twenty and Over.   The twenty and over category can also be divided into two types: (1) those who chose to become pregnant and (2) those for whom the pregnancy was not planned (Ahlburg & De Vita, 1992). The first group is older, more affluent, better educated, and not in a position to marry. They are generally thirty or older and have decided that if they are going to have a baby they must, for biological reasons, have one soon. This is normally a well-thought-out decision with issues ranging from options for impregnation (invitro, artificial insemination, a male partner, etc.) to adoption. Also, financial security generally is considered well in advance for this population. Furthermore, these women generally report satisfaction with their decisions (Ahlburg & DeVita, 1992).

The second group tends to be in their early twenties and less well off financially and educationally. They do not plan the pregnancy and frequently have neither the maturity nor the resources available to properly rear a child. It is important to recognize that even though the pregnancy was not planned, this does not mean that the baby was not wanted or loved at the time of birth (Ahlburg & DeVita, 1992).

Reflection...

Think about the structure of students' families when you were in elementary school. How do they differ from what you would see in a present-day classroom?

Teen Mothers. Unmarried teenagers give birth to approximately 13 percent of the children born in this country each year. Although this is still a considerable percentage, it is a significant decrease in the number of births to unmarried teens in the 1970s. But what has increased is the number of young women between the ages of fifteen and seventeen who are having babies. These births are particularly problematic because they bring many serious complications to motherhood, including a lack of maturity and limited financial resources. These mothers are clearly more apt to live in poverty, be unemployed, have low-level employment skills, possess narrow educational backgrounds, and have limited parenting skills, to name a few (Ahlburg & DeVita, 1992).

Due to the increase in the numbers of very young unmarried teenage mothers, there has been an increase in another kind of family structure—households headed by maternal grandmothers who are rearing the children of these young mothers. Sociologists call this phenomenon *skip generation parenting*. As a teacher, you may well be working with your student's grandparents. To complicate matters even more, you may be working with both the grandparents and the child's young mother.

There are those who point to the rate of unwed teenage mothers as evidence of a moral decline peculiar to the United States. However, this is an uninformed conclusion, because the rate of births to unwed teenagers in this country is about half of what it is in Sweden and is about the same as other Western countries (Canada, France, and the United Kingdom) (Ahlburg & De Vita, 1992). Using this birthrate as an index of morality suggests that the United States is no better and no worse than many other countries and, indeed, better than some. Perhaps it would be more appropriate to consider the ability of unmarried teen mothers to protect and provide for their children than to attempt to assess the morality of the situation.

You will be teachers for children of unmarried mothers and, as with all families, you will find great diversity among these families. A student from a home headed by an unmarried mother may be the child of a mature, well-educated, financially secure woman who is interested and involved in her child's education. Or the student may be the child of a mother who was fifteen years old at his or her birth, and this could be problematic. The young mother may be unable to attend school functions because she cannot take time away from her job, either because her employer won't let her or because she cannot sacrifice the income. The variances in these families are innumerable, as they are within all family structures.

Patterns of Marriage, Divorce, and Remarriage

The demographics describing the transition of families can often be confusing. Consequently, Figure 2.1 is presented to help you visualize this statistical flow. Please note that this figure pertains to all marriages and the statistics used for the following families (single-parent families/divorced and blended families) pertain only to families with children unless otherwise noted.

The following two family configurations to be explored are single-parent families due to divorce and blended families. These two families share a common attribute: In both types parents are married, or have been married at least once.

Single-Parent Families: Divorce

Though children of single-parent homes (through divorce) also are part of a diverse group, they do share some commonalities. In particular, there are two factors that

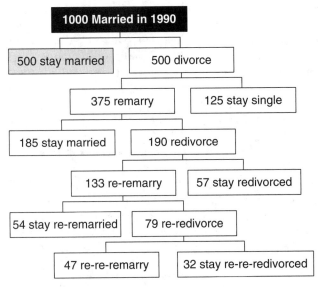

Totals after three remarriages

Married and stayed married to the same individual	500
Married, divorced, remarried and stayed married	286
Predicted total married	786

FIGURE 2.1   Patterns of Marriage, Divorce, and Remarriage

From: Burr, W. R., Day, R. D., & Bahr, K. S. (1993). *Family Science.* Reprinted with permission.

strongly influence the quality of the lives of children of divorced parents: (1) the length of time since the divorce, and (2) the family's economic resources.

Time Period.   Children who have recently experienced a divorce are children in a crisis that generally lasts about eighteen months. During this period, children can be expected to display grieving-cycle behaviors: denial, anger, depression, and finally acceptance (or in the case of divorce, adjustment). All children don't necessarily go through each of these stages, and the intensity and duration will vary according to the individual child. However, the majority of children will go through these stages. Grief is a response to loss (Fitzgerald & Kubler-Ross, 1992; Trozzi & Massimini, 1999), and even if a child's home situation has been undesirable, they will still feel a loss. The loss in those cases is the loss of a dream—the dream that they will become a happy family (Fuller, 1989).

It is common for children to feel guilt and fear during this period—guilt that they are in some way responsible for the divorce and fear that they might also lose the other parent. During this crisis period, children need understanding, sensitivity, and emotional support so their lives can continue as normally as possible when they have worked through their crisis. Too often, people focus solely on the crisis period of divorce because it is a high-profile, dramatic time marked by increased stress, heightened needs, and new or intensified behaviors. It is easy to think that the crisis will continue forever, but children are resilient and the majority of them will work through their grief.

Finances.   Income must be taken into consideration when trying to understand children from single-parent homes. A startling 57 percent of all female-headed households have annual incomes below the national poverty line (Field & Casper, 2001), and because more than 90 percent of all custodial parents are women, lack of financial resources is often a very real problem for these families.

Living in poverty has implications for the family experience, from inadequate nutrition (which may appear in the classroom as lethargy) and medical concerns (inadequate immunization means the family is not protecting children well) to quality of both the physical and emotional environment (when the custodial parent is distracted by inadequate resources, it is difficult to pay attention to children and their needs). In other words, fiscal matters must be considered when trying to understand the quality of the lives of your students from single-parent families. Often, problems that children of divorce experience are blamed on the structure of the family as opposed to the stresses and restrictions of poverty. An important question to ask would be "Are the problems your student brings to class due to the absence of a second parent or to the absence of adequate financial resources?"

Stigmatization.   We have all heard people explaining a child's behavior by saying, "She's from a broken home." If the divorce is recent, a better statement would be, "That child is going through a crisis," because that more correctly describes the situation. After your student has worked through his or her crisis, blaming the divorce for behavior is both inadequate as an explanation and inappropriate as a justification. Divorce (after the crisis period) no more produces juvenile misbehavior than marriage guarantees acceptable behavior. Moreover, the language that is used to describe these children and their families is often negative (for example, "broken home"). Broken means defective and surely no one would purposely purchase something that is defective. Yet the term is used frequently to describe divorced families. There was a break in the family at the time of divorce but then a new family evolved. Single-parent homes may be exemplary, undesirable, or, like most homes, somewhere in the middle—doing the best they can. Describing children of divorce as being from a broken home stigmatizes them and their families.

Unfortunately, such stereotyping of children of divorce is common. In the early 1980s, a journal of one of the leading educational administrators' organizations devoted an issue to children from single-parent homes. They based their findings on research they had commissioned. The findings stated that children of single-parent homes were deficient in many areas when compared to children from intact (original mother and father) families—in particular, academically. This news was passed on by the major news services and was displayed prominently in newspapers and other publications nationally and internationally. However, there was a major statistical flaw in the research design, the income level of the families was a confounding variable and was not considered. In a later issue of this organization's journal, in a small box in the back of this journal, was a retraction. Unfortunately, this was not reported by the media—it was not news and consequently there are still people who report these inaccurate findings.

Much of the negative view of children of divorce in recent years has been promulgated by Judith Wallerstein (Wallerstein & Blakeslee, 1989; Wallerstein, Lewis, & Blakeslee, 2000) through her books and subsequently, her numerous talk show appearances. Based on her research, Wallerstein asserts that over half the children of divorce experience long-term pain, worry, and insecurity that adversely affect their love and work relationships. The problem with these assertions is that they are based on her research, which was faulty and does not support her findings. As Coontz (1995) points out, this supposedly definitive study was based on a self-selected sample of only sixty couples. It did not compare the children of divorced couples with those of non-divorced couples to determine whether their behaviors stemmed from other factors. Moreover, the sample was drawn from clients that were in therapy at a mental health clinic. Only one third of the sample was seen as mentally healthy *prior* to the onset of the study. Unfortunately, Wallerstein influenced people who were either not acquainted with the specifics of her research or not knowledgeable about research on children of divorce.

Children from Single-Parent Homes: Divorce.   To complicate things even further, most of the research describing children from single-parent homes is about children of divorce and generally does not include the children of never-married women. Consequently, when looking at the research on single-parent families you need to ask, "Which single-parent families?"

What are children from single-parent homes like? Amato and Keith (1991) did a meta-analysis of the major studies addressing this question, and they concluded that children from single-parent homes are similar to children from two-parent homes.

As educators we are particularly interested in the academic implications of children of divorce and a number of recent studies have reported that there is little or no difference in the academic achievement between children of divorce and children from intact homes. (Hines, 1997; Painter & Levine, 2000; Shim, Felner, & Shim, 2000; Wadsby & Sven, 1996). Unfortunately, the media hasn't reported this research, which finds that the children of divorce, following the grieving period, are pretty much like other children. The media's omission results in the support of faulty perceptions of children of divorce.

There are a few differences between the children of traditional (intact) homes and children from single-parent homes. After all, children of these two families live in different structures and environments. The following cite some of these differences.

The parents in single-parent homes talk more to their children than parents in two-parent homes (there are no other adults around to talk with), and children in single-parent homes are more mature and have greater feelings of efficacy than children from two-parent families (due, in part, from spending more time talking with adults). Also, parents in single-parent homes are less likely to pressure their children into social conformity and more likely to praise good grades than parents in a two-parent household. On the other hand, single-parents on a whole spend less time supervising homework or interacting with the schools than do parents from two-parent homes (Acock & Demo, 1991). Also, two-parent homes can provide a more solid financial base and are less apt to be in poverty (Burr, Day, & Bahr, 1993).

It is important to note that there is often confusion about the statistics of single-parent homes. When you hear that half of all children will live in a single-parent home, it doesn't mean at a given time. Those figures mean at some time before they are eighteen years of age. Also, statistics concerning children from single-parent homes don't normally refer only to children of divorce. These figures generally include children of unmarried women and children who have lost a parent through death.

Blended Families

Blended families (stepfamilies) are growing in number. This is not surprising because there has been an increase in the number of single-parent families (unmarried and divorced).

The term *step*, as in stepparent, has an interesting history. It is derived from an early English term meaning deprived and describes the person who steps into a family after the death of an original parent. This was seen as a heroic act that often saved the family from economic ruin. Although the term *stepfamily* is commonly used, the term *blended* better describes this family unit and is used in this chapter.

In the past, death was the most common cause of blended families; currently, however, the marriage of divorced and unmarried mothers is the most common reason. In the past, death of either parent was problematic, but the death of the father was the most disastrous. Women generally were not part of the workforce and, furthermore, for much of history they were not allowed to own property or have wealth. In other words, remarriage could save a widow and her children from financial disaster.

Although children of single-parent homes are most apt to get the attention of the media, blended families may eventually become the largest family structure. The blended family is the most misunderstood of all family structures. Actually, the single-parent home is more like the intact home than the blended family. Educators are often uncomfortable with the single-parent family (Olsen & Haynes, 1993) and tend to breathe a collective sigh of relief when the single-parent family becomes a blended family. After all, it looks like the family we are most comfortable with—the traditional (intact) family.

However, the only thing that the intact family and the blended family have in common is their appearance. The blended family functions differently from other family structures. The members of a blended family bring with them to their new family a complex history as well as different traditions. Whereas there is diversity within any given family structure, none approach the complexity of the blended family. As an example of this complexity, the Institute for Clinical Social Work in Northbrook, Illinois, has defined thirty-two categories of blended families. As an educator, it is imperative that you have an understanding of this family if you are to serve them well.

Research on blended families is limited, and the findings are anything but conclusive. Some researchers view members of blended families as having more problems than the traditional family, while others view their problems as simply different. These latter researchers also see children from blended families as equally well adjusted as children from intact homes (Coontz, 1995).

Facts about Blended Families.   What is the truth about blended families? The following is a list of facts on which most researchers agree:

- Younger children tend to make the best adjustment to blended families.
- Adolescents, particularly those of the same sex as the stepparent, are apt to feel resentful of the stepparent.
- Children generally adjust better to a stepparent after the death of a natural parent than after a divorce.
- Following divorce, the attitude of the adults involved (custodial, noncustodial, and stepparents) will contribute significantly to the child's adjustment to a blended family. Not surprisingly, positive attitudes are more apt to result in a healthier adjustment than negative attitudes.
- Most blended families report being happy.

Reflection...

Consider the stereotype of the fairy tale stepmother. How many negative portrayals can you remember? How many positive? How might you explain this disparity?

Myths about Blended Families.   Unfortunately, too often the expectations for blended families are based on myths rather than facts. The following are four particularly dangerous myths (Fuller, 1992).

Myth 1.   Family roles in blended families are similar to those of intact families. Although another adult can replace a spouse, they cannot replace a parent. The role of the stepparent is ill defined and, as children often remind them, "You are not my parent!" While stepparents may nurture and support the children they seldom play the role assigned to the natural parent.

Myth 2.   The myth of instant love. It took the adults in the blended family time to build their relationship and yet there is an unrealistic expectation that the stepparent and stepchildren will automatically love one another. They need time to build a relationship, but even given time there are complicating factors. Mixed loyalties present problems for many blended families: "If I love my stepparent, am I being disloyal to my natural parent?" Also, jealousy of stepsiblings and stepparents is often a problem that must be addressed prior to the development of a functional family.

Myth 3.   Blended families function just like "traditional" families. Although traditional families share common histories, traditions, and relatives, blended families do not. In contrast, blended families share the richness that goes with diversity—although that diversity may require change. Family traditions (birthdays, Christmas, Hanukkah, family trips, etc.) provide opportunities for enjoyable and enriching new experiences, but they also may result in conflict. In addition, relationships between stepsiblings (custodial and non-custodial, etc.) must be negotiated. In many families stepsiblings add to the richness of the family as well as the friction.

Myth 4.   Life is just a family sitcom. Perhaps the most detrimental myth of all comes to us from television. Although the stepfamily myths of the past (e.g., Cinderella, Hansel and Gretel, Snow White) have been examined and found wanting, we have replaced them with a new set of myths about the blended family (i.e., the *Brady Bunch* and more recent shows about blended families). The *Brady Bunch* may technically be a blended family, but the script writers have them acting just like an intact family. It is important that you as an educator be aware of the realities of blended families. The Utopian adjustment made on television programs such as the *Brady Bunch,* and subsequently their never-ending reruns, is more dangerous than the myth of Cinderella. In Cinderella, the wicked stepmother is accepted as a storybook character while blended families may see the Bradys as a real possibility and feel guilty when they don't live up to this contemporary fairy tale.

When examining any family that differs from the traditional family there is a temptation to dwell on the differences between the two. Often the behaviors that are unlike those of traditional families are seen as undesirable. Also, the strengths of the nontraditional family are apt to be ignored. Coleman and her associates help us examine the strengths of blended families (Coleman, Ganong, & Henry, 1984).

Flexibility. Stepchildren often learn to adjust to different value systems. Thus they may adapt more easily and become more flexible to new traditions and situations. These children generally know how to negotiate in new situations and compromise when necessary. Consequently, when situations require new behaviors (new schools, teachers, etc.), the child from a blended family may have already developed some important coping skills that can be generalized to these other situations.

Multiple Role Models. There are generally more adults in the lives of children of blended families than those of other family structures, and these adults provide a variety of models from which a child can choose. Aunt Susan is a good business person, Cousin Jim is very creative, and Grandma Mae is a scholar, and they are all role models for the child from the blended family.

Experience with Conflict Resolution. It has been said that children from blended families should be excellent in politics or business management because they know how to negotiate. Their negotiation skills are generally well developed because they may have positive relationships with people who may otherwise be hostile to each other (i.e., their divorced parents).

An Extended Kin Network. The child of a blended family has more parents, grandparents, aunts, uncles, and cousins than children from other family structures. Not only are there more people to learn from, there are more people to love and support them.

Higher Standard of Living. Most children from blended homes previously lived in female-headed, single-parent homes with limited economic resources. With marriage, the total family income is generally increased. With the increase in resources, there is also a rise in the standard of living, as well as added opportunities available for the children. In addition, there is a decrease in the stress caused by worrying about financial instability.

Happy Parents. Remarriage may provide children with a more supportive emotional environment because their parents are happier. Children who have experienced hostility in a previous family may benefit greatly from a more caring, loving environment. Happier remarriages may also provide exposure to a good model of marital interaction.

Stepfamilies are not traditional families warmed over. They are families with their own unique strengths and needs. By understanding the realities of the blended family and dispelling the myths, you can work with these children and their families more effectively. Knowledge allows us to look past the differences and appreciate the strengths of the blended family.

In summary, it is necessary that educators know about, and appreciate, the families of their students. It is also necessary to know how changing family structures play out in the lives of children. Families have become a fluid concept and the following scenario is about one of your future students, Angie. Angie was born into an intact family, her parents divorced, she then lived in a single-parent family, her mother then remarried, and she then lived in a blended family. Angie's father also remarried and she was part of his blended family, but he has since divorced and is planning to remarry. Angie will have been a member of a number of family configurations during her childhood, not only with her custodial parent but also with her noncustodial parent. Angie's experience is representative of a large number of children.

In addition, as families change, so do their needs. For example, as the number of single-parent families increases, so does the need for child care. There is continual change in all families, even within traditional (intact) families. There may be changes in the parents' employment, child care arrangements, or the economic status of the family. Furthermore, families are more mobile and move more frequently than they have in the past. Families are in a continual state of change.

Reflection...

Think of a family that you feel is a functional (good) family. What would be the adjectives that describe this family?

Functional Families

What are the characteristics of a functional "good" family? What do good families look like and what do they do? What are the effects of a dysfunctional family on the lives of your students?

It is important to be careful in making judgments about families. Contrary to popular belief you cannot determine the effectiveness of a family by its structure. The intact family with two children, in an upper-income neighborhood, may or may not be more functional than the single-parent family with two children living in a working-class neighborhood. It is not the way a family looks, but rather the way it acts. For many years the body of literature on families was on the dysfunctional family—they were more obvious and easier to study. Presently, there is a considerable body of literature on the functional family, and some identifiable characteristics have emerged. We have a sense of what healthy families are and what they are not.

Functional families are not perfect. If a family seems too good to be true, they probably are. All families have problems; only the nature, severity, and ability of the family to solve problems differ. Because a family seeks professional help does not mean they are dysfunctional. In fact, it may be a good example of their ability to address the problems (problem solving).

Characteristics of Functional Families

David Olson (1984) discusses the findings of numerous research studies on the characteristics of functional families. Functional families (good families) do not mean perfect families. There are no perfect, problem-free families. Because families are always in a constant state of flux they must continuously adjust to their new living situation.

Family Pride.   Good families show unity and loyalty to family members. Members of these families are cooperative, see the family in a positive light, and deal with problems in a positive way.

Family Support.   A good family provides love and understanding to its members. It provides an environment that fosters growth and is sensitive to the needs of each individual member. An important aspect of family support is the commitment of time: Good families spend time together.

Cohesion.   A healthy balance between dependence and independence is found in good families. There is mutual respect and appreciation of the individuality of each family member.

Adaptability.   In our rapidly changing world, healthy families are flexible and able to compromise. Role flexibility is an excellent example of the contemporary family's adaptability. For example, cooking is no longer "women's work," nor do men have sole responsibility for the yard. Availability and skill, rather than gender, determine who performs a task in an adaptive family.

Communication.   Not surprisingly, good communication skills are important to a well-functioning family. This implies time to develop and practice those skills. Exhibiting good communication skills is important to a well-functioning family. This implies time to develop and practice those skills. Homes that exhibit good communication skills are particularly adept at listening.

Social Support.   Just as members of good families feel a pride in and commitment to their families, they are also active in their communities, neighborhoods, schools, and so forth. In other words, they demonstrate social responsibility. These families prepare their members to enjoy and feel a responsibility for the world in which they live.

Values.   Good families have a core set of identifiable values and their goal is to adhere to them. Parents in these homes try to model the behaviors that demonstrate these values. For many families this may mean an active involvement in a religious organization, although for some it does not.

Joy.   I would like to add another characteristic to the above list. Good families have fun. In my experience working with families, I have observed in functional families a joyfulness, a spontaneity, and an enjoyment of life.

Note that none of these describes the appearance of a family. A good family may be a single man and his adopted child, a young couple with children, a couple over the age of thirty who have just had their first baby, or an infinite number of other family configurations. What is important is not the appearance but how well a family functions.

Dysfunctional Families

Whereas functional families allow children to grow to independence in a safe and supportive environment, dysfunctional homes do not. They may or may not provide for basic physical needs, but they do not provide for the development of an emotionally healthy individual.

Dysfunctional families are often unpredictable, with little or no structure, leaving the children anxious and unsure of themselves; or they may be too structured, resulting in a lack of sense of self. It is difficult to identify an exhaustive list of characteristics for dysfunctional families. Consequently, it is more productive to examine some of the effects the dysfunctional family.

Characteristics of Dysfunctional Families

Distrust.   Often children reared in dysfunctional homes have a difficult time learning to trust others. During those important developmental years when most children are learning to trust, they find that it is emotionally safer to distrust. Consequently, they rely on no one other than themselves. The price they pay is high—the cost of distrust is a lack of intimacy with others.

Low Self-Esteem.   Frequently children from dysfunctional families are too self-critical, and often experience excessive feelings of guilt.

Inability to Have Fun.   Children from dysfunctional families are often full of anger, disgust, depression, and sadness. They take themselves too seriously and find it difficult to laugh at themselves (Taylor, 1990).

Shame.   It is common for children from dysfunctional families to feel that they deserve the treatment that they are getting. Their thinking is as follows: After all, adults are omnipotent so if they (children) are being treated poorly it must be because they deserve it. This is particularly true of children who are being physically or sexually abused, although shame is a common reaction of children from other dysfunctional settings as well. The result is that they grow up feeling that they are undeserving of better treatment.

What makes the effects of a dysfunctional family particularly disturbing is that these feelings do not cease, or in many cases even decrease, when children leave their dysfunctional home. Unless there is some sort of positive intervention, they will become adults that are handicapped by the messages they received from their dysfunctional families and are often doomed to repeat them. Their legacy is a lifetime of trying to prove that they are worthwhile people. In addition, they may become parents that perpetuate the pain of the dysfunctional family.

Summary

The family is a wonderful institution. It prepares children to fit into the larger world while teaching them that they have a responsibility to family, community, country, and others. It is a place where children are loved and nurtured and experiment with new behaviors in this secure social laboratory.

The idea of what constitutes a family has changed dramatically in the last fifty years. We know that it is the way a family functions, as opposed to its configuration, that tells us how successful a family is. No family is perfect. All families have problems and challenges, but in a functional family those become part of the learning experience.

We as educators handicap ourselves if we do not understand the nature of families. And, as part of this understanding, we are obliged to be generous with our appreciation of the efforts that parents make. We must also remember that the great majority of parents love their children and want the very best for them.

RECOMMENDED ACTIVITIES

1. Write a description of your family of origin. Include a description of family roles, rituals, relationships, and so forth. You may wish to include pictures and mementos to support your description.

2. Select a period of history and describe family life and compare it to your family unit.

3. Interview a parent of a single-parent home, a blended family, and an intact family. You might want to ask about family rituals, roles, decision making, and so forth.

4. Examine popular magazines, cut out pictures of fifty families, and make observations.

5. Invite a family therapist to discuss with the class functional and dysfunctional families and the therapeutic intervention for the latter.

ADDITIONAL RESOURCES

Families

Books:

Ahlburg, D. A., & De Vita, C. J. (1992). *New realities of the American family.*

This report examines the social, economic, and demographic trends that have contributed to the rapidly changing structure of the American family and the implications of these trends.

> Population Reference Bureau
> 1875 Connecticut Avenue NW, Suite 520
> Washington, DC 20009-5728
> Phone: 800-877-9881

Coontz, S. (1992). *The way we never were.*

This an excellent book that helps the reader understand families of the present and the past. It examines some of the myths and misunderstandings about families. Coontz's investigation of families is both interesting and informative. ISBN: 0-465-00135-1.

> Basic Books
> 10 E. 53rd St.
> New York, NY 10022
> Phone: 800-242-7737

Hamner, T. J., & Turner, P. H. (1996). *Parenting in contemporary society* (3rd ed.).

This research-based book focuses on acquainting students with parenting in three major areas: (1) concepts, challenges, and changes; (2) diverse family types; and (3) risks and alternatives. Although mainly directed toward early childhood specialists, it would also be helpful to other educators. 400 pp. ISBN: 0-205-16105-7.

> Allyn & Bacon
> Paramount Publishers
> College Book Orders
> 200 Old Tappan Road
> Old Tappan, NJ 07675
> Phone: 201-767-5937

Articles:

Scherer, M. (1996). On our changing family values: A conversation with David Elkind. *Educational Leadership, 53*(7), 4–9.

Videos:

The Child in the Family

This compelling video shows the roles of parents and functions of the family through interviews and profiles. This focus on families provides information and insight significant to all who seek to understand the child and support the family. Produced in live action format.

Magna System, Inc.
95 West County Line Road
Barrington, IL 60010
Phone: 800-523-5503

Families First

Bill Moyers examines a growing national movement that has achieved success in keeping troubled families together through the innovative strategy of working with them in their homes. It is modeled after a pioneer project called "home builders." (90 minutes, color)

Films for the Humanities & Sciences
P.O. Box 2053
Princeton, NJ 08543
Phone: 800-257-5126

Families Matter

This program with Bill Moyers examines why America has become an unfriendly culture for families and children and explores ways to rebuild a web of support for families. (60 minutes, color)

Films for the Humanities & Sciences
P.O. Box 2053
Princeton, NJ 08543
Phone: 800-257-5126

Family Influences

This video illustrates how family background influences the way people view themselves and others. It defines four types of parents—authoritative, permissive, authoritarian, and uninvolved—and compares the characteristics of children raised by each. It also examines the importance of birth order and considers non-traditional families. 1991. (30 minutes, color)

Insight Media
2162 Broadway
New York, NY 10024
Phone: 212-721-6316

Kids in Crisis—Self-Esteem Tips for Kids From Dysfunctional Families

This video offers kids from unstable families the self-esteem building tips they need to get through tough times and emotional crisis. Children are encouraged to see that they are not the cause of the problems at home and that they are special and capable of giving and receiving love. The full-color, animated video is approximately 20 minutes in length. This video is also available in the fourteen-part "Kid in Crisis" video series.

> The Bureau for At-Risk Youth
> 135 Dupont Street
> P.O. Box 760
> Plainview, New York 11803-0760
> Phone: 516-349-5520
> Email: info@at-risk.com
> www.at-risk.com

On the Home Front: The Influence of the Family

This program explores the effects of complex family interactions on child development. It defines bidirectional influences within the family and shows how different family structures (dual-income, single-parent, and blended family) affect children. 1991. (60 minutes, color)

> Insight Media
> 2162 Broadway
> New York, NY 10024
> Phone: 212-721-6316

Our Families, Our Future

This video, hosted by Walter Cronkite, highlights successful programs across the country that are seeking to assess the multiple stresses of family life. Indeed, this documentary puts a human face on the problems facing the American family and examines programs that are part of the burgeoning "family support" movement, which offers comprehensive services for both parents and children. Winner of two awards. 1995. (58 minutes, color)

> Filmmaker Library
> 124 East 40th Street
> New York, NY 10016
> Phone: 212-808-4980

Organizations:

> National Council on Family Relations
> 3989 Central Avenue NE, Suite 550
> Minneapolis, MN 55421
> Phone: 888-781-9331
> www.ncfr.com

> National Congress of Parents and Teachers
> 330 Wabash, Suite 2100
> Chicago, IL 60611
> Phone: 312-670-6782
> www.pta.org

Single-Parent Families

Books:

Coleman, W. (1998). *What Children Need to Know When Parents Get Divorced*. Minneapolis, MN: Bethany House.

Because it is often hard for children to express feelings, fears, and questions, it is easy to assume they are adjusting and coping with their parents' divorce when instead they may feel guilty that they are somehow to blame for the breakup. William L. Coleman provides an honest, understandable, and simple way for concerned adults to broach discussion of this sensitive subject with the children they care about. ISBN: 0-764-22051-9.

Dinkmeyer, D., McKay, J. D., & McKay, J. L. (1987). *A new beginning: Skill for single parent & stepfamily parents.*

This book focuses on the needs of single- and stepparent families. It contains case examples and many illustrations. Covers areas such as self-esteem, relationships and behavior, communication skills, and discipline. Excellent to use with parents or to help students understand some of the issues confronted by single-parent and stepparent families. 222 pp., ISBN: 0-87822-286-3.

> Research Press
> Department 96
> P.O. Box 9177
> Champaign, IL 61826
> Phone: 800-519-2707

Gouke, M. N., & Rollins, A. M., (1990). *One-parent children, the growing minority: A research guide.*

This is a very helpful book for those readers who want to examine the research on single-parent homes. This book contains over 1,100 abstracts of research, articles, and books. 494 pp., ISBN: 0-824-085-760.

> Garland Publishing, Inc.
> 1000A Sherman Avenue
> Hamden, CT 06514
> Phone: 800-627-6273

Chapters:

Hildebrand, V., Phenice, L. A., Gray, M. M., & Hines, R. P. (1996). Divorced single-parent families. In *Knowing and serving diverse families* (pp. 207–236). New York: Merrill Publishing Co.

Hildebrand, V., Phenice, L. A., Gray, M. M., & Hines, R. P. (1996). Single teenage parent families. Hispanic-American Families. In *Knowing and serving diverse families* (pp. 69–90). New York: Merrill Publishing Co.

Videos:

Do Children Also Divorce?

This film was produced to show teachers and parents the important role they must play in meeting children's needs during a divorce. It is normal for children to have negative reactions during the stress of divorce, with each age group exhibiting different behaviors. Special attention at this time will help them avoid serious psychological problems later on. 1988. (30 minutes, color)

> The Bureau for At-Risk Youth
> 645 New York Avenue
> Huntington, NY 11743
> Phone: 800-999-6884

Single Parenting

Hosted by actor Dick Van Patten, this video focuses on ways to minimize the adverse effects that a divorce or death may have on children. It offers positive techniques of effective single parenting. This video is primarily meant for families but would be excellent for use with a class interested in home–school relations. (20 minutes, color)

> The Bureau for At-Risk Youth
> 645 New York Avenue
> Huntington, NY 11743
> Phone: 800-999-6884

Teen Mothers

Deals with the issues surrounding teen pregnancy, guilt, courage, love, codependency, support, independence, the impact to the teen and her current family, and realistic decisions to be made for the future. A Linkletter Films video. Copyright 1999. (26 minutes)

> Magna System, Inc.
> 101 North Virginia Street
> Suite 105
> Crystal Lake, IL 60014.
> Email: magnasys@ix.netcom.com or
> www.magnasystemsvideos.com/index.html

Organizations:

> Parents Without Partners, Inc.
> 1650 South Dixie Highway, Suite 510
> Boca Raton, FL 33432
> Email: pwp@jti.net
> www.parentswithoutpartners.org/index.htm

> Single Parents Association Online
> 4727 E. Bell Road, Suite 45, PMB 209

Phoenix, Arizona 85032
Phone: 623-581-7445
Email: spa@singleparents.org
www.singleparents.org

Stepparents:

Books:

Shomberg, E. F., & Shimberg, E. F. (1999). *Blending families: A guide for parents, step-parents, and everyone building a successful new family.* Berkley: Berkley Publishing Group.

Today more Americans are part of a second-marriage family than a first. Inevitably, these newly blended stepfamilies will be confronted by their own special problems and needs. This insightful problem-solving guide offers solid solutions and includes real-life stories from families that have been through the adjustment process. ISBN: 0-425-16677-5.

Visher, E. B., & Visher, J. S. (1993). *Stepfamilies: Myths and realities.* Citadel Press.

Written by a husband and wife team consisting of a psychiatrist and a psychologist who drew on both their personal and professional experience, this book gives an overview of the stepfamily and explains the importance of understanding the special nature of the stepfamily and its differences from the nuclear family. ISBN: 0-806-50743-8.

Chapters:

Hildebrand, V., Phenice, L. A., Gray, M. M., & Hines, R. P. (1996). Step families. In *Knowing and serving diverse families* (pp. 237–259). New York: Merrill Publishing Co.

Videos:

An American Step Family

This video examines some of the problems faced by blended families. (26 minutes, color). Purchase and rental.

Films for the Humanities & Sciences
PO Box 2053
Princeton, NJ 08543
Phone: 800-257-5126

Divorce and the Family: When Parents Divorce

A clearheaded, unemotional look at the reality of a divorce. It takes viewers inside the minds of parents and teenage children to learn their fears and hopes as their world changes. Viewers witness courtroom hearings to gain a complete overview of divorce. They listen in on meetings with an evaluating psychologist and a teacher who explain how teens often react to divorce. Viewers learn about types of custody, alimony, mediation, child support, spousal maintenance, and visitation rights. A Learning Seed video. Copyright 1995. (24 minutes)

Magna System, Inc.
101 North Virginia Street
Suite 105
Crystal Lake, IL 60014
Email: magnasys@ix.netcom.com
www.magnasystemsvideos.com/index.html

Organizations:

Stepfamily Association of America
215 Centennial Mall, Suite 212
Lincoln, NE 68508
Phone: 402-477-7837
www.saafamilies.org/index.htm

Stepfamily Foundation
333 West End Avenue
New York, NY 10023
Phone: 212-877-3244
www.stepfamily.org

REFERENCES

Acock, A., & Demo, D. (1994). *Family diversity and well being*. Thousand Oaks, CA: Sage Publishing.

Ahlburg, D. A., & De Vita, C. (1992). New realities of the American family. *Population Bulletin, 47*(2).

Amato, P., & Keith, B. (1991). Parental divorce and the well-being of children. *Psychological Bulletin, 110*, 30.

Berger, E. H. (1995). *Parents as partners in education: Families and schools working together* (4th ed.). Columbus, OH: Merrill.

Berger, E., & Barger, B. (1975). *Sociology: A bibliographical approach* (2nd ed.). New York: Basic Books.

Bing, E., & Cowman, L. (1980). *Having a baby after 30*. New York: Bantam Press.

Burr, W. A. R., Day, R. R., & Bahr, K. S. (1993). *Family science*. Pacific Grove, CA: Brooks/Cole.

Coleman, M., Ganong, L. H., & Henry, J. (1984). What teachers should know about stepfamilies. *Childhood Education*, 306–309.

Coontz, S. (1992). *The way we never were: American families and the nostalgia trap*. New York: Basic Books.

Coontz, S. (1995). The American family and the nostalgia trap. *Phi Delta Kappan, 76*(7), K1–K20.

Demos, J. (1996). Myths and realities in the history of American life. In H. Grunebaum & J. Christ (Eds.), *Contemporary marriage: Structure, dynamics, and therapy* (pp. 9–31). Boston: Little Brown.

Field, J., & Casper, L. M. (2001). *America's families and living arrangements: Population characteristics* (Current Population Reports P20-537). Washington, DC: U.S. Census Bureau.

Fitzgerald, H., & Kübler-Ross, E. (1992). *The grieving child: A parent's guide*. New York: Simon & Schuster.

Fuller, M. L. (1992). The many faces of American families: We don't look like the Cleavers anymore. *PTA Today, 18*(1), 8–9.

Fuller, M. L. (1989). Children of divorcee: Things you should know. *PTA Today, 14*(5), 11–12.

Glick, P. (1989). Remarried families, step families and stepchildren. A brief demographic note. *Family Relations, 38*, 24–27.

Gordon, A., & Browne, K. (1993). *Beginning and beyond* (5th ed.). Albany, NY: Delmar.

Hines, A. M. (1997). A review of literature: Related transitions, adolescent development, and the role of the parent-child relationship. *Journal of Family and Marriage, 59*(2), 375–388.

Keniston, K., & Carnegie Council on Children. (1977). *All our children: The American family under pressure.* New York: Harcourt Brace Jovanovich.

Olson, D. (1984). *Families: What makes them work.* Thousand Oaks, CA: Sage.

Olson, M. R., & Haynes, J. A. (1993). Success of single parents: Families in society. *The Journal of Contemporary Human Services, 7*(5), 259–267.

Painter, G., & Levine, D. I. (2000). Family structure and youth outcomes. *Journal of Human Resources, 35*(3), 524–549.

Seward, R. (1978). *The American family: A demographic history.* Beverly Hills, CA: Sage.

Shim, M. K., Felner, R. D., & Shim, E. (2000). The effects of family structures on academic achievement. Paper presented at the Annual Meeting of the American Educational Research Association, New Orleans. April 24–28, 2000.

Skolnick, A. (1991). *Embattled paradise: The American family in an age of uncertainty.* New York: Basic Books.

Taylor, P. M. (1990). *Coping with a dysfunctional family.* New York: Rosen.

Trozzi, M., & Massimini, K. (1999). *Talking with children about loss: Words, strategies, and wisdom to help children cope with death, divorce, and other difficult times.* New York: Perigee.

U.S. Census Bureau. (1993). Poverty in the United States (*Current Population Research Series P60-185*). Washington, DC: U.S. Government Printing Office.

Usdansky, M. (1996). Single motherhood: Stereotypes Vs. statistics. *New York Times.* Retrieved August 10, 2002, from http://mbhs.bergtraum.K12.ny.us/cybereng/nyt/unwed-mo.htm

Visher, E. B., & Visher, J. S. (1993). *Stepfamilies: Myths and realities.* New York: Carol.

Wadsby, M., & Svedin, C. G. (1996). Academic achievement in children of divorce. *Journal of School Psychology, 34*(4), 352–336.

Wallerstein, J. S., Lewis, J. M., & Blakeslee, S. (2000). *The unexpected legacy of divorce.* New York: Hyperion.

Wallersein, J., & Blakeless, S. (1989). *Second chances: Men, women, and children: A decade after divorce.* New York: Ticknor & Fields.

Whitehead, B. D. (1993). Dan Quayle was right. *The Atlantic Monthly, 271*(4), 47–56.

CHAPTER

3

Diversity among Families

IVAN E. WATTS
Auburn University

SANDRA WINN TUTWILER
Washburn University

Diversity comes in many forms when discussing families. Even "mainstream" families (generally, white, middle class, etc.) are different from one another. However, there are some family characteristics that bind families together into various groups. This chapter examines some of those characteristics: ethnic/cultural, religious, and structural. The purpose of this chapter is to help you:

- Consider the degree of assimilation of ethnic/cultural families and recognize the importance of this information
- Understand what cultural pluralism means in relationship to ethnic/cultural families
- Consider some of the familial characteristics of Latino, Native American, Asian, and African American families
- Consider how religious diversity affects families
- Become better informed about non-traditional families: gay and lesbian families and grandparent-headed families

The Changing Family

Families in the United States have historically varied in structure, social and economic status, ethnic/cultural background, and religious tradition. These characteristics contribute to differences among families that suggest the diversity among the peoples of this nation. They underpin differences in language, customs, attitudes, behaviors, values, and everyday living circumstances existing among family units.

This chapter focuses on three attributes that contribute to family diversity: family structure, ethnic/cultural background, and religious traditions. Although each of these family characteristics is discussed separately, it is the particular combination of attributes that comprises a family's distinctiveness. But just as importantly, these family characteristics influence the manner in which the family conducts its day-to-day functioning. Understanding differences among families allows school personnel to structure a variety of strategies for working with families. School and home connections are likely to be enhanced when teachers and other school personnel are respectful of a family's living circumstances, as well as the unique ways a family might support the education of their children.

As noted in the previous chapter, conventional notions of a traditional or typical family are influenced by a family structure that gained prominence in the late eighteenth and early nineteenth centuries, and again in the 1950s. However, the family as a social institution has experienced many transformations that profoundly influence not only the ways in which we understand what constitutes "family" but also the function of the family unit. A discussion of diversity among families promotes more awareness and acceptance of differences among family units as they exist in contemporary life.

The relationship between parents and schools may be affected by faulty perceptions schools hold of given groups. Typically, school expectations of families reflect behaviors, value orientations, and capabilities of middle-class nuclear families. In this way, uniform standards for measuring familial competency exist that often ignore or negate the diversity among families as well as the contributions families bring to the educational setting. Stephanie Coontz, author of *The Way We Never Were*, points out that "myths (based on middle-class experience) that create unrealistic expectations about what families can, or should, do tend to erode solidarities and diminish confidence in problem-solving abilities of those whose families fall short" (1992, p. 6).

Although traditional bonds between white middle-class families and schools must be maintained, a need exists for recognition of the variety of ways in which families not fitting this form conceive of their roles in the educational lives of their children.

Family Structure

There are perhaps as many family types as there are individual families, but broad configurations of these families allow us to consider and understand families more easily. The previous chapter carefully examined single-parent families and blended families. This chapter will briefly examine the functioning of two-parent families, grandparents as parents, and the gay and lesbian families, but it is primarily dedicated to the ethnic/cultural diversity of families.

We all know the stereotype of the family—a mother, a father, and two children. In actuality, only 31 percent of families fits this picture of the stereotypical U.S. family, with twice as many families fitting into some other family model (Outtz, 1993).

Married-Couple Families

One form of married-couple family includes a husband, wife, and their biological and/or adopted children. Sociologists often call this family form an *intact family*. It is important to note that this is not a value judgment but merely a descriptive term. Another configuration of the married couple with children is the blended family. Although these two families function very differently, they have a similar appearance.

Slightly more than one third of all family households consist of married couples with children. This family structure is represented at all economic levels, as well as among all ethnic/cultural groups in the United States. A growing number of married couples, however, are childless. In fact, Outtz (1993) points out that in 1990 married couples without children outnumbered those with children.

Families are not static. Throughout the history of humankind they have and continue to change. A change that has greatly influenced married-couple families over the last fifty years is the increased number of women working outside the home. The number of married women with children under the age of eighteen in the work force has grown to a point that, currently, only three out of ten women in married-couple families are stay-at-home moms. While some women entered the work force out of economic necessity, others have entered to further a career.

Even though there have been dramatic changes in the structure and functioning of families, some things have not changed. Women still are the primary caretakers of children and have primary responsibility for the home. According to Demo and Acock (1993), household labor responsibilities for women that emerged with the nuclear family form are well established and resistant to change. Although men's contributions to household labor have increased over the last thirty years, mothers working outside the home add nearly forty hours a week in domestic labor to their outside-the-home employment responsibilities.

Women's entry into the work force dramatically changed the day-to-day needs and functioning of the married-couple family. The quandary over how to best attend to the needs of "latchkey" children has reached national discussion, and provides an excellent example of the impact of women's labor force participation on the nuclear family. Affordable and quality child care, flexible working schedules, and more flexible maternal and paternal leave policies from employers are major concerns, not only for married couple families but also for other families who have children home alone while adults are working. Just as employers are considering ways to accommodate the needs of working couples, many schools have also made changes to facilitate involvement of these parents in their children's education. A modification such as scheduling parent–teacher conferences for evening hours acknowledges the need for change in some school practices to adapt to the living circumstances of working couples.

Some working married couples meet the challenges caused when both parents are working by reaching out to an extended family. Ethnic minority couples who have maintained culturally valued extended family ties may not experience the same child-care dilemmas as those families who adopted a more nuclear family form. In this way, current issues facing working married couples are more closely related to the decline of the white middle-class nuclear family as the predominant family form.

Alternative Family Structures

The U.S. family is diverse in a variety of ways (culture/ethnicity, economic status, etc.). We tend to see this as a recent phenomenon when in fact there always has been diversity within and between family groups. However, the numbers and the nature of them are certainly changing: father-headed homes, foster homes, children living with a variety of relatives, and so forth. This section examines two of the non-traditional families: grandparent-headed homes and gay/lesbian families.

Grandparents as Parents

The number of homes in which grandparents are rearing the children of their children is increasing. This has long been a cultural practice with some Native American groups, but generally has not been a practice within mainstream society (Hildebrand, Phenice, Gray, & Hines, 1996). With the age of unwed mothers decreasing and substance abuse increasing, many mothers are unable or unwilling to care for their children. The increase in the number of grandparents rearing young children has reached such proportions that support groups for these grandparents have been formed across the country.

Although the number of grandparents as primary care givers has increased due to a variety of societal problems, there are other more positive reasons for this family configuration. It is common for grandmothers in some cultures (many Native American groups, for example) to assume parental responsibilities.

Gay- and Lesbian-Headed Families

Gay and lesbian families are more conspicuous and more numerous than in the past. Whereas this family structure may be controversial in some sections of society, an increasing number of children are being raised in gay and lesbian households. Although there are societal hesitations to label these households "families," their numbers are estimated to range from four to fourteen million (Hare & Richards, 1993; Outtz, 1993). The reluctance of many gay and lesbian parents to let their sexual orientation be known accounts for much of the difficulty in gathering exact numbers for this family type. Gay and lesbian parents often fear discrimination and the possibility of custody battles because they are automatically assumed to be unfit parents in some states.

For many gay and lesbian parents, children were the result of a previous heterosexual bond. However, artificial insemination and adoption are increasingly used as means for becoming parents. Gay and lesbian families may take a number of forms and span the social and economic ladders. Many families are headed by two women or two men in a partner relationship; some are blended families in which both parents bring a child or children to the family unit; some are single-parent families; and in some instances, a gay man may father a child with a lesbian and parenting is shared.

> ## Reflection...
>
> Explore your thoughts and feelings about gay and lesbian parents. How will your attitude affect the children of gay and lesbian parents?

Gay and lesbian parents differ in the extent to which they prepare their children for possible negative experiences in reaction to the parent's lifestyle. Some children are accepting of their parent's lifestyle, while others may feel they have a secret that must be kept. School personnel must reflect on their views of families headed by homosexuals. Behaviors that inhibit or support school–home relations will not go unnoticed by these parents. Attitudes that allow parents to interact on school- or family-related issues based on their chosen level of openness about their sexual orientation are more likely to enhance school–home relations.

Ethnic and Cultural Diversity

A position of dominance for European-American culture occurred in the seventeenth century. The English language, customs, laws, and religion were transported to the colonies by English immigrants, who made up the majority of early settlers. Although cultural shifts have evolved over the centuries, Euro-American cultural dominance has been maintained, and is now known as mainstream America— white and middle class. Native Americans and blacks who inhabited the colonies in the seventeenth century were viewed as unsuitable for assimilation into the Anglo-American way of life. Immigrants from Germany, Ireland, and Scandinavia were more readily accepted than were Italians, Jews, Croatians, Poles, and other southern and eastern Europeans who immigrated to United States.

Assimilation versus Cultural Pluralism

Immigrant groups were expected to conform to the established way of life in the United States. Families and schools were pivotal institutions in the process of conformity, with the latter positioned to play a major role in the process of assimilation. Assimilation is a cultural concept. It refers to the process whereby one group, generally a politically and economically inferior one, adopts the cultural traits of another group, usually one with political and economic superiority. This is a gradual process whereby both groups become virtually indistinguishable (Feinberg & Soltis, 1998). In the United States, assimilated individuals conform to the standards of life as set by European Americans, while abdicating cultural characteristics of their ethnic group. However, assimilation into a mainstream culture represents but one possible outcome of interaction between a dominant culture and various ethnic groups.

An earlier notion of the United States as a great melting pot of ethnicities never came to fruition. The melting pot ideology suggests a coming together of all ethnic/cultural groups would result in a new culture, one that melded the characteristics of each. However, rather than "melting" into a common culture, each new wave of immigrants was expected to give up distinctive cultural practices and to assimilate into an "American" culture which had been heavily influenced by populations from northern Europe. Many immigrant groups were pressured to take on the characteristics of the mainstream population while denying the richness of their own culture. The myth has been that the dominant culture would also change, influenced by other ethnic groups; the reality is very different.

A third possibility is enculturation. Bernal and Knight (1993) describe *enculturation* or *ethnic socialization* as a process by which developing individuals acquire cultural teaching from family, peers, and the ethnic community that allows for development of qualities necessary to function as a member of the ethnic group. The individual develops an ethnic identity. Ethnic group members, to varying degrees, may engage in enculturation.

These distinctions are especially important in attempting to understand how families identify themselves with respect to their ethnic backgrounds. Differences among various ethnic/cultural groups in language, customs, child-rearing practices, and values existing in the home could be explained in part by a family's beliefs in the value of assimilation and enculturation.

A number of issues emerge as families, particularly ethnic minority families, try to find a balance between their culture of origin (enculturation) and mainstream culture (assimilation). However, according to Ramirez and Cox (1980), society pressures minority parents to rear their children to be as much like mainstream children as possible. Unfortunately, this ignores the concern these parents have with regard to the cultural identity of their children. Will they lose their connections with the parents' culture(s) of origin?

Although it is important for school personnel to understand characteristics attributed to a given ethnic/cultural group, it is also important not to stereotype.

Traditional to Assimilated

Members of a culture whose behaviors, beliefs, and cognition are determined by a single culture are called *traditional* (e.g., a Navajo Medicine Man on the Navajo reservation), while those who forego their own cultural practices to take on all of the characteristics of the mainstream culture are said to be *assimilated*. Those people who are equally knowledgeable and comfortable in two cultures are *bicultural.*

Hence, it is important to view ethnic/cultural distinctions routinely associated with a particular group, not so much as prescriptions for the functioning of particular families, but rather as descriptions of possible characteristics, behaviors, or attitudes a family may incorporate into their day-to-day existence.

Reflection...

Consider the cultural behaviors of your family. Do your family traditions include special foods, activities, celebrations, and so on? How do these tie into your cultural background?

Mainstream Families

As mentioned early in this chapter, a "typical" U.S. family does not exist. Still, values, customs, and behaviors exist within certain families that are more reflective of values and attitudes accepted as mainstream cultural norms. For example, when compared with the norms of some minority ethnic group families, mainstream culture families tend to be more democratically oriented, with children having the opportunity to express their views and wishes. It would not be disrespectful for the child to question or challenge authority figures, including parents themselves.

Children are encouraged to be individuals and to make decisions for themselves early on, with parents in the role of providing support and guidance. Parents have high expectations that children will develop a sense of responsibility for their actions, learn to rely on themselves, and, over time, develop a level of independence believed necessary to function as an adult.

This focus on individualism envelops the family unit as well, because the nuclear or immediate family is valued over an extended one in the day-to-day functioning of the family. In fact, mainstream culture families generally confer less respect to the elderly when compared with some minority ethnic group cultures.

Another characteristic generally attributed to mainstream culture families is the focus on the importance of punctuality and attention to schedules. An adherence to both is seen as a sign of politeness and responsible behavior. The maxim "getting the job done" is an expression of an orientation toward completing tasks in a timely manner.

A competitive spirit underlines a drive for personal accomplishment in education, work, and play. A mainstream culture belief that the individual has some control over his or her destiny supports the notion that adversity can be overcome through hard work.

Although formal education is highly valued, children are given the opportunity, and expected, to achieve in other learning and performing situations as well. Activities such as athletics and vocal or instrumental music, whether an extension of school activities or privately arranged, are examples of areas in which hard work leads to personal accomplishment and contributes to the development of a well-rounded individual.

It is important to note that these family characteristics may be observable in any number of family situations. However, they are more likely observable in European-American middle-class families, as well as in more assimilated middle-class ethnic minority families.

African American Families

The history of African Americans in the United States, including two hundred years of enslavement, followed by years of segregation, discrimination, racial oppression, and both overt and institutionalized racism, plays a large role in characteristics exhibited in varying degrees among these families. Today, African Americans are approximately 12 percent of the population nationally, with substantial numbers living in urban cities where crime, poor housing, high unemployment, underemployment, and the lack of adequate services persist. Despite an increase in the number of African Americans acquiring post–high school education and attaining middle-class status, substantial numbers continue to live in poverty. Inequities continue in health care, employment, and quality of life between African Americans and European Americans.

Even with differences in social and economic class, survival and protection of one's family remains a predominant theme among African Americans. Concern over racism and biased treatment from both individuals and institutions influences many behaviors and attitudes among African American families. Valuing an extended family, for example, represents a belief that a larger, interdependent group stands a better chance of moving through barriers to survival. As part of the value of an extended family, the elderly are held in a position of respect, and African American children learn early to value and obey the elderly, even those to whom they are not related. Indeed, a sense of kinship often extends beyond blood relations to other members of the community.

Kinship ties also play a role in assuring that children are cared for. When parents and children were sold away from each other during slavery, children were taken care of by other adults on the plantation. Today informal adoptions by an aunt, uncle, grandmother, or even a cousin are common. Additionally, single parents (mother or father) faced with raising children without a spouse may turn to their kinship network for help and support.

The nurturance and protection of children is highly valued among African Americans. A strong belief that children need to be disciplined is complemented by the belief that children need time to be children. Hence, in many African American families, there is less focus on pushing the child toward independence and/or detachment from the family. When compared to peers in other ethnic groups, it is common to find African American young adults remaining with the family of origin for longer periods before establishing a home as an independent adult.

African American families have flexible family roles, a characteristic borne out of the social and economic circumstances faced by many African American families. Traditional gender roles for males and females may be reversed, based on the needs of the family. Children may also assume some roles normally taken by parents. Historically, because both African American parents had to work, it was expected that older siblings would look after and often discipline their younger siblings. Generally, family members adapt to whatever role is needed in order for the family to function (Burnett & Lewis, 1993).

Education is viewed as the way to a better life and thus has traditionally been held in high esteem by African Americans. This characteristic was supported by a study conducted by Ritter, Mont-Reynaud, and Dornbusch (1993), which focused on minority parent attitudes toward the education of their children. The study included students and parents from various ethnic minority groups, at various social and economic levels. Based on survey responses, African American parents emphasized hard work in academic areas (e.g., math, English, social studies) and more frequently reacted both positively and negatively to grades of their high school students. Although these parents also appeared to have more working knowledge of "school ways," including awareness of homework, school schedules, and the importance of course selection, they also tended to have higher levels of mistrust toward schools than some of the other ethnic minority parents included in the study.

Many African American families believe that it is necessary for children to understand racism, as well as the history and the contribution of African Americans in the United States, as a means for the child's self-protection and survival. African Americans are particularly sensitive to acts perceived as racist. They want children to be able to discern negative actions directed toward them that are based on the color of their skin and have little to do with their character. This distinction is seen as important in helping the child develop a positive self-esteem. The current movement by some African American parents and educators toward Afrocentric schools, particularly for African American males, highlights, in part, the importance of the development of this self-protective capacity.

Reflection...

Do you have African American or other ethnic minority friends? If not, why not? Describe ways we can develop friendships with people of different ethnic backgrounds and how we can model this for the children we teach.

Like many other ethnic minority families, African American families are challenged by the assimilation/enculturation dilemma. Historically, African Americans have come together as an interdependent group in order to address issues that might improve life circumstances (e.g., education, employment, housing) of the group. In fact, it is common to hear African Americans speak of "the community" as an entity that embraces all African Americans. There is an underlying expectation that the community should receive benefits from the successes of the individual. However, being successful in academic and work settings is often tantamount to leaving the community, an action believed to be an integral part of upward social mobility. This circumstance presents a dilemma for some African American families. Broadway (1987), for example, found that African American middle-class families were specifically concerned that their children learn to function in Euro-American middle-class contexts, while at the same time maintaining close cultural ties with the African American community.

Implied is a recognition among some African American families of the bicultural nature of African Americans. For example, many African Americans, particularly middle-class African Americans, are well versed in both standard and black English and can switch into using either, depending on the situation. W. E. B. Dubois referred to this talent as having a double consciousness. This consciousness basically allowed African Americans to exist in two different worlds, one black and one white (Lewis, 1993). African Americans have a prized oral tradition in which the use of language is highly valued. Indeed, some African Americans describe themselves as bilingual as well as bicultural, believing that some expressions lose the richness of meaning when translated into standard English.

As is the case with other ethnic minority groups, African Americans are a very diverse group. The extent to which they embrace the characteristics cited above will vary. School personnel are thus challenged to get to know individual families in order to understand more clearly how they identify themselves with respect to ethnic group characteristics.

Asian American Families

Asian Americans are the fastest growing minority group in the United States. With groups originating from countries including China, Japan, Korea, Cambodia, Laos, Vietnam, and India, Asian Americans are clearly a very diverse people. The experiences of Asian American families will depend to some extent on the circumstances surrounding their immigration to the United States. Some Asian Americans arrived in the United States as highly educated professionals, having marketable skills, and/or as bilingual and familiar with the mainstream culture in the United States. Still others arrived with low levels of education, languages other than English, and experiencing high levels of culture shock due to a lack of familiarity with this country. For example, Korean Americans have one of the highest levels of education among all ethnic groups, as well as high rates of self-employment. Like the first wave of Vietnamese, they were well educated in their homeland. More recent refugees from Vietnam, Cambodia, and Laos tend to have lower levels of education and experience higher levels of unemployment in the United States (Chan, 1992).

The assimilation/enculturation balance also influences the experience of Asian Americans. Throughout their history in the United States, Asian Americans have experienced varying levels of acceptance and rejection. For example, Chinese Americans, a culturally diverse group among themselves, were the first Asians to immigrate to the United States. Forty-two years later, they were banned from immigration as a result of the Chinese Exclusion Act of 1882. Anti-Chinese sentiment, fueled by racism and economic tension led to this federal law, which was not repealed until 1943. We might also remember the imprisonment of people of Japanese ancestry, the vast majority of whom were U.S. citizens, in relocation centers during World War II. Today, however, Asian Americans are stereotypically looked upon as a "model minority" (Lee, 1996).

Like other racial/ethnic minority groups, Asian American families are subjected to additional stereotypes that function to minimize the diverse cultural and historical backgrounds existing in this group. As Yao (1993) points out, it is impossible to describe a typical Asian American family. Although there is great diversity in the backgrounds, languages, religions, and customs among Asian Americans, there are some generalizations that can be stated about Asian American families.

The family is the primary social unit among Asians, hence its preservation is important to the maintenance of the social, political, religious, and economic order. The strongest familial bonds are between parent and child, rather than between parents themselves. The male is perceived as the head of the family. Unlike the democratic model existing in many mainstream culture families, parents are clearly the authority figures in Asian American families. Unquestioning obedience to parental control is expected from the child. In fact, the close supervision children receive from their parents is perceived as a sign of parental love. It is considered disrespectful for a child to question parental love and authority.

Asian Americans have high expectations for their children academically, and also value upward mobility. Achievement is considered part of the child's obligation to the family, rather than a personal accomplishment. The child's success, or lack thereof, is a source of pride or embarrassment to parents. Asian American parents believe that children should not be rewarded for what they are expected to do. In fact acknowledgment of accomplishments comes in the form of encouragement to do better, while failure to meet parental expectations results in punishment. The child may be chastised verbally and excluded from family social life (Espiritu, 1992).

At the same time, parents make many personal sacrifices for their children in order to facilitate their success. Family goals of achievement and upward mobility result in a high number of families in which both parents work outside the home. For recent immigrants who may have education and job skill limitations, it is not uncommon for parents to work long hours and/or have more than one job.

Asian American families tend to have distinct boundaries between educational responsibilities of the home and school. Teachers are highly respected and parents are not likely to contradict what is said by the teacher in his or her presence. Concurrently, matters more directly connected to the process of schooling (e.g., curriculum, discipline) are believed to be the province of the school. Within the home, parents closely watch the progress of the child, while encouraging the child to increase his or her performance.

Despite striking differences between behaviors, attitudes, and values of Asian American and mainstream culture families, it is often suggested that other ethnic minorities adopt Asian American child-rearing practices. Indeed, the label of "model minority" is viewed as a burden by some Asian Americans. The concomitant label of "superior students" assigned to Asian American children adds to the pressure these students already feel from high expectations emanating from the home. Additionally, the academic difficulty experienced by some Asian American students is often overlooked because of a perception that Asian American children are "smart students" (Shen & Mo, 1990). Academic pressures and other difficulties felt by Asian American students may go unnoticed, owing to some extent to the lessons taught in the home regarding social and emotional restraint. Discussing problems may be difficult for students, as well as for their parents.

Tradition passed through the ages continues to have a valued position within some Asian American families. The differences between Eastern and Western beliefs, customs, and values are often the basis of conflict between Asian American children and their parents. In fact, some families attempt to protect their children from outside influences by controlling those with whom the child comes in contact (e.g., peers, playmates). Nonetheless, influences of Western customs and values inadvertently cause tension in many Asian American families, especially families of more recent immigrants who may be less familiar with customs in this country. Schools and other social service institutions working to assist and support the transition of these families into their new home in the United States must take care not to undermine parental authority in the process.

Latino Families

Latinos in the United States include Mexican Americans, Cuban Americans, Puerto Ricans, and other Central and South Americans. Each of these groups has a different historical background that continues to influence their experience in contemporary U.S. society. Many Mexican Americans, or Chicanos, as many prefer, trace their ancestry to those who lived on the land that is today California, Texas, New Mexico, and Colorado. This land was ceded to the United States at the conclusion of the Mexican War of 1848. Others trace their ancestry to immigrants who fled Mexico in search of work during the Mexican Revolution of 1910.

Like Mexican Americans, Puerto Ricans are United States citizens as a result of land ceded to the United States following a war. The United States obtained Puerto Rico at the end of the Spanish American War, and later made the inhabitants of the island citizens of the United States. Today, Puerto Ricans live on both the island and mainland United States.

Cuban Americans immigrated to the United States as refugees beginning in 1959, with the reign of Castro. Early Cuban immigrants were wealthy professionals. However, the last wave of Cuban immigrants, those who were a part of the Mariel exodus of 1980, consisted of what Cuba referred to as its "social undesirables" (Suarez, 1993). The experience of the earlier Cuban Americans differs from that of the general population of Puerto Ricans and Mexican Americans, who tend to experience more discrimination, poverty, and higher school dropout rates. Approximately 26 percent of Latinos live in poverty (Ramirez, 1993), and, as noted earlier, this number increases when the family is headed by a single parent. Additionally, Fillmore (1990) estimates that approximately 40 percent of Latino children will drop out before completing high school.

Even with these differences, there are commonalities shared by Latino families that provide insight into the dynamics operating within these families. Regardless of class, religion, and length of time in the United States, Latinos traditionally value the family as an important resource for coping with life's stresses. Family is defined as a closely bonded group that may extend beyond blood lines. It is common for family members to prefer living close to each other, in order to more easily accommodate the financial and emotional support extended to family members.

Children hold an exalted position in the family. In fact, the birth of a child validates a marriage (Zuniga, 1992). Zuniga also points out that Latino families are generally less concerned about children reaching developmental benchmarks and tend to be more permissive and indulgent with young children when compared to mainstream culture families. Still, children have family-related responsibilities, such as helping with household chores or caring for siblings. Children are taught to respect elders and are expected to interact with others in a respectful and polite manner. Child-rearing practices among Latinos are traditionally geared to prepare children for their role in sustaining the function of the family in Latino culture.

There is concern, however, among some Latinos over what appears to be an erosion of traditional supports expected of the family. More-assimilated, younger Latinos who are focused on upward mobility are leaving the more traditional customs behind, including the traditional values of sharing and support among family members. The concern over the rift between old ways and new, more assimilated ways also extends to the implications these divisions have for the Spanish language as essential to maintaining a Latino culture. Younger Latinos may not speak Spanish, while the elderly may not speak English. This lack of communication contributes to the erosion of traditional ways.

Parents of children in public schools may have limited English as well. When combined with poverty, this lack of English proficiency often results in barriers between schools and Latino families, as well as for other language minority parents (e.g., Asian American parents). Language proficiency is to not be confused with parental competency. Hence, a number of schools seek ways to minimize language barriers (e.g., through translators), in order to maintain communication between the school and the home.

Native American Families

At the time of the arrival of Columbus in 1492, an estimated five million Native Americans (commonly labled Indians based on European explorers' mistaken belief that they had traveled to the far east) lived in North America. Nearly four hundred years later, the Native American population had decreased to approximately 600,000. Warfare and death due to new contagious diseases introduced by Europeans decimated tribes who inhabited the land before the Europeans' arrival. The remaining Native Americans were left without benefit of their warriors and their elders. The continuous loss of warriors left tribes unable to defend themselves in battle, and among some tribes the loss of elders equaled loss of historical and cultural knowledge that sustained the social order and way of life for tribal members.

The Native American way of life was further assaulted by continuous attempts at assimilation by European Americans. The English initially viewed Native Americans as unworthy of the land they lived on because they were not Christian, and later as unworthy of being included in an evolving European American way of life. By the late 1800s, however, concerted efforts were initiated to assimilate the now conquered indigenous peoples of North America. History is replete with descriptions of methods aimed at purging Native Americans of their culture. The young have been the major target of these efforts. For example, the Bureau of Indian Affairs made an intensive effort to assimilate Native Americans into the larger U.S. culture. This was accomplished by establishing industrial schools off the reservation. These schools were designed to eradicate the Native

American culture and customs, and replace it with European American culture (Trennert, 1990). Perhaps the most widely known effort of assimilation is the removal of Native American children from their families on the reservation. These children were sent to boarding schools in which they were discouraged from using traditional ways and inculcated with European American culture and values. Today, there is an effort among Native Americans to reestablish traditional values.

As we have observed with other ethnic minorities in this chapter, Native Americans are also culturally diverse. As noted with other families, the discussion of family characteristics of Native Americans is generally applicable to the group as a whole. The issue of assimilation and enculturation exists for Native Americans as for other groups, with families fitting at various points along a continuum of traditional and more European ways of life.

Not surprisingly, children are prized in Native American families. The family has traditionally played an intimate role in the education of children. In Native American families, the term *family* is broadened to include the immediate and the extended family, and all adults in the family are responsible for teaching children. In fact, biological parents may not have primary responsibility for the child's care. There is traditionally a strong bond between grandparent and grandchild in Native American cultures. The elderly are highly revered for their wisdom and experience in all areas, and are thus consulted on issues of child rearing as well. Aunts and uncles are also involved with child rearing; in fact, the same kinship terms are used for mother-aunt and uncle-father (Sipes, 1993).

Children are accorded respect in Native American families and are not scolded or admonished. Rather, they are taught through explanation and example and provided with the reason a behavior is expected. The lessons of an expected behavior may be embedded in stories, which are also commonly used to provide children with knowledge of Native American traditions, rituals, and beliefs.

The structure and functioning of Native American families, like those of African American and Latino families, are consistent with a value in collectivism over individualism. Actions that support the needs of the community are more positively regarded than accomplishments and achievements motivated solely by self-aggrandizement. One's personal well-being is enhanced by giving to and sharing with others. As a result of this focus on the group rather than the individual, some Native American children may exhibit behavior that could be labeled as shyness. They would rather not draw too much attention to themselves as individuals.

Native American families currently have the lowest income and employment rates in the United States, and their children have the highest drop-out rates of any group of students. In keeping with their cultural tradition, Native American parents are calling for a larger role in making decisions about their children's education. They are especially interested in a culturally relevant curriculum and an increase in the number of Native American teachers (Noley, 1992). Assimilationist educational practices historically disparage Native American culture. Thus, parents are also interested in cross-cultural training for teachers in order to reduce the discontinuity between home and school (Szasz, 1991).

> **Reflection...**
>
> Too often we focus on the negative stereotypes and characteristics of ethnic groups. What are some common strengths of African American, Latino, Asian American, and Native American families?

Religious Diversity

A majority of European immigrants during the colonial period were members of Protestant denominations. Not surprisingly, public education was founded on Protestant beliefs and values. Protestant denominations, including Lutheran, Methodist, Presbyterian, and Baptist, collectively make up the majority of religious affiliations in the United States today.

Students live in homes ranging from those in which religion is of little or no consequence, to those in which religion is integral to the everyday functioning of the family. In some cases, religious tradition is intimately tied to ethnic/cultural traditions. For example, among some Native American tribes spirituality is manifested through a belief that every living thing on earth is interconnected. Respect for all living things leads to harmony, an important attribute of Native American culture. Among Asian Americans, life values, social norms, and beliefs are supported by the religious-philosophical teachings inherent in Confucianism, Taoism, and Buddhism (Chan, 1992). And while Judaism provides a link among many Jewish Americans, some Jews view themselves as a cultural minority as well.

The previously mentioned assimilation/enculturation dilemma becomes an issue for ethnic/cultural groups for whom particular religious teaching is part of an ethnic/cultural group identity, because mainstream assimilation may lead to changes in religious beliefs and practices as well. In a similar manner, members of ethnic groups may follow non-mainstream religious practices and beliefs, albeit those that are not traditionally associated with their ethnic/cultural group. African Americans, for example, traditionally belong to Protestant denominations, although they may also follow the teachings of Catholicism, Judaism, and growing numbers are becoming Muslims. Latinos in the United States are traditionally associated with the Roman Catholic church; however, this number has decreased approximately 20 percent over the last twenty-five years because immigrant Latinos as well as those living in poverty are shifting to denominations believed to better serve their needs ("Latinos Shift Loyalties," 1994).

Even though schools have improved in their efforts to be more sensitive to the impact of school activities and practices on diverse religious traditions, instances continue to occur in which families perceive their religious values and beliefs to be in conflict with school practices. Moreover, the possibility of misunderstanding increases as religious beliefs and practices veer further away from traditional Protestantism. For example, the doctrine of Jehovah Witnesses forbids the celebration of holidays and birthdays. The children of these families will be in conflict if you expect them to join in the celebration. In addition, the rights of the family would be violated. Lunch menus with ham as the only entree overlook the Muslim and Jewish practice of not eating pork.

The freedom to worship at the church, synagogue, or mosque of one's choice contributes to the religious diversity of the United States. As educators, we must guard against making assumptions about the religion of our students. School personnel need only be prepared to listen to the family to accommodate the family's wishes, while taking care not to infringe on the rights of other families.

> **Reflection...**
>
> Consider your attitudes toward various religions. Do you have biases concerning other religions? Are there stereotypes that have affected your thinking? How could you investigate the accuracy of your perceptions?

Summary

Diversity among Families: Impact on Home–School Collaboration

Any general discussion of diversity among U.S. families is necessarily hindered by the richness and extent of that diversity. Additional family customs and values could be discussed within each of the broader ethnic/cultural groups mentioned. Characteristics of mainstream culture families discussed previously, for example, do not include the diversity of customs inherent in European American families. Additional families of African descent (e.g., Haitian, Ethiopian); Asian/Pacific Island families (e.g., Hawaiian, Samoan, Filipino); and Native American Eskimo families could be discussed within the context of their respective ethnic groups. At the same time, the needs and challenges facing the growing number of transracial families could be addressed as well. Extension of a discussion on family structure might include the growing numbers of grandparents now raising their children's children, as well as families with adopted children.

Addressing family diversity is central to building constructive home–school relations. The combination of family characteristics (e.g., middle class, African American, single parent, United Methodist) provides important information for understanding how to work with a particular family. It is even more important, however, to learn from families how they define themselves within the context of observable characteristics in order to understand more clearly the attitudes and values operating within the family.

Teachers must be prepared to work with families who challenge their personal notions and experiences of what constitutes family. For this reason, it is important to read and become familiar with cultures that are different from one's own. We may well be facing the eradication of the conforming role historically assigned to schools. An understanding of diversity among families is not meant to provide information for development of strategies to change families so that they fit the needs of the school. Rather, it provides information that allows schools to change, so that they are inviting to the variety of families represented in contemporary school settings.

RECOMMENDED ACTIVITIES

1. Interview (or videotape) families of two different ethnic/cultural groups and identify unique familial behaviors and those that are generally universal to all families.

2. Invite gay and lesbian parents to visit your class and share with you their family experiences.

3. Volunteer to work in a day-care center with children and families that are different from yours.

4. Visit churches different than your own and speculate how the doctrine of these churches would affect family life.

5. If families of particular ethnic or cultural backgrounds are not present in your community, identify such families in other communities and have a telephone conference call. It would be helpful to the family for you to send pictures of the class members so that they can visualize the people to whom they are speaking. Also, ask them to send you some family pictures.

6. Identify the cultural characteristics of your family and how those characteristics have affected your family life. Describe a family with a different cultural background you have known and compare and contrast the two families.

ADDITIONAL RESOURCES

Cultural Diversity

Books:

Dickenson, G. E., & Leming, M. R. (1990). *Understanding families: Diversity, continuity, and change.* Boston: Allyn & Bacon.

As a primary text for sociology of the family courses, *Understanding Families* delivers up-to-date research and a life-cycle approach spanning parenting, middle years, and retirement. Updated discussions of family crises include death and violence as well as traditional divorce.

Hildebrand, V., Phenice, L. A., Gray, M. M., & Hines, R. P. (1996). *Knowing and serving diverse families.* Englewood Cliffs, NJ: Merrill.

This book, divided into four parts, offers suggestions on how to serve individual families, and explores ethnic diversity and lifestyle variations among contemporary American families. It contains chapters that focus on African American, Hispanic American, Asian American, Arab American, Native American, and Amish American families.

Kendall, F. E. (1996). *Diversity in the classroom: New approaches to the education of young children* (2nd ed.).

This is a book of contributions by some of the leading proponents of multicultural education. This book has a number of selections that will be helpful to a classroom teacher (talking with parents, preparing for a multicultural classroom, affirming diversity, etc.). 192 pp.

Teacher College Press
P.O. Box 20
Williston, VT 05495-0020
Phone: 800-864-7626

Chapters:

Dauber, S. L., & Epstein, J. L. (1993). Minority parents and the elementary school: Attitudes and practice. In N. F. Chavkin (Ed.), *Families and schools in a pluralistic society* (pp. 73–84). Albany, NY: State University Press.

Ritter, R. L., Mount-Reynaud, R., & Dornbusch, S. M. (1993). Minority parents and their youth: Concerns, encouragement, and support for school achievement. In N. F. Chavkin (Ed.), *Families and schools in a pluralistic society* (pp. 107–120). Albany, NY: State University Press.

Organizations:

Institute for Responsive Education
605 Commonwealth Avenue
Boston, MA 02215
Phone: 617-353-3309

Intercultural Development Research Association
5835 Callaghan, Suite 350
San Antonio, TX 78228
Phone: 512-684-8180

African American Families

Books:

Hutchinson, E. O. (1992). *Black fatherhood: A guide to male parenting.*

Black men of different generations tell what it means to be a father in America. The book features interviews with fathers of different occupations, incomes, and family circumstances. 144 pp., ISBN: 1-881032-08-6.

Highsmith Company, Inc.
W5527 Highway
P.O. Box 899
Fort Atkinson, WI 53538-0800
Phone: 800-558-2110

Johnson, A. E., & Cooper, A. M. (1996). *A student's guide to African American geneal-ogy: Oryx American family tree series.*

This book is an excellent way to help African American students learn about their family history as well as informing non-African American teachers about native families. This book provides cultural background, an annotated bibliography, and interesting historical facts. In addition, it comes with color and black-and-white photographs and features a glossary and index. ISBN: 0-89774-975-8.

> Oryx Press
> Customer Service Department
> 4041 N. Central Avenue, Suite 700
> Phoenix, AZ 85012-9759
> Phone: 800-279-6799

Staples, R., & Johnson, L. B. (1992). *Black families at the crossroad.*

This book addresses the black family in America. It offers a comprehensive exami-nation of the black family unit as it has evolved in contemporary society by consid-ering how economics, racism, culture, and politics affect the dynamics of family relations. 315 pp., ISBN: 1-55542-486-4.

> Empak Publishing Company
> 212 East Ohio Street
> Chicago, IL 60611
> Phone: 323-642-8364

Williams, R. (1990). *They stole it but you must return it* (4th ed.).

Williams examines the historical roots of the African American family. He exam-ines what slavery did to the black family. The book is intended as a guide for black families. 130 pp., ISBN: 0-938805-01-0.

> Highsmith Company, Inc.
> W5527 Highway
> P.O. Box 899
> Fort Atkinson, WI 53538-0800
> Phone: 800-558-2110

Chapters:

Hildebrand, V., Phenice, L. A., Gray, M. M., & Hines, R. P. (1996). African American families. In *Knowing and serving diverse families* (pp. 69–90). Englewood Cliffs, NJ: Merrill.

Staples, R. (1988). The black American family. In C. Mindel, R. Haberstein, and R. Wrights (Eds.), *Ethnic families in America* (pp. 303–324). New York: Elsevier.

Articles:

Jones, E. (1993). An interview on the topic, "Changing church confronts the chang-ing Black family." *Ebony, 18*(10), 94–100.

Massaquoi, H. (1993). The Black family nobody knows. *Ebony, 18*(10), 28–31.

Videos:

Black History: Lost, Stolen, or Strayed

Although this film is old, starring a very young Bill Cosby, it is not dated. It is still the best video available that provides an in-depth examination of some of the influences which affect African Americans. 1965. (60 minutes, color)

> Insights Media
> 2162 Broadway
> New York, NY 10024
> Phone: 212-721-6316

I'll Fly Away

This is a PBS video series that helps the viewer understand a white and a black family in the 1960s. This series is not only very well done and entertaining but also allows the viewer to better understand the functioning and stresses of black families of that period, consequently better understanding today's families. (60 minutes)

> PBS Television Series
> Washington Educational Television Association
> Box 2636
> Washington, DC 20009
> Phone: 703-998-2600

Organizations:

> National Black Child Development Institute
> 1023 15th Avenue NW, Suite 600
> Washington, DC 20002
> Phone: 202-387-1281

Latino Families

Books:

Ryskamp, G., & Ryskamp, P. (1996). *A student's guide to Mexican American genealogy.*

This book is an excellent way to help Mexican American students learn about their family history as well as informing non-Mexican American teachers about native families. This book provides cultural background, an annotated bibliography, and interesting historical facts. In addition, it comes with color and black-and-white photographs and features a glossary and index. ISBN: 0-89774-975-8.

> Oryx Press
> Customer Service Department
> 4041 N. Central Avenue, Suite 700
> Phoenix, AZ 85012-9759
> Phone: 800-279-6799

SotoMayor, M. (Ed.). (1991). *Empowering Hispanic families: A critical issue for the 90's.*

This book is a collection of essays on various issues pertaining to Hispanic families. It deals with educational, sociological, and mental health issues. 214 pp., ISBN: 0-87304-243-3.

Family Service America
11700 West Lake Park Drive
Milwaukee, WI 53224
Phone: 414-359-1040

Vades, G. (1996). *Con Respeto: Bridging in the distance between culturally diverse families and the schools—An ethnographic portrait.*

This is a study of ten Mexican immigrant families, describing how such families go about the business of surviving and learning to succeed in a new world. Valdez examines what *appears* to be a disinterest in education by Mexican parents. This book examines a number of important issues and helps the teacher have a better understanding of these families. This is a well-written and informative book. 256 pp.

Teacher College Press
P.O. Box 20
Williston, VT 05495-0020
Phone: 800-864-7626

Valdivieso, R., & Davis, C. (1988). *U.S. Hispanics: Challenging issues for the 1990s.*

This booklet provides demographic information that will help the reader better understand the Hispanic population and consequently better understand the Hispanic family. ISBN: 0736-7716.

Population Reference Bureau
1875 Connecticut Avenue NW, Suite 520
Washington, DC 20009-5728
Phone: 800-877-9881

Chapters:

Carrasuillo, A. L. (1991). The family of Hispanic children and youth. In *Hispanic children & youth in the United States: A resource guide* (pp. 69–87). New York: Garland Publishing, Inc.

Hildebrand, V., Phenice, L. A., Gray, M. M., & Hines, R. P. (1996). Hispanic-American Families. In *Knowing and serving diverse families* (pp. 69–90). Englewood Cliffs, NJ: Merrill.

Videos:

The Latino Family

This video shows both the changes in and the endurance of traditional Latino families. In following three generations of one Mexican American family, it traces the pattern of migration and cultural change. It shows how the traditional roles of the Latino elderly are being altered by their families' needs and also how the traditional pleasures can still be celebrated.

Films for the Humanities and Sciences
P.O. Box 2053
Princeton, NJ 08543
Phone: 800-257-5126

The Status of the Latina Women

This video compares the Latina of the United States with those of Latin America. It also examines how Latino men perceive Latina women—the myth and reality, as well as the Latina woman's role in the family and in the community. 1993. (26 minutes, color)

> Films for the Humanities and Science
> P.O. Box 2053
> Princeton, NJ 08543
> Phone: 800-257-5126

Organizations:

> Mexican American Legal Defense and Education Fund
> 634 South Spring Street, 11th Floor
> Los Angeles, CA 90014
> Phone: 213-629-2512

Gay and Lesbian Families

Books:

Sherman, S. (Ed.). (1993). *Lesbian and gay marriages: Private commitments, public ceremonies.* Bulk of book consists of interviews with "long-term couples," some who had public ceremonies, some who did not. Appendices include directory of organizations. ISBN: 0-8772-297-5-9.

> Temple University Press
> USB Room 305
> Broad and Oxford Street
> Philadelphia, PA 19122
> Phone: 800-447-1656

Articles:

Hare, J., & Richards, L. (1993). Children raised by lesbian couples: Does context of birth affect father and partner involvement? *Family Relations, 42*(3), 249–253.

Videos:

We Are Family: Parenting and Foster Parenting in Gay Families

We Are Family won four major film awards. This video deals with what life is really like in three homosexual families. First, two gay fathers tell of their efforts to create a secure environment for their 16-year-old foster son. In another family, two lesbian mothers have helped their adopted 11-year-old boy overcome early neglect. In the third family we hear how two adolescent daughters have accepted their father's homosexuality. 1988. (57 minutes)

> Filmaker Library
> 124 East 40th Street
> New York, NY 10016
> Phone: 212-808-4980

Organizations:

> American Civil Liberties Union (ACLU)
> Lesbian and Gay Rights Project
> 132 West 43rd Street
> New York, NY 10036
> Phone: 212-944-9800, ext. 545

Miscellaneous

Videos:

Teenage Pregnancy

This video follows several teenagers through the births of their children and subsequent changes in their lives. It is a sobering look at the problems these girls face. (26 minutes, color)

> Films for the Humanities and Sciences
> P.O. Box 2053
> Princeton, NJ 08543
> Phone: 800-257-5126

Websites:

African American

> African American Resources
> www.blackquest.com/link.htm

> NAACP
> www.naacp.org

> National Urban League
> www.nul.org

Asian American

The Asian American Cybernaughts
www.janet.org/~ebihara/wataru_accyber

Asian American Resources
www.ai.mit.edy/people/irie/aar

Hmong Home Page
www.hmong.org

Hispanic/Latino

Anchor School Project: Migrant Education
www.anchorschool.org/family

Azteca Web Page
www.azteca.net/azteca/index.shtml

Chicano/Latino Net
www.latino.sscnet.ucla.tedu

Native American

American Indian Movement
www.aimovement.org

Indian Defense League of America
www.tuscaroras.com/IDLA

Native American Nations
www.nativeculture.com

Native Web
www.nativeweb.org/resources

Resources for Native American Families
www.familyvillage.wisc.edu/frc_natv.htm

Smithsonian Institution: Native American Resources
www.si.edu/resource/faq/nmai/start.htm

Other Diversity Sites

National Center for Research on Cultural Diversity and Second Language Learning
www.ncbe.gwu.edu/index.htm

Pathways to Diversity on the World Wide Web
www.diversityweb.org/about.htm

REFERENCES

Ascher, C. (1988). Improving the school–home connection for poor and minority urban students. *The Urban Review, 20*(2), 109–123.

Baca Zinn, M. (1987). Structural transformation and minority families. In L. Beneria & C. Stimpson (Eds.), *Women, households, and the economy* (pp. 155–171). New Brunswick: Rutgers University Press.

Banks, C. M. (1993). Restructuring schools for equity: What have we learned in two decades? *Phi Delta Kappan, 75,* 42–44, 46–48.

Bernal, M., & Knight, G. (Eds.). (1993). *Ethnic identity: Formation and transmission among Hispanics and other minorities.* Albany: State University of New York Press.

Broadway, D. (1987). *A study of middle class black children and their families: Aspirations for children, perceptions of success, and the role of culture.* Ph.D. Dissertation, Ohio State University.

Burgess, E., & Locke, H. (1945). *The family: From institution to companionship.* New York: The American Book Company.

Burnett, M. C., & Lewis, E. A. (1993). Use of African-American family structures to address the challenges of European-American post-divorce families. *Family Relations, 42,* 243–248.

Carter, M. (1994). Supporting the identity and self esteem of children in gay and lesbian families. Anaheim, CA: Annual Conference of the National Association for the Education of Young Children. (ERIC Document Reproduction Service No. ED 377 985)

Chan, S. (1992). Families with Asian roots. In E. W. Lynch & M. J. Hanson (Eds.), *Developing cross-cultural competence* (pp. 181–257). Baltimore: Paul H. Brookes Publishing Co.

Chavkin, N. F. (Ed.). (1993). *Families and schools in a pluralistic society.* Albany: State University of New York Press.

Coontz, S. (1992). *The way we never were: American families and the nostalgia trap.* New York: Basic Books.

Demo, D., & Acock, A. (1993). Family diversity and the division of domestic labor: How much have things really changed? *Family Relations, 42,* 323–331.

Espiritu, Y. L. (1992). *Asian American panethnicity: Bridging institutions and identities.* Philadelphia: Temple University Press.

Feinberg, W., & Soltis, J. (1998). *School and society* (3rd ed.). New York: Teachers College Press.

Fillmore, L. (1990). Latino families and the schools. *California Perspectives, 1,* 30–37.

Fraga, L., Meier, K., & England, R. (1986). Hispanic Americans and educational policy: Limits to equal access. *The Journal of Politics, 48,* 851–876.

Hare, J., & Richards, L. (1993). Children raised by lesbian couples: Does context of birth affect father and partner involvement? *Family relations, 42,* 249–255.

Hildebrand, V., Phenice, L., Gray, M., & Hines, R. (1996). *Knowing and serving diverse families.* Columbus, OH: Merrill.

Hill, R. B. (1993). Dispelling myths and building on strengths: Supporting African American families. *Family Resource Coalition Report, 12*(1), 3–5.

Hiner, N. R. (1989). Look into families: The new history of children and the family and its implications for educational research. In W. Weston (Ed.), *Education and the American family: A research synthesis* (pp. 4–31). New York: New York University Press.

Lasch, C. (1977). *Haven in a heartless world.* New York: Basic Books.

Latinos shift loyalties. (1994, April). *The Christian Century* (p. 344).

Lee, S. J. (1996). *Unraveling the "model minority" stereotype: Listening to Asian American youth.* New York: Teachers College Press.

Lewis, D. (1993). *W. E. B. Dubois: Biography of a race, 1868–1919.* New York: Henry Holt and Co.

McAdoo, H. P. (Ed.). (1993). *Family ethnicity: Strength in diversity* (pp. 164–176). Newbury Park, CA: Sage Publications.

McLemore, S. D. (1983). *Racial and ethnic relations in America.* Boston: Allyn & Bacon.

Mintz, S., & Kellogg, S. (1988). *Domestic revolutions: A social history of American family life.* New York: The Free Press.

Nieto, S. (2002). *Language, culture, and teaching: Critical perspectives for a new century.* Mahwah, NJ: Lawrence Erlbaum.

Noley, G. (1992). Educational reform and American Indian cultures. (ERIC Document Reproduction Service No. ED 362 341)

Outtz, J. H. (1993). *The demographics of American families.* Santa Monica, CA: Milken Institute for Job and Capital Formation. (ERIC Document Reproduction Service No. ED 367 726)

Pasley, K., Dollahite, D., & Tallman, M. I. (1993). Clinical applications of research findings on the spouse and stepparent roles in remarriage. *Family Relations, 42,* 315–322.

Ramirez, E. W. (1993). The state of Hispanic education: Facing the facts. Washington, DC: ASPIRA

Association, Inc., Institute for Policy Research. (ERIC Reproduction Service No. ED 357 132)

Ramirez, M., & Cox, B. (1980). Parenting for multiculturalism: A Mexican American model. In M. Fantini & J. Russon (Eds.), *Parenting in a multicultural society.* New York: Longman.

Ritter, P., Mont-Reynaud, R., & Dornbusch, S. (1993). Minority parents and their youth: Concern, encouragement, and support for school achievement. In N. Chavkin (Ed.), *Families and schools in a pluralistic society* (pp. 107–119). Albany: State University of New York Press.

Shen, W., & Mo, W. (1990). Reaching out to their cultures: Building communication with Asian-American families. (ERIC Document Reproduction Service No. ED 351 435)

Sipes, D. S. B. (1993). Cultural values and American-Indian families. In N. Chavkin (Ed.), *Families and schools in a pluralistic society* (pp. 157–173). Albany: State University of New York Press.

Suarez, A. (1993). Cuban Americans: From golden exiles to social undesirables. In H. McAdoo (Ed.), *Family ethnicity: Strength in diversity.* Newbury Park, CA: Sage Publications.

Szasz, M. C. (1991). Current conditions in American Indian and Alaska Native communities. Indian Nations At Risk Task Force. (ERIC Document Reproduction Service No. ED 343 7556)

Trennert, R. (1990). Educating Indian girls in nonreservation boarding schools, 1878–1920. In E. C. Dubois and V. L. Ruiz (Eds.), *Unequal sisters: A multicultural reader in U.S. women's history.* New York: Routledge.

U.S. Bureau of the Census. *Poverty in the United States: 1988 and 1989.* Current population report, Series P-60, No. 171, Washington, DC: Author.

U.S. Bureau of the Census. *Statistical abstract of the United States: 1990* (110th Edition). Washington, DC: Author.

Vanlenzuela, A. (1999). *Substractive Schooling: U.S.-Mexican Youth and the Politics of Caring.* New York: State of New York Press.

Wetson, W. (Ed.). (1989). *Education and the American family: A research synthesis.* New York: New York University Press.

Yao, E. L. (1993). Strategies for working with Asian immigrant parents. In N. Chavkin (Ed.), *Families and schools in a pluralistic society* (pp. 149–156). Albany: State University of New York Press.

Zuniga, M. (1992). Families with Latino roots. In E. W. Lynch & M. J. Hanson (Eds.), *Developing cross-cultural competence* (pp. 151–179). Baltimore: Paul H. Brookes Publishing Co.

4

Parents' Perspectives on Parenting

KAREN W. ZIMMERMAN
The University of Wisconsin–Stout

Too often the study of the relationship between home and school fails to address the component of parenting. Schools will be able to form better working relationships with the home if they understand parenting practices and problems. This chapter uses the parent's voice to investigate parenting. Sections 1 and 2 examine families from the perspective of demographics and structure. This chapter takes a different perspective—that of the parenting present in these families. The purpose of this chapter is to introduce the reader to:

- How parenting affects the lives of parents
- The nature and complexities of dual-employed parents
- The views of single-parent families
- The parenting concerns of non-custodial fathers and mothers
- The complexities of parenting in a stepfamily
- How parenting adults and children differ

Kenneth and Grace, a dual-employed couple, have two children. Joyce is raising her child as a single parent. Robbie and Kathy, along with their children from previous marriages, form a stepparent family. In this chapter, we will be looking at each of these family situations and the perspectives these mothers and fathers have on parenting.

This chapter focuses on parents and how they see themselves. It begins by examining how becoming a parent changes one's life and affects the marital relationship. Parenting styles and the parents' perspectives are explored. In addition, this chapter explores several familial structures from a parenting perspective. Dual-employed parents identify the coping patterns they use in dealing with role overload and role conflict between work and family. Viewpoints of single parents, divorced parents, and stepparents are shared. Finally, this chapter concludes with a discussion of what parents perceive as the rewards and satisfactions of parenting.

Becoming a Parent

New Parents

New parents are generally very concerned with how to raise their children. They want to incorporate their personal beliefs about child rearing and develop healthy parent–child relationships. These parents seek to understand and explore their feelings as they assume the parental role for the first time.

The changes in becoming a parent for the first time are abrupt (LeMasters, 1957; LeMasters & DeFrain, 1989). Newlyweds usually interact with each other as personally as possible, trying to mesh as a couple. But when the first child arrives, the couple will likely begin to respond to each other as mommy and daddy instead of as marriage partners. The responsibilities of parenthood take priority over personal gratification. LeMasters (1957) reports that new mothers feel tired, lose sleep, worry that their personal appearance and the appearance of the home are not up to par. In addition, they feel frustrated about having less time for friends and not having a social life.

New fathers also have many of the same complaints, but men and women differ in how they adjust to the new circumstances. Women tend to think of themselves in a *new* role, while men are more inclined to see themselves in an *additional* role. This can be especially frustrating for the husband, as the wife becomes more of a mother and less of a wife. Women are quicker to identify the change in the couple's relationship. One young mother describes this change as follows:

> We aren't able to pay much attention to each other, because Amy needs so much. She's great, don't get me wrong. But Daniel comes home from work cranky, I'm cranky because I haven't talked to anyone who says anything back to me, Amy's cranky because she wants to eat right now, and we don't have time to find out how each other's day went. So I'm making dinner for three cranky people. And as a consequence, we have not been as close as before she came. (Cowan & Cowan, 2000, p. 77)

Marital satisfaction declines somewhat in the early stages of the family life cycle when children are added to the family (Belsky & Rovine, 1990; Belsky, Spanier, & Rovine, 1983; Gable, Belsky, & Crnic, 1995; Rollins & Feldman, 1970). Infants and young children demand much time, energy, and attention, and parents have less time for each other. Both mothers and fathers miss the attention of their partner. Having children reorganizes the marriage along traditional sex-role lines (Cowan, Cowan, Heming, & Miller, 1991; LaRossa & LaRossa, 1981). The decrease in marital satisfaction is greater for women than for men. This is often attributed to women's feelings that their partners are not as involved as they are dealing with child care and household tasks (Cowan et al., 1991). Women assume more of the parenting and household tasks than men, even if they are employed outside the home.

One new mother of a six-month-old, who is doing more housework than ever before, describes this vividly:

> He wasn't being a chauvinist or anything, expecting me to do everything and him to do nothing. He just didn't volunteer to do things that obviously needed doing, so I had to put down some ground rules. Like if I'm in a bad mood, I may just yell: I work eight hours, just like you. Half of this is your house and half of this child is yours too. You've got to do your share. We planned this child together, and we went through Lamaze together, and Jackson stayed home for the first two weeks. But then—wham—the partnership was over. (Cowan & Cowan, 2002, p. 98)

Most educators agree that children thrive best in a home where some consistency between the parents is present. Significant differences between parents on developmental expectations, discipline, and nurturing styles could signal potential problems for the family. In a recent study, mothers and fathers of young children (ages one to four years) were asked to assess their own parenting and that of their spouse. Three parenting categories were examined: developmental expectations, discipline, and nurturing (Platz, Pupp, & Fox, 1994). Mothers and fathers had similar developmental expectations for their young children. However, fathers tended to see themselves as having a more disciplinarian approach than mothers. Furthermore, fathers gave mothers higher discipline ratings than mothers gave themselves. Mothers rated themselves as more nurturing than fathers. Mothers gave fathers higher ratings in developmental expectations than fathers gave themselves.

After the First Year

How does the role of parenting change during the second year of life? This is the question asked in a study of fathers and mothers (Fagot & Kavanagh, 1993). Parents with twelve-month-old children (infants) reported greater marital adjustment and more pleasure in parenting than parents of eighteen-month-olds (toddlers).

Meeting the daily hassles of parenting adds to parental strain as children make the transition from infancy to early childhood. Perceptions about the minor daily hassles and inconveniences associated with parenting were studied in families with young children (Crnic & Booth, 1991). Three groups of parents were studied: those with children aged nine to twelve months, eighteen to twenty-four months, and thirty to thirty-six months. Such things as "continually cleaning up the same messes," "difficulty getting privacy," "being nagged or whined to," "kids resisting or struggling over bedtime," and so on, were rated.

Parental reports of the daily hassles of parenting increased across the age groups—that is, as children grew older, the hassles increased. It seems that as children are developing and gaining more abilities, they may be presenting a greater range of behaviors and situations that parents find stressful. Furthermore, as the daily hassles of parenting increase, life satisfaction and parenting satisfaction decrease (Crnic & Booth, 1991).

Daily hassles of Head Start fathers were studied in relation to the play involvement with their children. Fathers reported 2.38 hassles per day related to work, travel, health, family finances, friends, and chance occurrences. For every additional hassle per day, fathers' play interaction with their children decreased by ten minutes on the same day (Fagan, 2000).

Parenting Styles

Parenting styles are shaped by values, attitudes, and beliefs of the parents. Baumrind (1967) identified three parenting styles that emerge when children are at the preschool stage of family development and continue on through adolescence. These three parenting styles are *authoritarian, authoritative,* and *permissive.*

Authoritarian Parents

The authoritarian parenting style emphasizes total parental control and the obedience of the child. The parent is definitely the person in power; conforming to the parent's standards is required. If necessary, the parent may use physical punishment to force the child to comply. The parent dominates the child by use of rewards and punishment. The child is not allowed to question nor given opportunities to discuss directives.

Authoritative Parents

Authoritative parents make use of reasonable limits and controls for the child's behavior, considering the child's stage of development and individuality. Authoritative parenting falls between authoritarian and permissive parenting. In this parenting style, the authoritative parent wants to develop responsible children by allowing input into discussion on rules and responsibilities. Children have some freedom, but not at the expense of rights and responsibilities of others.

Bogenschneider and Small (1997) found that mothers and fathers of teens who saw themselves as being more competent, had teens who reported they had more competent parenting behaviors. These parents monitored their teens at a higher level and were highly responsive to them.

Permissive Parents

Permissive parents strive to promote the child's regulation of his or her own behavior rather than regulating the child's behavior by intervening. In this approach, the child has more power than the parent. The permissive parent allows a child to regulate his or her own activities as much as possible, avoids the exercise of control, and does not encourage him or her to obey externally defined standards (Baumrind, 1966).

Most American parents see themselves as raising their children in an authoritative parenting style. When parents were asked to respond to problems dealing with children's misbehavior, most of the people selected responses that would fit with the authoritative parenting style (Bluestone & Tamis-LeMonda, 1999; Carter & Welch, 1981).

In addition, the popularity of the three parenting styles varies by social class. The authoritarian style is found to be more popular with blue-collar families. They are more likely to insist on obedience and to value teaching children to control their impulses. Middle-class parents are more likely to value explaining rules to the child, using verbal discipline, and prizing the child's individuality; this is consistent with the authoritative parenting style. Perhaps more important than style of parenting is that the parents provide guidance, consistency, and an atmosphere of caring.

Reflection...

Which parenting style did your parents use? What would be examples of your parents' discipline behaviors that would support your selection? If you are a parent, what parenting style do you use and why? If you plan to be a parent, what discipline style will you use?

Reflection...

Think of the stresses present in your life. How would these affect your parenting if you were a parent? If you are a parent, how are your life stresses evidenced in your parenting? How could you reduce these stresses?

Parenting Behaviors in Diverse Family Structures

Dual-Employed Parents

Kenneth (36) and Grace (38) are middle-class, African American parents with two children, Alicia (12) and Francine (10). They live in a four-bedroom house in a small city in California. Kenneth is an accountant for a large clothing firm and Grace teaches math in a local high school.

Kenneth, Grace, Alicia, and Francine experience a lot of family stress, as do most families in which both parents work. While Kenneth and Grace value enrichment experiences for their children, these activities do add to the complexities of their family life. The children are busy with Scouts, music lessons, ballet, after-school sports, and family activities. There is never enough time.

Kenneth and Grace, as dual-employed parents, are facing the many challenges of multiple roles: worker, parent, and a marital partner. People who have multiple roles gain benefits from each of their roles (e.g., a sense of accomplishment, financial gains, and enhanced self-esteem). These benefits can help to balance the role strain they also encounter. Role strain refers to the problems, challenges, conflicts, and difficulties one has as a result of being in a particular role and fulfilling the tasks and responsibilities that role requires.

Role Conflict and Conflicting Demands

Two types of role strain are role overload and role conflict. Role overload is the feeling that there is not enough time to accomplish everything one has to do. Grace teaches school all day and shuttles Alicia and Francine to music lessons, ballet, and Scouts before rushing home to fix supper. After supper, Grace has housework to do, a stack of math papers to grade, and to "catch up" with Kenneth on how his day went. The heavy work schedules of dual-employed families often leave limited time for parenting, the marital partner, household work, and leisure. Role conflict occurs when the demand of one of these roles interferes with doing what needs to be done in another role.

Kenneth's job requires that he be at the office until 6:00 P.M. each weekday. He is thankful that Grace can do the driving so Alicia and Francine can take part in after-school activities. He hates missing Alicia's soccer games and Francine's ballet and piano recitals.

Managing the demands of competing life roles, which Kenneth and Grace do daily, has become a common experience for many American men and women. Grappling with multiple life-role commitments is a key source of stress in dual-employed families, especially those with children in the home. Today dual-employed couples frequently have ambitions and commitments in both the work and family areas simultaneously. Men report career interests intruding on fathering roles. Women say that parenting is interfering with career roles. One first-time mother in her thirties described this conflict as follows:

> For the first time in my life I was having to make tradeoffs—work, to have a child, to be a wife, to take care of a home, and to try to do all of these things well meant that something had to get cheated a little bit in each area. Not enough so that anybody else would notice, maybe, but I did. I noticed it. (Daniels & Weingarten, 1984, p. 224)

Prioritizing Life Roles

Dual-employed couples' personal expectations concerning occupation, marital, parental, and home-care roles were examined in a study of parents with children (Zimmerman, Skinner, & Muza, 1989). Surprisingly, both husbands and wives independently rated their commitment to four life roles in the same priority order: parental as first, marital as second, home care as third, and occupational as fourth.

Reflection...

Which of your life roles (school, family, work, etc.) do you consider to be most important? How is this reflected in the life choices you make?

Although dual-employed couples agreed on the relative importance of these four life roles, they weighed these commitments differently. That is, wives were significantly more committed to the parental role than husbands, although both groups agreed that this was their highest priority. In contrast, husbands were significantly more committed to the occupational role than wives. Thus, both men and women placed a higher value on commitment to familial roles, particularly parental roles, than other life roles. For example, Kenneth and Grace are committed parents but, as discussed earlier, Kenneth's job prevents him from taking the girls to their after-school activities.

These dual-employed couples were divided into two employment orientation groups, worker and career, based on their education and the type of employment. Worker couples were significantly more committed to marital roles and to home-care roles than career couples. It is interesting to note that worker men, career men, and worker women all valued home-care commitment (e.g., working to have a neat, well-kept, and attractive home) to a greater extent than career women. Perhaps this dual-career mother's attitude toward housework illustrates this:

> You must begin with what one does not do. I have a cleaning woman...and what she doesn't do, doesn't get done. My kitchen shelves are cruddy, but it doesn't bother me. Dust sits around. It doesn't bother me that everything isn't shipshape.... The way a house is kept is not the most important thing in the universe. (Holmstrom, 1973, p. 71)

Moreover, the scores of career women on occupational commitment were similar to those of both worker and career men. Both groups of men and career women were committed to their occupation significantly more than worker women. One dual-employed father described how he prioritized his life roles in an account about his relationship with his daughter, Lisa.

> I drove truck for a while and I think it contributed to our being distant. Lisa felt like she didn't have a daddy. I came home and told her to clean something and she said, "You can't tell me what to do. You're not my daddy." That ripped me apart. I don't think it was really meant, but it hurt. I stopped driving a truck really fast and brought myself back home. She was more or less saying, "You should be home." (Dollahite, Hawkins, & Brotherson, 1996, p. 361)

Coping Patterns in Dual-Employed Couples

What coping patterns do dual-employed couples use to deal with stress from their work–family roles? Several studies have addressed this question. In one study of dual-employed parents with children, coping patterns parents identified using most frequently were examined (Zimmerman, Skinner, & Muza, 1989). Coping patterns are a broad range of behaviors used together to manage various dimensions of the dual-employed lifestyle simultaneously (Skinner & McCubbin, 1991). Maintaining a positive perspective on the lifestyle and reducing tensions and strains were the most frequently used coping patterns. This pattern includes behaviors that attend to personal needs focusing on reducing individual stress and maintaining an optimistic perspective on the situation. Examples include "maintaining health," "encouraging children to be more self-sufficient where appropriate," and "believing that there are more advantages than disadvantages to our lifestyle."

The second most frequently used coping pattern was modifying roles and standards to maintain a work–family balance. These couples modified their roles and standards by buying convenience foods, leaving things undone, and limiting involvement on the job.

Maintaining and strengthening the existing work–family interface was the third most frequently used coping pattern. The focus of this approach was using organizational skills in meeting family, work, and homemaking demands efficiently. An example would be planning schedules ahead of time.

Schnittger and Bird (1990) have identified the coping strategies that dual-career couples have found successful in dealing with the stresses in family life. Among these coping strategies are encouraging their children to help out whenever possible, eliminating some community activities, cutting down on outside and leisure activities, and lowering household standards. Also, parents find spending time alone with their spouses and making friends with other two-career couples helpful.

Coping with work and family demands by subordinating their careers, compartmentalizing work and family roles, and avoiding some responsibilities are strategies used both by career husbands and career wives. These couples contend with stress by limiting their involvement on the job, saying "no," and reducing the amount of time spent at work. They practice making efficient use of their time at work, plan ahead, and postpone certain tasks.

Single-Parent Families

Joyce Anderson, twenty-eight, is a single parent. Joyce, her daughter, Beth, a six-year-old, and Joyce's mother, Helen, are a family. They live in an apartment in a low-income neighborhood in Minneapolis. Joyce has worked at the same minimum wage job for a little more than two years. Beth is in first grade in a neighborhood school. One of their chronic problems is lack of health insurance. Although most single-parent families are functional families, their situation has lately become even more precarious than usual. Helen has suffered from a severe respiratory problem for a few years, and her doctor wants her to move to Arizona and live with her other daughter. If Helen leaves, not only will Joyce's resources be greatly reduced, she will have to pay for child care. The stresses Joyce and her family experience are good examples of those experienced by single-parent families.

Financial Concern

Problems occur in every family type, single-parent families included. Most studies have identified financial problems as a major problem of this type of family. One thirty-five-year-old single mother who is on welfare describes her current situation:

> I can't pay rent, I can't buy Keith clothes that will fit him, I don't have enough money for food, furniture, or clothes for Erin and myself. Everything and anything is a burden, right down to buying a roll of toilet paper. Not to mention Christmas …things are so bad that the thing the kids want most for Christmas is a kitchen table. (Richards, 1989, p. 398)

Worrying about finances can have a negative impact on parent–child relation-ships. One mother adds the following, "The lack of money is a real problem for all of us. My anxiety over not being able to find a job makes it hard to be attentive and concerned with the everyday demands of my children" (Richards, 1989, p. 398).

Other Areas of Concern

Whereas the lack of money is the single biggest problem reported by single par-ents, there are a number of other problematic areas. In a more recent study of single parents, lack of money was the number one problem reported by mothers (77 percent), followed by role/task overload (55 percent), and the lack of social life (30 percent) (Richards & Schmiege, 1993). For fathers, role/task overloads and problems with the ex-spouse were tied for first (35 percent), followed by lack of social life and lack of money (18 percent). In addition, problems with role overload were reported by over half the mothers and a third of the fathers. A mother of three adolescents describes role overload in her own words, "In this day and age of child rearing, it sure would be nice to be sharing the responsibility with some-one else. I get tired of being a full-time policeman and everything else" (Richards & Schmiege, 1993, p. 280). A single-parent father also mentioned a task and role overload. He especially hates cooking and believes a role overload has affected his parenting. He noted, "I would have to say that I tended to be more lenient than I should have been simply because I just didn't have the energy after I worked all day" (Richards & Schmiege, 1993, p. 280).

Children were also reported as a major source of stress. Most of these stress-ful encounters (50 percent) involved negative challenging behavior on the part of the child. These included noncompliance ("my youngest refused to take his nap," "fought with the kids to clean up their room"), irritating behaviors ("my daughter began whining during her nap," "the kids ran in and out all day and made a lot of noise"), defiance ("sassing and rebelling"), temper tantrums, and rule violations. These were followed by sibling conflict, demanding attention, being slow in get-ting ready for outings, illness, school failure, and misbehavior, as well as stressful interactions with child-care providers (Olson & Banyard, 1993).

Single parents, like all parents, have strengths as well as problems. Single moth-ers and fathers see themselves as supportive of their children, being patient, helping children to cope, and fostering independence in their children. They also describe themselves as well-organized, dependable, and able to coordinate schedules in man-aging their family. In an interview, one mother said of her parenting strengths:

> I think just communicating with my kids and listening to them and letting them make decisions and giving them choices…. They're very independent and respon-sible and they have very high self-esteem. I think I've helped them reach their po-tential and be good caring kids. (Richards & Schmiege, 1993, p. 281)

When these parents were asked whether single parenting becomes easier or more difficult over time, the majority agreed that single-parenting becomes easier over time. One father said, "Things go more into a routine, so it got a little bit easier that way.... You would learn how to do things, and again, I had a lot of support from my parents" (Richards & Schmeige, 1993, p. 282).

Divorced Noncustodial Fathers and Mothers

The divorce rate in the United States is high. Half of all marriages in the United States end in divorce and approximately 60 percent of these divorces involve minor children. Mothers are still much more likely to become the custodial parent than fathers. Relationships between noncustodial divorced fathers and mothers and their children are often strained and interaction may be infrequent.

Umberson and Williams (1993) held in-depth interviews with forty-five divorced fathers in Texas to identify the stress involved in noncustodial parenting. They found that visitation and custody issues presented major problems along with relationships with the ex-wife, as well as personal and social identity issues. Child support was also an area that these fathers found to be problematic. The unfairness of the system was pointed to by one divorced father:

> One thing that really irritates me about the court system here is that...you can be married for 10 years, and you can be a loving, wonderful father for 10 years. And ...in my instance, she met this other guy and decided to run off with him, and the minute that she left, I was no longer a worthy father. I got visitation! (Umberson & Williams, 1993, p. 389)

Some fathers in this study described the pain they felt after dropping off their children following a visitation. One father of a six-year-old son noted:

> I don't perceive any stress from being a single parent. When he's with me, it's not stressful at all. It's just hard bringing him back home.... All the way going back home he'll tell me how he wishes he could stay with me, he's going to miss me. (Umberson & Williams, 1993, p. 389)

Other divorced fathers reported that their former wives were good mothers. Knowing that their children are receiving good care is important to many divorced fathers. In the words of one of these fathers: "I think she does a real good job considering all the circumstances and everything" (Umberson & Williams, 1993, p. 392). In a second study, Thompson and Lawson (1994) examined divorced African American fathers in Kentucky and Missouri. These fathers had working- and middle-class jobs. From these in-depth interviews, two themes emerged: fathers seeing their children as the most important reason for marriage, and fathers seeing their children as the most significant reason for not divorcing. Most of these fathers were willing to stay married for the sake of their children. After divorce these fathers did not disassociate or think about disassociating from their children. The findings of this study conflict with the results of the study by Umberson and Williams (1993). Clearly, more studies need to be done to better understand the views of noncustodial divorced fathers.

Although the noncustodial father is a common occurrence and evident in most classrooms, the number of noncustodial mothers is significantly less. However, the number of noncustodial mothers is increasing. The activities of nonresident mothers and fathers with their absent children were studied by Stewart (1999). Overall, 41 percent of noncustodial parents engage only in leisure activities with their children. Thirty percent have not had contact with their children within the past 12 months. The remaining 29 percent of noncustodial parents mentioned school or organizational activities among the activities they participate in with their child. Stewart found that nonresident mothers and fathers have a similar pattern of interaction with their absent children. Nonresidential mothers spent 37.9 percent of their time in only leisure activities. Likewise, 24.8 percent of these mothers had no contact with their child. Nonresidential mothers spent 37.3 percent of their activity time with school and organizational activities.

In a study of thirteen noncustodial mothers in southwestern Virginia, mothers noted changes in the parent–child relationships following divorce (Arditti & Madden-Derdich, 1993). One 41-year-old mother missed the responsibilities of parenting:

> I don't consider myself a parent any more...I mean, I will always be their mother, but I don't look at it as a parent anymore without the day-to-day routine of getting meals, of making sure their homework is done because I am not living with them. (Arditti & Madden-Derdich, 1993, p. 313).

Another mother of 6- and 10-year-old sons discussed discipline as a noncustodial parent who only sees her children for a limited time:

> I enjoy being with the kids and look forward to seeing them all the time. Sometimes it is hard to discipline them because when I'm with them I don't want to be punishing them. I call them on the phone all the time. (Arditti & Madden-Derdich, 1993, p. 313)

These noncustodial mothers expressed dissatisfaction with custody arrangements and indicated that their ex-spouses were very satisfied. One mother expressed discomfort and guilt over the custody arrangements: "It's abnormal—a mother and child not being together. I think it's an injustice that's been done" (Arditti & Madden-Derdich, 1993, p. 313). With the growth of noncustodial mothers, we as educators must inform ourselves as to the needs and special circumstances of this parent population.

Stepparent Families

Challenges of Stepparenting

Kathy (35) is of European American extraction and the mother of Amy (9) and Jack (14). Both children are from a previous marriage. Robbie (35) is a Native

American who also has children from a previous marriage—Amanda (14), Jim (12), and Fred (7). Kathy and Robbie have been married four years and are both custodial parents. They live in a three-bedroom house in a medium-sized community in Colorado.

Robbie and Kathy started their new marriage with five children in the household—a blended family. In addition to working hard to form a strong, marital bond, Robbie and Kathy each had the challenge of performing in new roles as stepparents. Neither the role of stepfather nor stepmother is easy to carry out. Lacking clear role definition and being uncertain about how family roles should be carried out is called *role ambiguity*. Stepparents, such as Robbie and Kathy, frequently become confused and frustrated as they work out the role ambiguity of being a stepparent by the trial-and-error method.

Who Is in Charge?

Although Robbie was experienced in disciplining his own three children, he felt uncomfortable and wondered what he should be doing regarding disciplining Jack and Amy. The disciplining of stepchildren is a major issue confronting stepfathers. One study found that stepchildren reject stepparents who engage in discipline and control early in their relationship (Ganong, Coleman, Fine, & Martin, 1999). Even stepfathers who had children prior to stepparenting find it difficult. In one study, 30 percent of stepfathers believe that it is more difficult to discipline stepchildren than their own children (Marsiglio, 1992). Moreover, it is more challenging when the stepchild is an adolescent. One stepfather complained about his adolescent stepson as showing a "complete lack of any acknowledgment of my right to correct him or have him obey when asked (told) to do something—like clean up his room or be home at a certain time" (Giles-Sims & Crosbie-Burnett, 1989, p. 1071).

Stepfathers were asked what they would advise a friend about being a stepfather. Here is what they said:

> Live with them first, don't expect to ever replace the natural father in their eyes; win their respect; treat them as your own; love them and discipline them as your own; let nothing come between you and your woman—especially the kids. (Giles-Sims & Crosbie-Burnett, 1989, p. 1071)

A national study of stepfathers who were also natural parents found that the majority disagreed with the notion that it is harder to love stepchildren than their own children (Marsiglio, 1992). However, a third of these stepfathers also reported that they were apt to be more a friend than a parent to their stepchildren although the majority still felt that they had assumed the full responsibilities of parenthood. Kathy was concerned about Jack and Amy's reaction when Robbie tried to discipline them, especially during the first year of marriage. Mothers question how much to rely on the stepfather and how much authority he should have in disciplining the children. Typically, mothers remain in the disciplining role and stepfathers gradually begin assuming more of this role when they feel more comfortable with stepparenting. This is how Kathy and Robbie handled the situation. However, some mothers remain in the disciplining role. One mother relates:

> I have never counted on their stepdad to provide discipline, not even to put them to bed. That is not his responsibility. Those children are my responsibility and it is one that I choose to have. He married me, he only has to live with them, not discipline them. (Giles-Sims & Crosbie-Burnett, 1989, p. 1071)

There are indications that stepmothers have a harder time raising stepchildren than stepfathers do (MacDonald & DeMaris, 1996). Stepmothers report greater dissatisfaction with their family roles and higher levels of stress in carrying out family responsibilities than stepfathers (Ahrons & Wallish, 1987). Women are usually more responsible for the daily contact with and management of children. Therefore, they have the daily hassles of making decisions that may be unpopular with the children.

Coleman and Ganong (1997) found that the stepmothers who expressed the most frustration were those who indicated that they had high control needs. These stepmothers "had greater difficulty accepting messes children made, the noise and chaos children created, child's lack of gratitude for assistance, and the vying of the children for their father's attention" (Coleman & Ganong, 1997, p. 113). The husbands appeared to be passive, not wanting to take sides with their wives or to punish their children for the behaviors that caused problems between the stepmother and the children. Over time, these high control stepmothers said they learned to back off.

Successful Stepparenting

Six characteristics of adults who have successfully adapted to stepfamily life have been identified by Emily and John Visher, founders of the Step Family Association of America (Visher & Visher, 1990). These characteristics are:

1. These adults have mourned their losses and are ready for a new pattern of life.
2. They have a realistic expectation that their family will be different from a first marriage family.
3. There is a strong, unified couple.
4. Constructive family rituals are established and serve as a basis for positive shared memories.
5. Satisfactory step-relationships have formed (which takes time).
6. The separate households cooperate in raising the children.

Healthy stepfamilies may differ from healthy intact families according to Pill (1990). They are more flexible and adaptable because of the comings and goings of family members, and they allow for differences among family members. For example, they allow their children to decide whether to go on a family vacation or when to spend time with their other birth parent.

Rewards and Satisfactions of Parenthood

Nurturing children and being needed are sufficient rewards for parenthood. But would parents do it again? In one study, 93 percent of parents said yes—they would have children again. These parents felt that the greatest advantages of having children were the love and affection children bring; having the pleasure of watching them grow; the sense of family they create; the fulfillment and satisfaction they bring; and the joy, happiness, and fun they bring (Gallup & Newport, 1990).

Research studies on parental satisfaction have shown consistently that an overwhelming majority of parents report being satisfied with their parenting role (Cheng, Taylor, & Ladewig, 1991; Chilman, 1980; Ishii-Kuntz & Ihinger-Tallman, 1991). For some people, living childless even with a partner one loves is unacceptable. They want children as a creative expression of themselves. These parents find their own lives enriched by having children: to love and to be loved by them (Chilman, 1980).

A more recent study of young parents examined factors that appear to predict attitudes of childbearing rewards and regrets (Groat, Giordano, Cernkovich, Pugh, & Swinford, 1997). Young parents who found childbearing most rewarding were white, married, and had positive feelings about their first pregnancy. Those holding regretful childbearing attitudes were African American, materialistic, had three or more children, and expressed negative feelings about their first pregnancies.

In a study of the satisfying aspects of parenting, Langenbrunner and Blanton (1993) conducted in-depth interviews with mothers and fathers. Their statements regarding satisfaction clustered into six major areas: (1) the child's growth and accomplishments, (2) verbal and physical interactions between parent and child, (3) the child showing affection toward the parent, (4) parent–infant attachment processes, (5) positive evaluations of their performance of the parental role, and (6) experiencing a sense of cohesion in their family. Overall, these parents received the greatest amount of satisfaction from seeing their children's developmental accomplishments. One parent described this:

> I also derive a great deal of satisfaction from watching both of them, I have two children now, learning things. It's very interesting for me to see James learn to talk. I have also taken a great deal of satisfaction in seeing James take an interest in books. (Langenbrunner & Blanton, 1993, p. 184)

All the parents in this study expressed the good feelings they felt from physically interacting with and talking with their children. As one father said, "It is surprisingly relaxing to spend time with a small child and for me it is good therapy" (Langenbrunner & Blanton, 1993, p. 184).

The primary source of satisfaction for fathers in this study came from their experiencing a sense of family cohesion or family unity. For these fathers, a feeling of connectedness to the family was very important. As one father concluded:

> Well, I was thinking about it a lot. And the most satisfying times are just "feelings" that I have. There's not really anything happening specifically. But I have a sense of being a family unit or we're sharing our feelings. (Langenbrunner & Blanton, 1993, p. 185)

> **Reflection...**
>
> How do you think your parent(s) would respond to the question, "What has been the greatest satisfaction in your parenting?" After considering this question, call or write your parents and ask them.

Summary

Marital Satisfaction.   Becoming a parent involves a major transition for the couple and taking on a new life role. This changes the relationship between the husband and wife. Typically marital satisfaction decreases somewhat in the early stages of the family life cycle when children are in the home. The daily hassles of parenting add to parental strain especially when children are preschool age and younger.

Parenting Style.   Baumrind (1966) identified three parenting styles: authoritarian, authoritative, and permissive. These styles can be seen in the preschool through adolescent years. Working-class parents usually prefer the authoritarian style, while middle-class parents prefer the authoritative style. Consistency, guidance, and caring are very important in parent–child interactions.

Dual-Employed Parenting.   Dual-employed parents encounter role strain as they try to meet the expectations of their various roles. Role strain includes: role overload (having too much to accomplish in a limited time) and role conflict (demands of one life role interfere with meeting the demands of another life role). Dual-employed parents rate their life role commitments in the following order: parent, spouse, home care, and occupation.

   Coping patterns used by dual-employed parents to deal with work/family demands include: (a) maintaining a positive perspective on the lifestyle to reduce tensions, (b) modifying roles and standards to maintain a work/family balance, (c) maintaining and strengthening the existing work/family interface, and (d) finding support to maintain the family unit.

Single Parenting.   Single parents are faced with financial problems, role overload, and daily hassles of interactions with children. They see their parental strengths as parenting skills, managing a family, communicating, growing personally, and providing financial support. They believe that single parenting becomes easier over time.

Divorced Noncustodial Fathers and Mothers.   Divorced, noncustodial fathers report parental role strain due to visitation and custody issues, relationships with ex-wives, and personal and identity issues. They believe that the children are the most important reason for staying married. Noncustodial parents engage in mostly leisure activities with their children, or they have had no contact with them over the past year. Less than a third of noncustodial parents participate in school or organizational activities with their children. The pattern of activity is similar for both noncustodial fathers and noncustodial mothers.

Stepparenting.   Stepparent families find that the roles of stepfather and stepmother are not easy to carry out and lack clear role definition. They experience role ambiguity. Disciplining children is a major issue confronting stepfathers. Stepmothers report greater dissatisfaction with their family role and higher levels of stress. Healthy stepfamilies differ from healthy intact families. They are more flexible, adaptable, and allow for more differences.

RECOMMENDED ACTIVITIES

1. Watch the movie *Parenthood* (with Steve Martin) and analyze the parenting styles of the five families depicted in the film.

2. Invite an attorney, two noncustodial fathers, and two noncustodial mothers to speak to the class about legal and parenting concerns.

3. Put together pamphlets of resources that will help parents in your community with their parenting (e.g., organizations, mental health services, videos on parenting, books) and distribute them.

4. Monitor an evening of prime-time television and document the parenting behaviors you observe.

5. Invite parents from dual-employed families to class to discuss the mechanics of running a dual-employed family. What are the rewards and the stresses?

6. Have various students in the class interview custodial parents, noncustodial parents, a family therapist, and children from these homes, and share the various positions in class.

7. Examine the role of mediation in working out problems between the custodial and noncustodial parent. A panel comprised of a psychologist, family mediator, and an attorney could be helpful in reviewing this topic.

ADDITIONAL RESOURCES

Parenting

Books:

Binger, J. J. (2002). *Parent–child relations: An introduction to parenting* (6th ed.). Upper Saddle River, NJ: Prentice Hall.

This is an excellent text that covers parenting from a developmental perspective. It has a short, but good, section on the cultural meaning of parenthood and also includes contemporary parenting concerns (e.g., latch-key children).

Brooks, J. B. (2001). *The process of parenting* (3rd ed.). Toronto: Mayfield Publishing Company.

This is a superb resource book about parenting. It is thorough and well written. It explores parenting and the life cycle as well as the process of parenting. Brooks then looks at each stage of parenting and examines some special topics (e.g., children with special needs).

Galinsky, E. (1987). *The six stages of parenthood.* New York: Addison-Wesley.

Galinsky points out that parenting has stages just as childhood does. He examines these stages and discusses their implications as they relate to the individual parent.

Videos:

Basic Parenting Skills

This entertaining program examines the "three Rs" of parenting—routine, respect, and resources. Viewers learn specific skills and techniques for dealing with difficult behaviors constructively. The video also presents strategies for coping with the frustrations of being a new parent. 1990. (60 minutes, color)

> Insights Media
> 2162 Broadway
> New York, NY
> Phone: 212-721-6316

My Family, Your Family

Emily has a mother, a father, and a brother. Sam has no siblings. Cindy has a mother, a father, a stepfather, a stepbrother, and a half sister. Pointing out that there are all kinds of families, this program helps students understand that what makes a family a family doesn't depend on who is in it, but on the caring feelings members have for one another. Recommend by *School Library Journal.* Grade level K–2. (16 minutes, color)

> Sunburst Communication
> 39 Washington Avenue
> P.O. Box 40
> Pleasantville, NY 10570
> Phone: 800-231-1934

On Being an Effective Parent

This video is well done and is popular with parent groups. It helps parents develop positive skills in communicating with their children. It is often used with *Basic Parenting Skills.*

> Insights Media
> 2162 Broadway
> New York, NY
> Phone: 212-721-6316

Organizations:

> American Association of Family and Consumer Science
> 1555 King Street
> Alexandria, VA 22314
> Phone: 703-706-4660
> www.aafcs.org

National Congress of Parent and Teacher Associations
700 North Rush Street
Chicago, IL 60611
Phone: 312-670-6782
www.pta.org

National Council on Family Relations
33989 Central Ve. NE, Suite 550
Minneapolis, MN 55421
Phone: 612-781-9331
ncfr.org

Websites:

Children, Youth, and Families
www.cyfc.umn.edu

Family Fun
www.family.com

National Center for Fathering
www.fathers.com/research

National Child Care Information Center
www.nccic.org

National Center for Family Resiliency
www.nnfr.org

National Parent Information Network
www.npin.org

Parent's Place
www.parentsplace.com

Parent Soup
www.parentsoup.com

REFERENCES

Abbot, D. A., & Meredith, W. M. (1988). Characteristics of strong families: Perceptions of ethnic parents. *Home Economics Research Journal, 17*(2), 141–147.

Ahrons, C. R., & Wallisch, L. (1987). Parenting in the binuclear family: Relationships between biological and stepparents. In K. Pasley & M. Ihinger-Tallman (Eds.), *Remarriage and stepparenting* (pp. 225–256). New York: Guilford.

Arditti, J. A., & Maden-Derdich, D. A. (1993). Noncustodial mothers: Developing strategies of support. *Family Relations, 42,* 305–317.

Baumrind, D. (1966). Effects of authoritative parental control on child behavior. *Child Development, 37,* 887–907.

Baumrind, D. (1967). Child care practices anteceding three patterns of preschool behavior. *Genetic Psychology Monographs, 75,* 43–88.

Baumrind, D. (1991). Parenting styles and adolescent development. In J. Brooks-Funn, R. Lerner, & A. C. Peterson (Eds.), *The encyclopedia of adolescence.* New York: Garland.

Belsky, J., & Rovine, M. (1990). Patterns of marital change across the transition to parenthood:

Pregnancy to three years postpartum. *Journal of Marriage and the Family, 52,* 5–19.

Belsky, J., Spanier, G., & Rovine, M. (1983). Stability and change in marriage across the transition to parenthood. *Journal of Marriage and the Family, 45,* 567–579.

Bluestone, C., & Tamis-LeMonda, C. S. (1999). Correlates of parenting styles in predominately working-and middle-class African American mothers. *Journal of Marriage and the Family, 59,* 345–363.

Bogenschneider, K., & Small, S. A. (1997). Child, parent, and contextual influences on perceived competence among parents of adolescents. *Journal of Marriage and the Family, 55*(6), 345–362.

Boss, P. (1987). Family stress. In M. B. Sussman and S. K. Steinmetz (Eds.), *Handbook of marriage and the family* (pp. 695–723). New York: Plenum.

Carter, D., & Welch, D. (1981). Parenting styles and children's behavior. *Family Relations, 30,* 191–195.

Cheng, T. C., Taylor, M. R., & Ladewig, B. H. (1991). Personal well-being: A study of parents of young children. *Family Perspective, 25,* 97–106.

Chilman, C. (1980). Parent satisfactions, concerns, and goals for their children. *Family Relations, 29,* 339–345.

Coleman, M., & Ganong, L. H. (1997). Stepfamilies from the stepfamily's perspective. *Marriage and Family Review, 26,* 107–121.

Cowan, C. P., & Cowan, P. A. (2000). *When partners become parents: The big life change for couples.* Mahwah, NJ: Lawrence Earlbaum.

Cowan, C. P., Cowan, P. A., Heming, G., & Miller, N. B. (1991). Becoming a family: Marriage, parenting, and child development: In P. A. Cowan & M. Hetherington, (Eds.), *Family Transitions* (pp. 79–109). Mahwah, NJ: Lawrence Erlbaum.

Crnic, K. A., & Booth, C. L. (1991). Mothers' and fathers' perceptions of daily hassles of parenting across early childhood. *Journal of Marriage and the Family, 53,* 1042–1050.

Daniels, P., & Weingarten, K. (1984). Mothers' hours: The timing of parenthood and women's work. In P. Voydanoff (Ed.), *Work and family: Changing roles of men and women* (pp. 204–231). Palo Alto, CA: Mayfield.

Dollahite, D. C., Hawkins, A. J., & Brotherson, S. E. (1996). Narrative accounts, generative fathering and family life education. *Marriage and Family Review, 24,* 349–368.

Fagan, J. (2000). Head Start fathers' daily hassles and involvement with their children. *Journal of Family Issues, 21,* 329–346.

Fagot, B. I., & Kavanagh, K. (1993). Parenting during the second year: Effects of children's age, sex and attachment classification. *Child Development, 64,* 258–271.

Gable, S., Belsky, J., & Crnic, K. (1995). Co-parenting during the child's 2nd year: A descriptive account. *Journal of Marriage and the Family, 57,* 609–616.

Gallop, G. H., & Newport, F. (1990). Virtually all adults want children, but many of the reasons are intangible. *The Gallop Poll Monthly, 297,* 8–22.

Gangong, L., Coleman, J., Fine, M., & Martin, P. (1999). Stepparents' affinity-seeking and affinity-maintaining strategies with stepchildren. *Journal of Family Issues, 20,* 299–327.

Giles-Sims, J., & Crosbie-Burnett, M. (1989). Adolescent power in stepfather families: A test of normative-resource theory. *Journal of Marriage and the Family, 51,* 1065–1078.

Groat, H. T., Giordano, P. C., Cernkovich, S. A., Pugh, M. D., & Swinford, S. P. (1997). Attitudes toward childbearing among young parents. *Journal of Marriage and the Family, 59,* 568–581.

Holmstrom, L. L. (1973). *The two-career family.* Cambridge, MA: Schenkman Publishing Co.

Ishii-Kuntz, M., & Ihinger-Tallman, M. (1991). The subjective well-being of parents. *Journal of Family Issues, 12,* 58–68.

Langenbrunner, M. R., & Blanton, P. W. (1993). Mothers' and fathers' perceptions of satisfactions and dissatisfactions with parenting. *Family Perspective, 27*(2), 179–193.

LaRossa, R., & LaRossa, M. (1981). *Transition to parenthood: How infants change families.* Beverly Hills, CA: Sage.

LeMasters, E. E. (1957). Parenthood as crisis. *Marriage and Family Living, 19,* 352–355.

LeMasters, E. E., & DeFrain, J. (1989). *Parents in contemporary America: A sympathetic view* (5th ed.). Belmont, CA: Wadsworth.

MacDonald, W., & DeMaris, A. (1996). Parenting stepchildren and biological children: The effects of stepparent's gender and new biological children. *Journal of Marriage and the Family, 17,* 5–25.

Marsiglio, W. (1992). Stepfathers with minor children living at home. *Journal of Family Issues, 13*(2), 195–214.

McCubbin, H., & McCubbin, M. (1988). Typologies of resilient families. *Family Relations, 37,* 247–254.

Muza, R. A. (1988). *Family stress as related to coping strategies and life role salience of dual earner couples.* Unpublished master's thesis. Menomonie, Wisconsin, University of Wisconsin-Stout.

Olson, S. L., & Banyard, V. (1993). Stop the world so I can get off for a while: Sources of daily stress in the lives of low-income single mothers of young children. *Family Relations, 42,* 50–56.

Pill, C. (1990). Stepfamilies: Redefining the family. *Family Relations, 39*(2), 186–193.

Platz, D. L., Pupp, R. P., & Fox, R. A. (1994). Raising young children: Parental perceptions. *Psychological Reports, 74,* 643–646.

Richards, L. N. (1989). The precarious survival and hard-won satisfactions of white single-parent families. *Family Relations, 38,* 396–403.

Richards, L. N., & Schmiege, C. J. (1993). Problems and strengths of single-parent families: Implications for practice and policy. *Family Relations, 42,* 277–285.

Rollins, B., & Feldman, H. (1970). Marital satisfaction over the family life cycle. *Journal of Marriage and the Family, 32,* 20–28.

Schnittger, M. H., & Bird, G. W. (1990). Coping among dual-career men and women across the family life cycle. *Family Relations, 39,* 199–205.

Skinner, D. A., & McCubbin, H. I. (1991). Coping in dual-employed families: Gender differences. *Family Perspective, 25*(2), 119–134.

Stewart, S. D. (1999). Disneyland dads, Disneyland moms? *Journal of Family Issues, 20,* 539–557.

Thompson, A., & Lawson, E. J. (1994). Fatherhood: Insights from divorced black men. *Family Perspective, 28*(3), 169–181.

Umberson, D., & Williams, C. L. (1993). Divorced fathers: Parental role strain and psychological distress. *Journal of Family Issues, 14*(3), 378–400.

U.S. Census Bureau. (1989). Studies in marriage and the family: Singleness in America, single parents and their children, married-couple families with children. *Current Population Reports,* Series P-23 (162). Washington, DC: U.S. Government Printing Office.

Visher, E., & Visher, J. (1990). Dynamics of successful stepfamilies. *Journal of Divorce and Remarriage, 14,* 3–12.

Zimmerman, K., Skinner, D., & Muza, R. (1989). *The relationship of lifecyle stage and employment orientation to work/family stress, coping and life role salience in dual-earner families.* Paper presented at the meeting of the National Council of Family Relations, New Orleans, Louisiana.

5

Teachers and Parenting

Multiple Views

JUDITH B. MACDONALD

Montclair State University

This chapter begins by identifying why it is important for teachers and parents to be aware of each other's viewpoints and attitudes. A range of perceptions teachers have about parents—from an understanding of their vulnerability to a puzzlement about their indifference to school matters—is presented. In the last section, the attitudes various groups of parents have about teachers and parents are described. We believe students will ultimately benefit when parents and teachers better understand each other's frames of reference.

The purpose of the chapter is to help the reader to:

- Describe the similarities and differences of teaching and parenting
- Explain the changing roles of the teacher and the parent in the schools
- Compare teachers' perspectives on parents to parents' perspectives on teachers
- Identify ways for teachers to deal with parents' vulnerability and sensitivity about their children
- Compare and contrast time and work constraints for both parents and teachers
- Identify ways that the parent is a partner with the teacher in the education of their children

It is understandable that teachers and parents have been called "natural allies." They share the common goal of wanting children to develop their potential as fully as possible. But despite their similar aims, teachers and parents don't always work comfortably together to achieve them. The complexity of life today makes it hard for teachers and parents to connect with each other at a time when understanding one another may be even more critical than in the past. How teachers perceive parents and how parents view teachers and schools are subtle, but important, elements in providing optimal educational service to students.

When we talk about groups we tend to make generalizations. Although it may be easier or more efficient to talk "globally" about a group, we also know that talking in a general way can mask differences within a group that should be identified to understand its range and complexity. Just as we know that adolescents have certain characteristics and are driven by feelings that are particular to that age and stage of development, we also know how much they can differ from each other. When we talk about teachers and parents in this chapter, we will describe the varied perceptions that people from each group have about the other. We will explore teachers' views about parents and parents' perspectives on teachers and schools. We will consider how to help beginning teachers prepare for relating to the parents of the students they will teach.

Teaching and Parenting

Similarities

Although teaching and parenting are different experiences, as we have noted, they do share some common elements. We teach and nurture in both roles. The settings we work in as teachers and parents have similarities. The privacy (some teachers have called it loneliness) of the classroom has been compared to what Madeleine Grumet (1988) has termed "the exile of domesticity." Being a teacher or parent requires an energetic giving of oneself. Just listening to students and children demands a special attentiveness. Last, but certainly not least, is patience, an attribute essential in both teaching and parenting.

Differences

When teaching has been compared to other kinds of work, it is called unique because teachers, unlike other workers or professionals, confront "a unique set of difficulties...working with inherently changeful materials" (Lortie, 1975, p. 136). But parents also contend with the changeful nature of children and for longer periods of time than teachers. In fact, teachers who are also parents would be the first to say that hard as teaching can be, its challenges can't compete with those a parent faces. The vast number of books on raising children suggests that parents seem to need guidance and support.

In comparing teaching to parenting, the most obvious difference is the feeling of attachment one has to one's child versus one's student. Although the bond between teacher and student can be strong and meaningful, it lacks the elemental and enduring connections that usually develop between a parent and child. Lillian Katz (1980) identified important differences between mothering and nursery-level teaching, and the distinctions she identified also apply to parenting and teaching at higher levels.

Knowledge of Parents versus Pedagogical Knowledge

At this point in your preparation to become teachers, you may not yet have thought much about relationships with the parents of your prospective students. You are probably more concerned with issues of classroom management or of academic and pedagogical knowledge. Understanding parents, their views about their children, and those of the school may seem like a "back burner" issue. Without passing judgment on where it belongs in your hierarchy of topics in education, we suggest that knowing a parent's perspective will enrich your understanding of students. Because teaching is so fluid and unprescribed, and because there are concurrent classroom demands for attention, we contend with gaps in understanding students. Learning more about parents and their perspectives is one way of learning more about students.

Teacher Morale

Just as it is useful for you to know about parents, the parents should know about the challenges inherent in teaching. We know that parent attitudes affect teacher morale. Feeling valued and respected is crucial for teachers (and for most people), and its absence is the chief cause of teacher burnout or depression. A major cause of teachers leaving the profession is their perception of a lack of respect from parents.

Rob is an example of a teacher who became disenchanted with teaching due to a sense of growing disrespect from parents (and students). He teaches social studies in an ethnically, racially, and religiously diverse middle school. Rob is forty-two years old, married, and has two adolescent children. He has taught for twenty years and enjoyed teaching until the last five years. Rob told me that in recent years the parents in his school treated him as if he were their employee rather than a respected member of a profession.

> I had a student say to me, "Hey, take it easy, I'll have my mother get you fired".... So that lack of respect, the lack of returning the caring attitude that I have for them is very demoralizing. (MacDonald, 1994, p. 60)

We know that teachers are less valued in contemporary society than in the past. Reasons for this change in attitude deserve more analysis than we can provide here. But we do know that if teachers are to function effectively, efforts must be made to correct the misunderstandings that exist between parents and teachers who feel disrespected.

Changing Role of Parents in Schools

It is helpful in understanding how teachers perceive parents to note how the parent's role in schools has changed. In the first quarter of this century when "children were to be seen and not heard," parents, too, were not very visible or vocal in schools. Parents viewed teachers as experts and accorded them the respect appropriate to their position. Until the 1960s parent participation in schools was mainly confined to attending PTA meetings and was limited to those parents who were interested in school issues. Today, PTA events are still mainly supported by groups of interested parents, but most schools would welcome more parent involvement. A recent Gallup poll showed lack of parental interest and support is a primary factor contributing to teacher dissatisfaction.

Reflection...

Consider the responsibilities of working parents. Many parents' home and work responsibilities are such that they don't have enough time for everything they must do. Make a list of these responsibilities and consider the time required for each.

At the same time that teachers want parent support, they are also "wary of activist parents who have become more numerous since the 1960s and who act as if the schools belong to them" (Newman, 1994, p. 252). According to Lortie's study (1975) of teachers, "the good parent" is one who doesn't intervene and also supports teacher's efforts or acts as a "distant assistant." It is obvious there is a range of attitudes that teachers have toward parent involvement. It is a bit of a paradox that as parents have more opportunities to make educational choices—through the development of magnet schools and, in some systems of school vouchers—they have less time to make use of the expertise of teachers. Parents' stressful, busy lives and work schedules often prevent them from consulting with teachers on issues with which they could provide assistance.

Teachers' Perspectives on Parents

Teachers develop ideas about parents based on their interactions with them. As we consider teachers' perspectives, you will note the variety of opinions teachers seem to have about parents.

The Perspectives of Teachers Who Are Also Parents

It may surprise you to learn that more than 70 percent of teachers in the United States are also parents. Teaching parents are a useful source of knowledge about parents. Their perspective is especially instructive if they taught before becoming parents—which is the case for most teachers—and can compare their attitudes toward parents before and after being a parent.

Teaching parents find that a main effect of the dual role is an increased empathy for parents. They understand the complexities of the role of parent when they become parents themselves, and this positively affects their relationships with parents of students (MacDonald, 1994).

We think that sharing some of the attitudes teaching parents have about parents will be useful to you. Perspectives of teachers who are not parents are also presented in this section.

Attachment to Children

When teachers become parents they understand the profound attachment parents can have to their children. Although you may lack actual experience as a parent, awareness of a parent's attachment to a child may help you understand how it can affect the parent's perspective.

Consider Max, a forty-eight-year-old elementary school principal who began his career as a kindergarten teacher. He has a ten-year-old son and has been teaching and working in elementary education for more than twenty years. Max is the principal of a suburban school outside of New York City. Parents in this community are high achievers academically and economically, and, as Max said, "They are quite ambitious for their children.... You understand a parent's investment in their own child and how attached parents can be to their children.... As a parent you can understand why somebody would want everything for their child." So having his own child and feeling what he calls "that inexplicable love" helped Max, as a principal, understand and better cope with "irrational" attitudes of parents.

Understanding Limitations in Parents' Power

It goes without saying that parents are responsible for their children. Parents' values and priorities determine how they raise their children. Clearly they have the responsibility of setting rules and limits. Yet, there are situations in which a parent lacks control. For example, you might want your child to study for a test before doing something more enjoyable. Alice, a science teacher with two young children of her own, found that she could not actually force her child to study for a test. Alice teaches science in a white, middle-class school. She says she loves teaching science although, as a single mother and conscientious teacher, she is exhausted at the end of a school day. She said, "Prior to having my own children, I wouldn't understand how a parent couldn't make a child do his homework. Now I understand you can't force Johnny to study for a test, you can't force your kid to get A's."

Stanley is the father of three adolescents. He teaches English in a middle school which is ethnically, racially, and religiously diverse. He said, "you become sensitive to some of the problems that parents have. Before being a parent I thought 'well, you're the parent, you're in charge, why don't you do something about it.'" But Stanley also talked about parental responsibility:

> On the other hand being a parent also gives you the sense of what it is that parents *aren't* doing that they should be doing. You see children who come to school whose parents aren't involved in their lives, and that makes you wonder and get angry. So I think I'm more sensitive to that as well because I know what goes into parenting.

Awareness of Vulnerability, Sensitivity, Defensiveness

Teachers who realize how vulnerable and sensitive parents can be about their children will have an easier time communicating with parents. It is hard for parents to hear negative news about their child even when they ask you to tell them the truth.

Selma is an experienced fifty-year-old fifth-grade teacher in a suburban elementary school. She was very puzzled by her student Collin's lack of interest in school and lack of connection with the other students. Collin's mother is a well-educated woman in her forties who seemed worried about her son's lack of well-being and inability to fit in to the school. During a conference with Collin's mother, Selma focused on Collin's positive aspects. (He was a kind, sweet-natured boy who loved music.) The atmosphere Selma created encouraged Collin's mother to ask direct questions about Collin's adjustment to school. Selma was able to share more of the truth about Collin than if she had started the discussion with her very real concerns about him. Because the conversation was an honest sharing of knowledge about Collin, both the teacher and mother felt good about it and made plans to meet again.

We think it is useful to realize that if a student is not happily engaged in school, the parent may know it but may not know what to do about it. When a teacher is aware of the pain that a child's unhappiness causes the parent, the teacher is seen as an ally and not a judge. Together they can take steps to address the problem.

Maureen teaches elementary school and has four children. A parent of one of her students who had a learning disability was "resisting referral," as Maureen put it. After Maureen told the parent about her own learning-disabled child and how hard it was for her to face what she felt was the shame of this condition, the parent agreed to have her child evaluated.

When parents are hurting, it is hard for them to use their usual common sense. Parents feel vulnerable when school life isn't going well for their child. Parents of children with difficulties in school, such as learning disabilities, can be defensive about their child's condition, often denying it and thereby depriving the child of better educational alternatives.

Just as teaching isn't formulaic, there is no formula for helping parents see their child impartially. We suggest that you be aware of how sensitive parents of children with problems can be. It may be helpful to remember situations in which you felt vulnerable so as to become attuned to the parents' feelings. You may need to give them time to reveal their concerns, and often it is useful to talk first about less sensitive issues.

Reflection...

Why does there appear to be an uneasy tension between teachers and parents? Why can't teachers and parents trust each other to have children's best interests at heart?

Awareness of Insufficient Time, Being Overworked

Parents today, and especially mothers, have layers of responsibility. Many women work outside the home and have to attend to children and their activities, as well as take some if not all responsibility for household duties. Women who don't work outside the home may have other obligations such as caring for their parents.

Walter is a math teacher in an urban high school. He is in his early forties and has two children in elementary school. When his wife went back to work, he gained a new perspective on working women:

> When my wife went back to work, I really appreciated how hard it is for women who work.... You work all day just to come home and make the dinner, correct papers, and prepare for the next day's classes, and make lunches for the next day, and pretty soon it gets to be 10:00 at night.

We know that people today have less leisure time than their parents despite the labor-saving devices that many families have. Mothers with young children have the least free time and seem to have profited least from advances in labor-saving technology (Hall, 1991).

An awareness of parents' lack of free time will help you understand the constraints and stresses they contend with. Parents may not have the time to help with homework or other school-related tasks. Knowing the time limitations of parents may affect your decisions about what schoolwork should be done at home.

The Educated and/or Affluent Parent

In this section we describe the negative attitudes teachers have reported that some educated and/or affluent parents exhibit. These behaviors clearly don't apply to all educated or affluent parents. New teachers, in particular, feel uneasy teaching students of highly educated parents who may lack the sensitivity to understand the vulnerability of a new teacher. You might expect that the parent who is as educated or more educated than you would be your natural ally in school. Unfortunately, this isn't necessarily so. Teachers have varying perspectives about educated parents. They are clearly valued when they share an understanding of the teacher's educational objectives, but teachers also report that educated parents can be demanding and aggressive.

Experienced teachers claim that parental respect has declined in the last ten to fifteen years. Two groups in particular, educated and affluent parents, seem to be the culprits. Affluent parents can undervalue the teacher if they assess accomplishment in strictly monetary terms.

Cathleen, a high school teacher for twenty-five years, claims that affluent parents in her school (a suburb in the Northeast) are subject to a "stock market syndrome." She said, "When the economy is weak and people are in danger of losing their jobs, they show more disdain for teachers. Since they pay the teachers' salaries, they resent their security at a time when their own may be threatened."

We know it is difficult to work in a community where you expect educated parents to support your efforts but instead perceive themselves as experts and question your professional expertise. It is important for teachers, and especially beginning teachers, to realize that their professional knowledge is distinct and not interchangeable with the knowledge that educated parents may have. It may be a misnomer to call parents "educated" when they are disrespectful of teachers. We alert you to the existence of these parents but also reassure you that the truly educated parent will value and respect you as a teacher.

The Indifferent Parent

Teachers have found it frustrating to work with a parent who seems indifferent to their efforts. It is hard to understand why a parent wouldn't be responsive to a teacher's overtures for contact. We are usually not privy to the origins of a parent's indifference, although knowing why a parent seems apathetic might help you better connect with her or him.

Consider Melinda, a thirty-year-old kindergarten teacher who teaches in Newark, New Jersey, a large city with many urban problems. She has felt frustrated over the parents' lack of involvement and interest in their children's development and schoolwork. She feels it diminishes her job as a teacher when she cannot follow through on her commitment to children by connecting with parents.

We know that "back to school" nights usually draw the parents who don't need to come. That, too, is frustrating for teachers because it deprives them of the chance to interact with parents whose children they want to know more about. You should realize that the appearance of indifference may be masking other conditions. We know that life can be complicated for parents. They may be unable to come to school due to work or other familial obligations. They may feel uneasy in a conference situation. They may have unpleasant associations with school based on their own educational experience.

What can you do? Generally speaking, parents sense a teacher's earnestness. If you send home a note or make a telephone call that reveals your commitment to reaching the parent, that is an important step in connecting. We realize that you may ultimately have to accept the fact that, despite your efforts to reach out to parents, some will not be there for you.

The Bewildered Parent

Being a parent has never been easy. Parenting is one of the few jobs for which there is no preparation. Parents today may be more isolated and vulnerable than in previous generations. The extended family, which provided psychological support, has largely disappeared. In most two-parent households both parents work. In single-parent families, the parent bears even more responsibility. Today's parents may be more enlightened about child-rearing than their parents were. They clearly have access to more literature on the subject. But they have less first-hand knowledge of children. When both parents work, they not only have less time with their children, they also have less familiarity with their children's friends, and so have limited knowledge of the range of normal behavior. Teachers today are often called upon to provide support for bewildered parents.

Teachers expressed a range of opinions about bewildered parents. Rachel teaches English to special education students in a large, racially mixed suburban high school. She loves teaching and enjoys her students. However, she is appalled by the lack of maturity on the part of parents: "They simply don't know how to be parents. They don't know how to set limits; they don't know the importance of consistency." Her reaction to what parents didn't know was one of annoyance with what she felt was a lack of parental responsibility. She felt her students were being short-changed because of the parents' ignorance about their responsibilities.

Linda, a third-grade teacher in a suburban school, strongly believes that parents today need parenting skills. She was astonished at the lack of know-how a professional couple demonstrated regarding their child. They seemed to not know when a third grader should go to bed, let alone the kinds of limits and responsibilities they should set. Linda is troubled by the parents' fundamental lack of common sense.

Other teachers were more empathic toward parents who were unsure about how to cope with their children. Alex teaches social studies in a middle-class middle school. He empathized with parents who had adolescent children and found it "hard to know if you're doing the right thing." He understood how peer pressure can make life very difficult for parents as well as for children.

Reflection...

What is so difficult about parenting? Isn't it better we learn from our parents? If not, where do we learn how to parent and why do some parents seem to have such a hard time with parenting?

Max, the elementary school principal whom we described earlier, empathized with parents of pre-adolescent children, because he was going through the throes of that experience himself. He said:

> I feel for parents who are confused. My son is a pre-adolescent...he wants to be a baby one minute and the next minute he wants to be the independent teenager going off on his own and not wanting any questions asked of him. I know this is typical adolescence, but it's my first and only child, so the first time it hits you, it's a growth experience for the parent.

Being a parent means that you contend with uncertainty and change. Max enjoyed the challenge of growing as a parent and understood that parents must adapt to the stages their children go through. Alex understood the dilemmas of adolescents and their parents. Rachel and Linda are disturbed by what they perceive is a lack of parental responsibility where they believe it is sorely needed.

The Parent as Partner

Teachers found particular satisfaction when they encountered parents who seemed to profit from a relationship with them. These parents defy categorization in terms of age or socioeconomic status. What they seem to have in common is open-mindedness, respect for the teacher's knowledge, an eagerness to learn from the teacher, and a feeling of being at ease in a school setting.

> Dorothy, a second-grade teacher enjoyed having Jessica assist as a mother: She was so involved with all the kids, not just her own. Of course, we tell parents who come on trips with us or come to school to help out that those are the rules of the game— that you are there for all the children. But Jessica *really* was interested in all of them

and in my behavior with them. She watched me very closely and was very interested in picking up on my routines. She asked me a lot of questions. I could tell that she was storing away what she saw for use at home. I love having parents like that around because I do think after thirty years I know a lot and I wish I could share what I know more specifically with the parents. Jessica is like a sponge and I get such pleasure from sort of teaching her, too.

Dorothy isn't the only teacher to experience the satisfactions of developing a relationship with a parent. One of the pleasures of teaching is sharing what you know or have learned, and a likely recipient of this knowledge is a parent. But the parent has to be ready to receive and use this knowledge.

Understandably, teachers develop a perspective about parents based on the nature of their experiences. They feel frustrated with parents they cannot reach and they also know the satisfaction of connecting meaningfully with parents who need their help. We believe that in general parents want to do the best they can for their children. We think it is useful to have some familiarity with the perspectives teachers have about parents. These perspectives are presented to show the variety of ways parents present themselves to teachers, although parents may not be conscious of the effect they have.

As you know, teaching is more than teaching subjects. Who the students are and what they contend with at home affects the attitudes they bring to school. It may be helpful for you to think of your students as someone's child who goes home to a family after being in school and blends the school experience with the realities of home life.

Teachers are required to take on many roles today. We don't suggest that your teaching world extend to the home life of children. But we do believe that the parent is your partner in education, and you can learn from and teach each other—for the benefit of your students.

Parents' Perspectives on Teachers and Schools

For some people, one of the perks in growing up is not having to go to school anymore. But that advantage ends when you become a parent and your child goes to school. The discomfort you felt as a student can return when you are in an environment you never liked in the first place. Why talk about negative feelings as we begin to consider parents' perspectives on teachers and schools? Because many of us have them. Just walking into a school can suddenly make you anxious, remembering the tests on Friday and the Sunday night feeling that Monday was coming.

Are we exaggerating? Yes and no. For many people school was a haven—a place to learn, be with friends, and be nurtured intellectually and emotionally. For others, it was a place where people felt genuinely uncomfortable. The reasons vary. They may have been the victims of poor teaching; they may have had difficulty learning; they may have had problems with social adjustment. As we consider parents' perceptions about teachers and schools, we should remember that parents vary greatly, and the more we know about the range of their attitudes, the better we can address their needs.

Why Should Parental Perspectives Be Considered?

There are two principal reasons to pay attention to parents' feelings about school. First, their attitudes toward school influence their children's attitudes and affect their behavior in class (Seligman, 1979). Second, when parents demonstrate a supportive attitude about school, it has a beneficial effect on teachers. It makes them feel valued and contributes to keeping them in the profession (Newman, 1994).

Shift in Parents' Attitudes

We have already noted that before the 1960s most parents were not active in school affairs. School was the domain of teachers and children. Children went to school either knowing implicitly or being told explicitly that they should cause their parents no shame. Nowadays, however, according to one fifty-year-old teacher, "The parent is likely to blame the teacher for what the child hasn't taken the trouble to learn." Although this shift in parent attitude is not universal, it is sufficiently widespread to concern teachers.

Defining Parental Perspectives on Teachers and School

It can be difficult to assess parents' attitudes about school, and that isn't your primary task as a teacher. Still, if you have some sense of the feelings parents bring to school, you will better understand them and the environments from which your students come. We present viewpoints parents have about teachers and schools to make you aware of the array of feelings and beliefs parents can have on these issues. The circumstances of parent's lives—whether they are single parents, working parents, or stepparents, for example—will also affect their relationships with teachers and schools.

When we describe parents of a particular group, we don't mean to imply that all parents will have the attributes we have used in our example. We are identifying tendencies that people in a specific group may have.

Negative Feelings

Parents with a "Good Old Days" Mentality.   This view represents the belief that teachers are not as dedicated as they were in the past. These parents believe that teachers don't work as hard as they used to and that teaching isn't the "calling" that it once was. Parents assert that the caliber of people entering the profession has declined. They contend that teachers are in the profession for the security it provides and that they don't care sufficiently about students.

Parents who have these beliefs can undermine their child's education by their lack of support for the teacher. It is confusing to a child to hear his or her parent denigrate teachers. A student's success in school can be hampered by a parental attitude of alienation from school. We identify this attitude because you may encounter it. We think the mind-set of these parents can be altered as their children have positive school experiences.

Feelings of Discomfort Due to Disliking School.   As we have said, not everyone liked school as a student, and these feelings can re-emerge as a parent. Consider Joyce, who never enjoyed school. She saw it as a chore she had to get through. When her daughter, Beth, began going to school, Joyce felt the old apprehensions about school return. Fortunately, Beth seems to enjoy school and this pleases Joyce because of the potential for the better life education can give Beth. Joyce's jobs have been confined to minimum wage work from which she derives little satisfaction.

One of Joyce's lingering worries is that because she wasn't a good student, she will be unable to help Beth when she gets into higher grades. Being a single parent, she sees herself as having sole responsibility for helping Beth at home. In a conference setting, a teacher can usually sense a parent's uneasiness. Joyce would feel reassured learning how well Beth was doing in school. Beth's positive adjustment is likely to contribute to Joyce's level of comfort in school. With reduced anxiety about school, Joyce could get the help she might need to assist Beth if or when she will need it.

Effects of Feeling Discomfort in School.   It may be hard to understand how a parent's discomfort about school could be more important than attending to her child's problems. But there are such parents. Linda is an educated woman but she is also depressed by the emotional aspects of her life. She is not a joiner and has avoided school and parent association events. She has a son with learning difficulties and, despite being an educated person, she feels a sense of shame about her son's condition. Her uneasy feelings about school, coupled with an unwillingness to face her child's problems, interfere with finding an appropriate course of action for her son's problems.

A teacher cannot know a parent's frame of mind. We include Linda in our example of parents because, as we have said earlier, parent vulnerability is a subtle but frequent condition. With parents such as Linda, listening to them in a nonjudgmental, supportive way is a first step toward making them less anxious in school.

Positive Feelings

Single Parent—Child's Advocate.   As you might expect, not all parents of children with disabilities are vulnerable and take a "head in the sand" approach to solving problems. Louisa is a forty-year-old single mother of two elementary school–age daughters. The family lives in an integrated suburb. Louisa has sole responsibility for her children and is also working toward a college degree. One of her daughters has learning difficulties in math and reading. Louisa sees herself as the child's advocate and maintains frequent contact with the teacher. Although she describes herself as having emotional problems, she has the focus and the energy to get what is best for her child.

Maria is a single mother of three children, one of whom is severely learning disabled. Like Louisa, she does not shy away from finding solutions for her son. She has an optimistic outlook about what school can do for her son. She sees teachers as being on her side and feels nurtured by the efforts they have made for him.

Effects of Feeling Comfortable in School.   Parents who feel comfortable in a school setting tend to take leadership roles in parent–teacher associations. They are in a good position to use the school beneficially for their children.

Jean has three children. Her two daughters were very school oriented but her youngest child Tim was not interested in school. Jean did not work outside the home and so was fortunate in having the time to talk to Tim's teachers about him. She felt that informing teachers about one's child makes an important difference in their understanding of a puzzling student. Beside having the time to talk to Tim's teachers, Jean also had the inclination to work with them. She felt at ease in school and with teachers and so was able to help them address Tim's needs. She felt it was her obligation to share what she knew about Tim with his teachers.

Blended Family Perspectives

Blended families have many adjustments to make at home. Sometimes the school can be a haven of retreat from family conflicts. In other cases, family problems demand more solutions than the school can successfully provide. Gail was a thirty-eight-year-old teacher with a five-year-old son and three-year-old daughter when her husband died of a heart attack. After a period of three years she married a widower, Martin, who was ten years her senior. He had three children—daughters aged eighteen and eight, and a son aged fifteen. When they married, Gail moved into Martin's house. There were marked differences in Gail and Martin's style of parenting. Gail set very clear limits and was consistent while Martin was unable to deny his children anything. Martin's children were unaccustomed to rules, which made home life very hard for everyone.

Gail's children adjusted well to school because the orderliness their mother provided at home resembled the structure of school. Martin's children, however, were poorly adjusted at school (and at home). They no longer had the freedom at home that they were used to, and they were not involved at school.

With the help of psychological school services and family therapy, Martin's children began to function in school. They were moved to smaller schools where they could get more professional attention. Gail's children functioned well in their regular school but continued to have conflicts with their siblings at home.

As you can see, the different and conflicting parenting perspectives of Gail and Martin had an impact on their children at school as well as at home.

Teaching–Parenting Perspectives

It goes without saying that parents who also teach are comfortable in schools although they may not necessarily be in total agreement with a teacher's method of teaching. In general, though, parents who also teach feel a rapport with teachers and view them as colleagues and allies. Paula and Larry are both teachers and have three adolescent children. Paula said both she and Larry are very sympathetic to teachers. She described the atmosphere of her children's schools as "comfortable, inviting, and homey." She acknowledged that she and her husband are on the same economic and social level as the teachers, which she feels adds to the ease of communicating with them. She and Larry hold teachers in high regard and believe that most teachers work hard and seek to improve their teaching by taking courses to keep up with educational innovations.

Ruth is an example of a teaching-parent who is less contented with her children's teachers than Larry and Paula are. She has two pre-adolescent children and said:

> On several occasions my children have had teachers who were, in my judgment, doing a very poor job. Teachers who are parents must be very careful in the way they approach their own child's school and teachers. Over the years, I have felt uncomfortable at times having to walk that very thin line. To remember my place, and then when necessary to "go to bat" for my child.

Being a teacher and parent gives a parent the opportunity to interact as a colleague with the child's teacher. The success of the relationship depends on having similar educational goals. As we know, not all teachers share a common perspective. So while being an insider as a teacher is beneficial for a parent, it doesn't guarantee the parent the understanding he or she might expect.

Reflection...

How can teachers enable parents to better understand the complexities of teaching? How can parents help the non-parent teacher understand the total responsibility of parenting?

The Parent as Learner and Partner

We have referred to the parent, Jessica, in the section on teachers' perspectives, as someone who the teacher, Dorothy, perceived as benefiting from being in her classroom. Jessica valued what she learned from the teacher, such as routines and consistency, which she had not learned elsewhere. She sees the classroom as a unique setting in which to learn about children and then to use this knowledge as a parent. It is both instructive and nurturing for her. From Jessica's perspective, the school and teachers are sources of learning and collaboration.

Summary

We have presented a range of attitudes parents have toward teachers and schools. Despite the differences in their feelings about school, parents have a common desire for their children to succeed there.

We see the school as a place for teachers and parents to exchange knowledge and perspectives. The expertise of teachers should not be confined to the classroom. Most teachers have a natural desire to communicate what they know and this knowledge can be used by parents. Teachers have honed their skills in the laboratory setting of schools and parents can adapt these skills for use at home. Classroom techniques, such as questioning to stimulate thinking and giving students (children) time to think and respond, could be used by parents if they aren't engaging in these practices. Sigel (1991) has clearly described how parents' verbal interactions with children can affect their intellectual development.

We believe parents should know more about what it is like to be a teacher in today's society. Parents may not be sufficiently aware of the varied roles teachers are required to assume (i.e., social worker, surrogate parent) and the impact of these responsibilities on their teaching lives. We think that if parents better understood the complexity of teachers' professional lives, it would positively affect their relations with them.

Schools where the development of teacher–parent collaboration and trust is given priority produce students who take learning seriously and enjoy school. (Note: Two examples are James Comer's work in schools in New Haven, Connecticut, and Deborah Meier's in the Central Park East schools in New York City.) We hope this trend will grow, and as teachers you will contribute to it.

RECOMMENDED ACTIVITIES

1. Invite a panel of parents into class to discuss, from their perspective, the relationship between the parent and teacher. Make sure to include parents of children in preschool, elementary, middle, and high school classes.

2. Invite a panel of teachers into the class to discuss, from their perspective, the relationship between the teacher and parent. Make sure to include teachers from preschool, elementary school, middle school, and high school.

3. Interview teachers and/or administrators that have been teaching for over twenty years. Ask them to compare teaching today with teaching twenty years ago. Ask them specific questions about changes they see in the roles of teachers, parents, and children. What do they see as changes that are positive as well as negative?

4. Have a parent educator come into class and discuss the types of questions he or she hears from parents about parenting issues. How do these questions relate to teachers?

5. Identify various parenting discussion groups on the World Wide Web. Describe the different groups and the emphasis of their discussions. Ask parents you know if that is the type of format they would like to have available to answer their questions or if they prefer the face-to-face contact.

6. Interview parents and teachers and ask them what they perceive the role of the parent is in the school. If they identify roles, ask them to describe the differences they see with parent involvement in schools today compared to when they were growing up.

7. Survey different ages of children to determine what kind of role they would like to have their parents play in schools. Make sure to survey different age groups from four-year-olds to seventeen-year-olds.

ADDITIONAL RESOURCES

Parental Participation

Books:

Comer, J. B. (1989). Home, school, and academic learning. In J. Goodlad & P. Keating (Eds.), *Access to knowledge* (pp. 23–42). New York: College Board.

Delgado-Gaitan, C., & Trueba, H. (1991). *Crossing cultural borders: Education for immigrant families in America.* London: Falmer Press.

Meier, D. (1995). *The power of their ideas: Lessons for America from a small school in Harlem.* Boston: Beacon.

Neumann, A., & Peterson, P. L. (Eds.). (1997). *Learning from our lives.* New York: Teachers College Press.

Reitz, R. (Ed.). (1990). *Parent involvement in the schools.* Bloomington, IN: Phi Delta Kappa.

Winters, W. G. (1993). *African American mothers and urban schools: The power of participation.* New York: Lexington Books.

Articles:

Comer, J. B. (1986). Parent participation in the schools. *Phi Delta Kappan, 67*(6), 442–446.

Hulsebosch, P. (1992). Significant others: Teachers' perceptions on relationships with parents. In W. A. Schubert & W. C. Ayers (Eds.), *Teacher Lore* (pp. 107–132). New York: Longman.

Organizations:

Alliance for Parental Involvement in Education
P.O. Box 59
East Chatham, NY 12060
Phone: 518-456-1876

Center for Study of Parent Involvement
John F. Kennedy University
12 Altarinda Road
Orinda, CA 94563
Phone: 510-254-8820

National Committee for Citizens in Education (NCCE)
900 2nd Street, NW
Washington, DC 20002
Phone: 800-NETWORK

Parents as Teachers National Center
9374 Olive Blvd.
St. Louis, MO 63132
Phone: 314-432-4330

Parents' Rights Organization
12571 Northwinds Drive
St. Louis, MO 63146
Phone: 314-434-4171

Videos:

For Children's Sake: The Comer School Development Program Discussion Leader's Guide Videotape C—The Parents Program

Describes the Comer process, which puts children at the center of the educational process by calling on all significant adults in the community to work together to support and nurture every child's total development. 1992. New Haven, CT: Yale Child Study Center.

Involving Parents in Education

Examines how two schools, one rural and one urban, involve parents in their operations. Offers suggestions on how to build parent–teacher partnerships. 1992. Alexandria, VA: ASCD. (30-minute video and 54-page leader's guide)

Partnerships with Parents

Discusses how parents and teachers can work together for the benefit of preschool children, foster communications, and resolve difficulties with schedules of both parents and schools. 1989. (28 minutes)

Teacher TV: Parents as Partners, Episode #5.

Explores ways that teachers can get parents involved as their partner in education. 1993. (22 minutes) Washington, DC: National Education Association.

Working with Parents: Home School Collaborations

Examines how to improve communication between teachers and parents when they meet at parent–teacher conferences to better serve the student. 1984. (30 minutes)

Films:

Little Man Tate. 1991. MGM/UA. (99 minutes)

Music from the Heart. 1999. Miramax Films.

Websites:

COMPASS Resource Parents and Teachers
www.compassinc.com/resources.html

National Association for the Education of Young Children (NAEYC)
www.neayc.org

Parents as Teachers
www.txpat.org

Parents Planet
www.parents-planet.com

Parent Soup
www.parentsoup.com

Teacher/Parent/Trainer Site List
www.edpro.com

Texas Educational Network
www.tenet.edu

REFERENCES

Grumet, M. (1988). *Bitter milk: Women and teaching.* Amherst, MA: University of Massachusetts Press.

Hall, T. (1991, July 3). Time on your hands? It may be increasing. *New York Times,* pp. 1, 7.

Katz, L. G. (1980). Mothering and teaching: Some significant distinctions. In L. G. Katz (Ed.), *Current topics in early childhood education* (Vol. 3) (pp. 47–64). Norwood, NJ: Ablex.

Lortie, D. C. (1975). *Schoolteacher.* Chicago: University of Chicago Press.

MacDonald, J. B. (1994). *Teaching and parenting: Effects of the dual role.* Lanham, MD: University Press of America.

Newman, J. W. (1994). *America's teachers.* New York: Longman.

Seligman, M. (1979). *Strategies for helping parents of exceptional children.* New York: Free Press.

Sigel, I. E. (1991). Parents' influence on their children's thinking. In A. L. Costa (Ed.), *Developing minds* (Vol. 1) (pp. 43–46). Alexandria, VA: Association for Supervision and Curriculum Development.

CHAPTER

6

Parent–Teacher Communication

Who's Talking?

SARA FRITZELL HANHAN
University of North Dakota

My family is sad because my grandpa died.

(labels in drawing: my dad, my mom, Ann, me, Sarah)

Becca Olsen

After reading this chapter, the student will be able to:

- Identify principles for establishing two-way communication with parents
- Distinguish between effective and ineffective non-verbal communication
- Describe ways to establish a positive atmosphere for parent–teacher conferences

Although many of you may believe strongly that parents and schools should form true partnerships in order to maximize the benefit of parent involvement (Swap, 1993), this is not always an easy thing to achieve. It requires mutual commitment, action, trust, and understanding on the part of both parents and school personnel. One of the first steps teachers can take toward successful parent involvement and the possibility for true home–school partnerships is to learn the ins and outs of communicating with parents. This is not so different from skillful communication with anyone else, of course, but there are some purposes and nuances that can be particular to parent–teacher relationships.

In many teacher education programs, students are required to take a course in communication, usually a course in fundamentals of public speaking. When a rationale for the requirement is offered, it is usually that teachers need to learn to feel comfortable speaking in front of a group and to make an organized and articulate presentation. Although there are few occasions for teachers to give formal speeches to groups of parents, the direction of much parent–teacher communication nonetheless tends to be one-way, flowing from teacher to parent, with an expectation or perhaps even a hope that parents will receive teacher wisdom passively. As examples, some of the most common methods teachers use to communicate with parents are newsletters, parent handbooks, orientation meetings, and report cards, which typically involve the teacher *telling* parents about activities, school policies and procedures, student progress, curriculum, and so on. Even parent–teacher conferences are sometimes viewed as opportunities to *tell* parents how their children are doing in school. The idea is to have parents informed. Although just as important as the teacher education emphasis on speech, courses on *listening* are not only not required for teacher certification, they are seldom even available at any college or university in the country. Teachers, in other words, despite rhetoric about the importance of good home–school communication, are taught to talk rather than to listen to students and parents. To reap the benefits of parent involvement, however, parents too must speak and be heard. Communication must flow in at least two directions (National PTA, 1997), and for this to happen both parent and teacher need to consider each other their equal.

In most cases teachers need to take the initiative in order for this to happen. Problematic for a parent–teacher relationship based on equality is the inherent inequality of the relative positions of teacher and parent within the school. For many parents, their own children's initial school enrollment is their first contact with teachers and schools since they themselves were students, and school memories for many adults are not very pleasant (Seligman, 1979). Whether memories of school are pleasant or not, however, parents' childhood relationships with teachers were inherently unequal, and for many the nature of that relationship lives on, even though they are now adults. Teachers must also keep in mind that in some cultures parents cannot even imagine the idea of a parent–teacher partnership. In these cultures the expectation is that the teacher is always right and that it is best for the child and the parent to remain quiet about concerns they might have.

Reflection...

Think about your teachers from elementary or secondary school. Which teacher would you look forward to having a frank conversation with—and which would you not? What makes your memories different?

In addition to a perceived inequality between the teacher and the parent, parents are also keenly aware that they have placed the welfare of their children in the hands of teachers and that each teacher potentially has the power to make children's school lives either comfortable or difficult. For this reason, many parents tread lightly within the parent–teacher relationship, unwilling, from their perspective, to upset the child–teacher relationship for fear that the teacher might take it out on the child (Swap, 1993).

Finally, an important idiosyncratic quality of the teacher–parent relationship is that the stakes are so high. To be sure, this is true of some other relationships that rely on good communication as well, but in this case the quality of the relationship may affect what happens to a child's life—something that for many of us is of ultimate importance and weighs heavy with responsibility.

Building a Coequal Relationship

Although it may be difficult for teachers to affect the relationships children have with their parents, teachers can affect the nature of their own relationships with their students' parents. Most parents and many teachers consider schools to be teacher territory, not parent territory. The majority of parents probably feel uneasy, like fish out of water or guests in a strange place. They view teachers as authority figures, the experts in teaching and learning, and they are often even uncertain about their own expertise in parenting. When the relationship is unequal to begin with, the flow of communication generally goes from the person in the superior position (the one perceived to have more expertise) to the person who is viewed as inferior (parenting is seen as something everyone can do). It's much like pouring water from a pitcher into a glass (see Figure 6.1).

It is very difficult, under these circumstances, for the water (or conversation) to flow from lower vessel to higher vessel. If we truly want parents to be partners in our educational efforts, we must change the perceived positions of the players. Communication must begin to flow two ways. And considering the relatively powerful position of teachers, it becomes their responsibility to make the first move. Unfortunately, this is not always easy either, as there are many barriers that need to be avoided or overcome.

Barriers to Two-Way Communication

Language

In addition to the barrier of perceived inequality, language itself poses a number of stumbling blocks for those teachers and parents who wish to establish open and two-way communication. Language is often ambiguous. Mutual understanding requires both clear articulation on the part of the speaker/writer and accurate interpretation on the part of the listener/reader. The very acts of speaking, listening, writing, and reading, however, leave much room for misinterpretation. Teachers may, for instance, in the hopes of lessening parental disappointment, couch what they have to say about children in gentle terms, which in turn may be interpreted by one parent as teacher satisfaction or by another as a cover-up of serious problems. Another example that illustrates the importance of specificity and clarity comes from a first grade parent–teacher conference. The teacher told the parent in this conference that her child was "what we call immature." When the parent in-

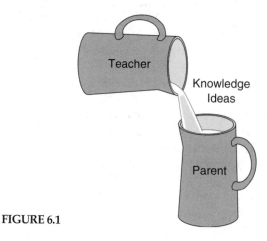

FIGURE 6.1

quired further about his immaturity, the teacher offered that "he was reluctant to try new things." The parent in turn asked what he was reluctant to do. The teacher said that he was unwilling to climb some bleacher-like stairs. At this point, the teacher's comments made sense to the mother because she knew of her son's fear of heights; only now could she be of some help to the teacher in offering both an explanation and the beginnings of a solution.

Although there is ambiguity in cases such as the above example, parents at least have the background to make some interpretation. When educational jargon is used, however, parents can be left feeling inept, ashamed, or even stupid or embarrassed to ask for an explanation. What does it mean to have an "auditory processing problem" or good "visual-spatial abilities" or "learning disabilities?" It seems best for teachers to forego jargon of all kinds in favor of using everyday language that is as descriptively specific and as free of value judgments as possible. This holds true for parents whose native language is not English as well, but there is even more risk of misunderstanding when everyday language may be difficult to understand. In such cases, if the school cannot provide a translator, it may be wise to invite the parent to bring in someone with whom he or she feels comfortable that can help translate both for the teacher and for the parent.

Body Language

The influence of nonverbal messages can also complicate the communication process. Body positions (e.g., arms and legs folded tightly), gestures (e.g., a shrug of the shoulders), facial expressions (e.g., a quivering lip or flaring nostrils), voice intonation or rate of speech (e.g., a firm and monotone voice), or an involuntary behavior (e.g., a quick inhale of breath) can all carry signals to the listener. If our nonverbal behaviors do not correspond with the message we wish to convey, or if we are unfamiliar with the meanings of nonverbal behaviors in other cultures, these behaviors can become obstacles to clear and sensitive communication.

Body language can provide information about a person's emotional state (see Table 6.1). The person who folds his or her arms and quickly turns away is most likely upset; this can be useful information. On the other hand, you do not want to overinterpret every movement. Some people are more comfortable sitting with their legs or arms crossed and it is their desire for comfort, rather than a nonverbal message, that may be the reason for the position.

You need to be aware of clusters of behaviors that seem unusual for that person. You can then use this information to help you rethink how you can best deal with the situation. It is also a good idea to monitor your own body language when dealing with parents—especially if it is a tense moment. What is it saying about you? Are you demonstrating defensiveness?

In addition, teachers sometimes deal with parents who are exhibiting contradictory nonverbal messages. Most seasoned teachers have had the experience of talking with a parent whose voice is calm, and face smiling but who has tears running down his or her face. In situations such as these you can say something such as, "I noticed that while we were talking about Beth's reading scores you were

TABLE 6.1   Nonverbal Communication

Attitude	Nonverbal Cue	Attitude	Nonverbal Cue
Openness	Open hands	**Nervousness**	Clearing throat
	Unbuttoned coat		"Whew" sound
			Whistling
Defensiveness	Arms crossed on chest		Cigarette smoking
	Crossing legs		Picking or pinching flesh
	Fist-like gestures		Fidgeting in chair
	Pointing index finger		Hand covering mouth while speaking
			Not looking at the other person
Evaluation	Hand to face gestures		Tugging at pants while seated
	Head tilted		Jingling money in pockets
	Stroking chin		Tugging at ear
	Peering over glasses		Perspiration, wringing of hands
	Taking glasses off, cleaning		
	Earpiece of glasses in mouth	**Frustration**	Short breaths
	Pipe smoker gestures		"Tsk" sounds
	Putting hand to bridge of nose		Tightly clenched hands
			Wringing hands
Suspicion	Arms crossed		Fist-like gestures
	Sideways glance		Pointing index finger
	Touching, rubbing nose		Rubbing hand through hair
	Rubbing eyes		Rubbing back of neck
	Buttoning coat—drawing away		
		Cooperation	Upper body in sprinter's position
Insecurity	Pinching flesh		Open hands
	Chewing pen, pencil		Sitting on edge of chair
	Thumb over thumb, rubbing		Hand to face gestures
	Biting fingrenails		Unbuttoning coat
	Hands in pockets		Tilted head
		Confidence	Steepled hands
			Hands behind back
			Back stiffened
			Hands in pockets with thumbs out
			Hands on lapels of coat

upset." It is then important to give them a few moments to think about what they are going to say about this emotional topic. This is also just as necessary with the parent whose body language suggests anger and hostility.

Still other barriers to effective two-way communication include such things as fatigue, lack of time, ego involvement (often manifested in defensiveness), differences in personality or communicative pace (most of us can think of people who speak annoyingly slowly or quickly), preoccupation with personal circumstances or other distractions, differing communicative purposes, or simply differences in status, age, sex, race, or culture. Obviously no matter how hard an individual teacher tries to establish a communicative flow that is two-way, there may be other contributing factors that make it impossible. But there are strategies that can be used successfully to lessen the impact of such factors.

Aids to Two-Way Communication

Active Listening

Speakers who are able to use everyday, but descriptive, language to clearly articulate ideas in nonjudgmental ways are obviously important in conducting effective two-way communication; but if he or she does not listen, even the most gifted speaker will not support a reciprocal conversation. A key to establishing a relationship in which two (or more) people communicate effectively is *active listening.* If you think of someone you consider a good listener, you can probably identify some of the visible outward characteristics that communicate close listening. Active listeners tend to maintain eye contact with the speaker; their posture communicates attentiveness, often with a forward lean; they may encourage the speaker by nodding, raising eyebrows or smiling appropriately in response to what the speaker is saying; they ask pertinent questions, sometimes to check their perceptions; they get rid of or ignore potential distractions; they acknowledge the feelings of the speaker; and mostly, they stop talking.

These are behaviors that are practicable and learnable, but active listening is more than just outward behavior: it is an attitude. The active listener *wants* to hear what is being said, and he or she listens with the goal of hearing—and empathetically understanding—what the speaker is saying; he or she is nonjudgmental. Active listening on the part of a teacher can communicate a wish to engage in real two-way communication, and this in turn begins to equalize the position of those in the relationship. Communication begins to flow two ways, with each party truly hearing the other and therefore responding appropriately.

When the teacher begins to listen and respond with empathy and understanding, mutual trust and respect begin to develop, and the parent(s) are able to speak out (and to listen actively and intelligently themselves).

Honesty

In addition to a context of mutual respect and trust, active listening and the use of descriptive and nonjudgmental language, communication must be based on a commitment to openness and honesty. If parents (and teachers) feel they are being manipulated or lied to, communications will break down. All of these qualities simultaneously interact to provide the atmosphere in which true partnerships can be developed and maintained. The foundation for the success of the following kinds of teacher–parent communication is the early establishment of relationships that embrace and enact the above qualities.

Initial Communication

There are many ways of initiating the parent–teacher relationship, and each of them should be planned with an eye to establishing a context in which teacher and parent are coequal, leading, in turn, to the establishment of communication that is two-way, respectful, honest, and productive.

Some schools or centers have *intake interviews* for parents when they enroll their children. These interviews should be viewed as occasions on which parents can ask for and receive information about the school and as occasions for the school to gather important information about the child from the parents. Parents can, for instance, provide medical information that could be relevant for teachers, especially in emergency situations. The name and phone number of the child's doctor, food allergies or other diet restrictions, medical conditions that might require special responses or that might affect the child's school performance are a few examples. The initial intake interview may also ask parents about such things as the child's interests or preferred ways of spending free time, or the family's linguistic, religious and/or cultural background, which in turn can help teachers build a relationship with the child as well as build a curriculum responsive to children's interests and needs. Schools, in turn, can use the intake interview to orient the family to the physical space, rules, and expectations of the school.

Information from and to parents may be made in writing (e.g., an enrollment form to be filled out by the parents or a policy manual for parents to take home), or the information may be offered and received verbally. Many educators advise using both an oral and a written method of communicating initial information— oral because it is more personal and written because there is no guarantee verbally stated information will be remembered. And in the case of the school receiving personal information about children, the sheer number of children precludes the possibility of a person remembering details for each child with any accuracy. Although such intake interviews are often conducted by principals or directors, teachers should attend, if at all possible, as a way of establishing initial communicative and two-way relationships as early as possible and as a way of coming to know and value the parents' perceptions of their children.

In the event that teachers cannot attend such interviews (often the case, as teachers have class preparation to attend to, and initial intake interviews most logically complement the administrative processes of registering), there are many other kinds of activities that can help establish early relationships both with families and among families, and with students. Some that I've heard about or used myself are: a beginning-of-the-year family picnic, a personal phone call to welcome each family to the school, a welcoming postcard sent prior to the beginning of school, a home visit by the teacher, a family/teacher start-of-the-year social, or an invitation to families and students to visit the classroom together. Such activities can take many forms, but the objective should be to exchange information and to make initial contacts; these efforts are crucial in building relationships that facilitate two-way communications on a regular and coequal basis. This requires initiative and personal attention from the teacher.

Reflection...

Describe how you would establish effective communication between yourself as a teacher and a family. Do you think your feelings about home–school communication would change if you had children in school and were teaching?

Regular Communication

Once initial communication has been established, methods of building and maintaining a communicative relationship need attention. Such methods, too, may be informal or formal, written or oral.

Informal Communication

The most common method of informal regular communication, especially with families of young children, is the casual conversation parents have with teachers while dropping off or picking up their children from school. For parents who do this, this may, in fact, be the most important place for tone setting. A casual conversation, if done with respect and with genuine interest in the parent's child, can go a long way simply because it does not occur in a more formal setting, such as a parent–teacher conference where parents may feel as if formal feedback is what goes on record. In the daily conversations parents have with teachers, feedback (two-way) is generally considered more helpful than threatening, more flexible than permanent.

For parents of children who are old enough to get themselves to school or for parents who are too busy or unable to make daily trips to the school or whose children ride buses, other means of regular informal communications can substitute. Perhaps one of the most common is the phone call. Although teachers may view this as an imposition on their personal time, a call to a parent of each child, well-spaced over the course of the first month of school, can be a key to parents realizing the teacher is approachable and genuinely concerned about children and parental opinions. You should be warned, however, that despite many classrooms now having their own phones, most teachers do not do this, and as a result a phone call out of the blue from a teacher may initially be frightening to parents. If no one has ever called the parent from school or there have only been calls when something is wrong (the child is sick or misbehaving), it may take more than one call to convince the parent that you are calling just to check in or to describe an interesting event. It is for this reason that I recommend that the first call of the year be a positive one. If this is the case, later calls that might not be so pleasant will be received much more willingly.

Written Communication

Written communication has a permanence about it that demands a particular kind of attention. Although it can take many forms and can be informal or formal, teachers are expected to write in proper English with correct spelling. When this is not the case, negative judgment of the teacher may occur, interfering with expectations of coequality. Likewise, teachers need to guard against negative judgment of parents who have poor writing skills or who are illiterate, lest this too interfere with a coequal relationship.

Newsletters

One of the most common methods of written communication with parents, besides the narrative report, which is discussed below, is the *newsletter*. These are written and regular publications which most often inform parents of the events in the classroom either prior to or following the events themselves. While many parents like these because they are interested in school curriculum and school happenings, others may find them relatively boring. One method that teachers employ to entice parents into reading the newsletter is to be sure to write something about each child in the class, highlighting their names. Another is to include announcements and news about things that would interest parents in general, interspersed with specific classroom news.

Computers have made the production of newsletters easier than ever, particularly if you use the same format each time. Most newsletters are sent biweekly or monthly, but how often they are published is up to the individual. Newsletters should not be more than two pages long. Parents are very busy and may feel put off by a multi-page document.

The newsletter provides you with an opportunity to share with parents the exciting things that are occurring in the classroom. It is important to use students' work, articles written by the students, and illustrations drawn by the students. Make certain that every student is mentioned several times over a period of time. The following is a list of possible newsletter items:

- Samples of the students' work
- Relevant quotations from the students
- Announcements
- Requests for needed materials (We need 2-gallon milk cartons, etc.)
- Special community announcements
- Reprints of short articles that might be of particular interest to parents
- Suggestions of things that parents and children can do together

- Thank you notes to parents who have in some way helped the class
- Suggestions for age-appropriate books for your students and books dealing with education, parenting, and so on for the parents
- Welcomes to new class members and their families
- A brief synopsis of what is being studied in class
- Articles or notes from parents for other parents

Unfortunately, most newsletters are a method of teacher-to-parent communication, which by itself is no problem, but when put together with other one-way communication has the potential for perpetuating the distance between parents and teachers. As teachers, you might want to consider how to involve parents in writing and planning part of the newsletter. This not only opens up possibilities for parental involvement in the program, it opens up possible parent-to-parent communications, may identify items more parents would like to see, and has the potential for lightening your own work load!

School–Home Journal

A form of two-way written communication, used most often for children with special needs, is the *school–home journal*. This is especially helpful when parents do not or cannot visit the school on a daily basis. It consists of a notebook in which teachers make comments about the child's school day on a regular basis. It is then sent home with the child, and the parent(s) respond to what the teacher has said and comment on the child's day at home. Of course, its success depends on the diligence of both the parent and the teacher, but you should not get discouraged easily. A parent may not be able to write in the journal every day, but may find the time to do so twice a week. Encouraging the child to write or draw his or her own occasional entry may also perk up the parent(s)' or the child's interest (and children can then help remind parents and teacher about their commitment to the journal).

Narrative Report

Another means of describing to parents the child's life in school is through *narrative reporting*. Although many parents cling to the traditional report card as a way of comparing their children with others, teachers who write narrative reports for parents are often rewarded for their time and effort with increased parental appreciation and support. It is important, however—especially because such reports are time-consuming for teachers—that the reports speak to the child's unique presence in the classroom. Comments such as "great student" or "needs some work" tend to be so generic that they are not helpful to parents. Nor do such remarks give specific enough information to enable the parent's helpful response. A good narrative report is one that describes only one child and is therefore not interchangeable with or substitutable for narrative commentary about other children. It is descriptive and sufficiently detailed to make the child's classroom work come alive for the reader.

Parent–Teacher Conferences

Although there was a time when parent–teacher conferences were not used except when there was trouble afoot, they are now probably the single most frequently used (and most institutionalized) method of parent–teacher communication in schools and other educational settings. The parent–teacher conference may vary in its frequency, length, and even purpose, but most often it occurs twice a year, lasting about fifteen or twenty minutes, largely for the purpose of parents becoming informed of their child's progress in school (Swap, 1993). Perhaps one reason that it has become such a stable method of home–school communication is that it has been relatively successful. For the most part, parents appreciate a time to talk to the teacher about their child's school life, and when done at regular intervals, with administrative time and support, it affords teachers an organized means of ensuring that each family has an opportunity to be personally informed. It is also interesting to note, however, that many teachers come to view these conferences as a chore rather than an opportunity and that both teachers and parents report some nervousness about them (Swap, 1993). The conferences can be emotionally draining for teachers and parents. Parents and teachers further complain that there is usually not enough time for meaningful conversation, and teachers often note, with regret, that the parents whom they most need to see do not come.

Even though it is improbable that parent–teacher conferences on their own can create two-way communication patterns between teachers and parents, there are a number of strategies that can be brought to bear at conferences that will maximize their potential for supporting other efforts at good parent–teacher communication. They can be scheduled, for instance, to accommodate parents' work schedules. Many schools now have parent–teacher conferences scheduled during one evening as well as during the day. It can also be helpful to parents to schedule conferences for siblings back-to-back, so that one trip to school will suffice to see the teachers of all the children in the same family.

The conference environment can be made less threatening as well. Seating parents next to the teacher at a table, rather than on the other side of a desk, can reduce the perception of unequal positions. Making parents comfortable with adult-sized chairs can help put them at ease. When possible, not keeping parents waiting and getting up to greet them at the door can communicate care and interest and help make parents feel welcome and valued. Engaging in a minute of small talk before addressing the conference agenda can also help put parents at ease and make the atmosphere more friendly.

Although fifteen or twenty minutes is a very short time to accomplish much in the way of communication, there are other things that can be kept in mind that can help maximize the success of the conversation itself. Experts recommend, for instance, that discussion about the child start out and end with something positive. If there is a concern to be communicated, it is best done in the middle of the conference (Rockwell, Andre, & Hawley, 1996). It is also important to limit the number of areas of concern expressed at any one time, especially if the advice and help of the parent is desired, as it is difficult for anyone to effectively deal with a litany of concerns at once. It is also important and very effective to be able to describe something about the child that shows the parent that you know the child in ways that go beyond grades on tests and academic performances. What engages her in class? Who are his friends? What role does he play in a group project? How does she express herself?

Two controversial activities related to parent–teacher conferences are note-taking and parents bringing others to the conference. Although there are some advantages to either a parent or a teacher taking notes at conferences, there are also disadvantages. Note-taking both helps the note-taker remember what has been said and conveys to the other person that he or she takes what is said seriously. On the other hand, note-taking can convey an impression that the note-taker is creating a written record which could be used against the speaker. This becomes a particularly touchy issue in a litigious time and culture such as ours. Whatever your inclination, however, permission to take notes should be asked before doing so.

Although some teachers react strongly to the presence of anyone but the parents in a conference, parents do have a right to bring others with them, and there are sometimes sound reasons for doing so (Schulz, 1987). Especially when issues such as special education diagnosis or placement are being discussed, it helps to have a second pair of ears. When we take in difficult or disappointing information, we tend to focus on only the most shocking elements of the conversation. We can miss such things as suggestions for action or possible alternative interpretations. For this reason, we should welcome friends or relatives who come to help parents hear. We should also welcome child caregivers when parents have invited them to be part of the conference, as they often have as much information to contribute to the conversation as the parents do. For non-English speaking parents, a friend who can serve as a translator, if the school or center does not provide one, is often a welcome relief for both teacher and parent. If, however, parents have been accompanied by someone and they seem to be uneasy about the person's presence, or if a neighbor has just come along for the ride (and may be a possible gossip), it is appropriate to request that such individuals wait outside while you confer with the parent(s). Decisions about children attending their own or their siblings' conferences depend on the preference of the teacher and the parent, the age of the children, and the purpose for their attendance, and need to be determined on an individual basis. Similarly what happens if the parents are divorced or separated? Frequently the teachers, when presented with those situations, will hold separate conferences with the parents.

Reflection…

How would you make sure fathers are included in conferences? What if both parents were female (a lesbian relationship)?

These suggestions can help make the parent–teacher conference pleasant and productive, but they don't go very far toward increasing the reciprocal nature of information flow. It's important to save time for parents' questions and discussion of any agenda they might bring to the conference. And if time runs out during the regularly scheduled conference, arrangements should be made for a second conference. In fact, parents need to feel that they can request a conference with the teacher at any time during the year, without suspicion.

Effective parent–teacher conferences require planning, thoughtful action, and timely follow up on the part of the teacher and the parent. Figure 6.2 offers a helpful checklist for teachers as they engage in their parent–teacher conferences. Of course the most important element in supporting parental participation in a conference is to stop talking and start listening!

Communication with Parents of Middle School Students

Student–Parent–Teacher Conferences

A fast-growing model for conferences includes the student in the conference. This model can be used from first grade through high school but is particularly successful with middle school students. Because middle school takes a team approach, this "team" conference is particularly appropriate.

It is important to note that the student must be an active member of the team who has input into the conference. There are several methods of conducting this type of conference and numerous variations. The following is one possible scenario.

Beginning of the School Year.   Meet during the first weeks of school to set goals for the school year and discuss how these goals will be met. At this time the responsibility of each participant should be determined and written down for future reference. The time and date for the next conference might be determined at this point as well.

Mid-Year.   This conference should begin with a collective evaluation of the success of the previously set goals. At this time, adjustments to the goals and responsibilities should be made as needed. These adjustments may involve knowledge not available to the participants earlier in the semester. An appointment may be made for the next conference.

Final Conference.   Again, it is important to review the original goals and the modifications made during the second conference. This is a time to evaluate the year's progress. It is important that all areas be evaluated—areas of strength as well as areas of concerns. It is also a time for parents, teachers, and students to enjoy the successes of the year.

FIGURE 6.2   **Conference Checklist**

Pre-Conference

_____ **1.** Notify—Purpose, place, time, length of time allotted

_____ **2.** Prepare
                    –Review child's folder
                    –Gather examples of work
                    –Prepare materials

_____ **3.** Plan agenda

_____ **4.** Arrange environment
                    –Comfortable seating
                    –Eliminate distractions

Conference

_____ **1.** Welcome
                    –Establish rapport

_____ **2.** State
                    –Purpose
                    –Time limitations
                    –Note taking
                    –Options for follow-up

_____ **3.** Encourage
                    –Information sharing
                    –Comments
                    –Questions

_____ **4.** Listen
                    –Pause once in awhile!
                    –Look for verbal and nonverbal cues
                    –Questions

_____ **5.** Summarize

_____ **6.** End on a positive note

Post-Conference

_____ **1.** Review conference with child, if appropriate

_____ **2.** Share information with other school personnel, if needed

This has been modified from material developed by Roger Kroth and the Parent Involvement Center, University of New Mexico.

Teachers and parents both have reported this as a productive format. By including students in conferences, not only are parents and teachers responsible but students are also. The number of conferences may vary according to individual need and school policy.

Homework Hot Line

Parents often feel intimidated by their middle school child's homework. They may have found a subject difficult when they were in school, not have been exposed to the material, or have forgotten it—after all, it has been a number of years since these parents were the age their children are presently. Whatever the reason, parents and students may need additional help. Schools that have implemented *homework hot lines* have found this a positive way to help both parents and students. They enable students and parents to call for help during evening homework hours.

Homework hot lines can be used in a variety of ways. For example, they could be used to assist callers with their assignments or to verify homework assignments. The following is a list of guidelines for running a successful homework hot line. It is important to remember that there are many variations of this program and that a school must tailor it to meet its own needs.

- Determine what the greatest homework need is for your school and for students. Include parents and students in planning efforts. In most schools, it is math—particularly pre-algebra and algebra. The second pertains to writing skills and is very broad in nature—everything from punctuation and grammar to how one structures a term paper. After determining your needs, decide how you are going to meet them.
- How often is this service going to be available? Mondays through Thursdays are generally busy homework nights for middle school students. Remember that it is usually better to start small and increase the service as needed.
- Who is going to staff the homework lines? Some schools use volunteers as "homework helpers" and some use paid personnel. Those programs that pay "helpers" tend to be the most successful. If volunteers are the most practical option for your school, then consider hiring a part-time coordinator who will set up schedules, find replacements for those helpers who cancel, and so on. If this program becomes an added burden for busy teachers and/or administrators, it will fail.
- After the program is planned, determine how to best inform parents and students about the Homework Hot Line.
- Have regular meetings of the hot line staff to identify problems and improve the service.
- Give the program time before trying to determine its success. It generally takes a while to build a clientele for any program of this nature.

Reaching Out to Parents through Computer Classes

Many parents are not computer literate and feel uncomfortable that their children are so much more knowledgeable about computers and their use than they. Many schools have provided evening classes to teach parents some basic computer skills and the response is normally excellent.

These classes should be as informal as possible. Classes offered for credit with homework assignments are generally not as well received. You must remember that the parent may already feel inadequate due to lack of computer skills. Those classes that are friendly, less structured, and reinforce success are the most successful. Parents that have been in the class for awhile, or who have computer skills, can be used to help new class members. This has been a particularly successful strategy.

Although many parents don't have computers in their homes, it doesn't mean that they are not interested in computers. And, as libraries and other public facilities make computers available to the public, those parents without computers can now more easily find access to computers. Still, a lack of a computer is a handicap. Schools generally have computer labs that are not utilized in the evenings, making these labs an ideal parent resource. If parents can drop by the lab to use the word processor, learn programming skills, or "surf the Net," they can develop better feelings about themselves and feel more a part of the school. The benefits to the school are numerous: The parents feel more a part of the school community, see the school as being concerned about the family as a whole, can better understand the child's curriculum, and develop a relationship with other parents in the school community. Everyone wins!

Email can be used for regular communication with some parents, either between parent and teacher or among parents. Because email messages may be written at convenient times, this may increase the frequency of communication, but should not completely replace face-to-face communications.

Other Ways of Communicating on a Regular Basis

Parent Bulletin Boards

Still another vehicle for communicating with parents is a *parent bulletin board.* Strategically placed so that parents come upon it when they are at the school or center, a bulletin board containing attractive and interesting information for parents can be an effective way to communicate with parents. Unfortunately, depending on the program, all parents may not come to the school or center, and the communication on bulletin boards moves from displayer to onlooker, generally not in the other direction. This kind of communication tends to be one-way. Nonetheless, there are strategies that can be employed to encourage both parent attention and parent participation. One key to interesting bulletin boards is the relevant and attractive displays of information. Interesting information for parents might include pictures and documentation of children's work at school (both product and process) (Edwards, Gandini, & Forman, 1993), information about parenting, notices of community events that might be interesting for parents, children, or families, interesting (and positive) news clippings about the parents, announcements about school events, and so forth.

To ensure continued attention over time, the bulletin board needs to be changed on a regular basis. Although using a bulletin board for parents to communicate to teachers is probably inappropriate, given other more direct modes of communication, using the bulletin board as a place for parents to communicate with one another is certainly possible. The bulletin board then becomes interactive, not passive. If a section of the bulletin board were set aside for parents' use, they could bring in items that they know would be of interest to other parents, which in turn could lead to more parental interest and ownership as well as the establishment of a vehicle for parents to find and communicate with others who share similar interests and concerns related to their children in school.

Home Visits

Teachers in some schools and other educational programs such as Head Start visit parents in their homes for a variety of reasons. Although a frequently cited reason for such home visits is that they allow teachers opportunities to see the home contexts of children as a way of understanding them better and gaining some empathy for their families, other reasons may be just as compelling. Home visits at the beginning of the school year can establish an early context for two-way communication. Parents generally appreciate the teacher's efforts to come to their territory—a place where they are in charge and where the teacher is a guest in a strange place. Making a home visit can signal to a parent that the teacher is interested in the family and a partnership, and when this occurs, parents often start the year ready to work together rather than spending valuable time trying to find their role with the teacher (Burian, Haveman, Jacobson, & Rood, 1993). In addition, children are often quite taken by the presence of their teacher in their home, and they too start the school year more enthusiastically. The relationships in these cases are already initiated before school even gets started.

There is need for some caution related to home visits as well. It is important to allow parents to refuse a home visit. They may be self-conscious about the conditions of their home, or they simply may not be individuals who are pleased to welcome others into their home. Also, some teachers recommend doing home visits in pairs, both to help collect multiple perspectives and to guard against the possibility of a threatening visit. It should be noted, however, that each additional person from the school upsets the balance of equality. Unfortunately, lack of funding often means that teachers cannot be paid to conduct home visits, but many teachers, after experiencing the good will that comes from them, are willing to do them on their own time.

Communication on Special Occasions

Initial communication and regular communication are important contexts for parent–teacher communication, as they first set the stage and later work toward maintaining relationships that are open and productive for all concerned, and especially for the students. There are, however, times that require other strategies for other kinds of communication.

Communication with Groups

There are occasions when those required classes in public speaking can come in handy. Parent nights, parent education classes, school programs, and even school orientation programs all are events at which teachers may be asked to speak to groups of parents en masse. When such opportunities arise, however, there must also be room for parent voices to be heard. Whenever such meetings occur, for instance, there needs to be ample time for parents to ask questions and to give their opinions. Parent speakers might share the podium with teachers and other school personnel. Structuring the schedule for parent or parent/teacher discussion groups can help parents feel ownership in the events and know that their opinions also have weight.

Times of Crisis and Truly Difficult Parents

Even given the most successful and productive efforts at open and effective parent–teacher communication, there are both times and individuals that can test the commitment of the most well-meaning teacher. Despite parents who are generally cooperative (if sometimes or initially reluctant) about working with the teacher in partnership, a few, no matter what the teacher does, cannot easily be reached. Some examples are the very irate parent or the chronic complainer. Parents who are irate are obviously unhappy people, but frequently they are people who have had trouble getting themselves heard. If a parent is irate, one strategy is to swallow your pride and your defensiveness and concentrate on listening alone, without responding. Try, in such instances, to hide your own emotions, take out pencil and paper and concentrate on writing down every complaint the parent has. Do not interrupt with explanations or even apologies. Simply write. When they begin to slow down, ask if they have anything else to add. Continue this until they exhaust their list. Doing this will generally have an effect on their demeanor. Anger will usually dissipate, and in the meantime, you have a clear record of what the complaints are. When you have everything recorded, calmly read the parent(s) what you have listed and assure them that you will look into the issue(s) and then get back to them. Give yourself some time, and then return to the list when you have more emotional distance from it (usually overnight will do it). Confer with others who can help you think about the course of action you can take, changes you can make, and principles on which you wish to take a stand. Be prepared and calm when you get back to the complainer. Chances are, he or she will be much more willing to hear your thoughts on the matter now.

Chronic complainers can also benefit from knowing they are being heard, but sometimes such individuals continue looking for problems no matter how many you've solved for them. One strategy for working with such parents is to invite them into the classroom to observe and participate, as appropriate, in classroom activities. (They can, for instance, be invited to read to children.) When they become part of the inside, rather than staying on the outside, and when they discover the difficult and complicated nature of teaching and learning, they often become the teacher's best allies, spreading the word to other parents about the teacher's good work.

We, as educators, work toward a cooperative environment where individuals are respected. We work with students to resolve their problems in non-confrontational ways. In fact, many schools employ conflict resolution as a way of dealing with conflict. Consequently, we often feel uncomfortable with discord. Table 6.2 provides some guidelines for working with aggressive people. It also helps you to be less defensive and more centered on solving the problem at hand.

Some parents prove difficult for teachers because they come to rely on their listening skills *too* much. For some parents, you will be the only other adult who cares about them enough to listen to their problems. You, after all, have a mutual concern for their child, and you may have chosen this profession to be of help to others. Although such parental trust can be helpful for two-way communication, if it gets out of hand and becomes excessive, the teacher may feel (uncomfortably) as if he or she is expected to be a counselor to the parent. Under such circumstances it is important to remember that you have been trained as a *teacher*, not as a counselor. Having knowledge of community resources is helpful in such situa-

TABLE 6.2   Tips for Dealing with Aggression

DO	DON'T
1. Listen—without interruptions.	1. Argue.
2. Write down main points of what has been said.	2. Defend or become defensive.
3. When they slow down, ask if anything else is bothering them.	3. Promise things you can't produce.
4. Exhaust the list of complaints.	4. Own problems that belong to others.
5. Ask for specific clarifications when complaints are too general.	5. Raise your voice.
6. Show them the list of complaints.	6. Belittle or minimize the problem.
7. Ask for suggestions in solving the specific problems, and write down the suggestions.	
8. As they speak louder, you speak softer.	

These practices take practice. Our first reaction is almost always anger or hostility and these only serve to make matters more volatile. Also, remember that all of us have, upon occasion, acted in an angry, inappropriate way, and usually wish we had behaved with more temperance. Give the parent the same understanding that you would like to receive.

This has been modified from material developed by Roger Kroth and the Parent Involvement Center, University of New Mexico.

tions, as the most appropriate help you can give such individuals is probably to refer them to professional services that meet their counseling needs.

Summary

Working with parents can be very rewarding—for you, for parents, for your school or center, and especially for the children who are under your care and tutelage. In order for this work to be most fruitful for all concerned, a concentrated effort at open and two-way communication is required. Without communication, mutual goals are less likely to be met. Here is a list of some principles to keep in mind when planning for such an effort:

Principles for Effective Communication with Parents
- Choose or create an environment that puts parents on an equal footing with you.
- Care about the parent(s)' child. Ask about him or her.
- Care about the parent(s). Ask about them.
- Listen to understand.
- Use descriptive, rather than judgmental, language when relating a child's school life. Avoid educational jargon.
- Don't talk about other parents or their children. Respect the confidentiality of all families.
- Take the initiative to establish a coequal relationship. Don't be discouraged by limited initial success.
- Establish communications early in the school year, before problems occur.
- Find time to spend with parents.

RECOMMENDED ACTIVITIES

1. Think of a time when you know you were not being listened to. How did you know? What was the behavior of the person to whom you were speaking? How did you feel? What was your response?

2. Ask three friends to think about a person they consider a good listener. Interview them about the qualities they think makes the person so. Make a list of these qualities and compare them with what you know about yourself as a listener.

3. Interview three teachers. Ask them about the principles and the techniques they use for communicating with parents. Where appropriate and possible, obtain examples of written communications, such as newsletters. Analyze what was described and given to you for communicative flow. Note especially where parent voices were heard.

4. Interview three parents of school age children. Ask them about parent–teacher conferences. How do they prepare for them mentally and emotionally? Ask them to describe the worst and best conferences they have had with teachers.

5. Interview three teachers. Ask them about parent–teacher conferences. How do they prepare for them mentally and emotionally? Ask them to describe the worst and best conferences they have had with parents.

6. Ask teachers about the role technology—other than the telephone—plays in their communication with parents.

7. Interview parents of children in early childhood, elementary, middle, and secondary schools. Ask them to describe the most effective style or pattern the school/center or teacher(s) use with them. How could it be more effective? Compare the results among the four groups.

8. Interview teachers to discuss how report cards or narrative reporting is being done. Does it change from elementary to middle to secondary? If so, how does it change?

ADDITIONAL RESOURCES

Communicating with Parents

Books:

Henderson, A. T., Marburger, C. L., & Ooms, T. (1986). *Beyond the bake sale.* Columbia, MD: National Committee for Citizens in Education.

This book is a guide for educators to help them work with parents to improve schooling. It is particularly geared to dealing with some of the problems that have become greater in recent years owing to changes in family life such as high divorce rates, teenage parents, and working mothers.

Kroth, R. L. (1985). *Communicating with parents of exceptional children.* Denver, CO: Love Publishing.

This book serves as a practical handbook for educators and parents of children with disabilities. It combines innovative strategies with daily activities designed to improve communication between the school and the family.

Articles:

Gomby, S. S., Larson, S. L., Lewit, E. M., & Berhman, R. E. (1993). Home visiting: Analysis and recommendations. *The Future of Children, 3*(3).

Weiss, H. B. (1993). Home visits: Necessary but not sufficient. *The Future of Children, 3*(3).

Websites:

National PTA
www.pta.org/programs

University of Illinois Extension
www.urbanext.uiuc.edu/success/09-communication.html

Teacher web site for communication
www.4teachers.org

Videos:

Conducting Effective Conferences with Parents

This program offers suggestions about how to prepare and conduct conferences with parents. It considers what kind of questions to ask, what information should and should not be exchanged. 1998. #TP93 (22 minutes)

Insight Media
2162 Broadway
New York, NY 10024
Phone: 212-721-6316

Working with Parents: Home-School Collaboration

This video will help teachers understand the concerns and fears of parents. Parents explain what they want from parent–teacher conferences and ways to improve the exchange of information. The video provides specific suggestions for how teachers and parents can work together to create a positive learning environment, and discusses when counselors should be called upon to resolve an impasse. 1984. #TP93 (30 minutes)

Insight Media
2162 Broadway
New York, NY 10024
Phone: 212-721-6316

REFERENCES

Burian, B., Haveman, S., Jacobson, M., & Rood, B. (1993). Implementing a multi-age level classroom: A reflection on our first year. *Insights into Open Education, 26*(2), 23–32.

Edwards, C., Gandini, L., & Forman, G. (Eds.). (1993). *The hundred languages of children: The Reggio Emilia approach to early childhood education.* Norwood, NJ: Ablex.

Kroth, R. (1985). Communicating with parents of exceptional children. Denver, CO: Love Publishing.

National PTA. (1997). National Standards for Parent/Family Involvement Programs. Chicago, IL.

Rockwell, R. E., Andre, L. C., & Hawley, M. K. (1996). *Parents and teachers as partners.* Fort Worth, TX: Harcourt Brace.

Schulz, J. B. (1987). *Parents and professionals in special education.* Boston: Allyn & Bacon.

Seligman, M. (1979). *Strategies for helping parents of exceptional children.* New York: Free Press.

Swap, S. M. (1993). *Developing home–school partnerships: From concepts to practice.* New York: Teachers College Press.

7 Parent Involvement in Education

SOO-YIN LIM

University of Minnesota, Crookston

Children learn and grow in three influential contexts: family, school, and community. There is a strong connection on the positive effects for the children, families, and school when schools reach out to parents and actively involve parents to support and encourage their children's learning and development. The purposes of this chapter is to help you:

- Define parent involvement
- Identify and explain the benefits of parent involvement for children, parents, teachers, and school
- Describe ways schools and teachers can involve parents
- Identify and explain the basic foundations of planning and implementing a successful parent involvement program

Defining Parent Involvement

Parent involvement is a widely used term, which among educators is sometimes used synonymously with terms such as *partnership, parent participation, parent power,* and *school, family, and community partnerships* (Epstein, 1996; Wolfendale, 1989). According to Moles (1992), parent involvement may take a variety of forms and levels of involvement, both in and out of school. It includes any activities that are provided and encouraged by the school and that empower parents in working on behalf of their children's learning and development. Epstein (1996) extended the term from parent involvement to "school, family, and community partnerships" to describe how children learn and develop in these three main contexts: school, family, and community. Therefore, these three influential contexts need to be integrated into every facet of children's education and development.

The concept of parent involvement is not new to the field of education and has played a significant role in U.S. education. Frobel, who made primary contributions to the establishment of U.S. kindergarten programs, commented:

> All are looking for reform in education.... If building is to be solid, we must look to the foundation—the home. The home education of rich and poor alike must be supplemented.... It therefore behooves the state to establish institutions for the education of children, of parents, and of those who are to be parents. (cited in White, Taylor, & Moss, 1992)

The U.S. Department of Education launched GOALS 2000 so that "every school will promote partnerships that will increase parental involvement and participation in promoting the social, emotional, and academic growth of children"

(Children's Defense Fund, 2000, p. 64). The legislature also encourages school and community collaboration to assist families in supporting their children's success in education. This support prompts schools across the United States to examine and revise their current policies, practices, and programs on parent involvement. To achieve this goal, school, parents, and community must see their interconnectedness with each other, come together to build a shared vision, and understand their individual roles in relation to the roles of others. Such cooperation is necessary to ensure that all children receive the support and services they need to succeed in school.

The Benefits of Parent Involvement: What Research Has to Say

Researchers have evidence for positive effects of parent involvement on children, families, and school when schools and parents continuously support and encourage the children's learning and development (Bronfenbrenner, 1974, 1979; Eccles & Harold, 1993; Henderson, 1987; Illinois State Board of Education, 1993). According to Henderson and Berla (1994), "the most accurate predictor of a student's achievement in school is not income or social status but the extent to which that student's family is able to:

1. Create a home environment that encourages learning
2. Express high (but not unrealistic) expectations for their children's achievement and future careers
3. Become involved in their children's education at school and in the community" (p. 160)

Henderson and Berla (1994) reviewed and analyzed eighty-five studies that documented the comprehensive benefits of parent involvement in children's education. This and other studies show that parent involvement activities that are effectively planned and well implemented result in substantial benefits to children, parents, educators, and the school.

Benefits for the Children
- Children tend to achieve more, regardless of ethnic or racial background, socioeconomic status, or parents' education level.
- Children generally achieve better grades, test scores, and attendance.
- Children consistently complete their homework.
- Children have better self-esteem, are more self-disciplined, and show higher aspirations and motivation toward school.
- Children's positive attitude about school often results in improved behavior in school and less suspension for disciplinary reasons.
- Fewer children are being placed in special education and remedial classes.

- Children from diverse cultural backgrounds tend to do better when parents and professionals work together to bridge the gap between the culture at home and the culture in school.
- Junior high and high school students whose parents remain involved usually make better transitions and are less likely to drop out of school.

Benefits for the Parents
- Parents increase their interaction and discussion with their children and are more responsive and sensitive to their children's social, emotional, and intellectual developmental needs.
- Parents are more confident in their parenting and decision-making skills.
- As parents gain more knowledge of child development, there is more use of affection and positive reinforcement and less punishment on their children.
- Parents have a better understanding of the teacher's job and school curriculum.
- When parents are aware of what their children are learning, they are more likely to help when they are requested by teachers to become more involved in their children's learning activities at home.
- Parents' perceptions of the school are improved and there are stronger ties and commitment to the school.
- Parents are more aware of, and become more active regarding, policies that affect their children's education when parents are requested by school to be part of the decision-making team.

Benefits for the Educators
- When schools have a high percentage of involved parents in and out of schools, teachers and principals are more likely to experience higher morale.
- Teachers and principals often earn greater respect for their profession from the parents.
- Consistent parent involvement leads to improved communication and relations between parents, teachers, and administrators.
- Teachers and principals acquire a better understanding of families' cultures and diversity, and they form deeper respect for parents' abilities and time.
- Teachers and principals report an increase in job satisfaction.

Benefits for the School
- Schools that actively involve parents and the community tend to establish better reputations in the community.
- Schools also experience better community support.
- School programs that encourage and involve parents usually do better and have higher quality programs than programs that do not involve parents.

Six Types of Parent Involvement

It is clear and beyond dispute that parent involvement has significant and wide-ranging positive effects. Although most educators and schools agree and embrace the concept of parent involvement and its impact on children from preschool through high school, many have not transferred their knowledge or beliefs into plans, plans into practice, and practice into results (Eccles & Harold, 1993; Epstein 1986; Gestwicki, 1996; Simon, Salinas, Epstein, & Sanders, 1998). Few parents understand or are aware of the resources of their children's school system, program, and activities that are available for their children (Epstein, 1996). Many studies indicate that parents are interested in participating at all levels from playing the role of an audience to decision making. Unfortunately, many parents often do not know how to get involved. Thus, it is the parents' lack of knowledge, not lack of interest in supporting their children's education, that prevents them from participating (Nichols, 1991; Williams and Chavkin, 1985). Lynn Kagan (1989) concluded that even though everyone agrees that parent involvement is beneficial, it cannot be achieved until there is real agreement about its value and a shared understanding of the complementary roles of the parents and educators in the entire educational process.

The National Network of Partnership Schools established by Joyce Epstein and her colleagues at John Hopkins University responded to the challenge by developing six types of parent involvement based on the theoretical model of "overlapping spheres of influence." This model indicates that children do not learn and grow in the context of home alone or school alone, but in three influential contexts—home, school, and community (Epstein, 1987b). There is no one single formula or blueprint that will create a successful home–school–community partnership. However, there are basic guidelines for schools, districts, and state departments to create meaningful, positive, and permanent programs that actively involve families in their children's education.

Each of the six types of involvement consists of many different activities that promote or enhance partnership. Each will likely yield different results for children, parents, teachers, and the school, depending on how well the activities are designed, planned, and implemented, thereby leading to either positive or negative results. Schools may choose to use the framework of six types of parent involvement developed by Epstein. But each school must be aware of the local needs of its families and children while designing its own parent-involvement program (Epstein, 2001; National PTA, 2000).

Type 1: Basic Responsibilities of Families

The most basic involvement of parents is their continuous responsibility for raising their children and providing them with food, clothing, shelter, health, and safety. The National Education Goals for Year 2000 indicate that "all children in America will start school ready to learn" (Children's Defense Fund, 2000, p. 63). What does "ready to learn" mean? It goes beyond teaching children across the nation their basic ABCs and numbers. It means parents should form the foundation for their children's success in school by providing and maintaining a positive home environment that is conducive to learning and the development of physical, intellectual, social, and emotional skills and values. This is a continuous process of teaching and guiding children throughout their school years and helping them build self-confidence and self-esteem (Epstein, 1987a; Gonzalez-Mena, 1998; National PTA, 2000).

Parents vary in their experiences and parenting skills. Thus, schools will have to take an active role in assisting parents with parenting and child-rearing skills, helping in understanding child and adolescent development, and providing ideas for creating a home environment that supports children's learning at each age and grade. Research indicates that families want to learn and receive ongoing information on how to help their children succeed and excel in school. Concurrently, teachers and administrators need the families to assist schools in becoming better informed about their children and families. Information about children and family backgrounds, cultures, needs, interests, goals, and expectations can be provided by families. Therefore, Type 1 involvement consists of a combination of information *for* parents and *from* parents about children and families (Epstein, 2001).

Sample Activities That Support and Assist Parents in Parenting and Child-Rearing Practices

1. Provide ongoing information to all parents in a variety of ways:
   - Workshop, parent education, and grade-level meetings
   - Newsletters and pamphlets
   - Videos and audiotapes
   - School websites and email
   - Computerized phone messages
2. Establish a parent resource room—a family-friendly center where parents can come together and discuss parenting issues and check out resources and materials.
3. Organize a family support program—encourage parents to organize a parent-led support group where families can connect and share their experiences and their knowledge with each other.
4. Provide home-visit opportunities for teachers to learn and to become more aware of the families, as well as for the families to understand school expectations.
5. Provide information on community services, such as free immunizations and clinics, services offered by social services, community parent education, parent–child community activities, and religious services. (Epstein, 2001; National PTA, 2000)

Tips on Successful Planning and Implementation of Parenting Activities

1. *Relevance and meaningfulness of topics.* It is critical that topics selected are relevant and meaningful for parents regarding the age or grade level of their children. An ongoing survey of needs and wants from parents is highly recommended throughout the year. The survey allows the parents to be a part of the decision-making process when their topics of interest are selected and presented.
2. *Disseminate information to all families.* Information should be distributed to all parents regardless of whether they are able to attend workshops or parent

meetings. Workshops should not be limited to school premises; instead, the content of topics discussed can be viewed, heard, or read at times and locations that are convenient for the families (Epstein, 2001). For example, the workshops can be videotaped or audiotaped, allowing families to receive the information at their convenience. Workshops can be summarized and put in a variety of forms, such as newsletters, school websites, or computerized phone messages. Parents can read them at home, in the school's parent room, or public library. Allow parents who were unable to attend meetings or workshops to discuss them online with other parents and speakers.

3. *Provide sufficient notice to parents.* Workshops or meetings that require parents to come together at the same time and place need sufficient notice. Such notice should include location, date, and time of the meeting, a brief description of the topic, and name of the presenter of the workshop.
4. *Location should vary.* Workshops may be offered at the school building as well as other locations in the community that represent families' neighborhoods.
5. *Time schedules.* Workshop information should be made available at various times rather than one scheduled time. Additionally, families have other obligations; therefore a conscious effort to start and end on time is critical.
6. *Concise, clear, easy to understand information.* Ongoing verbal and written information on parenting should be concise and clear and should use plain language that is free from educational jargon. Translation of information is needed for families whose first language is not English. (Epstein, 2001; National PTA, 2000)

Type 2: Communication

Effective communication is essential for building a successful partnership between school and home. It requires the school to build two-way sharing of information, with conscious efforts from the school to engage in give-and-take conversations, establish common goals, and follow up with consistent interactions between school and home (National PTA, 2000). Without good two-way communication between the school and the family, other levels of involvement are made much more difficult to achieve (Moore, 1991). Children often play an important role in the success of Type 2 involvement. Children are involved as couriers in taking messages from school to home and bringing them back to school from home.

The school's basic obligation is to consistently and effectively provide information about school programs and children's progress through school-to-home and home-to-school communications. When successful, this reduces the potential for conflict and stress between all parties involved. A common practice utilized by many schools is to share information about their programs and children's progress through school and class newsletters, report cards or narrative progress reports, parent–teacher conferences, and phone calls. With the advance of technology, schools are increasingly using email to communicate with families, and using voice mail and the school's website to relay messages to parents.

Sample Activities That Are Effective in Establishing Two-Way Communication

1. Create newsletters and bulletin boards that are interactive, through which parents are able to respond to teachers, administrators, and other parents. The following are a few examples: include a question for parents to respond to and then provide the responses or answers in the next newsletter; provide a venue for interaction between parents regarding carpooling, exchange of outgrown clothing, weekend child care, recipes, a source of "take-away" coupons, and parenting articles.

2. Send weekly or monthly folders of children's work home for parents to review and comment on their child's progress.

3. Establish online discussion with teachers and administrators. The purpose is to exchange and clarify information and perceptions; to support parents, teachers, and administrators; and to provide suggestions or ideas. Email addresses of school staff should be included in the school handbook as well as on the school's website.

4. Place a suggestion box or create an online suggestion box to encourage parents to ask questions and offer ideas. Encourage conversations that will help their children's learning. Parents who speak other languages should be encouraged to write in their own language.

5. Conduct parent–teacher conferences with follow-ups as needed. Provide language translators for written and verbal communication to assist families who do not speak English. Arrange and plan for phone conferences when parents are unable to come to school for the conferences.

6. School or parent handbooks should have clear information about school policies, roles, and responsibilities of the school, family and community, and curriculum. Provide easy two-way communication for parents to make comments and ask further questions after reviewing the handbook. This can be implemented through a short open-ended questionnaire at the back of the handbook or by encouraging parents to drop a note in the suggestion box.

7. Establish regular schedule of distributing notices such as school and classroom newsletters, calendars, and other communication activities that notify parents about important school dates, school events, parent–teacher conferences, parent meetings, and other important information.

Tips on Successful Planning and Implementation of Two-Way Communication

1. *Clarity, readability, and usefulness of information.* Periodically review all written communication to make sure that content is current, clear, understandable, relevant, and meaningful to families.

2. *Special consideration for families who do not speak or read English well.* A language barrier between educators and families presents the greatest obstacle to effective communication. The challenge increases when there are several different languages spoken within one school. This makes school and parent–teacher meetings difficult. Stenomask or TALK System (TS) allows translators to translate what is being said and then transmit to the audience

members with receivers and earphones. This system can accommodate five different translators at the same time (National PTA, 2000)

3. Provide a variety of ways for parents to communicate with the school. Communication methods such as notes, journals, email, websites, computerized messages, and voice mail allow parents to access messages at their convenience. This gives flexibility to parents who work irregular shifts or have difficult schedules.

4. Develop "telephone trees" or family directories with phone numbers and email addresses of school staff (teachers, administrators, counselors, family coordinator, nurses, class parents, and parent organizations). This will serve as a great reference for the families.

Type 3: Volunteering

The typical activities in this category are parental assistance to teachers and administrators in supporting the school program and helping with children's schoolwork and activities, including field trips, class parties, and class performances. Volunteering ranges from low to high levels of participation. Parents can either act as audience with minimal commitment in advocacy, or they can act in decision-making roles with higher levels of commitment.

Many schools face the challenge of having too few volunteers. Often the same group of parents repeatedly does the volunteer work. Approximately 70 percent of parents have never helped the teacher in the classroom, and only 4 percent of the parents (about one or two parents per classroom) were highly active at school (Epstein, 2001). Despite the low percentage of involvement in this area, parent involvement in the school is still highly desirable among teachers and administrators (Epstein, 2001; Moore, 1991). The number of children with parents working full-time or part-time during school hours has dramatically increased. Seven out of ten children ages six to thirteen have both parents or a single parent in the work force (Children's Defense Fund, 2000). To meet this challenge, Epstein (2001) suggests there is a need to redefine volunteerism to include parents' supporting school goals and children's learning in any place and at any time.

Schools are starting to provide flexibility in time and place to enable parents to volunteer their talents and interests. For example, parents can volunteer in schools, at home, or in other community locations, and at convenient times such as evenings, weekends, and during school closing or vacation days. Schools that create flexibility for families found an increase in the number of parents and others who volunteer. Flexibility also allows regular and occasional volunteers to come together to work on common goals for the school program, share common interests, and acquire other talents while providing volunteers with the opportunity to work in various areas of the school.

Sample Activities for Volunteering in and out of School

1. For teachers:
   - *Volunteers in the classrooms.* Listen to a child read and encourage a child to write; assist in a computer laboratory; serve as chaperones for field trips,

school dances, class parties, or sporting events; share hobbies and cultures by integrating them into curriculum; celebrate diverse cultures represented in the class, school, and community.

- *Volunteers outside the classroom.* Translate children's books or written communication such as newsletters; update classroom website or search for Internet links that support children's learning; lead cooking or craft activities at home; contribute to long- and short-term projects such as making costumes and plots for dramatic play centers or a school play; gather necessary resources or materials for special events; be coaches, tutors, or mentors for middle or high school students.

2. For administrators:
   - *Volunteers in the school.* Encourage parents to come to school for their light exercise by walking around middle and high school hallways. This increase of adult presence will decrease behavioral problems. In addition, parents can volunteer as chaperones at school dances, sporting events, and school plays or join advisory committees such as PTA, PTO, or other groups.
   - *Volunteers outside the school.* Create and maintain school websites; take or compile pictures or videos of students and develop presentation for school use; organize letter-writing campaigns on education issues; plan and organize school exhibits (such as art, science, clubs) at local malls or stores; compile "yellow pages" of parent resources regarding family hobbies, expertise, special interests, and places of work; recruit, train, and organize recognition ceremonies for volunteers.
   - *Volunteers as audiences.* Attend school or class events, sporting events, open houses, and recognition and award ceremonies.

Tips for Successful Planning and Implementation of a Volunteering Program.   To implement and maintain Type 3 involvement (volunteering) successfully, schools need to include ongoing activities such as recruitment, training and supervision, and recognition.

1. *Recruitment.* In general, there are two important issues that relate to recruitment:
   - *Identify potential volunteers.* Volunteers should not be limited to parents of children who attend the school. Instead, volunteers should represent parents and people from the community that cut across categories of age, sex, education, socioeconomic status, race, ethnicity, religion, occupation, and various neighborhood communities. Volunteers may be recruited by exploring a variety of places in the local community. Such locations include colleges, senior citizen or retirement communities, television and radio stations, businesses, museums, libraries, parks, and churches.
   - *Strategies for finding people to volunteer.* The methods of recruitment depend on the size of the school and number of volunteers needed. Schools need to reach out to the community and communicate the what, why, and how of volunteer service in schools. The school can arrange to speak at different community events and local meetings such as senior centers and retirement

communities; businesses, agencies and organizations; and local committees and organizations meetings. This kind of recruitment elicits discussions, answers questions, and clarifies information. Other recruitment methods include:

- Working with local media such as television, radio, and newspapers to promote the school's volunteer programs.
- Develop brochures, posters, and fliers that can be posted and distributed in retirement communities, hospitals, social service agencies, banks, churches, and grocery stores.
- Set up booths in local malls or community fairs.

2. *Training and Supervision.* Even before recruiting volunteers, schools need to assess and review their needs for volunteer services. During the assessing and reviewing process, school staff, including teachers, counselors, coaches, club advisors, janitors, secretaries, and administrators, should help in identifying the needs of the school. Similarly, the need for volunteers in classrooms of a specific age or grade level or on a particular subject matter can be assessed and reviewed. When a list of needs is identified, it can be translated into a clear and concise job description for volunteers (see Figure 7.1).

FIGURE 7.1   Sample Job Description for Classroom Volunteers

Classroom Volunteer Job Description

Teacher: Lisa Myers   **Grade:** Preschool I

Job Responsibility: Supervise painting area

Time and Day Needed: 10:00–11:00/3:00–4:30 (Monday through Friday)

Volunteer roles:
- Help children put on aprons if they are painting. First, encourage them to do this themselves.
- Discuss colors, mixing of colors, shapes, sizes, etc. with children. Some children like to tell you about their painting, but do not insist on this. You may ask, "Would you like to tell me about this?"
- Write child's name on the upper left corner or ask child where he or she wants it. Use upper- and lowercase letters (e.g., John)
- Help children put their work on the drying rack, put their aprons away, and wash their hands.
- Extra paints are in the art cupboard (above the sink) if needed.
- Wash brushes and containers as needed.

Helps develop the following:
- Concept of colors, shapes, sizes, and textures
- Hand–eye coordination
- Expression of ideas and feelings

It is highly recommended that before being accepted, all volunteers should be interviewed to assess their skills, interests, and placement. Program orientation and ongoing training are crucial for the success of volunteer programs. Orientation sessions should include the following:

- *Tour of building.* Provide a map and tour of the facility (both internal and external), highlighting key places such as bathrooms, main office, library, lounge, and space for volunteer workers to store their personal belongings.
- *Policies and procedures.* Provide a school handbook for volunteers to refer to when needed. Discuss the school's philosophy and mission, operating policies and procedures, children's guidance and discipline, confidentiality, ethics on working with students and school staff, attendance, and dependability.
- *Meeting with school staff.* Introduce volunteers to school staff such as administrative and office staff, teachers, and cafeteria and custodial staff.

Orientation should lead into training that is ongoing and can be done on-the-job or through individual or small group sessions. Training sessions should be informal (friendly and supportive), hands-on, clear, and relevant to the specific skills and responsibilities of each volunteer. All volunteers should have their job description to refer to when needed. Effective training will reduce conflict between school staff and volunteers, such as communication problems and confusion over expectations and responsibilities. It also eases fear and anxiety for the volunteers and increases a positive and cooperative relationship with school staff.

Supervision is needed for all volunteers. Volunteers are entitled to receive feedback from supervisors. This also provides opportunities for volunteers to share their experiences and to provide input on the work they performed. This initiates an informal evaluation, and such systematic evaluation allows for volunteers to self-evaluate their contributions to the program, for school staff to evaluate volunteers, and for the program to evaluate whether the goals and objectives are being met.

3. *Recognition.* Regardless of the amount of time each volunteer contributes to the school, every volunteer should receive recognition of their commitment and services. Individual staff that works with a volunteer must make a continual effort to regularly acknowledge and express appreciation for work done. A year-end acknowledgment such as a reception, dinner, or recognition night should be held to recognize all volunteers who have made a difference for the school program and children's education. There are numerous ways of recognizing volunteers throughout the year. For example:

- *Create a special, visible area in the school dedicated to volunteers.* Display pictures of volunteers working in different projects and places. Include names of volunteers, number of hours volunteered, and brief descriptions of their contributions.
- *Provide incentives.* Issue coupons in exchange for hours volunteered that can be redeemed at "volunteer store" to "purchase" donated materials,

such as household and personal products, nonperishable food, greeting cards, and gifts.
- *Publicize volunteers.* Recognize volunteers in monthly newsletters, school websites, or stories in local newspapers. (National PTA, 2000; Rockwell, Andre, & Hawley, 1996)

Type 4: Learning at Home

In the field of early childhood education, one of the basic beliefs is that parents are their children's first and most influential teachers. Parents have influence over what children do at home—the amount of time and type of programs children watch on television, amount of time spent playing video games, types of music they listen to, and amount of time spent studying and doing their homework. When children reach school age, the amount of time spent at school is less than that spent at home and in child care combined. Thus, the amount of time spent away from school is valuable for learning and building positive attitudes about education.

Home-based learning not only enhances children's learning experiences but also serves many purposes. It "should reinforce, support, and strengthen learning that has been introduced and shared at school" (Trahan & Lawler-Prince, 1999, p. 65). It involves families with their children via gamelike activities, homework, and curriculum-related activities such as mathematics, science, and social science. This also includes parents assisting their high school children to set goals for the school year or for the future, making joint decisions on what courses to take. These activities may or may not have directions or suggestions from the teacher. Activities typically cover the "general skills or behaviors" and "specific skills" (Epstein, 1987a, p. 8). General skills activities are those that promote critical-thinking or problem-solving skills, promote language skills, enhance social and emotional skills, or reinforce certain behaviors using consistent child-guidance techniques agreed on with the teacher. Specific skills activities are those that involve families in helping children "to review, complete, or extend skills that the student is working on with the teacher in class" (Epstein, 1987a, p. 8). Specific skills activities occur more often for children in grade school.

Most parents help their children through their past school experiences and knowledge of school subjects. Most parents across all grades want more information about their children's homework, homework policies, and tools for helping their children. According to Epstein (1986), 85 percent of parents spent 15 minutes or more helping their children at home when requested by teachers. These parents stated that they were willing to spend an average of 40 minutes with their children if they had directions from the teacher about how to help their child. Over 90 percent of parents reported that they assisted their children with homework occasionally, and fewer than 25 percent received requests and directions from teachers on how to assist children with specific skills.

Sample Activities for Involving Parents in Children's Home-Learning Activities
1. *Backpack reading.* Children bring home a book each night for parents to read or listen to their child read. Materials include a book and inventory list for parents to complete.

✳ **2.** *Mobile learning centers.* Each bag includes two or three hands-on activities to either promote several developmental areas or a specific skill. Each bag consists of a letter to the parents, directions for each activity, parents' feedback journal, and materials needed for the activities. The activity bags are sent home with each child for a week or two and then returned. The teacher replenishes the materials and prepares the activity bag to go to the next child.

✳**3.** *Home kits.* Activities are theme based, and the kit includes a book with follow-up hands-on activities. Kits are checked out by the child for a week.

✳ **4.** *Home learning enablers.* This is an inexpensive way of promoting parents' involvement with their children's learning by showing them how to use household materials to teach children without having to spend a large amount of money on materials. Each week HLE activities are sent home with the child. An activity card includes the name of the activity, the purpose of the activity, materials needed, directions on how to do each activity, time needed for completion, adaptation ideas, and an evaluation form for parents to complete.

5. *Family lending library.* Parents have the opportunity to check out books, materials, and audio- and videotapes in which teachers demonstrate or model a certain skill or activity. Children also have the opportunity to check out books, magazines, toys, and home-learning activity kits.

6. *Interactive homework.* This is geared more for older children in elementary, middle, and high school. Interactive homework is directly linked to course objectives and requires children to interact and communicate with family members or community members. (Epstein, 2001; Gorter-Reu & Anderson, 1998; Patton & Jones, 1997; Shoemaker, 1996; Trahan & Lawler-Prince, 1999)

Tips for Successful Planning and Implementation of Home Activities

1. *Provide information and training sessions.* The goal is to explain what home-learning activities entail early in the year, such as during an open house or parent meeting. Training sessions are offered throughout the year to provide opportunities for teachers to demonstrate sample activities, and for parents to practice the strategies. This also allows teachers and parents to share ideas.

2. *Incorporate activities into the family's schedule.* Activities are designed to be completed in short periods of time. For families with very young children, design activities that can be incorporated into the child's daily routine, such as mealtime, bedtime, and bathtime.

3. *Make homework interactive.* Create homework that requires interaction and discussion with parents, family and extended family members, or community members.

4. *Easy access of activity resources or materials.* If materials are not provided for parents, then the materials should consist of common household items with special precaution for safety and age-appropriateness of the materials used.

Type 5: Decision Making

Parent involvement in decision making takes a variety of forms, such as choice of school, review and evaluation of school program, review of fiscal budget, hiring of personnel, advisory role for school committees, and advocate for school, families and children. The types of decision-making practices each school has are dependent on the school's philosophy and parent involvement goals and policies. Decision making involves a partnership process in which parents and educators come together and share their ideas and views, solve problems, and take actions toward a shared vision that contributes to school goals and policies.

Parents can act as leaders for other parents by representing their opinions, ideas, and concerns on behalf of their children's learning and development. Equally important is that parent leaders take the information about school decisions and policies back to the families. For parents to act as true leaders, teachers and administrators will need to provide the necessary background information and training for parents to effectively carry out their responsibilities and make sound decisions.

Parents can also participate as advocates for the school, families, and children. In subtle ways, most parents, individually, have acted as advocates for their children. An example is when parents stand up and voice their views and ideas to improve their children's experiences in school. Another level of advocacy is to have parents come together as a group to represent group objectives on issues that affect the quality of school and improve children's education and families' lives. Parents can be seen as advocates at the local, regional, state, and national levels. To be an advocate requires parents and educators to work together to identify an issue, research it, disseminate the information researched, attend meetings to discuss the issue, find solutions and identify strategies, provide updates, and last but not least, recruit and train advocates to write and articulate their messages to lawmakers, media, and community members (National PTA, 2000).

Sample Activities for Involving Parents in Decision-Making

1. *Parent organizations, advisory committees.* Advisory committees can be long- or short-term. Short-term committees are parents and educators coming together to work on short-term projects, such as selecting a math curriculum, reviewing and developing school evaluation forms and processes, forming a student club, selecting materials for parent room, or organizing a specific school events such as an open house, a school dance, or an awards and recognition ceremony for students and volunteers. Long-term committees (e.g., PTA/PTO) entail parents and educators who meet regularly to discuss issues pertaining to school plans and policies, fiscal budget, school curriculum and activities, and personnel.

2. *Advocacy groups.* These groups target specific activities that educators and parents work on together to lobby for school, children, and family improvement on a local, regional, state, or national level. Issues include teacher–child ratio in the classroom, safety and health regulations, services offered to children with or without disabilities, teachers' salary, and need for new building expansion.

3. *Town meetings.* These meetings are set up in the community not only inviting parents and school staff but also involving and networking with community members to discuss issues on school goals, children's education, and family needs.

4. *Training sessions for parents and educators.* Parents, educators, and community members are invited to assist in identifying training needs, develop training sessions, and offer training sessions that will help parents and educators to effectively implement their various responsibilities in the area of decision making and advocacy.
5. *Classroom committees for parents and teachers.* Parents and teachers get together to discuss and plan curriculum-related activities for school and home, plan summer learning packets or activities, plan special events and celebrations, and address children's needs and experiences.

Tips for Successful Planning and Implementation of Decision-Making Involvement

1. *Number and diversity of parents represented within a committee.* Parents must be numerous or equally represented by parents and educators. A diversity of parents representing voices for families and schools should come from a balance of age or grade levels, racial and ethnic groups, fathers and mothers, different neighborhoods, and special interests.
2. *Provide information to make sound decisions.* Educators need to consistently provide relevant, clear, background information for parents so that they can effectively contribute to any decision-making. Teachers should allow parents sufficient time to read any information sent home and to review and reflect on issues to be discussed during the next meeting.
3. *Provide continual training for parents.* Parents need a variety of training in skills that allow them to effectively play their role as leaders and team members, contribute to the decision-making process, and advocate at different political levels (see Figure 7.2).
4. *Establish regular meetings.* Regular meetings allow committee members to form a closer teamwork relationship, stay focused on important issues, and spend less time updating and recalling issues discussed. Meeting times and locations should be flexible to meet parents' needs and other family obligations.
5. *Develop and maintain collegiality between and among educators and parent.* Some educators believe that there should be a boundary between parents and professional educators in order to "preserve the power and authority gained through formal training and experience" (National PTA, 2000, p. 117). Although the professional training and expertise of administration and teachers is crucial to provide quality education and safe environment for children, parent involvement activities and practices should not be seen as a threat to teacher authority. Parents actively involved in PTA/PTO "may be perceived by administrators (and other parents not in PTA/PTO) as insiders who are interested in school matters" (National PTA, 2000, p. 118). This creates boundaries between parents, and parent leaders need to make extra efforts to include all parents so that they feel that ideas, insights, and concerns of all parents are welcomed.

Type 6: Collaborating with the Community

Since 1970, the American family and social structure has dramatically changed in complex ways that can have an impact on families and can create stress in families. Families are increasingly facing not one, but several, difficult issues such as financial concerns; an increase in single-parenting; the absence of extended families for assistance and support; and an increase in families that are in the "sandwich generation," providing care for their own children as well as their elderly parents (Fredriksen-Goldsen & Scharlach, 2001; Rockwell, Andre, & Hawley, 1996; U.S. Census Bureau, 2001). There is interconnectedness between quality of family life and children's development and learning. When families are struggling and in crisis, schools will need to step in by networking and collaborating with the community to gain access to services and resources to strengthen families and children's success in learning.

Schools and teachers should also see the community in a broader context by including community members who are interested in improving the quality of education. Community members can provide the schools with materials, people, and natural resources; therefore, schools need to make connections with various community members such as large and small businesses, religious communities, cultural groups, government agencies, and other organizations. Service learning is relatively new and is usually offered by colleges and universities that encourage college students to share their talents and assist school and community needs.

Sample Activities in Collaborating with Community

1. Provide information to parents and school staff on the availability of community resources and services in a variety of ways:
   - Create yellow pages of community resources and services that are interested in helping families, children, and schools. Include the names of agencies, address, telephone number, email address, and website if available, and a brief description of resources or services available (e.g., free training sessions such as parenting, ESL classes, and GED programs).
   - Inform, encourage, and support individual families to access available services or resources needed.
2. Regularly seek, network, and collaborate with community businesses, agencies, organizations, and groups in strengthening the other types of involvement mentioned previously (Types 1 through 5).

Foundations of Facilitating a Meaningful Parent Involvement

Parents, regardless of their income level, educational background, family structure, or past experience with schools, want to be actively involved with their children's education. They would like the schools to show them how to get involved (Epstein & Sanders, 1998; Nichols, 1991). Educators are increasingly aware of parents' desire to communicate with their children's teachers, receive frequent feed-back on the children's academic progress, and have the opportunity to share in decision making that affects their children's education. Once administrators and teachers decide to form collaborative relationships with families and share responsibilities in providing quality education to the children, the first step is to create partnership (Gestwicki, 1996). Following are some common factors found in programs that are successful in reaching out to families and forming productive school-family partnerships.

1. Positive School Climate

For schools to successfully reach out to parents, the first and foremost step is to create a positive social atmosphere and culture in the school and classrooms. The school climate has a direct effect on the extent to which parents are involved in the school and their children's education (Comer, 1986; Comer & Haynes, 1991; Dauber & Epstein, 1993).

Administrators should be leaders in creating an environment in which teachers and staff demonstrate to parents a sense of full partnership. Administrators should also develop an organized, well-structured plan that allows active, meaningful participation by parents. For schools to have and maintain positive climate and attitudes, all school personnel (office staff, custodial staff, cafeteria staff, administrators, and teachers) should be examined. Below are some examples of attitudes and behaviors that facilitate positive school climate:

- *Friendliness and approachability.* Greet visitors and answer telephone in friendly and professional way.
- *Openness and enthusiasm.* Provide parents a sense that "we are all in this together"; make time to listen to concerns, ideas, and questions of family members.
- *Empathy, compassion, and patience.* Acknowledge and recognize parental time and other family obligations, show patience while developing relationships with parents, be sensitive to the uniqueness of parents' reactions and feelings.
- *Respect for others.* Understand and show tolerance and respect for students and families with diverse cultural values, child-rearing practices, diet, views, values, and so on.

2. Regular Communication

Communication is one of the most crucial components for creating and maintaining a constructive partnership with families. A regular, ongoing, two-way communication from school to home and home to school is needed. All families have different reading abilities and ways to communicate. Not all families are available during school hours due to different work schedules and familial obligations. Schools need to use a range of communication techniques that enable all schools and families to share information. Some examples are:

- Teachers set flexible time options that meet parents' schedules. Options include prearranged phone conversations, evening conferences, and teacher's availability during parents' prime time or dropping off and pick up times.
- Administrators compensate teachers who need to meet parents after hours, such as in the evening or early in the morning.
- Teachers use print and nonprint communications, including written information such as school or classroom newsletters and parent education newsletters that can be transferred onto video- or audiotapes if needed.
- Explore technology possibilities such as voice mail, computerized phone messages, email, and school websites. This allows parents to access information or leave messages for the teachers or schools at any time and any place.

Schools and teachers need to make special efforts and considerations when communicating with families in which English is not the first language and who have little formal education. Articles or any print resources sent to families should be translated to the family's native language. Transferring information onto audiotapes, videotapes, or summarizing articles to lower reading levels is needed for families with lower literacy levels. School staff and teachers sometimes may need to read to the family and ask questions to make sure that they understand. This may take time, but it reduces conflict and promotes and enhances positive relationships between home and school.

3. Diversity

An inclusive parent involvement program requires schools and teachers to understand and recognize the diversity of children and families that are represented in their schools and classrooms. Families differ in their structures (two- or one-parent homes; teenage or young parents; working, nonworking, or unemployed parents; families with or without children with disabilities), economic status, racial and ethnic backgrounds, and educational backgrounds. Awareness of students' and families' beliefs, attitudes, and cultural customs and values is also essential for the effectiveness of the planning and implementation of parent involvement. Acknowledging the presence of family diversity is beyond visual representations of culturally diverse materials in the school or classroom settings. It includes but is not limited to the following:

- *School representatives should reflect families from diverse backgrounds.* An effort is needed to encourage and support parents of minority groups to actively participate in all types of parent involvement activities, from leadership roles in decision making to attending parenting classes and assisting their children's learning at home.
- *Listen and look for clues and cues of individual families.* Encourage families to share their cultural backgrounds that have significance influence over their parenting and child-rearing practices, diet, communication styles, and education beliefs.

- *Instill sense of belonging in children and families.* Educators must seek and involve families and other elders and cultural community experts to help incorporate the children's home cultures into school curriculum.
- *Involve parents in child's assessment and recommendation.* Assessment of children should not be limited to standardized tests or formal checklists but should include observations and gathering of children's work by teachers and parents. When schools actively include parents' feedback and suggestions during children's recommendations for remediation, it results in appropriate recommendations that match with the children's home culture and social practices.
- *Written and verbal communications to parents should be meaningful.* Schools and teachers need to be sensitive and responsive to families' cultural and educational backgrounds when talking to them or writing messages and sending informational materials to parents.
- *Respect the individuality of families.* Educators do need to be aware of different cultural groups, but at the same time must avoid generalizing families into their distinct groups, such as low-income families, single-parent families, or Native American families. Families within the same cultural group can also have individual differences. (Coleman & Wallinga, 2000; Hoover, 1998; Walker-Dalhouse & Dalhouse, 2001)

4. Training for Educators and Parents

Administrators need to support teachers, school staff, and parents in order for them to effectively carry out a productive home–school partnership. Administrators will have to provide emotional and social support, as well as seek and secure funds to provide adequate training for teachers, school staff, and parents.

For Educators.   Provide frequent and regular professional development for administrators, teachers, and school staff that will adequately allow them to plan and implement parent involvement activities, improve communication skills and parent–teacher relationships, become aware and work effectively with diverse students and families, and identify parents' needs and interests. When educators have adequate training in establishing positive home–school partnerships, it will significantly improve the climate of the school.

Administrators will need to have organized and well-structured plans and implementations of parent involvement in order to communicate effectively with school staff and teachers and provide a consistent approach to parent involvement practices.

For Parents.   Parents need ongoing guidance, training sessions, and information on how to become actively involved in their children's education, work as team and parent leaders, and contribute to school goals that require decision-making efforts.

5. Providing Comprehensive Parent-Involvement Programs

When schools develop parent-involvement programs that are comprehensive and offer a variety of different types of involvement, it acknowledges the diversity of parents served in the school. All parents have different skills and abilities, interests and needs, schedules and family obligations, and ages and grade levels of children. Therefore, all parents and families will respond differently to requests for involvement in their children's education. Some parents are able to participate at the school during school hours, yet many will have to choose activities that allow them to stay at home. This comprehensiveness and flexibility will acknowledge the parents' needs and interests and will allow parents to build on their strengths and resources. All this will affect the amount and type of parent involvement in the school.

RECOMMENDED ACTIVITIES

1. Form a parent-involvement panel; invite principals and teachers from different levels of education (e.g., early childhood, elementary, middle, and high school) to speak about best practices in parent involvement activities. Look for the differences and similarities of practices in each level of education.

2. Form a panel and invite parents that have children at different age and grade levels (e.g., infants and toddlers, preschool, elementary, middle, and high school) to discuss their roles in their children's education and how schools can support their roles. Compare and contrast parents' roles for children of different age groups.

3. Visit a Head Start program (center-based) and Early Head Start program (home-based) and interview the parent coordinator to investigate and understand their parent-involvement programs.

4. You are a classroom teacher. Choose an age or grade level and design your own parent-involvement program for the school year.

5. You are an administrator for a school. Choose level of education and design a parent-involvement program for your school.

ADDITIONAL RESOURCES

Books:

Barbour, C., & Barbour, N. H. (1997). *Families, schools, and communities: Building partnerships for educating children.* Columbus, OH: Prentice Hall.

Epstein, J. L. (2001). *School, family, and community partnerships: Preparing educators and improving schools.* Boulder, CO: Westview Press.

Gestwicki, C. (1996). *Home, school, and community relations.* Albany, NY: Delmar.

Rockwell, R., Andre, L., & Hawley, M. (1996). *Parents and teachers as partners: Issues and challenges.* Orlando, FL: Harcourt Brace & Company.

Turnbull, A. P., & Turnbull, H. R. (1997). *Families, professionals, and exceptionality: A special partnership.* Columbus, OH: Prentice Hall.

Videos:

Helping Parents Flourish

> NAEYC
> 1509 16th Street, N.W.
> Washington, DC 20036-1426
> Phone: 800-424-2460

Parent Involvement

This video examines techniques for encouraging parents to become more involved in their children's education. It makes some very specific suggestions. With the busy schedule of today's parents this video is most timely. 1994. (22 minutes, color)

> Films for the Humanities & Science
> P.O. Box 2053
> Princeton, NJ 08543
> Phone: 800-257-5126

Partnerships with Parents

Young children benefit most from programs in which teachers and parents work together as partners. The program dramatizes the importance of the parent–teacher relationship for children and demonstrates how to establish and maintain positive communication. It also shows how to handle common problems teachers face when working with parents. 1989. (28 minutes, color)

> Insight Media
> 2162 Broadway
> New York, NY 10024
> Phone: 212-721-6316

Shared Decision Making

This video examines two school communities that involve parents, teachers, school-board members, and students working together to make decisions that result in better schools. 1994. (22 minutes, color)

Working with Parents: Home-School Collaborations

This video will help teachers understand the concerns and fears of parents. Parents explain what they expect from parent-teacher conferences and discuss ways to exchange information. The video provides specific suggestions for how teachers and parents can work together to create a positive learning environment. 1984. (30 minutes, color)

Organizations:

Alliance for Parental Involvement in Education
P.O. Box 59
East Chatham, NY 12060-0059
Phone: 518-392-6900
www.croton.com/allpie

Center on Families, Communities, Schools and Children's Learning
Johns Hopkins University
3505 North Charles Street
Baltimore, MD 21218
Phone: 401-516-0370
www.jhu.edu/news_info/educate/experts/epstein

Hispanic Policy Development Project
Suite 5000A, 250 Park Avenue South
New York, NY 10003
Phone: 212-523-9323
www.infolit.org/members/hpdp.htm

North Central Regional Educational Laboratory
1120 East Diehl Road, Suite 200
Naperville, IL 60563
Phone: 800-356-2735
www.ncrel.org

National Coalition for Parent Involvement in Education
Box 39
1201 16th Street NW
Washington, DC 20002
Phone: 703-684-3345
www.ncpie.org

National Congress of Parent Teacher Associations
700 North Rush Street
Chicago, IL 60611-2571
Phone: 312-670-6782
www.pta.org

National Network of Partnership Schools
Dr. Joyce L. Epstein, Director
Johns Hopkins University
3003 North Charles Street, Suite 200
Baltimore, MD 21218
Phone: 410-516-8890
www.csos.jhu.edu/p2000

National Parent Teacher Association
700 Rush Street
Chicago, IL 60711
Phone: 312-787-0977
www.pta.org

REFERENCES

Bronfenbrenner, U. (1974, November). Is early intervention effective? *Day Care and Early Education, 44,* 14–18.

Bronfenbrenner, U. (1979). *The ecology of human development: Experiments by nature and design.* Cambridge, MA: Harvard University Press.

Children's Defense Fund. (2000). *Yearbook 2000: The state of America's children.* Washington, DC: Author.

Coleman, M., & Wallinga, C. (2000, Winter). Teacher training in family involvement: an interpersonal approach. *Childhood Education, 76*(2), 76–81.

Comer, J. (1986, February). Parent participation in the schools. *Phi Delta Kappan, 67*(6), 442–446.

Comer, J., & Haynes, N. (1991). Parent involvement in schools: An ecological approach. *Elementary School Journal, 91*(3), 271–278.

Dauber, S. L., & Epstein, J. L. (1993). Parents' attitudes and practices of involvement in inner-city elementary and middle schools. In N. Chavkin (Ed.), *Families and schools in a pluralistic society* (pp. 53–71). Albany, NY: SUNY.

Eccles, J. S., & Harold, R. D. (1993). Parent–school involvement during the early adolescent years. *Teachers College Record, 94*(3), 568–587.

Epstein, J. L. (1986). Parents' reactions to teacher practices on parent involvement. *Elementary School Journal, 86,* 277–294.

Epstein, J. L. (1987a, February). Parent involvement: What research says to administrators. *Education and Urban Society, 19*(2), 119–136.

Epstein, J. L. (1987b). Toward a theory of family–school connections: Teacher practices and parent involvement. In K. Hurrelmann, F. X. Kaufmann, & F. Losel (Eds.), *Social intervention: Potential and constraints* (pp. 209–246). Mahwah, NJ: Lawrence Erlbaum.

Epstein, J. L. (1996). Improving school-family-community partnerships in the middle grades. *Middle School Journal, 28*(2), 43–48.

Epstein, J. L. (2001). *School, family, and community partnerships: Preparing educators and improving schools.* Boulder, CO: Westview Press.

Epstein, J. L., & Sanders, M. (1998). What we learn from international studies of school–family–community partnerships. *Childhood Education, 74*(6), 392–394.

Fredriksen-Goldsen, K. I., & Scharlach, A. E. (2001). *Families and work: New directions in the twenty-first century.* New York: Oxford University Press.

Gestwicki, C. (1996). *Home, school, and community relations.* Albany, NY: Delmar.

Gonzalez-Mena, J. (1998). *The child in the family and the community.* Upper Saddle River, NJ: Prentice Hall.

Gorter-Reu, M. S., & Anderson, J. M. (1998). Home kits, home visits, and more. *Young Children, 53*(3), 71–74.

Henderson, A. (1987). *The evidence continues to grow: Parent involvement improves student achievement.* Columbia, MD: National Committee for Citizens in Education.

Henderson, A. T., & Berla, N. (1994). *A new generation of evidence: The family is critical to student achievement.* Washington, DC: National Committee for Citizens in Education.

Hoover, J. (1998, Winter). Community–school alliances: The road to successful learning. *Winds of Change, 13*(1), 28–31.

Illinois State Board of Education. (1993, March). *The relationship between parent involvement and student achievement: A review of the literature* (ERIC Document Reproduction Service No. ED 357 848). Springfield, IL: Department of Planning, Research, and Evaluation.

Kagan, S. L. (1989). Early care and education "tackling the tough issues." *Phi Delta Kappan, 70,* 433–439.

Moles, O. (1992). Synthesis of recent research on parent participation on children's education. *Educational Leadership, 44.*

Moore, E. K. (1991). Improving schools through parental involvement. *Principal, 71*(1), 17, 19–20.

National PTA. (2000). *Building successful partnerships: A guide for developing parent and family involvement programs.* Indianapolis, IN: National Educational Service.

Nichols, G. J. (1991). *Helping parents help their children toward literacy.* (ERIC Document Reproduction Service No. ED 335 632)

North Central Regional Educational Laboratory. *Critical issue: Creating the school climate and structures to support parent and family involvement.* Retrieved November 4, 2001, from www.ncrel.org.

Patton, M., & Jones, E. (1997, March/April). CHILD-PACs make for happy families. *Teaching Exceptional Children, 29*(4), 62–64.

Rockwell, R., Andre, L., & Hawley, M. (1996). *Parents and teachers as partners: issues and challenges.* Orlando, FL: Harcourt Brace.

Shoemaker, C. J. (1996). Home learning enablers and others helps: Home learning enablers for ages two to twelve. *Program Enrichment Paper.* (ERIC Document No. ED 394 694)

Simon, B. S., Salinas, K. C., Epstein, J. L., & Sanders, M. G. (1998). Proceedings of Families, Technology, and Education Conference, Chicago, IL, October 30–November 1, 1997. See PS 027 175.

Trahan, C., & Lawler-Prince, D. (1999). Parent partnerships: Transforming homework into home-school activities. *Early Childhood Education Journal, 27*(1), 65–68.

U.S. Census Bureau. (2001, June). *America's families and living arrangements.* Washington, DC: U.S. Department of Commerce.

Walker-Dalhouse, D., & Dalhouse, M. (2001, July). Parent–school relations: Communicating more

effectively with African-American parents. *Young Children, 56,* 75–80.

White, K. R., Taylor, M. J., & Moss, V. D. (1992). Does research support claims about the benefits of involving parents in early intervention program? *Review of Educational Research, 62*(1), 91–125.

Williams, D. L., Jr., & Chavkin, N. F. (1985). *Final report of the parent involvement in education project* (project No. p-2, grant NIE-400-83-007). Washington, DC: U.S. Department of Education.

Wolfendale, S. (1989). *Parental involvement: Developing networks between school, home, and community.* London: Cassell Educational Limited.

CHAPTER

8

Families and Their Children with Disabilities

AMYSUE REILLY

The lives of families with special needs children are the same as other families and, at the same time, very different. Family love, affection, and pride are similar, but families of children with disabilities often experience stresses not normally a part of other families' lives. This chapter examines the dynamics of these special families. The purpose of this chapter is to help the reader explore the:

- History of special education and parental involvement
- Legislation that has affected students with special needs and their families
- Reaction of family members upon learning of their child's disability
- Accommodations and adjustment made by the family
- Adjustment of fathers, siblings, and mothers
- Community response

Two Sculptors
I dreamed I stood in a studio
And watched two sculptors there,
The clay they used was a young child's mind
And they fashioned it with care.

One was a teacher; the tools she used
Were books, music and art.
One, a parent who worked with a guiding hand
And a gentle, loving heart.

Day after day the teacher toiled
With touch that was deft and sure,
While the parent labored by her side
And polished and smoothed it o'er

And when at last their task was done,
They were proud of what they had wrought;
For the things they had molded into the child
Could neither be sold nor bought

And each agreed he would have failed
If he worked alone,
The parent and the school,
The teacher and the home.

Author Unknown (in Salisbury, 1992).

Excerpted from Salisbury, C. L., & Dunst, C. J. (1997). Home, school, and community partnership: Building inclusive teams (pp. 57–88) in R. Rainforth & J. York-Barr (Eds.), *Collaborative Teams for Students with Severe Disabilities: Integrating Therapy and Educational Services*. Reprinted with permission from Brookes Publishing Co.

Families of children with disabilities are no different from others in wanting their offspring to have an opportunity to develop, learn, socialize, and enjoy life. In order to enhance these possibilities, however, families and professionals must work together to ensure that these children are provided with the needed experiences to grow through exploration of the world around them.

This chapter will familiarize the reader with the dynamics surrounding families who have a child with a disability. By way of introduction, a useful synopsis of the progression of integrating individuals with disabilities into homes, schools, and community settings will be provided. This will be followed by a statistical overview of the numbers of students with special needs being served in recent years. Finally, a summary of relevant legislation will be offered.

Historical Perspective

For centuries, a societal laissez-faire attitude has been responsible for the generally insensitive standard of treatment of people with disabilities. Consider, for example, that some cultures abandoned or destroyed babies and toddlers if they developed or exhibited disabilities, while others used youngsters with disabilities as social curios and sideshow entertainment. Twentieth-century history reveals that most institutions for those with disabilities were more reminiscent of penal, rather than medical, facilities.

Antiquity and the Middle Ages

Interestingly, however, two significant visionaries of ancient times spoke of a more humane social treatment of these individuals. Hippocrates (physician, c. 460–377 B.C.) believed emotional problems were a result of natural forces rather than supernatural powers. Likewise, Plato (philosopher, c. 427–347 B.C.) hypothesized that people who were mentally unstable were not accountable for their behaviors.

During the Middle Ages, a limited number of religious orders provided basic care and shelter for individuals with disabilities who were removed from their families. These children were often cared for in monasteries. They participated within their range of ability in the day-to-day activities of the monasteries, performing housekeeping chores, grounds-keeping duties, and tending crops. Unfortunately, these persons were often thought to be possessed by demons and subjected to cruel treatments intending to exorcise these demons.

Nineteenth-Century Developments

Jean Marc Gaspard Itard found an abandoned, naked boy living in a dense forest near Aveyron, France. Given the name Victor, this "Wild Boy of Aveyron" was reared in a nondomestic and isolated environment. Jean-Marc Gaspard Itard, who was a physician and researcher for the deaf, believed that learning was best acquired through hands-on experiences that provided challenging opportunities. Based on Itard's success with Victor, he came to believe that anyone could learn if properly stimulated. Edouard Sequin, a student of Itard's, brought this educational philosophy to the United States in the mid-nineteenth century, and actively promoted it in residential programs for people with mental retardation.

In the nineteenth century, residential schools for individuals who were deaf and/or blind were established in the United States. These schools were based on European residential schooling that had demonstrated the benefits of appropriate education. In 1817, Thomas Gallaudet established this country's first residential school for the deaf at Hartford, Connecticut.

In 1829, Samuel Howe founded the Perkins School for the Blind in Watertown, Massachusetts. Anne Sullivan was trained at the Perkins School and, subsequently, recruited by the Keller family to provide an on-going intense education for their daughter Helen. Through Ms. Sullivan's teachings and the family's perseverance and unwavering commitment, Helen became a nationally recognized inspirational speaker and a respected author. What was once thought to be impossible now became possible. In essence, individuals with severe sensory disabilities could become functional community members.

Twentieth-Century Developments

Pearl Buck's *The Child Who Never Grew,* a heartfelt story about raising a child with mental retardation, provided parents of similarly affected youngsters a level of support and encouragement sorely missing in their lives. By sharing her frank and moving account of raising her child, many parents of children with disabilities also began to share their experiences with each other, thus fostering a grass-roots prototype for parental support groups.

Other twentieth-century efforts were prompted by the increase in society's concern with the incidence of infant mortality, childhood diseases, and abusive child labor. Coupled with these concerns was John Dewey's educational reform, which emphasized a more child-centered philosophy of teaching and parenting. The results of these outcries and teachings, which were influenced by involved families, educators, and physicians, led to significant reform of societal attitudes toward those with disabilities, especially the treatment and services provided individuals with mental retardation and mental illness.

The mid-twentieth century was distinguished by an international leader with a disability. President Franklin D. Roosevelt demonstrated through his own perseverance that he could perform efficiently despite his ineffectual polio-afflicted legs. He was a productive chief executive despite performing the majority of his duties from a wheelchair.

President John F. Kennedy grew up with a sister who was mentally retarded, and, while in office, he established the Task Force on National Action to Combat Mental Retardation, the President's Commission on Mental Retardation, and the Bureau of Education for the Handicapped (now the Office of Special Education Programs). President Kennedy's strong convictions regarding the right to full opportunities for individuals with mental retardation (and all other disabilities) strongly influenced the development of special education.

Several years later, Vice President Hubert Humphrey, whose granddaughter had Down syndrome, showed a strong interest in early education for young children with disabilities. He also supported the notion that early stimulation would provide a youngster the additional learning opportunity necessary to progressively acquire skills later in life.

Another contemporary public official who supported the development and passing of landmark legislation was Connecticut Senator Lowell Weikert, whose son had a disability. The Education for All Handicapped Children Act, known as Public Law 94-142, was implemented in 1975 and laid the ground work for this country's educational reform and commitment to infants, toddlers, children, youth, and young adults with disabilities.

Number of Children Receiving Special Educational Services

A national count of children receiving special education services began in 1976 with the passing of Public Law 94-142 (Education for All Handicapped Children Act), which required special educational services be provided for all children with disabilities. Since 1976–1977, there has been a steady annual increase (overall, approximately 25 percent) in the numbers of children receiving special education services.

Over 4.5 million children with disabilities, ranging from six to twenty-one years of age, or approximately 10 percent of the population, received special education services during the 1991–1992 school year (U.S. Department of Education, 1993). This was a 3.9 percent increase from 1990–1991, the largest increase since 1976–1977 (U.S. Department of Education, 1993).

The increase of younger children served in special education was due directly to early intervention programs implemented in 1986. Public Law 99-457 mandated state-determined services for infants and toddlers (birth to age 2) and required appropriate educational opportunities for preschoolers (3 to 5 years of age). Since then, the population growth of youngsters receiving early intervention services has increased significantly. An estimated 35,000 infants and toddlers (birth through age 2) and 422,226,000 preschoolers (ages 3–5) were among those receiving special education services during 1991–1992 (U.S. Department of Education, 1993).

The empirical data presented above indicates that an even larger number of young children with disabilities and their families will be seeking various early intervention and transition services into community educational programs. The legislation concerning special education is critical to these children and their families.

Federal Special Education Laws and Legislation

Parental involvement in the legislative process dates back to the early 1950s, with the establishment of the National Association of Parents and Friends of Mentally Retarded Children (now, the American Association for Retarded Citizens). ARC has a long history of representing the interests of people with mental disabilities and their families. Other parent groups have been organized through the strong efforts of family involvement (e.g., United Cerebral Palsey Association and the National Society for Autistic Children). In the late 1960s a group of parents of children with mental retardation collaborated with the Pennsylvania Association for Retarded Citizens to sue the state. They won their lawsuit and the court held that all children with mental retardation must be provided with a free public program of education and training (*Pennsylvania Association for Retarded Children v. Commonweath of Pennsylvania*, 1972). As a result, the time was right to establish federal legislation (Turnbull, Turnbull, & Wheat, 1982; Turnbull, Turnbull, Shank, & Leal, 1995).

The Individuals with Disabilities Education Act (IDEA, 1997) provides states and local education agencies funding to help them educate students from birth to age three (Early Intervention), age three to nine (Early Childhood Special Education), from six to twenty-one (Special Education and Transition Programs). IDEA defines special education as specially designed instruction that meets those specific needs of a student with a disability.

IDEA has six principles or legal frameworks that govern and rule the educational services of individuals with disabilities. *Zero rejection* is a rule against excluding any students with disabilities. *Nondiscriminatory evaluation* is a rule that requires schools to evaluate a student fairly and without bias to determine if that student has a disability, what kind of disability it is, and how extensive the disability is. *Free, appropriate education* is a rule that requires schools to provide individually designed education for each student based on the evaluation and any necessary related or supplementary services. *Least restrictive environment (LRE)* is a rule that requires schools to educate students with disabilities with non-disabled students to their maximum extent appropriate. *Procedural due process* is a rule that safeguards for students and their families against schools' actions. *Parental and student participation* is a rule that requires schools to collaborate with parents and students to determine their special education programs.

Public Law 94-142 (1975)

The various parental organizations (ARC and other parental organizations representing all areas of exceptionalities) joined to develop a strong political advocacy. These groups were striving for federal legislation mandating that all students with disabilities be provided with a free, appropriate public education (FAPE). Through the concerted efforts of parents and professionals, Congress passed the Education for All Handicapped Children Act in 1975. In addition, this law recognized the critical role that families play in the decision-making process in their children's lives.

One of the earliest programs for youngsters considered disadvantaged by society's standards was established by President Lyndon B. Johnson in 1965. To remedy the lack of learning opportunities, Johnson initiated the development of a federally funded educational project called Head Start. Prior to the late 1960s and early 1970s, few programs existed for any preschoolers, much less for those with disabilities. Even fewer programs were available for infants and toddlers.

In 1975, President Gerald R. Ford signed landmark legislation that dramatically altered the educational rights of individuals with disabilities ages six to twenty-one and their families. Among other things, the spirit of this legislation, the Education for All Handicapped Children Act (Public Law 94-142), advocated families to be actively involved with their child's educational programs.

Public Law 105-17 (1997)

Congress has amended Public Law 94-142 four times (1983, 1986, 1990, and 1997). In the most recent amendments, the title of the law also was changed to the Individuals with Disabilities Education Act (IDEA). This change reflects the philosophy that the main focus should be on an individual's *abilities* rather than his or her *disabilities.*

The overall basic features and requirements of the original 1975 act have remained essentially unchanged despite its three amendments, including the rights of parents of children with disabilities. These entitlements have strengthened parental participation and input by guaranteeing to parents their legal rights and opportunities for involvement (Hanson, 1985; Turnbull et al., 1995).

Five fundamental rights are guaranteed to parents of children with disabilities, as is their subsequent involvement in the special education process. Specifically, parents and the served child are to:

1. Be provided free appropriate public education.
2. Be provided safeguards by the school system to protect these rights (e.g., parental consent must be given for any assessments or placement regarding the served children).
3. Be educated with their nondisabled peers to the maximum extent possible. This is also referred to as the concept of *least restrictive environment.*
4. Participate as full members of the individual education plan (IEP) team developing and implementing the child's IEP.
5. Play an active role in the educational decision-making process concerning their child. If the parents are not satisfied with any educational decision regarding their child, they have recourse.

Public Law 99-457 (1986)

The second amendment, made in 1986 (Public Law 99-457), required states to develop and implement, within five years, comprehensive interdisciplinary services for infants and toddlers (birth through age 3) with disabilities, and to expand services for preschool children (aged 3 through 5). As a result, individual states now provide free, appropriate education for all 3- to 5-year-olds with disabilities who are eligible for federal preschool funding.

An extension of the comprehensive interdisciplinary service for infants, toddlers, and preschool programs was the *Individualized Family Service Plan* (IFSP), which required educational services to develop a family plan that would enhance both the child and the child's family (Howard, Williams, Port, & Lepper, 2001). Too frequently, professionals need to be reminded of the various dimensions of a child's life and behavior. The educators' and parents' perceptions of the child often differ depending on the context and depth of discussions (Dunst, Trivette, & Deal, 1988). Some professionals may present a picture of the child that is not an accurate representation of the child as a whole.

> To sit and listen—as one after another of the other participants (teachers and therapists) describe Bill's deficiencies and the almost minuscule progress that he has made from year to year—has almost left me feeling sad and hopeless. For that one day each year, I see Bill as I know other people see him and not the unique person I live with and know and love. (Statum, 1995, p. 65)

The Program for Infants and Toddlers with disabilities (Part C of IDEA) assists states in providing comprehensive programs of early intervention services for youngsters with disabilities and their families. Services must be family-directed and, to the maximum extent appropriate, services are provided in the child's natural environment. These special services, evaluations, assessments, and program planning occur only if the family approves and only with the family's participation at the level they feel most comfortable (Howard et al., 2001). In addition, effective early intervention for infants and toddlers with disabilities is guided by five general principles of IDEA, Part C. Early intervention services are to be rendered in the child's least restrictive and most natural environment. They also must be family-centered services that use a transdisciplinary service delivery model (roles are shared among team members including the family). The services are also guided by empirically and value-driven practices, and those practices are developmentally and individually appropriate (Davis, Kilgo, & Gamel-McCormick, 1997; Howard et al., 2001).

Americans with Disabilities Act (ADA), Public Law 101-376

ADA is another landmark federal law that addresses civil rights legislation for persons with disabilities, ensuring nondiscrimination in a broad range of activities. This civil rights legislation, enacted in 1990, prohibits discrimination because of an individual's disability. ADA benefits all people with disabilities, without regard to their age. ADA benefits people in a wide range of public and private sectors (not just employment and education). It mandates that local, state, and federal government programs be accessible, that businesses make reasonable accommodations for those with disabilities, and that public accommodations make reasonable modifications to ensure access for individuals with disabilities. ADA also mandates access to public transportation, communication, and other areas of public life. ADA requirements apply to day-care programs, nursery schools, and even Head Start programs.

Rational of Inclusion

Inclusion is a term generally applied to educating students with and without disabilities within the regular class in neighborhood schools. IDEA addressed specialized instruction for students with disabilities, stating that a free, appropriate public education and inclusion in education with their non-disabled peers, to the maximum extent possible, be provided to these students. Public Law 99-457 indicates that interdisciplinary services provided to infants and toddlers with disabilities must be family-directed and, to the maximum extent appropriate, those services be provided in the child's natural environment (Etscheidt & Bartlett, 1999; Howard et al., 2001). This is also referred to as the concept of least restrictive environment. This legal term is used to define the rights of children with disabilities to be educated in settings that are not segregated from children without disabilities (Howard et al., 2001). There is a preference for including children with disabilities in the regular classrooms along with their specialized services. Inclusion is a continuum of services that depends on the child's needs, the preferences of parents, the need for related services, and the level of progress in the regular setting (Howard et al., 2001).

How a child performs in one setting rarely constitutes a complete picture of how that given child performs in all settings. It is for this and other reasons that professionals should readily provide the family ample opportunity to share their perspectives regarding their child (Salisbury, 1992; Turnbull et al., 1995). Parental input has definite value in that it may furnish the professional(s) with critical information not easily obtained during the course of clinical observation or the teaching regimen. Also, such input reminds the professional that the child is a unique individual with various needs which are met in different settings by many providers.

In summary, these significant pieces of legislation have provided a tremendous increase in new educational programs and opportunities for all infants, toddlers, preschoolers, school-aged children, youth, and young adults with disabilities. The importance of family involvement in the collaborative educational pursuit of their children's opportunities is central to much of this legislation. It is for this reason that professionals must continue to learn how to work more effectively within the family system.

Family Systems

This section is based on the premise that families of children with disabilities, like families of all other children, want their offspring to have meaningful, enjoyable, and successful lives. Furthermore, it recognizes that in order for this to be possible professionals must respect and appreciate each family's unique position as they strive toward this end. The overall family dynamics that are impacted by the presence of a child with a disability are first presented. Second, the reader is introduced to fathers and siblings and their perspectives, which are often neglected in a literature that has traditionally emphasized the mother's role within the family system. Finally, the parental viewpoints and opinions regarding community inclusion for their children with disabilities is discussed.

Adjustments: Dealing with the Disability

Reactions.   When a family is first told their long awaited "bundle of joy" has a disability, it is not easy to predict how each family member will react (Powers, 1993). Most families first receive this information from medical professionals while they are dealing with the hospitalization of their infant or toddler (Long, Artis, & Dobbins, 1993; Pearl, 1993). Receiving information pertaining to the birth (or diagnosis) of such a child is indeed overwhelming (Buck, 1950; Long et al., 1993; Meyer, 1986b).

Each family member's reaction stems from intense feelings and draining emotions, often leaving them in a state of confusion, questioning, and bewilderment. Of course, a major key to working effectively with such families is to respect their right to express this intense and constantly varying range of emotions (Fewell, 1986; Gibbs, 1993).

> Over the years I have often heard that parents must learn to accept the fact that their child has disabilities. I know no parent who hasn't accepted their child's disabilities. When you get up in the morning and force your child's legs into braces, put them in a wheelchair, feed them breakfast, give their antiseizure medication, you have accepted and are dealing with your child's disability. (Statum, 1995, p. 68)

Professionals naturally may make generalizations regarding how parents might react and respond to their child with a disability. This action is usually in hope of working more effectively with the families. Often, however, the parental feelings, emotions, and behaviors are unpredictable. After all, few families are prepared to face the complex issues confronting them (Singer & Powers, 1993).

Emotional Impact.   Parental expectations regarding their child's disability can be strongly influenced by the different types and severity of the disability (Fewell, 1986; Kroth & Edge, 1997). Parents have long anticipated the birth of their child and their anticipation is full of hopes and dreams. Parental grief and reactions to the birth of their child with a disability is a result of the loss of their "normal" child (Murray & Cornell, 1981).

Thus the birth of a child with a disability is frequently a stressful event for families due to the variety of feelings, reactions, and responses felt by the various family members (Dunst, Trivette, & Jordy, 1997; Featherstone, 1980; Murray & Cornell, 1981; Turnbull, Brotherson, & Summers, 1985). Farber (1975) indicated several adaptations that families develop when having a child with a disability. Murray (1980) indicated that families frequently go through a series of reactions and responses. Kirk and Gallagher (1989) and Kübler-Ross (1969) found that some parents and other family members, including siblings, grandparents, and other extended family members, are faced with a variety of feelings, reactions, and responses when having a child with a disability. These feelings, reactions, and responses may change as life goes on, especially as the internal and external resources increase (Kroth & Edge, 1997).

Professionals have become more aware of how family members are affected by the presence of a child with a disability. Professionals also need to take into consideration the roles and needs of each family member (Goldenberg & Goldenberg, 1980; Turnbull et al., 1985). Turnbull's and Turnbull's (2001) framework for understanding the emotions, dynamics, and elements of family systems has allowed professionals to work more effectively with these families. The four elements of this framework are (1) family resources, (2) daily interactions among family members, (3) different individual family needs, and (4) changes that occur over time which affect family members (Turnbull & Turnbull, 2001).

Accommodations: Getting On with Life

Adaptiveness.   Families are remarkable adapters to the needs of their child (Seed, 1988; Lobato, 1990; Pearl, 1993). Moreover, the role of each family member assumes varying dimensions depending on the respective attitudes and behavior displayed regarding the child's disability (Meyer, 1986b; Nixon, 1993; Seed, 1988).

A broad range of emotion is experienced while attempting to reconcile those feelings regarding the family's child with a disability (Hawkins, Singer, & Nixon, 1993; Meyer, 1993; Seed, 1988). The anguish and stress is often tremendous, yet somehow each family member learns to cope with a mechanism that is frequently quite efficient to carry other family members through the substantial turmoil. In other words, the family often draws closer as they depend on one another.

Balanced Lifestyle.   A family's daily routine typically focuses around the child with the disability. Thus, their attempt to find a balance in a family routine is an arduous task at best, given they often are having to juggle appointments dealing with various medical specialists, therapists (physical, occupational, speech and language), and early interventionist home visits. Clearly, it is time-consuming to visit a multitude of professional offices while trying to find answers to questions regarding the diagnosis or treatment of a child with a disability. Also, it is an exhausting pursuit for families to find the best services and newest information regarding their child's condition. Again, the family's attempt to find a requisite balance and perceived normalcy is an issue with which they frequently wrestle.

Child–Peer Relations.   Parents are constantly seeking opportunities for children with disabilities to actively engage in typical early childhood experiences with their peers (Boswell & Schuffner, 1990; McLean & Hanline, 1990; Ruder, 1993; Statum, 1995). Also, critical to these children's development is the growth they continually experience from interactions as members of their own families (Frey, Fewell, Vadasy, & Greenberg, 1989; Pearl, 1993; Statum, 1995). Thus, an additional difficulty is the family's effort to continually locate positive peer-interactions so their exceptional child has an opportunity to enhance his or her learning experiences (Bailey & Bricker, 1984; Guralnick, 1990; McLean & Hanline, 1990; Ruder, 1993).

Child Care.   Finding an appropriate child-care program for any family often is a trying event and even more stressful to families attempting to locate such a program that will accept a child with a disability (Fewell, 1986). Quite frankly, child-care providers are not customarily informed on how to work with young children with disabilities and thus are reluctant to accept responsibility for such children. They are, however, increasingly being asked to care for these children.

Seeking Services.   Families seek the best services to provide for their child. Consequently, their homes are often like New York's Grand Central Station in trying to schedule various needed services. Furthermore, opening one's home to the numerous specialists arriving to provide services to their child and family is an intrusion on family privacy with which other families do not have to contend (Hanson, Lynch, & Wayman, 1990; Pearl, 1993). Nevertheless, these families are frequently required to carry out the programs prescribed for their child if they want to ensure their child's progress.

Early childhood special education interventionists attempt to work with families and their children with disabilities in a caring, sensitive, and supportive manner (Fewell, 1986; Pearl, 1993). Obviously, the services provided must be flexible and responsive to the diversity of family needs and resources (DeGangi, Wietlisbach, Possison, Stein, & Royeen, 1994; Hanson et al., 1990).

In addition to handling everyday life stressors, families learn how best to provide for the various needs of their child. Therefore, early intervention services must strive to be family friendly, family focused, and family centered. Moreover, services need to be provided to families in the various settings that each family requires, such as home, day care, or community.

Values.   Cultural and religious values heavily influence a family's structure as well as their views of disabilities (DeGangi et al., 1994; Hanson et al., 1990; Howard et al., 2001). Families will differ by cultural, economic, and religious influences, as well as by membership and structure of the family itself (Hanson et al., 1990; Howard et al., 2001). Such values can impact the effectiveness of the family's acceptance and willingness to implement intervention strategies. Therefore, professionals must be respectful of families' value systems and their services flexible enough to be in accordance with differing family value systems and cultures (DeGangi et al., 1994; Hanson et al., 1990).

Extended Family.   Another important factor is the extended family, which is often a wonderful resource for providing that additional assistance needed in dealing with their child. An extended family can include grandparents, aunts, uncles, cousins, neighbors, and close friends who have joined the family circle. These members frequently provide the continual encouragement, respite relief, moral support, comfort, and unconditional understanding needed by the parents and other family members (Fewell, 1987; Gallagher, Cross, & Scharfman, 1981; Long et al., 1993; Pearl, 1993).

Support Groups. Parents of children with disabilities often need additional support other than that provided by professionals (Long et al., 1993; Meyer, 1993). Consequently, there is a growing network of parent support groups across the nation. Networking is a process linking parents interested in talking to other parents who have coped with similar situations—felt anguish, needed relief, and paved the road for tomorrow (Frey et al., 1989; Gibbs, 1993; Grossman, 1972). These networks of extended support allow family members to grow through personal shared experiences.

Perspectives of Family Members

Fathers. Traditionally, professionals have focused on mothers' perspectives regarding parental concerns of families and their children with disabilities. Interestingly, however, these mothers have long recognized the need to facilitate the father's involvement with their child's intervention program (Gallagher et al., 1981). In response, professionals have begun to address the significant needs of fathers and their active involvement in their child's intervention program (Lamb & Meyer, 1991; Young & Roopnarnine, 1994).

"A man's pride in his child's abilities influences his perspective of his parenting abilities, which increases his pride in his abilities as a parent" (Meyer, 1993, p. 83). A father's attitude toward his child's disability frequently influences the attitude of the family as a whole (Frey et al., 1989; Lamb & Meyer, 1991).

Typically, when a man becomes a father he evaluates his future in respect to his ability to provide and influence the development of his child. He assesses his accomplishments, career satisfaction, family, and marriage. The diagnosis of a disability can directly influence how a man assesses his family life (Meyer, 1986b), which in turn can directly influence the overall family unit's perception.

As a result of their recognized importance, there are now support programs specifically designed to meet the individual needs of fathers (Meyer, 1986a; Young & Roopnarnine, 1994). One example provides an opportunity for fathers to participate in discussions regarding how their views of accomplishment and family have changed in the wake of the child's diagnosis (Meyer, 1993). Fathers bring their children to the program and are given the opportunity to be primary care givers, thus increasing their feelings of "expertise" regarding their child's disability. Father-focused support groups assist the family in handling everyday life stressors while attending to the various needs of their child.

> When people speak of acceptance, they imply that parents must learn that their child's disability prevents them from having all the things normal people have, that these children can't be a real part of our society. They must be separate even though it is bad and painful. But it isn't the job of a parent of a child with disabilities to accept things the way they are. It is our job to do anything we possibly can do to change things. (Statum, 1995, p. 68)

Siblings.   Professionals, while providing services to the child with a disability, have also unintentionally overlooked siblings. Fortunately, professionals now have begun to address the significant need of siblings, and their sincere interest to be involved in the intervention program.

Siblings are curious about their brother's or sister's disability and genuinely want to increase their knowledge and understanding of their sibling's condition. Also, according to Meyer (1993), "Nondisabled siblings frequently complain about people who view their sibling *as* the disability" (p. 85). Thus, siblings need more information as well as the skill to share with others what they have learned.

Several sibling programs have been established to provide brothers and sisters opportunities to meet others who share the experience of having a sibling with a disability (Meyer, Vadasay & Fewell, 1985; Powell & Ogle, 1985). Through these programs, "participants share strategies to address common sibling concerns, such as what to do when classmates make insensitive comments about people with disabilities or when siblings embarrass them in public" (Meyer, 1993, p. 84).

In spite of the challenges due to their brother's or sister's disability, there are unanticipated benefits that contribute to their lives (Gibbs, 1993; Meyer, 1993). Some of the reported sibling benefits of these shared experiences include increased understanding of other people, more tolerance and compassion, and greater appreciation of their own good health and intelligence (Grossman, 1972). After acquiring these (and other) benefits, "brothers and sisters frequently express pride in their siblings' accomplishments and view their siblings in terms of what they can do" (Meyer, 1993, p. 85).

Mothers.   Mothers, like fathers and siblings, are individuals and respond accordingly. But there are also some experiences that are common to many mothers. It is not uncommon for some mothers to feel a personal responsibility for the their child's condition. They blame themselves for not having been more careful during pregnancy. They wonder if it is something they did, or perhaps something they didn't do. Thoughts such as these often result in feelings of self-recrimination and condemnation (Buscaglia, 1975).

Mothers often find their lives dramatically changed after the birth of a child with a disability. The woman who had been actively involved in the community, with personal interests, employment, and so forth, may find that her world becomes very small. Because of the demands of time, energy, and emotion, the mother may find that her whole life is changed, leaving little time for her own interests and needs. Burnout is often a consequence of this change in life circumstances (Berger, 1995).

As with the other family members, the mother will need to grieve her loss—the loss of the dream of the "perfect child." This may be complicated by the fact that mothers often feel they are responsible for helping other family members deal with their grief, and neglect their own need to grieve, thus prolonging it.

Diverse Background Families.   Consider the importance of significant people with whom the child and the family interacts. The child's family members, peers, friends, and religious association influence the child. A family's cultural background has a major impact and influences the behaviors of each family member

(Nieto, 1996; O'Shea, O'Shea, Algozzine, & Hammitte, 2001). The family's culture has a set of values and beliefs that guides the members' diversity and dynamics (Shimoni & Baxter, 1996). Thus, understanding the child's cultural and ethnic background will influence the understanding of the family's customs and traditions (O'Shea et al., 2001). Acceptance of diversity and effective communication increase the opportunities to value diversity, including a disability. This can be shared by the family, and will influence the decisions being made on the behalf of the child and family (Kroth & Edge, 1997; Shimoni & Baxter, 1996).

Extended Families.   Some extended families include relatives or close friends who reside in the same house permanently (Shimoni & Baxter, 1996). Other extended families include relatives or close friends who do not reside in the house, but have significant roles or responsibilities to the family. Extended families provide support for both the child with a disability and for the other family members (Shimoni & Baxter, 1996). Understanding family structure and how it effects the family dynamics is crucial in providing effective services for the family.

Blended Families.   Blended families are becoming more common. Nearly one out of three individuals is a member of a stepfamily (Larson, 1992). Complex family situations frequently arise because various family traditions and values are blending together. The quality of family functioning is increasingly important as the family members bond. Family members build effective links of communication, togetherness, and trust, which enable them to better cope with and manage family situations.

Community

> Full inclusion affords children with disabilities an opportunity given to other people: to live a meaningful life. I know that every day Anna spends in an integrated environment is a meaningful day. Every transaction she has with another child counts for something. Every day she is teaching lessons that no one else can teach. She is bringing out the best in others who bring out the best in her. She deserves that opportunity, and so do they. (Statum, 1995, p. 68)

As expected, parents and families are concerned with providing supportive and nurturing environments for their children with disabilities (Rainforth, York, & Macdonald, 1992). The new IDEA legislation (PL 102-119) specifically ensures that professionals will address the issue of transition from early intervention programs for infants and toddlers to preschool programs. The smooth and successful transition of these children (and their families) from early intervention programs to community-based programs should be a primary concern of all individuals involved (Seed, 1988; Singer et al., 1993).

Parents and families are often concerned that children with disabilities will experience isolation from their nondisabled peers. The fact is that all children (disabled or not) can and do learn through shared experiences with their peers. In return, nondisabled peers also benefit and begin to recognize that these new friends are a part of their neighborhood. Several studies have shown that in integrated settings, nondisabled children develop at the expected rate, and children with disabilities make progress (McLean & Hanline, 1990; Odom & Strain, 1984). An important lesson is that children are cruel only because such experiences are lacking (Seed, 1988).

> I withdrew her from the special center she had attended for several years and enrolled her in a Head Start program. Anna was the only child in her class in a wheelchair, the only one who couldn't speak. The teacher had never taught a child with severe disabilities before. That first morning when we came rolling into that room full of noisy, active 4-year-olds, the teacher said to me, "Go home and don't worry; everything will be fine." And it was. Whatever problems we had, we worked out together. By year's end, Anna was beginning to speak. And I learned that it doesn't take a special person to teach children with disabilities. It simply takes a special person to be a good teacher. (Statum, 1995, p. 66)

Summary

The general perspectives held by professionals, communities, and families of children with disabilities have matured. No longer is the birth of a child with a disability viewed as a burden. As families and parents are empowered through their experiences (e.g., coping, adapting, seeking support), they have become active leading members in their child's learning opportunities. Families have also learned to effectively implement strategies and techniques that best fit their families' goals and objectives.

All families, including families of children with disabilities, have hopes, dreams, and desires for their children. For families with children with disabilities these expectations are more difficult to attain. In order to pursue their goals, families and professionals must learn to work in a collaborative partnership. Together, professionals and parents must in turn learn how to be more respectful and genuinely sensitive in their collaborative partnership efforts. There is always an undying hope and belief that, as a result of their efforts, the community will accept their children with dignity and respect (Santelli, Turnbull, Lerner, & Marquis, 1993; Seed, 1988).

> There is a hitherto unacknowledged place in the world for our children and we need to claim it. The current movement toward full inclusion gives us a hope that no other generation of parents of children with disabilities has had; the hope that when our children are grown they will be accepted as full members of the human community. We are luckier than we thought. (Statum, 1995, p. 68)

ADDITIONAL RESOURCES

Families of Children with Disabilities

Books:

Bateman, B., & Linden, M. A. (1992). *Better IEPs: How to develop legally correct and educationally useful programs*. (3rd ed.). Longmont, CO: Sopris West.

Developed for special educators, regular educators, and parents as a guide to developing individualized educational program plans that are both legally and educationally useful. The authors highlight the five main components of IDEA (Part B) and address the IEP's role. Included also is a child-centered three-step IEP process that is quite helpful.

Buzzell, J. (1996). *School and family partnership: Case studies for special educators.* Albany, NY: Delmar Publshers.

This book is a collection of case studies to help prepare students for the real world of teaching. Each case is a short story that describes a problematic situation that a teacher has actually faced. It includes a number of cases that help special education students better understand these special families and develop skills they will need to be supportive. 160 pp.

Curran, D. (1989). *Working with parents.* Circle Pines, MN: American Guidance Service.

Topics covered in this book for professionals working in the parent education field include: conducting groups that empower parents, reexamining traditional assumptions about parents, and listening to identify parents' needs.

Cutler, B. C. (1993). *You, your child, and "special education:" A guide to making the system work.* Baltimore: Paul Brookes.

A handbook for parents describing and explaining the special education system. Topics covered: rights to education, school system's power structure, and effective strategies for dealing with school personnel.

Davis, M. D., Kilgo, J. L., & Gamel-McCormick, M. (1998). *Young children with special needs: A developmentally appropriate approach.* Boston: Allyn & Bacon.

A book for both general and special education teachers to design effective, appropriate learning programs for young children with disabilities. Classroom modifications made to make learning appropriate for children with disabilities are often effective for other children.

Featherstone, H. (1980). *A difference in the family: Living with a disabled child.* New York: Penguin Books.

A woman shares her own personal story regarding the impact a disability has on the family as a whole as well as on each individual family member. She shares the family dynamics and frank discussion of their decisions regarding the child with a disability.

Harry, B. (1992). *Cultural diversity, families, and the special education system: Communication & empowerment.* New York: Teachers College Press.

This timely and thought-provoking book explores the quadruple disadvantage faced by the parents of poor, minority, handicapped children whose first language is not that of the school that they attend.

Howard, V. F., Williams, B. F., Port, P. D., & Lepper, C. (2001). *Very young children with special needs: A formative approach for the 21st century* (2nd ed.). Upper Saddle River, NJ: Merrill Prentice Hall.

Provides an introduction to early childhood and early childhood special education professionals who provide child and family services as well as intervention to very young children with disabilities. This foundation book offers the philosophy, history, family impact, legal issues, and medical concerns that are important to early intervention and early childhood services to very young children with disabilities and their families.

Kroth, R. (1996). *Communicating with parents of exceptional children* (3rd ed.). Denver, CO: Love.

Kroth's work in the area of parent involvement acted as a foundation for many other researchers and writers. You will see his influence in most major works in this area. Although this book was meant for those working with parents of special needs students in particular, it is also valuable in working with parents in general. He provides the reader with a philosophical basis for planning, as well as practical suggestions. This is a book that all educators interested in parent involvement need for their library.

Kroth, R. L., & Edge, D. (1997). *Strategies for communicating with parents of exceptional children.* (3rd ed.). Denver, CO: Love.

A book of techniques, based on the premise that all parents have strengths from which to contribute to their child's education, as well as needs to be met. It is aimed at teachers who would like to improve their skills in working with parents.

Lobato, D. J. (1990). *Brothers, sisters, and special needs: Information and activities for helping young siblings of children with chronic illness and developmental disabilities.* Baltimore: Paul Brookes.

This is a curriculum and activity guide for children 3 to 8 years of age with siblings who are disabled. Provides workshop activities to assist children in understanding their "disabilities."

Meyer, D. J., & Vadasy, P. F. (1994). *Sibshops: Workshops for siblings of children with special needs.* Baltimore: Paul Brookes.

The easy-to-use Sibshop is a practical resource that brings together 8- to 13-year-olds to express their feelings about brothers and sisters with disabilities.

O'Shea, D. J., O'Shea, L. J., Algozzine, R., & Hammitte, D. J. (2001). *Families and teachers of individuals with disabilities: Collaborative orientations and responsive practices.* Boston: Allyn & Bacon.

This book is written for general and special educators who work with diverse families. This resourceful book provides practical information on understanding and learning about various family issues and needs that impact their children's educational needs.

Powell, T. H., & Gallagher, P. A. (1993). *Brothers & sisters: As special part of exceptional families* (2nd ed.). Baltimore: Paul Brookes.

This contains personal stories shared by brothers and sisters of exceptional siblings. Topics include sibling adjustment, effective listening, and innovative teaching programs.

Rainforth, B., York, J., & Macdonald, C. (1992). *Collaborative teams for students with severe disabilities: Integrating therapy and educational services.* Baltimore: Paul Brookes.

A text on how to establish effective transdisciplinary teaming with professionals and parents. Various models of effective collaboration in educational settings are discussed.

Rosenkoetter, S., Hains, A., & Fowler, S. (1994). *Bridging early services for children with special needs and their families.* Baltimore: Paul Brookes.

A practical guide for service providers via a step-by-step process of planning coordinated, uninterrupted services for children and their families. A series of case studies illustrate a variety of early childhood transitions.

Stainback, W., & Stainback, S. (1990). *Support networks for inclusive schooling: Interdependent integrated education.* Baltimore: Paul Brookes.

Written for administrators, educators, parents, students, and interested citizens as a primary tool for developing schools into inclusive communities. A guide for designing classrooms where students are valued for their talents and not characterized only by their limitations.

Articles:

Davern, L. (1996). Listening to parents of children with disabilities. *Educational Leadership, 53*(7), 61–63.

Videos:

Parents' Views of Living with a Child with Disabilities

This video features candid interviews with parents of children with disabilities and shows the daily life conflicts and frustrations they encounter. (30 minutes, color). Purchase.

> The Bureau for At-Risk Youth
> 645 New York Avenue
> Huntington, NY 11743
> Phone: 800-999-6884

Parenting Special Children

A two video set that discusses issues parents face when their newborn has health problems. It contains three interviews with parents of exceptional children. The video addresses the psychological stages that parents experience and discusses early intervention, communication with caregivers, applicable federal laws, and ways of dealing with health care professionals.

Organizations:

> Council for Exceptional Children
> 1920 Association Drive
> Reston, VA 22091
> Phone: 703-620-3660

National Clearinghouse on Family Support and Children's Mental Health
Portland State University
P.O. Box 751
Portland, OR 97207-0751
Phone: 800-628-1696

National Information Center for Children and Youth with Disabilities
P.O. Box 1492 Washington, DC 20013
Phone: 800-999-5599

Websites:

Clearinghouse on Disability Information
www.ed.gov/offices/orers

The Council for Exceptional Children
www.cec.sped.org

Eric Clearinghouse on Disabilities and Gifted Education
www.ericec.org

Family Village (new site with broad range of disability-related information
    for parents and professionals with lots of links to other sites)
www.familyvillage.wisc.edu

Friends of Inclusion Resource Page
www.inclusion.com

National Information Center for Children and Youth with Disabilities
www.nichcy.org

REFERENCES

Americans with Disabilities Act of 1990, Public Law 101-336.

Bailey, E., & Bricker, D. (1984). The efficacy of early intervention for severely handicapped infants and young children. *Topics in Early Childhood Special Education, 4*(3), 30–51.

Berger, E. (1995). *Parents as partners in education: Families and schools working together* (4th ed.). New York: Merrill Publishing Co.

Boswell, B., & Schuffner, C. (1990). Families support inclusive schooling. In W. Stainback & S. Stainback (1990), *Support networks for inclusive schooling: Interdependent integrated education* (pp. 219–230). Baltimore: Paul Brookes.

Buck, P. (1950). *The child who never grew.* New York: John Day.

Buscalglia, L. (1975). *The disabled and their parents.* Thorofare, NJ: Charles B. Slack, Inc.

Davis, M. D., Kilgo, J. L., & Gamel-McCormick, M. (1998). *Young children with special needs: A developmentally appropriate approach.* Boston: Allyn & Bacon.

DeGangi, G., Wietlisbach, S., Possison, S., Stein, E., & Royeen, C. (1994). The impact of culture and socioeconomic status on family–professional collaboration: Challenges and solutions. *Topics in Early Childhood Special Education, 14*(4), 503–520.

Dunst, C. J., Trivette, C. M., & Deal, A. G. (1988). *Enabling and empowering families: Principles and guidelines for practice.* Cambridge, MA: Brookline Books.

Dunst, C. J., Trivette, C. M., & Jordy, W. (1997). Influences of social support of children with disabilities and their families. In M. J. Guralnick (Ed.), *The effectiveness of early intervention* (pp. 499–522). Baltimore: Paul H. Brooks.

Education for All Handicapped Children Act (1976) (EHA), 20 U.S.C.A. 1400 *et seq.*

Etscheidt, S. K., & Bartlett, L. (1999). The IDEA amendments: A four-step approach for determining supplementary aids. *Exceptional Children, 65*(2), 163–174.

Farber, B. (1975). Family adaptations to severely mentally retarded children. In M. J. Begab & S. A. Richardson (Eds.), *The mentally retarded and society: A social science perspective* (pp. 247–266). Baltimore: University Park Press.

Featherstone, H. (1980). *A difference in the family: Living with a disabled child.* New York: Penguin Books.

Fewell, R. (1986). A handicapped child in the family. In R. Fewell & P. Vadasy (Eds.), *Families of handicapped children: Needs and supports across the life span* (pp. 87–104). Austin, TX: PRO-ED.

Frey, K. S., Fewell, R. R., Vadasy, P. F., & Greenberg, M. T. (1989). Parental adjustment and changes in child outcome among families of young handicapped children. *Topics in Early Childhood Special Education, 8*(2), 38–57.

Gallagher, J., Cross, A., & Scharfman, W. (1981). Parental adaptation to a young handicapped child: The father's role. *Journal of the Division of Early Childhood, 3,* 3–4.

Gibbs, B. (1993). Providing support to sisters and brothers of children with disabilities. In G. Singer & L. Powers (1993), *Families, disability, and empowerment: Active coping skills and strategies for family interventions* (pp. 27–66). Baltimore: Paul Brookes.

Goldenbreg, I., & Goldenberg, H. (1980). *Family therapy: An overview.* Monterey, CA: Brooks/Cole Publishing Company.

Grossman, F. K. (1972). *Brothers and sisters of the retarded children: An exploratory study.* Syracuse, NY: Syracuse University Press.

Guralnick, M. (1990). Major accomplishments and future directions in early childhood mainstreaming. *Topics in Early Childhood Special Education, 10*(2), 1–17.

Hanson, M. J. (1985). Administration of private versus public early childhood special education programs. *Topics in Early Childhood Special Education, 5*(1), 25–38.

Hanson, M. J., Lynch, E. W., & Wayman, K. I. (1990). Honoring the cultural diversity of families when gathering data. *Topics in Early Childhood Special Education, 10*(1), 112–131.

Hawkins, N., Singer, G., & Nixon, C. (1993). Short-term behavioral counseling for families of persons with disabilities. In G. Singer & L. Powers (1993). *Families, disability, and empowerment: Active coping skills and strategies for family interventions* (pp. 317–341). Baltimore: Paul Brookes.

Howard, V. F., Williams, B. F., Port, P. D., & Lepper, C. (2001). *Very young children with special needs: A formative approach for the 21st Century* (2nd ed.) Upper Saddle River, NJ: Merrill Prentice Hall.

Kirk, S. A., & Gallagher, J. J. (1989). *Educating exceptional children* (6th ed.). Boston: Houghton Mifflin.

Kroth, R. L., & Edge, D. (1997). *Strategies for communicating with parents of exceptional children.* (3rd ed.). Denver, CO: Love.

Kübler-Ross, E. (1969). *Death and dying.* New York: Macmillan.

Lamb, M. E., & Meyer, D. J. (1991). Fathers of children with special needs. In M. Seligman (Ed.), *The family with a handicapped child* (pp. 151–179). Boston: Allyn & Bacon.

Larson, J. (1992). Understanding step families. *American Demographics, 14,* 360.

Lobato, D. J. (1990). *Brothers, sisters, and special needs: Information and activities for helping young siblings of children with chronic illness and developmental disabilities.* Baltimore: Paul Brookes.

Long, C., Artis, N., & Dobbins, N. (1993). The hospital: An important site for family-centered early intervention. *Topics in Early Childhood Special Education, 13*(1), 106–199.

McLean, M., & Hanline, M. (1990). Providing early intervention services in integrated environments: Challenges and opportunities for the future. *Topics in Early Childhood Special Education, 10*(2), 62–77.

Meyer, D. J. (1986a). Fathers of children with special needs. In M. E. Lamb (Ed.), *The father's role: Applied perspectives* (pp. 227–254). New York: John Wiley & Sons.

Meyer, D. J. (1986b). Fathers of handicapped children. In R. Fewell & P. Vadsey (Eds.), *Families of handicapped children* (pp. 35–73). Austin, TX: PRO-ED.

Meyer, D. J. (1993). Lessons learned: Cognitive coping strategies of overlooked family members. In A. Turnbull et al. (Eds.), *Cognitive coping, families & disability* (pp. 81–92). Baltimore: Paul Brookes.

Meyer, D. J., Vadasy, P. F., & Fewell, R. R. (1985). *Sibshops: A handbook for implementing workshops for siblings of children with special needs.* Seattle: University of Washington Press.

Murray, J. N. (1980). *Developing assessment programs for the multi-handicapped child.* Springfield, IL: Charles C. Thomas.

Murray, J. N., & Cornell, C. J. (1981). Parentalplegia. *Psychology in the Schools, 18,* 201–207.

Nieto, S. (1996). *Affirming diversity: The sociopolitical context of multicultural education* (2nd ed.). New York: Longman.

Nixon, C. (1993). Reducing self-blame and guilt in parents of children with severe disability. In G. Singer & L. Powers (1993), *Families, disability, and empowerment: Active coping skills and strategies for family interventions* (pp. 175–201). Baltimore: Paul Brookes.

Odom, S., & Strain, P. (1984). Classroom-based social skills instruction for severely handicapped preschool children. *Topics in Early Childhood Special Education, 4*(3), 97–116.

O'Shea, D. J., O'Shea, L. J., Algozzine, R., & Hammitte, D. J. (2001). *Families and teachers of individuals with disabilities: Collaborative orientations and responsive practices.* Boston: Allyn & Bacon.

Pearl, L. (1993). Providing family-centered early intervention. In W. Brown, S. Thurman, & L. Pearl (1993), *Family-centered early intervention with infants & toddlers: Innovative cross-disciplinary approaches* (pp. 81–101). Baltimore: Paul Brookes.

Pennsylvania Association for Retarded Children v. Commonwealth of Pennsylvania, 343 F. Supp. 279 (E. D. Pa., 1972).

Powell, T. H., & Ogle, P. A. (1985). *Brothers & sisters—A special part of exceptional families.* Baltimore: Paul Brookes.

Powers, L. (1993). Disability and grief: From tragedy to challenge. In G. Singer & L. Powers (1993), *Families, disability, and empowerment: Active coping skills and strategies for family interventions* (pp. 119–149). Baltimore: Paul Brookes.

Rainforth, B., York, J., & Macdonald, C. (1992). *Collaborative teams for students with severe disabilities: Integrating therapy and educational services.* Baltimore: Paul Brookes.

Rehabilitation Act of 1973. Section 504, 19 U.S.C. section 794.

Ruder, M. (1993). The provision of early intervention and early childhood special education within community early childhood programs: Characteristics of effective service delivery. *Topics in Early Childhood Special Education, 13*(1), 19–37.

Salisbury, C. (1992). Parents as team members: Inclusive teams, collaborative outcomes. In B. Rainforth, J. York, & C. Macdonald (1992), *Collaborative teams for students with severe disabilities: Integrating therapy and educational services* (pp. 37–56). Baltimore: Paul Brookes.

Santelli, B., Turnbull, A., Lerner, J., & Marquis, J. (1993). Parent to parent programs: A unique form of mutual support for families of persons with disabilities. In G. Singer & L. Powers (1993), *Families, disability, and empowerment: Active coping skills and strategies for family interventions* (pp. 27–66). Baltimore: Paul Brookes.

Seed, P. (1988). *Children with profound handicaps: Parents' views and integration.* Philadelphia: Falmer Press.

Shimoni, R., & Baxter, J. (1996). *Working with families: Perspectives for early childhood professionals.* Reading, MA: Addison-Wesley Publishers Limited.

Singer, G., Irvin, L., Irvin, B., Hawkins, N., Hegreness, H., & Jackson, R. (1993). Helping families adapt positively to disability: Overcoming demoralization through community supports. In G. Singer & L. Powers (1993), *Families, disability, and empowerment: Active coping skills and strategies for family interventions* (pp. 67–83). Baltimore: Paul Brookes.

Singer, G., & Powers, L. (1993). *Families, disability, and empowerment: Active coping skills and strategies for family interventions.* Baltimore: Paul Brookes.

Statum, S. (1995). Inclusion: One parent's story. In P. Browning (Ed.), *Transition IV in Alabama: Profile of commitment.* State Conference Proceedings, January 1995 (pp. 65–68). Auburn, AL: Auburn University.

Todis, B., Irvin, L., Singer, G., & Yovanoff, P. (1993). The self-esteem parent program: Quantitative and qualitative evaluation of a cognitive-behavioral intervention. In G. Singer & L. Powers (1993), *Families, disability, and empowerment: Active coping skills and strategies for family interventions* (pp. 203–229). Baltimore: Paul Brookes.

Turnbull, A. P., Brotherson, M. J., & Summers, J. A. (1985). The impact of deinstitutionalization on families: A family systems approach. In R. H. Bruininks (Ed.), *Living and learning in the least restrictive environment* (pp. 115–152). Baltimore: Paul Brookes.

Turnbull, A. P., & Turnbull, H. R. (2001). *Families, professionals, and exceptionality: A special partnership* (4th ed.). New York: Merrill.

Turnbull, H. R., Turnbull, A. P., Shank, M., & Leal, D. (1995). *Exceptional lives: Special education in today's schools.* New York: Merrill.

Turnbull, H. R., Turnbull, A. P., & Wheat, M. (1982). Assumptions about parental participation: A legislative history. *Exceptional Education Quarterly, 3*(2), 1–8.

U.S. Department of Education. (1993). *Fifteenth annual report to Congress on the implementation of the Individuals with Disabilities Education Act.* Washington, DC: Government Printing Office.

Young, D., & Roopnarine, J. (1994). Fathers' childcare involvement with children with and without disabilities. *Topics in Early Childhood Special Education, 14*(4), 488–502.

9 Family-Involvement Models

In this chapter, six writers will identify different models of family and parent involvement in the schools. The models will cover programs that serve children from infancy to fifteen years of age. The authors will identify national models (McLean, Shaeffer, Lim, and Glessner) or identify a model that can be used at any middle or secondary level (Johnston and Fogelberg). Please keep in mind that these are only representatives of many models that are available for discussion. After reading the chapter you should be able to:

- Identify various parent/family-involvement models at the preschool, elementary, middle, and special education level
- Compare and contrast models in and between levels
- Recognize the components of successful parent- and family-involvement models
- Comprehend why one model may work at one level and not at another level

Family Involvement in Special Education

Mary McLean

University of Wisconsin, Milwaukee

Margaret (Peggy) Shaeffer

University of North Dakota

Inclusion has made all children the concern of the "regular" classroom teacher. Unfortunately, most classroom teachers are not prepared to work with the parents of children with special needs. The special education segment of this chapter shares successful parent-involvement models and other information that will be most helpful to educators.

Models of family involvement in special education have been strongly influenced by the legal system established by federal law, which regulates the education of students with disabilities. Chapter 10 will provide you with information on special education law and the parental rights, which are ensured through the law. The Individuals with Disabilities Education Act (IDEA), formerly known as the Education of the Handicapped Act, is the law that has had the greatest impact on the involvement of parents in the education of their children with disabilities. The reauthorization of this law in 1975 (PL 94-142) established the rights of students with disabilities to a free and appropriate public education. Prior to PL 94-142, parents were frequently turned away from public school programs that did not provide educational services for children with disabilities. As described in Chapter 10, this law also established procedural safeguards for parents, such as the right to access their children's educational records (and the right to limit access by others), the requirement of parental consent prior to initial evaluation and initial placement of a child in special education, and the right to written notice in the event that the school proposes to change or refuses to change services. Furthermore, in cases in which a disagreement occurs between parents and the school in relation to children's educational programs, the right to due process of law is assured.

The requirements of the law clearly have a significant impact on the relationship between parents of children with disabilities and school personnel, and, to a great degree, these requirements structure the interactions that occur. However, many programs have gone beyond the requirements of the law in providing services that are not only individualized to meet the needs of the child but also individualized to meet the needs of the family. These programs see their role as one of providing support as the family undertakes activities necessary for family functioning, including the activities necessary to provide for the child with a disability. Such programs incorporate a *family-centered* philosophy.

Interestingly, two of the most recent amendments to IDEA that authorize services for infants and toddlers with disabilities, PL 99-457 and PL 102-119, incorporated aspects of a family-centered philosophy into the law. This law requires a "family-directed" assessment and the development of an Individualized Family Service Plan that identifies outcomes for the child and family as well as the services to be provided in order to facilitate these outcomes.

A Family Systems Conceptual Framework

During the late 1970s and early 1980s, family systems theory emerged as a foundation for intervention in the helping professions. Family systems theory views the family as a social system wherein all members have an impact on each other (Minuchin, 1974). When applied to special education, this theory emphasizes the idea that intervention with one family member will affect all members. In other words, professionals should recognize that the provision of special education services to a child not only affects the child but will also affect family functioning in a manner that may be beneficial or detrimental.

Turnbull and Turnbull (2001) presented a family systems conceptual framework that incorporates information from family systems theory and the special education literature to provide a framework for evaluating the impact of special education services on family functioning. Applying this framework to the provision of educational services to children with disabilities leads the educator to consider the impact of educational activities on the family and to attempt to see the world from the family's perspective. The framework requires us to consider input variables, characteristics of family interactions, and life-cycle changes. It becomes apparent that each family is unique and complex; there will be considerable diversity among families in beliefs and values, in resources, in the challenges they face, and in coping and interaction patterns of the family members. Furthermore, educational intervention will have an impact on the entire family system and will not be confined to the member with a disability. Families also change over time. Intervention systems will need to be able to accommodate changes in the family system, which will impact the child with a disability. The reader is referred to Turnbull and Turnbull (2001) for more information on the family systems framework.

Reflection...

Family systems theory or a family-centered philosophy seems to be such an important part of the models in this section. Why do you think this is the case? Has this theory or philosophy been evident in other parts of the text? Or is this just author bias?

Family-Centered Intervention

As educators have become more aware of how families function and the impact of the family on the success of intervention efforts, a philosophy of intervention has emerged, known as family-centered intervention. Family-centered philosophy moves intervention efforts from an agency-oriented approach to a family-oriented approach. It is eloquently described by the following passage from Turnbull and Summers (1985):

> Copernicus came along and made a startling reversal—he put the sun in the center of the universe rather than the Earth. His declaration caused profound shock. The earth was not the epitome of creation; it was a planet like all other planets. The successful challenge to the entire system of ancient authority required a complete change in philosophical conception of the universe. This is rightly termed the "Copernican Revolution." Let's pause to consider what would happen if we had a Copernican Revolution in the field of disability. Visualize the concept: the family is the center of the universe and the service delivery system is one of the many planets revolving around it. Now visualize the service delivery system at the center and the family in orbit around it. Do you recognize the revolutionary change in perspective? We would move from an emphasis on parent involvement (i.e., parents participating in the program) to family support (i.e., programs providing a range of support services for families). This is not a semantic exercise—such a revolution leads us to a new set of assumptions and a new vista of options for service. (p. 12)

Over time, the philosophy and practices of family-centered intervention have been revisited and modified to meet the changing needs of children and their families.

For example, many different terms have been used to describe this philosophy of family-centeredness: *family-guided* (Slentz & Bricker, 1992), *family-focused* (Bailey et al., 1986), and *parent empowerment* (Dunst, 1985; Dunst, Trivette, & Deal, 1988). The components and interplay of the critical features of these philosophies have evolved over time. Dunst (2000) examined multiple ways of identifying and operationalizing key components of the family systems approach to intervention that considers the complex factors of family, environment, and planned and unplanned events. This new generation of a family-centered model is taking us deeper into the arena of maximizing the child's and family's natural environments for supporting development. The context of the family is expanded to include not only the home but also the school and the community at large (Bruder & Dunst, 2001). Regardless of the terminology or the exact way in which the philosophy is implemented, the common idea held by all is that intervention should be provided in collaboration with family members, in a manner that facilitates the family's decision-making role, and in a manner that is in line with the family's priorities. To incorporate a family-centered philosophy, a paradigm shift must occur. Intervention must move away from being child focused and agency directed to being family focused and, to a large extent, also family directed. The following three programs exemplify a family-centered philosophy.

Parent to Parent Programs

The Parent to Parent Model was established in 1971 as the foundation for the Pilot Parents Program in Omaha, Nebraska. At its foundation is the belief that parents of individuals with disabilities can serve as resources to other parents of individuals with disabilities as well as to professionals (Turnbull, 1999). Basically, it serves as a matching program between "veteran" parents of an individual with a disability to parents who are just beginning the journey of meeting the challenges of a disability within the family. It was reported that nearly 650,000 families were receiving services through approximately 600 local and statewide Parent to Parent programs (Turnbull, Turnbull, Shank, & Leal, 2001). More than one third of the programs are funded through Part C (Turnbull, 1999).

The Parent to Parent programs are run by volunteer parents and range in size from perhaps two or three parents to statewide networks of programs supported by volunteer and professional staffs. Referrals to the program come from a variety of sources, from medical, educational, and social service agencies to personal contacts through family and friends. Once a family has been contacted, care is taken to determine the best family match considering such multiple dimensions as location, disability, and family structure and lifestyle, and cultural influences. The new families' strengths and concerns also dictate the method and type of interactions that occur between the matched families. For example, in some instances the contacts may be minimal in terms of telephone interactions with occasional conversations, and in other instances there may be more intensive support provided such as problem-solving sessions, identification of community resources, and training in advocacy skills.

The efficacy of using parents as providers of education to parents and professionals is documented. As Turnbull (1999) reports, parents who use the Parent to Parent services are better able to cope with the challenges of living with a disability in the family. In addition, the participating families were living the experiences with families who were like them, and the feeling of sameness was beneficial as well as providing a support system for developing coping skills and serving as a resource for gathering necessary skills and information.

COACH

Choosing Options and Accommodations for Children (COACH) (Giangreco, Cloninger, & Iverson, 1993) is actually an assessment and planning tool for developing and implementing educational plans that meet the needs of students with moderate to severe disabilities in inclusive environments. COACH assists in planning for special education services to be provided in general education classrooms. It is chosen here as an example of family-centered special education services because of the emphasis placed on the family as " the cornerstone of relevant and longitudinal educational planning" (p. 6). One goal of COACH is to assist families in becoming partners with professionals in the educational process as well as becoming better consumers of the services provided to their children. The following five beliefs are specified as the basis of establishing partnerships between parents and professionals:

- Families know certain aspects of their children better than anyone else does.
- Families have the greatest vested interest in seeing their children learn.
- The family is likely to be the only group of adults involved with a child's educational program throughout his or her entire school career.
- Families have the ability to influence positively the quality of educational services provided in their community.
- Families must live with the outcomes of decisions made by educational teams all day, every day.

The COACH system begins with a family prioritization interview that identifies family-chosen priorities for the students' educational program. This aspect of COACH establishes the role of the family as codesigner of the educational program rather than simply being asked to approve a program that was predetermined by professionals. COACH then utilizes collaborative teamwork, coordinated planning, and problem-solving strategies in the process of developing goals and objectives and determining options for addressing these goals and objectives in the general education setting.

Coinstruction

As indicated above, the implementation of family-centered services requires professionals to make a shift from involving families in the approval of professionally determined intervention plans to family involvement as partners throughout the entire assessment and intervention process. This shift has been difficult for some professionals because it may be very different in orientation from their preservice training and experience (Bailey, Buysse, Edmonson, & Smith, 1992).

One strategy for enhancing the ability of professionals to form partnerships with the families they serve is coinstruction in higher education. According to Whitehead and Sontag (1993), the primary purpose of coinstruction is to give students the consumer's perspective on intervention efforts. This broader perspective should result in increased sensitivity to the impact of their actions on families.

The participation of family members in the professional development of special education personnel is not particularly new; however, it has traditionally been accomplished through rather limited means such as a guest speaker or panel of parents; videotape or film portraying a family's story; or articles, poems, or books written by families (Featherstone, 1980; Fialka, 1994). There has been a recent increase in efforts, particularly in early intervention, to include family members much more extensively in the planning and implementation of both preservice and inservice training (Bailey, McWilliam, & Winton, 1992; Gilkerson, 1994; McBride, Sharp, Hains, & Whitehead, in press). This trend toward family involvement in the training of professionals has brought new meaning to the term *parent trainer*, which in the 1960s and 1970s referred to a professional who taught parents how to teach their children. In the 1990s, *parent trainer* refers to a parent who has agreed to teach professionals about working with families.

According to McBride et al. (in press), approaches to coinstruction vary widely across personnel development programs. They suggest thinking of the various possible coinstruction roles as points on a continuum. Parents are frequently involved in courses related to working with families but may also participate in coursework addressing assessment and curriculum. Parents may participate in limited activities or in every class session. Parents may provide only the family perspective or may also teach core content. Each situation will be different depending on the parent's experience and desire to participate, the consent for instruction, and the strength and comfort level of the parent–faculty team.

Parents who are providing the family perspective may be asked to share their family's experience relative to a particular topic, such as receiving the initial diagnosis of disability, participating in assessment experiences, choosing intervention services, and so forth. This can be done in many ways: by using prepared speeches, slides or overheads, or informal conversation. Faculty can help family members determine their preferred mode of sharing experiences. An instructional videotape is now available to help parents in telling their stories (King, 1994).

Reflection...

Is coinstruction being used at your college or university? If not, describe the benefits of this model for your college or university. If coinstruction is used, how could the model be strengthened at your school or university?

Some parents will gain a good deal of expertise as a result of their experience in parenting a child with a disability. These parents will have information to present on topics such as particular diagnoses and disabilities, medical procedures, aspects of the law, particular intervention strategies, funding mechanisms, and advocacy efforts. Demonstrating the expertise parents have to offer can be a very valuable lesson for professionals as they learn to work in partnership with families.

Coinstruction is a model of personnel development that has only recently begun to be utilized in preservice and inservice training. It occurs in many different forms and has the potential to impact the family's perspective on professionals who work with children. This ability to understand the world from the perspective of family members is critical to providing educational services to children and families that reflect a family-centered philosophy.

The three models described in this section reflect the family-centered approach. The models are attempts to improve the family's role in providing educational services for their children. It is important for all of us to continue to discover programs that work and look at ways to improve those programs or incorporate them into our own educational systems.

Family-Involvement Models in Early Childhood Education

Soo-Yin Lim

University of Minnesota, Crookston

Early childhood educators have for a long time recognized the need for parents to actively involve and influence their children's development and learning at an early age. Early childhood education is also based on the beliefs that parents are their children's first teachers, know their children best, and have valuable insights and information to share with teachers. Teachers have the background knowledge in child development and experiences with young children that become a valuable resource for parents (Balaban, 1985). Together, teachers and parents share a common perspective and interest—the children's optimal growth and development and to reach their fullest potential as learners.

The following section describes several current program models that are national and state initiatives to facilitate family and school partnerships.

Head Start

Head Start, established in 1965, is the nation's most extensive investment in the education of preschool children from low-income families. The program has many years of developing and refining strategies to involve families in the program

(Zigler & Freedman, 1987). Head Start provides holistic, comprehensive services for children ages three to five and their families. Head Start's services include four components: health and nutrition, education, social services, and parent involvement. The program's services are designed to respond appropriately to each child's developmental level as well as each family's cultural, ethnic, and linguistic milieu. Head Start serves over 800,000 children and is administered by the Head Start Bureau, the Administration on Children, Youth and Families (ACYF), the Department of Health and Human Services (DHHS), and the Administration for Children and Families (ACF). Head Start funding comes from two sources: 80 percent of the funds come from federal monies through the Department of Health and Human Services, and the remaining 20 percent must come from sources at the community level of each individual program.

The overall mission of Head Start is to increase school readiness and foster the healthy development of young children in low-income families. In most communities, Head Start programs incorporate both center- and home-based services. Children typically attend half-day preschool classes and receive periodic home visits from teachers and parent and family service coordinators. Head Start classes generally follow the schedule of local public school systems, but some programs include full-day and full-year child-care services. A child who is enrolled in Head Start will generally receive a comprehensive screening before the start of preschool classes. This includes assessment of the child's developmental areas, language and speech, hearing, vision, nutrition, physical health and development, and immunizations. The results of the screening are shared with the child's parents. Children's growth and development are assessed on an ongoing basis throughout the year.

Parent-Involvement Practices

In Head Start, parent involvement is viewed as essential, and parents are supported as the most important educators, nurturers, and advocates for their children. According to the Head Start Parent Involvement handbook, parent participation should lead to positive effects in five outcome areas: effective parenting, self-esteem and confidence, family life, education (of the parent), and employment. The Head Start Policy Manual mandates performance standards for four areas of parent involvement:

1. Provide opportunities for parents to have direct involvement in the area of decision-making on program planning and operations.
2. Provide opportunities for parents to work with their own children in cooperation with Head Start teachers and staff.
3. Provide opportunities for parents to participate in the classroom as volunteers, and with the possibility of becoming paid employees.
4. Provide opportunities for parents to plan and implement parent activities.

Parents are not only encouraged, but are expected to work with Head Start staff members to set goals for their children and their families, and to participate in the program as much as possible. They are encouraged to visit their children's classrooms, to serve as volunteers or aides to teachers and staff, and to contribute their talents and services for the good of the program. Parents have opportunities to share their opinions and ideas when planning curriculum, and evaluate Head Start curriculum and services. All parents of enrolled children are members of Head Start Parent Committees. The committee meets on a regular basis and discusses issues relating to curriculum, services, and policies. The Parent Committees elect representatives to the Head Start Policy Council, which is the governing body of the program. These parents can also be elected to serve as officers on local, state, and national Policy Councils.

Classes and workshops concerning families and parenting are offered for parents on a regular basis. These classes cover a wide variety of topics, which are chosen by parents through the use of an interest survey. Head Start programs are often linked to adult learning and job placement programs within a community. Parents are supported in their efforts to reach educational and career goals.

Classroom teachers typically carry out individual home visits to meet with families and children at the beginning and the end of the school year. During the teacher's initial home visit, teachers review curriculum with parents, and complete a planning form on which parents have the opportunity to include ideas and suggestions. The year-end home visit comprises assisting children and parents in planning for the child's transition to kindergarten. Parents are provided with information on helping their children to make the transition, as well as on local kindergarten registrations. Additional home visits by parent and family service coordinators are scheduled throughout the year. At least two parent–teacher conferences are scheduled for parents during the year.

Early Head Start

Early Head Start was created as an extension of the Head Start program to serve low-income families with infants and toddlers, as well as pregnant women. In 1994, the U.S. Congress passed a reauthorization of the Head Start Act, which mandated the Head Start Bureau to initiate a new program to provide comprehensive early intervention for these families. The Early Head Start was established in 1995 and has grown from the original 68 programs to 635 community-based programs nationwide, serving 45,000 children. Grants for Early Head Start programs are administered by the Administration for Children and Families (ACYF).

The mission of Early Head Start is "to promote healthy prenatal outcomes for pregnant women, enhance the development of very young children, and promote healthy family functioning" (Head Start Bureau, 2001). The program goals include enhancing the physical, cognitive, social, and emotional development of children; helping parents learn how to best care for and teach their children; and assisting parents in moving toward economic independence. Early Head Start programs work closely with community agencies including child-care providers in meeting the needs of children and families.

Children are eligible for Early Head Start until age three and are later transitioned into a regular Head Start or another appropriate preschool program. Services are provided through home-based, center-based, and combination options as a response to the individual needs of families and specific community needs. Home-based programs include weekly home visits and bimonthly group socialization events. Center-based programs include periodic home visits by the child's teacher and other center staff. Certified family child care is also an option designed to serve families and children.

Parent-Involvement Practices

Early Head Start mandates parent involvement similar to the performance standards of Head Start programs discussed earlier. The programs have governing systems such as parent committees, policy councils through which parents can participate in the process of planning curriculum, policymaking, and decision making. Along with Early Head Start staff, parents participate in developing and updating an individualized plan for their own children's growth and development, and individualized family partnership agreement. This helps to ensure that services are responding to the goals and needs of families. Prenatal education and health care is provided to pregnant women, and programs must establish procedures to record and follow the provision of health care services to families. Parents with very young children are provided with opportunities to increase their knowledge and understanding of child development, parenting skills, and their children's education needs (Jerald, 2000).

Title I/Even Start

Even Start is a family-centered education program authorized as part of Chapter 1 or Title 1 of PL 100-297, which provides funds to local educational agencies to "improve the educational opportunities for the nation's children (ages 1 through 7) and adults by integrating early childhood education and adult education for parents into a unified family-centered program" (Gestwicki, 1996, p. 96). At present, there are approximately eight hundred sites across the nation that serve approximately one million parents and children. Home-based programs are one of the outreach mechanisms; they promote (1) adult literacy, including basic skills, GED certificate, and workforce skills; (2) preparation of parents to support their children's education and growth; (3) helping parents understand their roles and influence in their children's education; and (4) preparation of children for school success.

National Association for the Education of Young Children (NAEYC)

The National Association for the Education of Young Children has developed standards of professional practice and serves as a guide for accrediting high-quality early childhood programs. One of the ten components used to accredit high-quality programs includes relationships among teachers and families. The rationale for parental involvement is that "young children are integrally connected to their families. Programs cannot adequately meet the needs of children unless they also recognize the importance of the child's family and develop strategies to work effectively with families. All communication between centers and families should be based on the concept that parents are and should be the principal influence in children's lives" (National Academy of Early Childhood Programs, 1998, p. 30).

There are eleven specific areas of staff–parent interaction that should be included in the accredited early childhood program's parental involvement plan:

1. Provide information to parents on the program's philosophy and operating policies and procedures.
2. Provide orientation for new children and families.
3. Maintain regular, ongoing communication with families to build trust and mutual understanding.
4. Welcome parents into the program at all times and encourage them to get involved in various ways.
5. Establish verbal and written systems to allow sharing of day-to-day happenings that may affect children.
6. Encourage joint decision making on how best to support children's development and learning.
7. Provide information to parents on program activities in a variety of ways.
8. Provide and communicate transition plans to parents to ensure smooth transition from one program to another.
9. Show acceptance of and respect for various family structures and cultural perspectives.
10. Become familiar with community services and resources and connect families with needed services and resources.
11. Establish policies and techniques on ways of negotiating difficulties and differences.

Minnesota Early Childhood Family Education (ECFE)

The Early Childhood and Family Education program was founded in Minnesota in 1974 and is the oldest state-funded effort. The development of ECFE progressed from 1974 to 1983, through a series of pilot programs that were coordinated by the Minnesota Council on Quality Education and funded by Minnesota Legislature. In 1984, the Legislature ruled that any school district with a community education program could establish an ECFE program. These programs are now funded through a combination of local levies, state aid, registration fees, and funds from other sources.

The mission of ECFE is to strengthen families and help parents create an environment that will encourage the healthy growth and development of their children. The program is available to all families with a child or children between birth and five years of age, and regardless of family structure, income, or special needs. ECFE also works with education, health, and human service agencies to connect families and children to needed services.

Classes are designed to provide learning experiences for children, interaction time for parents and children, and parent group discussion time. Classes may be offered for specific age groups or for children of mixed ages and typically run for two or 2½ hours a week throughout the school year. Field trips and special events are often scheduled outside of regular class times. Other activities and services include home visits and lending libraries of books, toys, and learning materials.

Parent-Involvement Practices

The ECFE program recognizes parents as children's first and most important teachers. An underlying premise of ECFE parent-involvement practices is that, during the early years of a child's life, parents are often most receptive to information and support. Classes and events are specifically designed for parents to participate in activities with their children. These experiences are to help parents become aware and understand their children's interests and abilities. A licensed parent educator leads parent group discussion, and his or her role is to provide information and facilitate discussion on a variety of topics related to parenting. Support and encouragement from other parents is also an important component of parent group discussion time. Individual ECFE programs are required to have an advisory council in which parents make up a majority of the membership. The advisory councils assist program staff in planning, developing, and monitoring the ECFE programs (a typical ECFE parent and child session structure is shown in Figure 9.1).

FIGURE 9.1   Typical Components in an Early Childhood Family Education Session

The typical ECFE schedule includes parent–child interaction, parenting education, and early childhood education.

Parent–child interaction includes approximately 30 to 45 minutes for children and parents to participate together in activities. The experiences are designed to help children develop and to help parents understand their children's interests and abilities.

Parenting education is planned for a time between 60 to 90 minutes to provide an opportunity for adults to discuss family concerns, such as self-esteem, sibling rivalry, and nutrition. A licensed Parent Educator guides discussions and offers current information. Support and encouragement from other parents is an important part of this component.

Early childhood education is provided for children to have learning experiences with other children while their parents are in the parent education group. A licensed Early Childhood Teacher plans and supervises activities such as painting, block and truck play, reading, and puzzles.

Reprinted with permission from the Minnesota Department of Children, Families, & Learning, St. Paul.

AVANCE

The AVANCE Family Support and Education Program is a private, nonprofit organization located in San Antonio, Texas. Gloria G. Rodrigquez established the program in 1973 with funding from the Zale Foundation to provide comprehensive, community-based, family support programs targeted for at-risk and Hispanic populations. *AVANCE* is a Spanish word meaning "to advance" or "to progress." At present, there are ten AVANCE chapters located throughout Texas, supported by a Funding Consortium consisting of the Carnegie Corporation of New York and various other foundations. In 1995–1996, over 7,000 adults and children received AVANCE services. AVANCE is open to all families with children under age four residing within the designated boundaries of each program.

The mission of AVANCE is to provide support and education services to low-income families. The program provides services that will "strengthen the family unit; enhance parenting skills, promote educational success, and foster the personal and economic success of parents" (AVANCE, 2000). AVANCE offers parent education, social support, adult education, early childhood education, youth programs, personal development, and community empowerment (AVANCE, 2000; Hyslop, 2000; Sandell, 1998).

Parent-Involvement Practices

AVANCE parent education is a nine-month center-based program in which families attend once a week for 3 one-hour segments. The classes are offered in English and Spanish, and typically the first hour focuses on toy making, followed by an hour on child development and parenting topics, and ends with information on the availability and accessibility of community resources and services. While parents are attending the parenting classes, the children participate in early childhood education. Other services include home visits that are made monthly for observing parent–child interactions, special programs for fathers, and literacy training. AVANCE established a public policy center to address policy issues that are pertinent to Hispanic children and families, encourage families and individuals to participate in the policy making process, and work on representing and supporting the voices of the families. AVANCE also operates a national training center that disseminates information to over forty states and other parts of the world. Curriculum resources are sold in fifteen states, and training for individuals has reached twenty-four states (AVANCE, 2000; Hyslop, 2000; Sandell, 1998).

Parent and Child Education (PACE)

Kentucky's Parent and Child Education program was established in 1986 and became the first government-sponsored family literacy program. Currently known as PACE for Family Independence, the program is funded through the school districts and administered by the Department for Adult Education and Literacy (DAEL) in the Workforce Development Cabinet. The program expanded from six pilot sites during 1986 to thirty-six sites in 1995 and served as a model for the federally-funded Even Start program and other state programs.

The mission of PACE is to improve the educational future for undereducated parents, and at the same time to provide quality early childhood education for their children. The rationale is based on the premise that illiteracy and academic failure tend to repeat themselves in generations to come. The eligibility requirement is that parents have not obtained a high school diploma or have high school diplomas but function at a very low literacy level, and have a child or children ages zero to eight.

Parents and children who have not yet enrolled in public schools attend classes three days a week. The program consists of four components: adult basic skill education, early childhood education, parent education and support, and regular opportunities for parent–child interaction. Other services include screening transportation, meals, and free GED testing. A typical PACE class has parents and children arriving at school in buses provided by PACE. Adult education classes consist of preparation for the GED and basic skills. The early childhood education program promotes and enhances the developmental needs of the young children and adopts the High/Scope preschool curriculum. Parent education provides parents with support groups and discussion of parenting topics that meet the needs of the families (Peyton, 1999; Sandell, 1998).

Summary

The seven models discussed in this early childhood education section represent programs that encourage active parent participation in early childhood education settings. Early childhood education supports the basic fundamental beliefs that: (1) parents are their children's first and most influential teachers at a very young age, (2) parents have valuable insights and information to share with program staff and other parents, and (3) parents and children are a family unit and cannot be seen as a separate entity, thus, creating an environment in which parents and children can interact together is one of the crucial components in parent involvement.

Family-Involvement Models
in Elementary Education

Marci Glessner

The way schools care about children is reflected in the way schools care about the children's families (Epstein, 1995, p. 701).

Educators have long known that involving parents in the education of their children can provide benefits such as higher achievement, better attitudes, and higher aspirations. Although it may be easy to research a program and to want to try to fully develop it within a school district, it is important to look at a variety of programs for family involvement. As Trevett and McMillan (1998) state, "Successful programs are not carbon copies of efforts in other cities or states; they each contain unique features that incorporate the advantages of their community and address the areas of need" (p. 9).

Therefore, when looking at various models, it is important to realize that no one model is a best fit for all schools; each has its strengths to be examined and utilized as seen fit. The following examples illustrate a continuum of models for family involvement beginning with a teacher-centered approach and moving toward whole family involvement in school decision making.

Teachers Involve Parents in Schoolwork (TIPS)

The Teachers Involve Parents in Schoolwork (TIPS) process, developed in 1987 by Joyce Epstein at Johns Hopkins University, highlights and utilizes the critical bond between teachers, parents, and students in a child's education at the elementary, middle, or high school level. With TIPS, families are encouraged to actively participate in learning activities and homework; this helps them stay informed and involved, and leads to greater success at school. Presently, TIPS activities are available for the curricular areas of language arts, science and health, and mathematics (Epstein, 1993).

The goals of TIPS include designing homework activities that increase students' academic and communication skills, helping parents understand what their children are learning in school, and enhancing the communication between parents and teachers (Epstein, Jackson, & Salinas, 1992).

One classroom teacher, an entire school, or an entire district can implement the TIPS program. As educators utilize it, they first review TIPS activities for ones that match curricular goals. If they prefer, teachers can also choose to design new interactive homework that matches their own curricula. After homework has been chosen or designed, teachers explain the TIPS process to students and their parents through discussion, letters sent home, and parent meetings. Then, on a weekly or biweekly basis, the classroom teacher assigns homework activities. The homework may take as little as ten minutes or as long as an hour to complete. After each student completes the homework assignment with a family partner or parents, the family partner then provides feedback for the teacher directly on the TIPS activity form and sends it back to school. Once the form has been returned, the teacher evaluates the student's work, as well as the comments made by the family partner, and adapts existing activities as needed (Landsverk, 1996).

TIPS is an easily managed program for classroom teachers and gives them an avenue of communication between themselves, their students, and the parents of their students. In addition to providing parents with information and knowledge about school, it gives a message to the students that both the classroom teacher and family partners care about the work they do in school.

MegaSkills

MegaSkills, a program based on uniting and strengthening the bond between home and school, has conducted programs in 4,000 schools in forty-eight states. Over 100,000 families, including African American, Hispanic, Native American, Pacific American, and at-risk families, have successfully participated in MegaSkills workshops.

Dorothy Rich (1992, p. 5), the developer of MegaSkills, believes basic values, attitudes, and behaviors play a strong role in determining a child's achievement in school; these basic tenets comprise the "megaskills" needed to become a lifetime learner. Even though these skills are reinforced in a classroom setting, their real power comes from being taught, modeled, and encouraged in the home.

To accomplish this task, MegaSkills workshops are conducted for parents and educators at individual schools or districtwide. The materials, available in Spanish as well as a number of Asian languages, are provided to the participants over the course of twelve workshops. Through their participation in these workshops, families learn new ways to support their children's education and become more involved in school activities. For example, one suggestion for helping elementary-aged children learn about teamwork is for parents along with their children to examine the newspaper for articles describing events affecting families in a foreign country. Family members then discuss the articles and develop ideas or ways to help the families in need.

Data gathered from Maupin Elementary School in Louisville, Kentucky, demonstrated that the adoption of the MegaSkills schoolwide program resulted in higher student interest in school, increased responsibility among its students, improved school climate, and increased parent involvement in school activities and attendance at parent–teacher conferences (Edge, 1996).

Center for the Improvement of Child Caring (CICC)

Since 1974, the Center for the Improvement of Child Caring (CICC), through its nonprofit community service, training, and research, has strived to support parents in gaining education, training, and support so they will be able to raise healthy, responsible, and productive young people effectively and humanely (Alvy, 1994).

To meet this goal, CICC cooperates with schools and other organizations to provide parenting programs appropriate for individual community populations. CICC trains the instructors who then work for their local schools and institutions to strengthen the home–school bond. As of 1999, CICC had trained over 5,000 instructors in forty-four states.

The wide range of parenting classes and seminars varies from special classes for parents of infants, toddlers, elementary schoolchildren, and adolescents to programs designed for specific cultural groups. For example, CICC's Effective

Black Parenting Program teaches parenting strategies and child management skills from an African American perspective.

Depending on a community's needs, CICC's programs can be taught as a fifteen-week course for small groups of parents or as a one-day seminar for larger groups. During class time, parents learn to put child management skills such as effective praise, time-out, and the point system to work in their own family situations. Parents who participate in the fifteen-week class session are then encouraged to practice the learned skills and strategies at home and receive helpful encouragement and feedback on their implementation of those strategies when they return to the next class session.

National Network of Partnership Schools

Begun in 1995, The National Network of Partnership Schools was established through Johns Hopkins University to help education leaders establish and strengthen programs of school–family–community partnerships. When the program began, there were twenty-eight initial sites across the United States. Currently, every state in the union has established a parent information resource center designed to increase family involvement in education. The U.S. Department of Education Goals 2000 Title IV Parental Assistance Program has provided funding for these programs (Epstein, 1995).

Let's use Wisconsin as an example. As a member of the National Network of Partnership Schools, Parents Plus of Wisconsin focuses on family–school–community partnerships, family resource centers, and home visits to increase family involvement in children's education. In the area of partnerships, they specifically utilize Epstein's six types of family–school–community involvement to train participants to work together to build effective partnerships. The six types of involvement are parenting, communicating, volunteering, learning at home, decision making, and collaborating with the community (Epstein, 1995). Soo-Yin Lim addressed these six types in more depth in Chapter 7.

Schools form action teams consisting of at least three parents of children in varying grade levels, three teachers in different grade levels, an administrator, community members, and, at the middle and high school levels, students. They receive training in the six types of involvement, after which they work together to determine the goals that will best meet the needs of their population. The action team is then responsible for devising partnership activities that will help them achieve these goals.

Along with training teachers, parents, and administrators in partnerships, Parents Plus of Wisconsin also utilizes family resource centers to help parents stay involved in their children's education. The resource centers provide parents with information regarding parenting and education, as well as links to other available resources within the community. For first-time parents who are interested, staff members from family resource centers also provide home visits. Although these specific services do not directly affect the school system, their benefits are noteworthy. Through a combination of direct and indirect services, over one million people in Wisconsin were served through this project (S. Werley, State Director of Parents Plus of Wisconsin, personal communication, December 12, 2001).

School Development Program (SPD)

James Comer founded the School Development Program (SDP) in 1968 at Yale University's Child Study Center to promote the development and learning of children by building supportive bonds between children, parents, and school (Comer, 1988, p. 42). Comer believes a good education should help students become responsible problem solvers who are "motivated, contributing members of a democratic society" (Comer, 2001, p. 1). To accomplish this, schools need to be a place where students feel comfortable, valued, and secure and are enabled to form positive emotional bonds with their parents and school staff. This bonding then leads to positive attitudes toward school and promotes the overall development and academic learning of students (Comer, 1993).

The SDP accomplishes this task by implementing a program based on staff collaboration and parent involvement. Although each school implements the program based on its own specific needs, each has three governance teams in place: the School Planning and Management Team, the Mental Health Team, and the Parents' Group.

Together, these three teams create comprehensive school plans that include identifying specific goals, periodic assessment and modification of these, and staff development to achieve the goals. Each team, however, is charged with a specific task.

The first team, the School Planning and Management Team, is composed of parents, teachers, administrators, and support staff. They identify target goals for social and academic programs and devise and monitor program activities. For example, some teams have designed a Discover Room where students who have lost interest in learning work to regain that interest.

The second team, the Mental Health Team, meets to discuss social and behavioral patterns within the school setting and determines solutions for recurring problems. Members of this team work with individual children who may exhibit behavior problems, but members also look at school conditions that aggravate the problems and advocate for positive changes (Comer, 1993, p. 9). Its members consist of teachers, administrators, psychologists, social workers, and nurses.

The third governance team is the Parents' Group. Their mission is to involve parents in all aspects of school, ranging from volunteering in classrooms to school governance.

From its roots in the 1960s until now, SDP has been successfully implemented in more than 250 schools in nineteen states.

Summary

Family involvement in a child's education can have lasting benefits, both academically and emotionally. Research has demonstrated that the majority of parents do want to be involved in their children's education but do not know how to help. By providing parents with a variety of opportunities through which they can become involved, schools strengthen the bond between home and school.

Family-Involvement Models in Middle Schools

J. Howard Johnston
Aimee L. Fogelman
University of South Florida

Middle schools are based on a student-centered concept. It is a team approach, and parent involvement is a logical extension of the team concept. In the past, parent involvement has dropped significantly as the children get older, and by the time they reach the middle grades, those parents who appeared in great number in first grade have dwindled to a few. These developmentally sensitive years demand the team effort of educators and parents.

There is one irrefutable truth in education: parent involvement in the schools promotes student success and achievement. This involvement is the very heart of most school reform efforts and is advocated directly by local, state, and national policy makers. Indeed, one of the national educational goals stated explicitly that "By the year 2000, all schools will promote partnerships that will increase parent involvement and participation in promoting the social, emotional and academic growth of children" (Goals 2000, 1994).

For middle school educators, however, it is widely believed that securing parent involvement is extraordinarily difficult, largely because students would prefer that their parents not exert a strong influence on their educational or social lives. Although there may be a grain of truth in that belief, the positive effect of parent involvement at the middle school level is so clear that schools and communities should work diligently to overcome impediments to parental involvement and promote significant, important parental participation in the school life of their children.

The Outcomes of Involvement

Although less research has been done at the middle level than the elementary level, the results are clear: family and parent involvement in the educational process has a profound and positive effect on students' achievement, school adjustment, and behavior. Conversely, students whose families do not collaborate with schools are likely to exhibit more behavior problems, experience achievement difficulties, and drop out of school. For those families that establish strong partnerships with the school, the benefits are obvious and enduring.

Higher Aspirations and Stronger Commitment to Life-Long Education

Students whose families are involved in school tend to express higher aspirations for their careers and educational attainment. Such students are inclined to set career goals in scientific, technical, and professional areas and to aspire to higher levels of education and training than students who see their parents as uncommitted to the school. Students with involved parents are much more likely to be motivated to continue their education beyond high school. At the middle level, students of involved parents are more likely to select advanced courses in high school and engage in more academically rigorous programs of study. These students also tend to use terms such as *learners* or *students* when asked to describe themselves and their strengths.

Avoidance of High-Risk Behaviors

Alcohol use, drug use, crime, and other antisocial behaviors decrease among adolescents as the amount of family participation in schooling increases. Students of involved parents tend to avoid high-risk and other dangerous behaviors at the same time they form relations with peers who also avoid problematic situations and behavior. When students of involved parents do encounter difficulty in school or in the community, it is likely to be a single incident rather than part of a pattern of disruptive or delinquent behavior. These encounters, if handled in a supportive way by the parents, are treated as learning experiences by the student and are unlikely to be repeated.

Increase School–Community Participation

Students with involved parents are nearly three times more likely than young people with uninvolved parents to engage in school-sponsored activities such as athletics, the arts, academics, or service clubs and projects. Because these activities tend to help the students bond more closely with the school, this type of engagement virtually ensures that students will become supportive, contributing members of the school community. Typically, students who feel connected to the school exhibit higher achievement, better social adaptability, and high levels of self-esteem.

Avoidance of School Problems

As might be expected, students with involved parents are much less likely than those with noninvolved parents to have problems in school. Students whose parents are uninvolved are twice as likely as those with involved parents to be in the bottom half of their class or repeat a grade. In fact, there is some indication that the degree of parent involvement is more significant in the school success of students than virtually any other variable, including race, social class, and native language.

Reflection...

The middle school population is composed of young adolescents. How do parents get involved, yet give the children at this age some autonomy, without embarrassing their adolescents? Given what you know about adolescent development, how do parents walk this fine line compared to parents of elementary schoolchildren?

Impediments to Family Involvement

With such compelling evidence of its positive effects, it seems that every parent would want to work diligently to become involved in his or her child's education program, and that every school would make meaningful parent participation its first priority. Unfortunately, the impediments to parent engagement are just as clear as the benefits of that involvement.

Low Involvement and Declining Involvement

As students get older, parent involvement declines dramatically. All types of parent involvement decline between the sixth and twelfth grades, by which time a relatively small number of students benefit from active parent involvement, ranging from simply inquiring about the student's schoolwork to actually helping with that work and participating in parent functions at the school.

Various studies conducted by the Search Institute, the Center for Research on the Education of Students Placed at Risk (CRESPAR), and the U.S. Department of Education report disturbingly low rates of parent involvement at the secondary level. In these studies, it was found that only 42 percent of secondary students reported that their parents helped them with their homework, 53–54 percent of parents contacted the school about their child's academic performance, 52 percent of parents attended meetings scheduled by their child's teacher, and 27 percent volunteered or served on a committee.

Because students with high participating parents tend to have fewer school problems, most parent contact with the school is among parents whose students are doing well. The parents least likely to become involved with the school are those whose children are having academic or behavioral difficulty. Thus, the students who need the strongest collaboration between home and school are often those least likely to have it.

Poor Communication between Home and School

Often, parents who are not involved in their children's education avoid contact with the school because their prior contacts have been unproductive, frustrating, or hostile. If parents believe that contacts with the school will result in their being blamed for problems, judged as inept or incompetent as parents, or confronted with demands that they simply cannot meet, they can hardly be expected to seek such contacts with any enthusiasm.

Destructive patterns can evolve in a number of ways, but typically, they begin when parents are poorly informed about ways they can help their children be successful. If the child is not successful, and the parents do not know what to do to support success, the parents feel helpless and powerless. When the school continues to convey messages about their child's problems without offering concrete ways for the parents to support the child's achievement, parents often become withdrawn, defensive, resentful, and hostile.

Different Expectations Regarding Norms and Behaviors

Often, parents and schools disagree markedly on what is best for students. In most instances, these differences arise because of beliefs, values, and norms that are held by the parents and the teachers involved. Someone who holds a different value perspective may view behavior that may be perfectly normal or acceptable to one person as inappropriate, irresponsible, or immoral. Attempts to solve problems between home and school are often thwarted by the clash of two essentially reasonable but contradictory value positions.

A common example is found when students have obligations outside school that conflict with school requirements. Many young people, particularly those from impoverished backgrounds, are expected to contribute to the family's economic resources in material ways. This might take an indirect form, such as providing child care for a younger brother or sister, or direct forms, such as contributing income from a job.

If a student arrives at school late every morning because he must provide before-school child care for younger siblings, or a student fails to complete homework because she must work after school and in the evenings, school personnel can easily interpret these actions as indictors that the parents lack interest in their child's school program or are not supportive of school achievement. The parents, on the other hand, might see the school's efforts to compel on-time attendance or punish the student for failure to complete homework as unfair and unnecessary intrusions into the family's economic life. Resolution of these kinds of conflicts is made even more difficult because each party in the disagreement sees its position, quite accurately, as reasonable and right.

Trivialization of the Parent's Role

As students progress through the curriculum, the nature of the subject matter becomes more specialized and more difficult. Parents who are able to provide academic assistance for their children throughout the elementary grades may suddenly, despite their best intentions, find themselves unprepared to help their children with their schoolwork. These conditions are particularly prevalent among parents who were not themselves successful in school, especially those who are impoverished, are limited in English proficiency, or have dropped out of school.

Even among well-educated parents, the increasing complexity of the curriculum, especially in mathematics and science, may make direct assistance impossible. For virtually all parents, skill deficiencies associated with sophisticated technology use may render them helpless to provide their children with direct assistance in fields that make heavy use of technology.

For other parents, though, especially those with few resources or little personal success with schooling, the potential for such direct assistance may be even more limited. The frustrations produced by their own difficulties with school are reinforced by their inability to help their children be successful.

Despite the best intentions, schools often reinforce this sense of powerlessness by the nature of the tasks they ask parents to perform in support of their child's education. Volunteering in the library, sponsoring fundraising events, or serving on the PTA council, although important for the overall functioning of the school, may be seen as trivial by parents because, although these activities support the school and its programs, they do little to directly support the success of a parent's individual child. Rather than volunteering for an activity that is seen as having a relatively low payoff for the success of their own children, many parents simply withdraw from school participation by the middle school years.

Conflict between Family Resources and School Requirements

Often, schools require parents to become involved in their children's educational program in ways that are beyond their personal or material resources. The parents' inability to provide such resources may result in a student failing to meet course requirements or to engage in the kind of cocurricular activity that is clearly associated with school success. Although it is patently unfair for a student to be punished with poor grades or lack of access to school, such occurrences may be quite inadvertent on the part of the school.

One common example of these conflicts may be found in project assignments. Students who come from families with sufficient resources may have access to both the money and the parental assistance that will enhance their likelihood of success. Most educators have seen professional-quality projects submitted for science fairs, social studies courses, or other academic competitions and have harbored the vague hunch that the students submitting the work received more than a reasonable amount of adult assistance in completing the assignment.

Other examples are not so obvious. Simple assignments, which assume the presence of certain resources (Internet access, books, a TV, newspapers in the home, an employed parent, transportation), may be impossible for a student to complete. If the student is embarrassed by his family circumstances, a teacher may never know what is preventing the successful completion of assigned work. All the teacher sees is a consistent pattern of noncompliance with respect to out-of-class assignments.

School Behaviors that Make Parents Feel Unwelcome

Even though schools say they encourage parents to be involved in their child's education, some of the school's actions can contradict that. Parents who attempt to become involved in the child's education, but are made to feel unwelcome are unlikely to continue communicating with the school. Unwelcoming acts on the part of the school are often inadvertent, but the messages they send are destructive to the relations between home and school.

Teachers should be aware of common practices that alienate parents. Withholding information about performance expectations is one of these practices. By not providing information about expected academic and social behaviors, a disjuncture between the home and school occurs. Schools that share expectations with parents increase the likelihood that what is being taught at home will parallel what is being taught at school, resulting in reinforcement of desirable skills and behaviors. Also, parents' schedules should be considered when planning special events and volunteer times for the classroom or school. Scheduling special events or asking parents to volunteer when they are unable to be at the school sends a strong message that the parent is not wanted there.

Reflection...

We, as educators, often hear the comment by teachers, "The parents whose children are not a problem show up for open house, parent–teacher conferences, and so forth. Why can't we get the other parents involved? We could really help them, and they could help us with their child."

A Model for Family Involvement

As with all levels of schooling, it is no longer sufficient to provide opportunities for parent participation in the education of their children or to admonish parents about its importance and their responsibility to provide it. Instead, schools must *actively support* parent participation in tangible ways. First, they must work to mediate the barriers to home–school collaboration outlined previously; then, they must take a proactive stance in helping families to become major participants in the education and school lives of middle school students.

A model proposed by Shea and Bauer (1991) for the support of special education parents can easily be adapted to support parent involvement in middle schools. The model is hierarchical, requiring that conditions at each level be satisfied before parental participation at the next level can be expected.

1. *Crisis assistance.* Among the families of middle school students, crises often arise that prevent either the parents or the student from focusing their attention on school or academic matters. For many students, divorce, substance

abuse, legal troubles, family financial difficulties, and a host of other problems make school-related problems appear trivial indeed. Although schools can often do little to resolve specific crises that exist outside of their domains of influence, they can do several things to help solve problems, or at least keep them from becoming worse.

a. *Referrals.* Often, when families confront a crisis, they are not sure what resources are available for help. Schools that support parental participation keep them well informed about the support services that are available in a community to assist families in crisis. Because family crises are often first noticed in school, or even reported to a child's teacher or counselor, it is important that everyone in the school be aware of the range of social services available and be equipped with information about contacting those services. Domestic abuse, arrests of older siblings, drug-related crime, pregnancy, forced eviction, and a host of other problems seem far removed from the purview of the school, but it is essential that school personnel be able to direct families to the available support and assistance in their community. Without the resolution of these crises, students affected by them are likely to remain unsuccessful in school.

b. *Do no harm.* The physician's Hippocratic oath stipulates that the first criterion for selecting a treatment for a patient is that it "do no harm." Schools would be well advised to follow the same policy for students in crisis. Often, school policies or practices exacerbate family crises, sometimes to the point of overwhelming a student so that he or she drops out of school. An attendance policy that punishes a student for staying home to care for a seriously ill parent or sibling, a grading policy that does not permit make-up work for a student who has been in foster care or some other emergency care facility, and a teacher who makes insensitive jokes about jails and convicts in front of students with an incarcerated parent or sibling all may be sufficient to convince a student that the school is part of the problem and needs to be avoided.

To avoid doing harm, teachers must be alert to the signals students may give that they are in distress: excessive absence, extreme fatigue, changes in mood or disposition, extreme irritability, dramatic physical changes such as sudden weight gain or loss, or evidence of abuse. Then, in a gentle and sympathetic way, teachers must be able to express their concern to the student and offer to secure help if it is needed. Although specific assistance needs to be provided by specially trained professionals in accordance with district policy and state law, initial training in sensitive observation and first-line interviewing skills should be a fundamental part of every teacher's in-service development.

Fortunately, genuine crises are rare among most students, so teachers are not often called on to confront them. Sensitivity and commitment to the success of every student, however, will help ensure that the school is seen as a helpful resource in a crisis rather than an aggravating factor.

2. *Information and resources.* For most parents, the most important form of support a school can provide is in the form of information. The nature of that information is crucial in supporting parent participation. Information should be specifically related to the child, his or her program, and his or her performance in it. General information about the school is not particularly interesting to most parents. If their child is not involved in the new physical science program, for example, they are not especially keen to receive a lot of information about it. At the same time, they are interested in the programs their child is participating in, the services that are available to him or her, and the way the child is performing in school. Many parents find traditional open houses a waste of time; the school showcases its achievements without providing specific information parents about their child's achievement.

Information shared with parents should be routine, balanced, and specific. Email and voice mail makes it easier than ever for teachers and parents to communicate. Advances in technology now permit teachers to select comments from extensive menus to produce detailed progress reports for parents; report cards can now carry extensive comments about a student's work and achievement. Informal notes can supplement routine communication to note a special achievement or a special problem the child is facing.

In each type of communication, parents should be told what they could do to help their child perform more effectively in school. A problem should not be identified without providing the parent with direction on how to correct it. Once again, the use of technology makes it possible for teachers to select from a menu of suggestions that will provide specific guidance as they promote school success at home.

3. *Supporting parent engagement.* Beyond information, it is important to help parents develop skills of effective parenting and support for their children. These skills not only help parents work more effectively to resolve the problems of adolescence, which often divert attention from school achievement, but also provide them with the support and encouragement they need to parent their children in these demanding times.

   a. *Parenting and supportive skills.* Parent training can be offered by the school not only to enhance the overall effectiveness of the parents but also to help them develop the skills that will support their children's success and achievement. This training may be general (such as effective parenting skills) or quite specific, focusing on a specific need in the school (such as helping SLD students with homework or how to start planning for high school course selection).

   The most effective parent training is provided when parents and professionals are involved in planning and delivering the training; the school can be sure it is topical, relevant, and interesting to parents. The use of parents also broadens the scope of community resources that can be used, including other community agencies or individual experts on specific topics.

   b. *Social and emotional support systems.* Parenting in modern U.S. society can be a lonely and difficult job. Many parents are single and are solely responsible for their children. Most U.S. citizens no longer live in tightly knit communities where extended family and kin provide support and assistance in raising children. All parents are coping with new influences and demands on their children that are often beyond their control.

The school can play a valuable role in providing a center for social and emotional support of parents. Schools can help parents organize support groups in which individual parents can receive help from people who share common interests and concerns. Although these groups work best when they are organized by parents themselves, the school might begin the process by inviting parents to consider forming such a group to help each other through the tumultuous times of adolescence and early adulthood.

c. *Enabling activities.* It is essential that the school not only encourage parent involvement but also remove barriers and impediments to parent participation. Scheduling meetings that respect parents' work schedules or providing phone access to teachers or counselors at predictable times enables parents to remain in touch with the school. Some districts have even run the school buses on "back to school" night to serve poor parents who do not have access to transportation. Similarly, a child-care service at the school during parent meeting times may allow parents with younger children to attend events they might otherwise have to miss. Other districts in which students are bused great distances may conduct parent conferences in the churches and community centers in the school's community, rather than trying to get parents to travel to attend school functions. In short, it is essential for schools to assess all of their practices, identify those that stand in the way of meaningful parent participation, and work to change or eliminate them. Most important, though, the school must demonstrate a genuine commitment to securing parent involvement.

4. *Securing support for school programs and operations.* When crises have been resolved, parents are well informed, and they feel supported by the school with the monumental job of raising adolescent children, then they are ready to support the school's programs and operations by volunteering their time and effort, sharing their resources, and participating in the governance of the school. Once again, schools must work carefully to provide opportunities for parent involvement and services that do not discriminate against any particular parent or group. As a beginning, parents should be surveyed to determine what their strengths are and what kinds of contributions they can make to support the school. Often, parents, particularly those who are poorly educated, are reluctant to volunteer because they are not certain what they could possibly do to enhance the school's program. However, many of them possess skills and strengths that can contribute much to the school if they were asked to do so.

Reflection...

Encouraging parents to share their talents and expertise with the school not only makes them feel like a part of the school community, but it also provides exceptional experiences to the students. What are some other ways in which parents can be included in the school?

Contextual Considerations

In planning any parent involvement program, it is very important to consider the environment and context in which the school operates. It may not be necessary to provide transportation and child care to secure parent attendance in an affluent school, but it may be necessary to plan conference dates and school activities far ahead of time to accommodate busy professional calendars. In some communities, particularly those populated heavily by recent immigrants from Third World countries or by adults with low rates of literacy, communication with the home may have to proceed through informal means: a network of parents who speak the native language of the other parents, a church, or a social group. Many schools produce and duplicate tapes and videos regarding parent involvement, ensuring that parents who are not literate in English are not excluded from meaningful school participation.

The most important consideration though is that the school understand its community, its culture, and its needs in order to provide opportunities and support for parent involvement. No single set of practices works equally well for all parents and all communities. Each school community, indeed each family, is unique, with special needs, interests, resources, and commitments. Part of a school's commitment to diversity, which has come to characterize the U.S. school system, must be a strong, explicit, and sincere commitment to supporting families and students, regardless of their economic, social, or educational circumstances.

Engaging Culturally Diverse Parents

Engaging parents can be a challenging task, one that is complicated further when working with parents from culturally diverse backgrounds. These parents face the same barriers as others, as well as some unique to their situation. In many cases a language barrier exists. Also, differences in cultural values and beliefs can be an obstacle. Parents from different cultures may have had bad experiences with schools, may feel uncomfortable in the schools, or may not believe it is their place to interfere with what they consider to be the school's job—teaching their child. In any case, involvement of these parents is important to the success of the student. Furthermore, they can be an invaluable resource for the school.

When initiating contact with culturally diverse parents the teacher must be sensitive and respectful of their customs, values, and beliefs. Though every individual in a cultural group differs, cultural styles should be considered when communicating with families from different backgrounds. Depending on the culture, the amount of personal space one is comfortable with varies. Typically Americans feel comfortable with three feet of space between themselves and another person. Hispanics, however, tend to stand closer during conversations. Physical contact is another consideration. In some cultures hugging when greeting is customary. In others, such as Asian cultures, one should not shake hands with members of the opposite sex when meeting. Eye contact is another concern. Making direct eye contact may be seen differently in various cultures. In some it is a sign of interest or admiration. In others it shows disrespect and even aggression. A final consideration is the ordering of business. Though in American it is customary to "get down to business," in other countries socializing before and during the discussion of serious matters is common.

Learning about the parents' cultural norms is only the first step in engaging culturally diverse parents in school. Other things can also be done to help them feel comfortable in the school, such as having bilingual staff in the reception areas of the school, offering to meet them at their home or at a neutral location, making sure that any written correspondence is in their native language, basing communication on the needs and interests of the parent, and encouraging the parent to share talents with the school community.

Parents from culturally diverse backgrounds bring with them rich experiences that can benefit all of the school's children. In one school, a group of parents with limited English proficiency might work with a teacher after school to provide Spanish language tutorials for students studying that language. The parents benefit from interaction with English-speaking students, and the school benefits from a rich instructional resource. In another setting, recent immigrants might stage a cultural festival that raises money for the school's library, while teaching children about the art, music, food, and customs of their country. Not only will the child of parents who come from diverse cultural backgrounds benefit from involvement of their parent in school but also if the teacher can tap into the vast array of experiences these parents bring with them, the whole school can benefit.

Reflection...

Parents from culturally diverse backgrounds bring with them the unique ability to open doors to other cultures by sharing their customs and traditions. What are some other ways in which your school can involve these parents?

The Model in Operation

The model outlined above looks quite different in each school setting. However, in a successful parent-involvement program, it is essential that each component of the model be in place for the community served by that school. The following example shows how one middle-level school, located on the suburban fringe of a large city, supports significant parent involvement.

Lee Junior High School serves eleven hundred students in grades 7 through 9. Located in an older suburb near a large midwestern city, Lee's student population reflects the diversity of its community. Nearly a third of its students are African American, 20 percent are Hispanic, 40 percent Caucasian, and 10 percent Asian and Pacific Islander. Virtually all of its Hispanic and Asian and Pacific Islander students are recent refugees and immigrants from Central America and Southeast Asia. Just under a third of the students qualify for free or reduced-price lunch. ESOL programs are provided for approximately 15 percent of the students. Lee provides a comprehensive parent-involvement program designed to accommodate the needs of diverse groups in the community and to support student achievement.

Crisis Assistance

Parent volunteers staff Lee's Assistance Line, which has a directory of community services available for virtually any kind of family difficulty. The line's volunteers, parents and retirees from the surrounding area, are trained to make referrals but not to engage in counseling or other direct assistance. For times when the assistance line is not covered, a recording device allows parents to leave questions, which can be answered when a volunteer is present. The line is not used in the case of emergencies.

In addition, Lee's staff and faculty are provided with directories and contact numbers of social service agencies, clinics, shelters, and a variety of other community resources, which can guide them if a parent seeks help during a conference or phone call. Under the laws of the state in which Lee is located, teachers are protected from liability in making such recommendations, and they are required by law to report suspected child abuse to a specific governmental authority for investigations.

Lee's faculty has also conducted a family impact assessment of the policies and practices in their school, particularly those affecting attendance and grading. They attempted to identify those practices that might have a substantially negative impact on families who are coping with other difficulties, and have either modified those polices and practices or developed procedures whereby a student can be granted relief from punitive policies while involved in a family crisis. Faculty have also been trained by the counselors to conduct interviews of students who appear to be experiencing some form of stress or difficulty. Normally, these students are referred to a counselor for additional consultation and assistance.

Information

Lee's information plan is comprehensive, systematic, and responsive to changing conditions in a student's performance or program. It is designed to share important information and provide opportunities for parents to contact teachers and administrators who work with their children.

Each year, an orientation packet is sent to each parent in the school. It includes a schoolyear calendar, which lists meetings, significant dates, and tips to parents for remaining engaged in the education of their children. This packet includes a description of school policies, rules, and expectations. It also contains course descriptions; information about the school's support services, such as counseling and special education; and its cocurricular and arts programs. Every significant parent meeting is listed for the entire year, as are special training sessions, parent support and social groups, and special booster activities, such as band parents or math club parents. The calendar is a comprehensive planning resource for parents and includes significant dates for each grade level. For example, eighth grade parents are advised that the grade level dance is from 6:00–9:00 P.M.; ninth grade parents are informed about "moving-up" ceremonies. In this way, information is not distributed haphazardly throughout the year, nor does the school depend on students to keep parents informed of special school events.

Also in the orientation packet, parents will find a printout of their child's schedule and the name of each of his or her teachers. In addition, the teacher's planning period and the school's phone number is listed so that parents know when it is best to contact them. Each teacher also posts "phone conference appointment hours" in the school office so parents can schedule calls at times other than the planning period.

Progress reports are very detailed, with the aid of a computer program designed specifically for the task. Teachers can select from hundreds of descriptive comments in all areas of student performance, behavior, or social adjustment. After selecting a descriptive comment, they are given another menu of recommended actions for parents to take to correct a problem or support a student's strength. Progress reports end with an invitation to contact the teachers with questions and a reminder about the teacher's conference hours and phone number. Report cards also provide for extensive comments, and both report cards and midterm progress reports are kept in a cumulative computer file so that parents and teachers can review student progress at any time.

Parent conferences are held twice each year, early in the fall and in the middle of the spring semester. They are scheduled between 3:00 and 9:00 P.M. so that working parents may attend. At the beginning of each year, every teacher is provided with a printout of computer labels for each student, bearing their parents' names and home address. This allows teachers to write informal notes to parents quickly and easily without having to look up an address.

Recently, Lee has begun experimenting with technologically enhanced communication, including a computerized bulletin board, which may be accessed through one of the popular online computer services. Information about the school, its programs, calendar events, and services is available twenty-four hours a day to parents or students who need it for planning or decision making. Lee has also begun producing a weekly show called "Focus on Lee," which is aired over the community's cable TV public access channels. This show replaces much of the "show and tell" about the school that is normally conducted at open houses. Community groups may borrow videos for home viewing. All of Lee's publications are available in Spanish and Vietnamese, translated by parent volunteers, and special editions of its videos are translated into each language as well. Anticipating an upgrade of its phone system, Lee is also planning to provide voice mail boxes for each of its teachers, which will allow them to leave or receive messages from parents and students without going through the school's cumbersome switchboard.

Supporting Parent Involvement and Securing Assistance for the School

Lee seeks to provide opportunities for all forms of parent involvement. To that end, its parent council has provided a large array of opportunities and services for parents.

In addition to a host of specialized booster groups, which support everything from band to basketball to the computer club, the school invites parent participation in its Educational Foundation, an independently chartered, nonprofit organization devoted to supporting the school through fundraising and sponsorship of specific activities. The Foundation provides specialized equipment for the computer and video facilities, offers minigrants to teachers to encourage innovation and advanced training, and provides financial support for students who may not be able to afford specific school activities, such as the purchase of a yearbook or the expense of a class trip.

The parent council also organized orientation meetings for parents of incoming seventh graders, parent-training sessions, support groups, and numerous other opportunities based on a needs assessment conducted by the group. Every parent in the school is asked to volunteer ten hours of service per year, although some are not able to do any and some do much more. These volunteer resources are used to support telephone trees to disseminate information about upcoming meetings, translation services, and a variety of other activities. For all school-sponsored activities, parents organize a ride share program for parents who lack transportation, and the student council provides child care at the schoolsite for parents who are unable to find or afford child care.

The school also indirectly supports parents by providing academic support for students whose families may not be able to do so. An after-school homework club is available for all students, staffed by parent volunteers, teachers, and students who use it as an opportunity to fulfill a community service requirement for graduation. In addition, the after-school latchkey program, sponsored in conjunction with a local community agency, is operated in the school building. This program offers tutorial assistance, service opportunities, and educational programs in technology, sports, and the arts.

What Advice Can We Give Parents?

It is not uncommon for teenagers to experience difficulty in school at some point in their academic careers. Though some students make it through these periods with little or no help from their parents or teachers, others need intervention. When teachers contact parents about problems their children are having, it is imperative that they not only explain specific concerns they have, but that they also give specific suggestions about how they can help.

The first step is to identify students who are at risk for failure. Students with a history of poor performance in school, trouble focusing, consistently low grades, a high number of absences, or a lack of self-confidence are considered at risk. Other signals of at-risk students include disruptive behaviors or withdrawal from school or classroom activities. Most commonly students transitioning from one school to another and girls from linguistically or culturally diverse backgrounds exhibit these signs.

Providing concrete suggestions to parents about how they can help their children is the most effective way a teacher can be of assistance. The first suggestion a teacher should make is that parents set clear boundaries and expectations for their children's behavior and performance. This is one of the most important ways an at-risk child can be supported. After clear expectations are in place, parents should encourage their teens to talk about their fears or concerns, and the parent should listen and try to understand them. Making school a priority in the home by encouraging good study habits and hard work can also be effective. For teens struggling academically, finding tutoring services may help improve the school performance. Also, parents should encourage their teens to participate in community groups, after-school programs, or other organizations. Encouraging their teens to volunteer is another option a parent should be offered. Helping teens to find an interesting place to volunteer not only gives them a chance to aid others, it also gives them experience in a work environment, which can translate into future career interests.

In conclusion, by studying carefully the needs of its community, mobilizing committed parents who are willing to serve in leadership capacities, and creating both opportunities for and the expectation of parent participation, Lee has established a comprehensive, effective parent-engagement program. Most important, it is a dynamic program; it changes constantly to adjust to new needs and opportunities in the community. Such a comprehensive program obviously requires the attention, commitment, and support of school personnel, but by creating a school culture that nurtures parent involvement, the school is able to provide high quality service to parents and students without additional money—just a deeply committed human resource.

> **Reflection...**
>
> Lee Junior High School offers a comprehensive program that encourages parent involvement on all levels. How would you modify this program to make it successful in the school setting in which you teach?

Summary

The models of parent involvement for special educators, early childhood, elementary, and middle school are just that—models. In schools today, there are variations on this and other models, as well as teachers, parents, administrators, students and other community members trying to get families involved in schools in a variety of ways. The ultimate reason, obviously, is that students do better in school when their parents and families are involved.

RECOMMENDED ACTIVITIES

1. We know there are more models or examples of programs that involve parents and families in school. Identify two other models or examples currently being used in your state or region.

2. Identify schools or programs that are using any of the models presented in this chapter. Have teachers or administrators that are using those models come into the class to discuss the model presented and how it is being specifically used.

3. Develop your own models of what you think a successful parent- and family-involvement program should look like in the schools.

4. Write to the organizations that have developed the various models to obtain detailed information about how the models work.

5. Discuss family system theory. Is the theory identified in other parts of this book? What is it and how do psychiatrists or psychologists use it?

ADDITIONAL RESOURCES

Organizations:

AVANCE-Hasbro National Family Resource Center
Suite 310, 301 South Frio
San Antonio, TX 78207
Phone: 210-270-4630
Fax: 210-270-4612
www.avance.org

Center on Families, Schools and Children's Learning
Johns Hopkins University
3505 N. Charles Street
Baltimore, MD 21218
Phone: 410-332-4575
www.csos.jhu.edu/p2000/center.htm

ECFE
Early Childhood Family Education
Minnesota Department of Education
992 Capitol Square Building
550 Cedar Street
Saint Paul, MN 55101
Phone: 612-296-6130
Fax: 612-297-5695
www.educ.state.mn.us/ecfi

Family Literacy Branch Department for Adult Education and Literacy
Third Floor, Capital Plaza Tower
550 Mero Street
Frankfort, KY 40601
Phone: 502-564-5114
Fax: 502-564-5436
www.adulted.state.ky.us

Head Start
National Head Start Association
1651 Prince Street
Alexandria, VA 22314
Phone: 703-739-0875
Fax: 703-739-0878
www.nhsa.org

Head Start Bureau
330 C Street, SW
Washington, DC 20447
Phone: 202-205-8572
www2.acf.dhhs.gov/programs/hsb

Home and School Institute
MegaSkills Center
1500 Massachusetts Avenue, NW
Washington, DC 20009
Phone: 202-466-3633
www.megaskillshsi.org/default.htm

Homeschooler Information Network
www.homeschooler.com

Homeschool World
www.home-school.com

Minnesota Early Learning Design
219 N. 2nd St., Suite 200
Minneapolis, MN 55401
Phone: 612-332-7563
Fax: 612-344-1959
Email: info@meld.org
www.meld.org

Middle School Partnership
www.middleschool.com

National Association for the Education of Young Children
1509 16th St. NW
Washington, DC 20019
Phone: 800-424-2460
www.naeyc.org

National Middle School Association
2600 Corporate Exchange Drive, Suite 370
Columbus, OH 43231
Phone: 614-895-4730
www.nmsa.org

National PTA
www.pta.org

Parents as Teachers National Center, Inc.
10176 Corporate Square Drive
Saint Louis, MN 63146
Phone: 314-432-4330
Fax: 314-432-8963
www.patnc.org

The Search Institute
Suite 210, 700 South Third Street
Minneapolis, MN 55415
Phone: 612-376-8955
www.search-institute.org

Title 1/Even Start
National Even Start Association
2225 Camino del Rio South, Suite A
San Diego, CA 92108
Phone: 800-977-3731
www.evenstart.org

REFERENCES

Alvy, K. T. (1994). *Parent training today: A social necessity.* Studio City, CA: Center for the Improvement of Child Caring.

AVANCE. (2000). *AVANCE.* Retrieved November 10, 2001, from www.avance.org

Bailey, D. B., Buysse, V., Edmondson, R., & Smith, T. (1992). Creating family centered services in early intervention: Perceptions of professionals in four states. *Exceptional Children, 58*(4), 298–309.

Bailey, D. B., McWilliam, P. J., & Winton P. J. (1992). Building family-centered practices in early intervention: A team-based model for change. *Infants and Young Children, 5,* 73–82.

Bailey, D. B., Simeonsson, R. J., Winton, P. J., Huntington, G. S., Comfort, N., & Isbell, P. (1986). Family-focused intervention: A functional model for planning, implementing and evaluating individual family services in early intervention. *Journal of the Division for Early Childhood, 10,* 156–171.

Balaban, N. (1985). *Starting school: From separation to independence.* New York: Teachers College Press.

Bruder, M., & Dunst, C. (2001). Expanding learning opportunities for infants and toddlers in natural environments: A chance to reconceptualize early intervention. *Zero to Three,* pp. 34–36.

Comer, J. P. (1988). Educating poor minority children. *Scientific American, 259*(5), 42–48.

Comer, J. P. (1993). *James P. Comer, M.D., on the school development program: Making a difference for children* (ERIC Document Reproduction Service No. ED 358 959). New York: Columbia University, National Center for Restructuring Education, Schools, and Teaching.

Comer, J. P. (2001). Schools that develop children. *The American Prospect, 12.* Retrieved April 30, 2001, from www. prospect.org/print/v12/7/comer-j.html

Dunst, C. J. (1985). Revisiting, rethinking early intervention. *Analysis and Intervention in Developmental Disabilities, 5,* 165–201.

Dunst, C. (2000). Revisit, rethinking early intervention. *Topics in early childhood special education, 20*(2), 95–104.

Dunst, C. J., Trivette, C. M., & Deal, A. G. (1988). *Enabling and empowering families: Principles and guidelines for practice.* Cambridge, MN: Brookline.

Edge, D. (1996). *Maupin MegaSkills school-wide program: Final evaluation report [and] executive summary* (ERIC Document Reproduction Service No. ED 396 846). Louisville, KY: University of Louisville, School of Education.

Epstein, J. L. (1993). School and family partnerships. *Instructor, 103*(2), 73–76.

Epstein, J. L. (1995). School/family/community partnerships: Caring for the children we share. *Phi Delta Kappan, 76*(9), 701–712.

Epstein, J. L., Jackson, V. E., & Salinas, K. C. (1992). *The TIPS manual for teachers: Language arts and science/health interactive homework in the middle grades.* Baltimore: Center on Families, Communities, Schools, and Children's Learning, Johns Hopkins University.

Featherstone, H. (1980). *A difference in the family: Living with a disabled child.* New York: Penguin.

Fialka, J. (1994). You can make a difference in our lives. *Early-On Michigan, 3*(4), 6–11.

Gestwicki, C. (1996). *Home, school, and community relations.* Albany, NY: Delmar.

Giangreco, M. F., Cloninger, C. J., & Iverson, V. S. (1993). *Choosing options and accommodations for children: A guide to planning inclusive education.* Baltimore: Paul Brookes.

Gilkerson, L. (1994). Supporting parents in leadership roles. *Zero to Three, 14*(4), 23–24.

Goals 2000: Educate America Act, The. (1994, April 11). *Washington Social Legislation Bulletin, 33,* 31.

Head Start Bureau, U.S. Department of Health and Human Services, Administration for Children and Families. (2001). *Head Start policy manual.* Washington, DC: Author.

Hyslop, N. (2000). *Hispanic parental involvement in home literacy* (ERIC Document Reproduction Service ED No. 446340). Indianapolis, IN: Clearinghouse on Reading, English, and Communication.

Jerald, J. (2000). *Early head start.* Retrieved November 10, 2001 from www.headstartinfo.org/publications/hsbulletin69

King, S. (1994). *Telling your family story: Parents as presenters.* Madison: Wisconsin Personnel Development Project, Waisman Center, University of Wisconsin–Madison.

Landsverk, R. A. (1996, Fall). *Families, communities, schools learning together* (ERIC Document Reproduction Service No. ED 408 029). Madison: Families in Education Program, Wisconsin Department of Public Instruction.

McBride, S. L., Sharp, L., Hains, A. H., & Whitehead, A. (1995). Parents as co-instructors in preservice training: A pathway to family-centered practice. *Journal of Early Intervention, 19*(4), 343–355.

Miller, S. (1985). *Report to the Ford Foundation.* New York: Ford Foundation.

Minuchin, S. (1974). *Families and family therapy.* Cambridge, MA: Harvard University Press.

National Academy of Early Childhood Programs. (1998). *Accreditation criteria and procedures of the National Academy of Early Childhood Programs.* Washington, DC: Author.

Peyton, T. (1999). State family literacy legislation: Kentucky. *Family literacy legislation and initiatives in eleven states.* Retrieved November 28, 2001 from www.famlit.org/policy/states.html

Rich, D. (1992). *MegaSkills: In school and in life—The best gift you can give your child.* Boston: Houghton Mifflin.

Sandell, E. (1998). Family involvement models in early childhood education. In M. Fuller & G. Olsen (Eds.), *Home–school relations* (pp. 177–184). Boston: Allyn & Bacon.

Shea, T. M., & Bauer, A. M. (1991). *Parents and teachers of children with disabilities* (2nd ed.). Boston: Allyn & Bacon.

Slentz, K. L., & Bricker, D. B. (1992). Family-guided assessment for IFSP development: Jumping off the family assessment bandwagon. *Journal of Early Intervention, 16,* 11–19.

State of Kentucky. (1995). *PACE: Parent and child education handbook.* Frankfort: State of Kentucky, Department for Adult Education and Literacy.

Stayton, V., & Miller, P. (1993). Personnel competence. In *DEC recommended practices: Indicators of quality in programs for infants and young children with special needs and their families.* Reston, VA: Council for Exceptional Children.

Trevett, S., & Mcmillan, J. H. (1998). *Enhancing parental involvement in urban schools: Types of programs, characteristics of successful programs, and proven strategies* (ERIC Document Reproduction Service No. ED 443 923). Richmond, VA: Metropolitan Educational Research Consortium.

Turnbull, A. (1999). From parent education to partnership education: A call for a transformed focus. *Topics in Early Special Education, 19*(3), 164–171.

Turnbull, A. P., & Summers J. A. (1985). *From parent involvement to family support: Evolution to revolution.* Paper presented at the Down Syndrome State-of-the-Art Conference, Boston, MA.

Turnbull, A. P., & Turnbull, H. R. (2001). *Families, professionals, and exceptionality: A special partnership.* (4th ed.). Columbus, OH: Merrill.

Turnbull, R., Turnbull, A., Shank, S., & Leal, D. (2001). *Exceptional lives: Special education in today's schools* (3rd ed.). Upper Saddle River, NJ: Merrill Prentice Hall.

Whitehead, A., & Sontag, J. (1993). *Co-instruction: A case study.* Madison: Wisconsin Personnel Development Project, Waisman Center, University of Wisconsin-Madison.

Zigler, E., & Freedman, J. (1987). Head Start: A pioneer of family support. In S. L. Kagan, D. R. Powell, B. Weissbourd, & E. F. Ziegler (Eds.), *America's family support programs: Perspectives and prospects* (pp. 57–76). New Haven, CT: Yale University Press.

10 Education Law and Parental Rights

GLORIA JEAN THOMAS

Idaho State University

In this chapter, the author will present information on the legal rights and responsibilities of parents and schools. The author will describe the history of the legislation between the home and the school. Court cases will be cited as they relate to issues such as curriculum, special education, students' rights, harassment, and liability.

After reading the chapter, the student should be able to:

- Discuss the history of the legal relationship between parents and schools
- Identify the origins of local taxes for schools, compulsory attendance laws, academic standards for schools, and state credentials for teachers
- Understand how the issue of religion has been a constant source of tension between parents and schools
- Recognize the significance of sexual harassment lawsuits in the K–12 school system today
- Comprehend the significance of *Brown* v. *Board of Education of Topeka, Kansas* (1954) in relation to school and parents, then and now
- Distinguish between school rights and student rights
- Understand the effect Title IX has had on extracurricular issues

Parents have always been a child's first teachers. Only in recent history have governments assumed responsibility for much of a child's formal education. Even when schools are organized, parents retain their rights to influence and guide a child's upbringing. This chapter discusses the legal rights and responsibilities of parents and schools in today's litigious society. The history of the legal relationship between parents and schools will first be explained, followed by a discussion of the legal role of the states in the education of their citizens. Court cases will be used to demonstrate the role of the federal and state courts in resolving disputes between parents and schools. Issues to be discussed include compulsory attendance, vaccinations, the curriculum, religious exercises, school fees, special education, student rights, liability, and discrimination.

History of the Legal Relationship between Parents and Schools

In 1642 the colonial legislature of Massachusetts Bay became concerned that parents were so busy eking out survival in the harsh New World that they were shirking their responsibilities to educate their children. Children who were not taught to read the Bible were sure to fall prey to "ye olde deluder Satan." Therefore, the legislature passed a statute charging all parents to see to the education of their children. In 1647 the legislature required towns of fifty households to appoint a teacher and towns of one hundred households to build a school. Taxes could be levied to support these schools, which were not only to ensure that children could read the scriptures but to facilitate a literate society for the good of the colony. Thus, these laws became the first compulsory education laws, the first school funding laws, and the first official recognition of a legal relationship between schools and parents.

However, the legal rights of parents for the education of their children predate any written law. From the beginning of time, parents have been a child's first teachers, assuming responsibility for instructing the child in survival skills and tribal or community mores to enable society to exist and perpetuate. Because the right of parents to guide the upbringing and education of their children is recognized as natural and inherent, that right is regarded as fundamental for citizens of the United States.

Fundamental rights are those rights that citizens of this country take for granted because they have always existed in a free society. Other fundamental rights include the right to marry whomever one chooses (or not to marry), the right to have children (or not to have children), and the right to choose one's job, career, or profession. These rights are not written down in any federal or state constitution or statute. Yet, they are protected as if written into the U.S. Constitution, the supreme law of the land. Therefore, the right of parents to guide the upbringing and education of their children is a protected right.

The legal status of children as minors means that children under the age of majority (age 18 for most purposes in the United States) are not expected to have adult judgment to determine what is best for their own welfare. Because minors are not considered capable under the law of exercising responsibility for their own decisions, laws prohibit them from signing binding contracts, from buying harmful substances (such as alcohol and tobacco products), and from being held to the criminal and civil codes of law as adults. Children are under the protection of their parents, who are charged with ensuring the safety and welfare, including the education, of their minor children.

Because parents have the ultimate legal authority for the education of children, the role of schools is *in loco parentis* (in place of the parent). The concept of *in loco parentis* dates back to old English law that allowed schoolmasters to have power over pupil conduct. However, the schoolmaster had only that portion of parental powers necessary for the conduct of the school. Parents could never give up all authority over their child because of the "natural relation of parent and child…the tenderness which the parent feels for his offspring, an affection ever on the alert, and acting rather by instinct than reasoning" (*Lander* v. *Seaver*, 1859).

Therefore, when children go to school, the school as an entity and teachers as individuals are *in loco parentis* to those children. School personnel are responsible for the safety, welfare, and education of the child in place of the parents. However, parents do not abdicate their ultimate authority over the upbringing of their children simply because they comply with state compulsory attendance laws by sending their children to school.

The issue becomes one of finding the balance between the school's right and responsibility, delegated to it by the state, to prepare children to be knowledgeable, productive citizens of a democratic society and the parents' right and responsibility, inherent because of their being parents, to guide the upbringing of their children. All legal issues involving parents and schools are based on the tension between these two sets of rights and responsibilities.

> ### Reflection...
>
> Should the rights of parents or the rights of schools weigh more heavily when a dispute reaches the courts? What else needs to be considered?

State Constitutions and Education

Education is not mentioned in the U.S. Constitution, perhaps by conscious design but more probably because the writers of the Constitution had themselves been educated in private schools, by tutors, and by self learning. The idea of public schools, even though in existence since the Massachusetts Bay Colony time, had not become universally accepted. In the late 1700s, a few pauper schools existed for the children of the poor, orphans, and other wards of the colonies, but education was generally a private concern of parents.

However, interpretation of the Tenth Amendment gradually resulted in education becoming the responsibility of the states. The Reserved Powers Clause of the Tenth Amendment meant that education would come under the authority of the states:

> The powers not delegated to the United States by the Constitution, nor prohibited by it to the States, are reserved to the States respectively, or to the people.

Over time, the states recognized the importance of education for all children if the experiment in democracy was to succeed. Colonial legislatures wrote education into their state constitutions. Later, territorial legislatures were required to include provisions for education in their constitutions prior to applying for statehood. Most territorial authorities followed the lead of older states, resulting in the education clauses in many state constitutions being worded very similarly. The North Dakota Constitution, written in 1889, is similar to that of many states admitted to the Union after the Civil War. Article VIII, with variations, could be found in the constitutions of many states:

> Section 1. A high degree of intelligence, patriotism, integrity and morality on the part of every voter in a government by the people being necessary in order to insure the continuance of that government and the prosperity and happiness of the

people, the legislative assembly shall make provision for the establishment and maintenance of a system of public schools which shall be open to all children of the state of North Dakota and free from sectarian control. This legislative requirement shall be irrevocable without the consent of the United States and the people of North Dakota.

Section 2. The legislative assembly shall provide for a uniform system of free public schools throughout the state, beginning with the primary and extending through all grades up to and including schools of higher education, except that the legislative assembly may authorize tuition, fees and service charges to assist in the financing of public schools of higher education.

After writing lofty ideals into their constitutions, most states did not get involved in the local control of schools for many years. Frontier villages were so isolated that parents were the only teachers, fundraisers, architects, builders, administrators, and evaluators for tiny, one-room schoolhouses. As communities grew and state governments became more organized and stable, the role of the states, as defined in state constitutions, became important.

Reflection...

What does your state constitution include about education?

State Legislatures and Education

From the days of the Massachusetts Bay Colony, state legislatures assumed limited responsibility for the schools. As populations of cities grew, the problems of low educational standards, inadequate curricula, minimal training for teachers, inconsistent school funding, and lack of school governance structure became apparent. Relying on state constitutions that indicated state responsibility for schools, state legislatures slowly became involved in schools.

In the 1800s, reformers such as Horace Mann and Charles Barnard took their causes to state legislatures and encouraged laws to be passed to improve the physical facilities of schools, to mandate compulsory attendance of children, to require local tax support for schools, to require state credentialing of teachers, and to establish minimal academic standards for schools. Other state legislatures followed the lead of Massachusetts, Connecticut, and other progressive states of the nineteenth century.

As the nation's population grew, school districts were formed with school boards elected from the citizenry of the district in accordance with state laws. School board members were officers of the state, charged with implementing state statutes in the local schools. As schools became more complex, state legislatures became more involved in the day-to-day operation of the schools, passing laws regulating teacher qualifications, the curriculum, teacher evaluation, high school graduation requirements, the school calendar, extracurricular activities, school consolidation, bond elections, personnel records, student records, disciplinary procedures, fees, bus service, textbooks, vaccinations, religious exercises, and testing. To enforce the myriad of laws being passed, many state departments of education evolved from advisory to regulatory bodies and assumed responsibility for enforcement of state statutes.

As education became accepted as one of the primary responsibilities of the state, responsibility for the funding of schools shifted from the local community to the state. Prior to this shift, the funding for schools had depended on the goodwill of local tax assessors and city councils because the school tax was usually a tax on local property.

As the twenty-first century begins, state responsibility for schools is an accepted fact. As that responsibility for the funding of schools shifted from the local community to the state, the control of decision making for the schools also shifted from the local community to the state education agencies. The result has been a loss of control and sense of responsibility for schools at the local level for all persons involved in the school, but especially parents. Where once they hired, evaluated, and fired the teachers; chose the textbooks and the curriculum; held box lunch auctions, passed the hat at school concerts, and donated land to finance equipment, supplies, books, furniture, and teacher's salary; and designed and built the school building, parents now pay state taxes and are asked to adhere to their elected state legislators' decisions about their schools. The legal distance between parents and schools has increased as the state has exercised its legal authority over the educational system.

> **Reflection...**
>
> Why are school boards comprised of lay persons, not professional educators?

State and Federal Courts and Education

Although most disputes between parents and the schools never go beyond discussions before the local school board, the courts have long been involved when disputes cannot be resolved easily. Because education is a state responsibility, most disputes arise over state laws or policies passed by school boards acting as agents of the state. Therefore, the majority of court cases involving schools are brought in state courts. Only when the dispute involves the federal Constitution or a federal law can a case be heard in federal court. Involvement of the federal courts to any great extent arose in the 1950s with the conflicts over desegregation of the schools.

When a dispute arises between parents and the schools, generally the courts are asked to balance the fundamental rights of the parents to guide the upbringing of their children against the delegated rights of the school to educate productive citizens for the democratic state. Figure 10.1 illustrates the historic role of the courts in weighing the rights of one party (the parents) against the rights of the other party (the school).

The question of whose rights weigh more heavily, those of the parent or those of the state, has been the subject of court cases that have been appealed all the way to the U.S. Supreme Court. This fundamental right of parents to guide the upbringing of their children was the core issue of a case brought before the U.S. Supreme Court in 1925. In *Pierce* v. *Society of Sisters* (1925), an Oregon law requiring all parents to send their children between the ages of eight and sixteen years to only public schools was challenged successfully. This Supreme Court decision allowed parents the right to send their children to parochial or other types of private schools.

> [W]e think it entirely plain that the Act of 1922 unreasonably interferes with the liberty of parents and guardians to direct the upbringing and education of children under their control.... The child is not the mere creature of the state; those who nurture him and direct his destiny have the right, coupled with the high duty, to recognize and prepare him for additional obligations. (*Pierce* v. *Society of Sisters*, 1925)

In resolving disputes between parents and the school, the courts almost always must interpret state laws or school board policies. Fundamental rights of parents will weigh very heavily in these cases, but reasonable laws and policies of the school will be upheld if parents' fundamental rights are not in jeopardy.

Court Involvement to 1954

Very few cases against the schools were brought by parents before the 1950s, for several reasons. Before World War II, local communities were still in control of their schools, with parents feeling that they knew the school personnel and the activities going on at the school. People did not leave their small towns, and the

Rights of School   Rights of Parents

FIGURE 10.1

teachers, administrators, and board members were their next door neighbors. The curriculum had not changed drastically since parents had been in school. Radio brought the world closer to the hometown, but national and international news was of places that had little to do with the local community. Therefore, parents rarely used the courts to make changes in their local schools.

The federal courts were seldom involved in the schools prior to the desegregation cases of the 1950s. Therefore, court cases prior to the 1950s were almost all heard in state courts because usually state laws or school board policies were the subject of disputes. Prior to 1954, the courts heard a few cases dealing with issues such as vaccinations and religion.

In spite of the fundamental rights of parents to guide the upbringing of their children, parental requests are not always honored by the courts. When parental desires or requests endanger the health, safety, or welfare of their child or others, the courts rule against the rights of parents. In an era before medical science stopped deadly diseases from causing epidemics in communities, schools were often closed when smallpox, tuberculosis, diphtheria, influenza, and other contagious diseases struck. When vaccinations were developed against some of these diseases, schools often required students to be immunized before they were allowed to go to school. However, some parents were against vaccinations, often citing religious reasons. The school's right to require vaccinations has been upheld (see *Viemeister* v. *White,* 1904), and the parent's right to circumvent compulsory attendance laws by not complying with vaccination requirements has been denied (see *People* v. *Ekerold,* 1914). In later cases, the court ruled against parents even when smallpox and diphtheria were on a decline, stating, "A local board of education need not await an epidemic, or even a single sickness or death, before it decides to protect the public. To hold otherwise would be to destroy prevention as a means of combating the spread of disease" (*Board of Education of Mountain Lakes* v. *Maas,* 1959). Changes in medical sciences beginning in the 1950s would ease the terror brought by formerly fatal diseases and result in the courts amending earlier decisions relating to vaccinations.

When disputes about the school curriculum involve religion, the federal courts have long been involved because these disputes always center on the First Amendment of the U.S. Constitution. Questions related to the relationship between church and state, as defined by the First Amendment, can be brought before the federal courts. The key religion clauses of the First Amendment are the Establishment and Free Exercise Clauses:

> Congress shall make no law respecting an establishment of religion, or prohibiting the free exercise thereof.

In 1943 the Supreme Court handed down the first of its many controversial decisions dealing with religious exercises in the schools. A West Virginia school board had adopted a resolution ordering that the salute to the flag become a regular part of the curriculum of the schools. The children of parents who were Jehovah's Witnesses refused to participate because the flag salute is against the tenets of their religion. Jehovah's Witnesses literally interpret the second of the Ten Commandments from the Bible:

> Thou shalt not make unto thee any graven image, or any likeness of anything that is in heaven above or that is in the earth beneath, or that is in the water under the earth; thou shalt not bow down thyself to them nor serve them. (Exodus 20:4–5)

The parents brought suit in U.S. District Court, asking for an injunction to stop enforcement of the policy. In ruling for the parents, the U.S. Supreme Court noted that "the refusal of these persons to participate in the ceremony does not interfere with or deny rights of others to do so" (*West Virginia State Board of Education* v. *Barnette*, 1943).

The flag salute case was brought in the patriotic heat of World War II, and the conclusion of that war brought a cry for a return to values of the past. Attempts were made by many parents and religious organizations to bring religious instruction into the schools. In Illinois, parents and clergy of Jewish, Roman Catholic, and a few Protestant faiths formed an association and obtained permission from the school board to offer religious instruction in school. The classes were voluntary in that parents signed cards requesting that their children be permitted to attend the religion classes. However, those students who did not enroll had no other class option but merely were sent to another room to study. Parents and others who believed that bringing in rabbis, priests, and ministers to teach religion classes was a violation of the Establishment Clause brought suit. The U.S. Supreme Court agreed that these classes fell "squarely under the ban of the First Amendment" (*McCollum* v. *Board of Education*, 1948).

However, in 1952, the Supreme Court upheld a released time program in which students were released by their parents from school to attend religion classes held at nearby churches. The court ruled that schools may accommodate religion because there is "no constitutional requirement which makes it necessary for government to be hostile to religion" (*Zorach* v. *Clauson*, 1952). Thus, the stage was set for the battle over the separation of church and state to be waged in the public schools.

These early cases all set precedents for the many cases that would soon follow as society became more complex. With the end of World War II, the nation grew rapidly, not only in numbers but in diversity and complexity. Immigrants were no longer from primarily Judeo-Christian, European countries, and they brought their own cultural and religious beliefs, plus memories of traumatic experiences during the war. Farming became mechanized, forcing small farmers out of business and requiring fewer farmers' children to remain on the farm. Immigrants, farmers, and others looking for a better life flooded the cities, multiplying urban problems for the first time. People became mobile, not staying in one place long enough to know their neighbors. Communication systems improved, and people became aware of changes and trends in other states and cities across the country. Compulsory attendance laws began to be enforced by the states, and parents realized that the only way their children could get jobs and improve their lives was by staying in school through high school. The United States took center stage in world affairs, and the schools were pressured to revise and expand the curriculum to ensure that the nation was the best in everything from military armaments to space travel to industrial output. The casual, informal, neighborly relationship between parents and the schools changed to a formal, legal relationship because of the changing world.

Reflection...

What changes did the end of World War II bring to your community, including the schools?

Court Involvement after 1954

The year 1954 is often used as the watershed year for school law and the relationship of parents and schools. In the 1950s the National Association for the Advancement of Colored People (NAACP), along with many other organizations and individuals, began a campaign to end segregation of the schools on the grounds that separation of the races forever branded minority people as second class citizens. In Topeka, Kansas, the case of Linda Brown and several other black children who were forced by Kansas state law to attend all-black schools provided an appropriate test case. With Thurgood Marshall as the attorney for the plaintiffs, *Brown* v. *Board of Education of Topeka, Kansas* (1954) became the most important school law case ever brought before the courts. Declaring that the doctrine of "separate but equal" has no place in the field of public education, the U.S. Supreme Court changed forever the relationship between the schools and the federal government and, hence, the relationship between parents and the schools. The *Brown* case officially desegregated the schools, but it also brought the federal court system into the schools to a degree never before known. Because of continual resistance to desegregation, the federal courts took on the role of overseers of some school districts, imposing mandates on hiring of teachers and administrators, enrollment systems, district boundaries, busing, and school board elections. The 9–0 vote of the Supreme Court in *Brown* signaled to the nation that the time had come for society to change, for the civil rights of all people to be recognized and protected, and for the schools to provide an education for all children. That decision also indicated that the courts would be used to enforce mandated changes when society refused to make the changes voluntarily.

Reflection...

Why is *Brown* v. *Board of Education* often considered by many to be the most important school law case ever heard by the U.S. Supreme Court? Did the case have any effect on your local school district?

Parents were often the ones reluctant to accept court mandates for change. The images of adults screaming at black children walking to school under the protection of federal marshals have been imprinted on the national conscience. As one group's rights came to the forefront in the media, other minority groups began seeking their children's rights. Individual rights became important to persons who had previously given little or no thought to their fundamental or constitutional rights. As society became more complex, as awareness of rights grew, as disenchantment with the public schools increased, and as local communities lost control of their schools, parents turned to the courts to resolve their problems and to reclaim their right to guide the upbringing of their children. Educators became threatened when parents wanted to become more involved in the schools than school personnel desired, and an adversarial relationship developed. Controversies led to court cases dealing with compulsory attendance, school fees, the curriculum, special education, student rights, liability, and discrimination and harassment. All of these issues raise questions that are still debated by school personnel and parents today.

Compulsory Attendance.   Although some southern states attempted to circumvent desegregation orders by repealing their compulsory attendance laws, all states had such laws in place by the 1970s and started enforcing the laws even for groups that had previously been exempt. In Wisconsin, the Amish had traditionally allowed their children to attend public schools through only the eighth grade. Fearing a threat to their lifestyle and their religion if their children were exposed to worldly values, several Amish parents did not enroll their children in high school and were convicted of violating the state compulsory attendance law. The U.S. Supreme Court in *Wisconsin* v. *Yoder* (1972) once again upheld the fundamental right of parents to guide the upbringing of their children:

> Thus, a State's interest in universal education, however highly we rank it, is not totally free from a balancing process when it impinges on fundamental rights and interests, such as those specifically protected by the Free Exercise Clause of the First Amendment, and the traditional interest of parents with respect to the religious upbringing of their children.... The primary role of the parents in the upbringing of their children is now established beyond debate as an enduring American tradition. (*Wisconsin* v. *Yoder,* 1972)

The U.S. Supreme Court carefully stated that the *Yoder* decision applied only to the Amish or other religious groups with a similar history. However, many other religious sects, private schools, and home schools have used the rationale in the *Yoder* decision as a basis for challenging compulsory attendance laws.

Compulsory attendance laws continue to be challenged by parents who do not wish to comply with vaccination rules. Although many contagious diseases have been eradicated or at least controlled in the United States, the courts still uphold reasonable requirements for vaccinations for smallpox, tuberculosis, and other diseases. When the argument is forwarded that vaccinations are against the parents' religion, the courts often respond with statements such as the following made by the Arkansas Supreme Court:

> Anyone has the right to worship God in the manner of his own choice, but it does not mean that he can engage in religious practices inconsistent with the peace, safety and health of the inhabitants of the State, and it does not mean that parents, on religious grounds, have the right to deny their children an education.... A person's right to exhibit religious freedom ceases where it overlaps and transgresses the rights of others. (*Cude* v. *Arkansas*, 1964)

As new contagious diseases proliferate (AIDS and Ebola), previously controlled diseases emerge with new deadly strains (hepatitis, meningitis, and tuberculosis), the threat of and biological terrorism looms, debates over vaccination (if available), quarantine, and school attendance by stricken children will arise as parents feel their children's lives are threatened. Although many persons in this nation may have felt at one time that deadly diseases would soon no longer threaten lives in the United States, the courts are likely going to be asked to continue to weigh the rights of parents to exercise their personal and religious beliefs about disease and vaccination against the right of schools to protect the health and welfare of all children and personnel.

As HIV and other sexually transmitted diseases become rampant among students, the issue of sex education in the curriculum remains a topic of debate. Until the 1970s, some teachers handled topics related to human sexuality in health classes, but when those topics were labeled "sex education," many parents became concerned about the content of such courses. They claimed that their rights to guide the upbringing of their children certainly included the right to teach them about sex and intimacy according to family or religious values. However, sex education was purported to be a solution to the explosion in number of teen pregnancies. Recognizing the susceptibility of the teenage population to the still fatal effects of HIV and the harmful, disfiguring effects of other sexually transmitted diseases, some schools argue that sex education must be compulsory because all students are at risk and parents may not have the knowledge to teach their children about the new dangers that accompany sexual behavior. The courts are divided in their rulings about sex education courses, upholding those that include an excusal system (see *Medeiros* v. *Kiyosaki*, 1970; *Smith* v. *Ricci*, 1982) as well as those that mandate the course for all students (see *Cornwell* v. *State Board of Education*, 1969).

As parents become disillusioned about public schools, more challenges to compulsory education laws may be anticipated. Private schools, including parochial, for-profit, charter, and home schooling, will be established, some adhering to state guidelines for licensure and some claiming that such guidelines merely perpetuate the problems the new schools are attempting to combat. Some parts of the curriculum will continue to be challenged by parents who want more control over what their children are being taught at school. When parents feel that the schools are failing in their responsibility to prepare students for productive lives, then parents will challenge the validity of compulsory attendance laws. Teachers will have to deal with parents who question the purpose of schools and at least some parts of the curriculum. The courts will continue to be faced with the task of balancing the rights of parents to guide the upbringing of their children and the right of states to require school attendance. School personnel will want to ensure that district policies about controversial topics such as home schooling, vaccinations, and sex education are in place prior to questions arising about compulsory attendance laws. Teachers and administrators will need to be prepared to defend the role of public schools in society and how the curriculum will aid in preparing a child for the future.

Reflection...

Should children be compelled to attend school? Why? What types of schools exist in your community?

School Fees.   Public school education in the United States has always been free, that is, no tuition is charged when a student enrolls in the school. However, the charging of fees has a long history, dating back to when every student took a turn bringing a bucket of coal for the pot-bellied stove. In today's more sophisticated world, fees are charged for everything from the school yearbook to towels for physical education classes to anticipated breakage in laboratory classes to participation in extracurricular activities to textbook rental. When a state constitution guarantees a free, public education for every child in the state but then fees are assessed, some parents have challenged the legality of such fees. Courts are then faced with having to interpret what the state constitution writers meant when they included the word *free* in the description of public schools.

A North Dakota school district's authority to charge rental fees for textbooks was challenged by a group of parents in 1978. The state supreme court ruled in favor of the parents:

> The term "free public schools" without any other modification must necessarily mean and include those items which are essential to education. It is difficult to envision a meaningful educational system without textbooks. No education of any value is possible without school books. (*Cardiff* v. *Bismarck Public School District*, 1978)

However, other state courts have ruled that "free" applies only to the lack of tuition and that charging for essentials like textbooks is legally tenable.

Other fees have been challenged in other states. In California, for example, the charging of fees for extracurricular activities was ruled unconstitutional under their state law that requires the Legislature to "provide for a system of common schools by which a free school shall be kept up and supported in each district" (*Hartzell* v. *Connell*, 1984). Extracurricular activities were shown to be a vital part of public schooling in California, and fees were not allowed. The outcome in some of these states has been by the elimination of extracurricular programs because of lack of funding.

Court challenges by parents against school fees will likely continue as the resources of school districts diminish, costs of educating students increase, and parents are called upon to bear more of the cost of their children's "free" education. Teachers will have to be careful not to waste any of the district's resources or expect parents to provide too many expensive items, such as elaborate treats, costumes, or supplies, to replace what the school was once expected to provide. School administrators may want to consider including parents as members of committees that develop fee levels and structures and that determine which academic and extracurricular activities and programs may have to be dropped in the face of rising costs.

Reflection...

With three children in middle school, Kathy and Robbie are faced with having to pay substantial school fees. Amy and Fred want to play basketball, and Amy wants to play soccer and volleyball as well as audition for the school play. The school charges a fee for each extracurricular activity plus towel fees for each sport and for the required physical education classes. In addition, there are fees for a card to get admitted to school activities (games, plays, concerts, etc.), for the school newspaper, for the yearbook, for having one's picture taken for the yearbook, and for class expendables (workbooks, paper, etc.). Kathy and Robbie do not see how they can afford the fees; yet, they understand the value of their children participating in and attending school activities.

- What legal questions should Kathy and Robbie ask?
- What does your state constitution, statures, and case law precedent say about school fees?
- What questions should they ask of the school district? Of their building principal?

Curriculum.   The curriculum has long been considered the prerogative of professional educators, and those who challenge the curriculum have been considered troublemakers. Yet, parents have a right to know what their children are learning and should have a voice in determining the curriculum. Too often, school personnel forget that parents can be the best allies of the school in assisting children to learn. The curriculum is becoming too complex and too fragmented for parents to be left out of the teaching–learning process. Today's parents have a difficult time cooperating with schools in guiding the upbringing of their children if they have no idea what the schools are teaching their children.

Challenges to the curriculum are made for many reasons but are usually settled at the local school board level. The majority of those cases that reach the courts are brought on the basis of religious arguments. These cases are often brought by parents who believe that the schools are fostering secular humanism (usually defined as a belief in the supremacy of man instead of supernatural beings) instead of a belief in God or teaching values antithetical to family values. On the other hand, our national history as a haven for persons of all religious creeds has led to an increasing number of diverse religious backgrounds and beliefs being represented in the schools. The school has been called the battleground for the struggle to define the separation of church and state. The conflict becomes especially difficult when the two religion clauses of the First Amendment become pitted against each other, as so often happens when the school claims that allowing a religious practice to occur on school property would be a violation of the Establishment Clause but parents claim that not allowing that religious practice to occur on school property would be a violation of the Free Exercise Clause.

In 1963 the U.S. Supreme Court unleashed a furor when it ruled in *Abington School District* v. *Schemmp* that vocal prayers in school violate the Establishment Clause of the First Amendment. Many accused the Supreme Court of being atheist when the ruling went in favor of arguments made by the "professed atheist," Madeline Murray, on behalf of her son in the companion case, *Murray* v. *Curlett* (1963). Church–state cases comprise the school-related issue on which the U.S. Supreme Court has made the second greatest number of rulings (the first being desegregation).

In 1985 a Mobile, Alabama, attorney, Jaffree, sued the state of Alabama (represented in the title of the court case by its governor, George Wallace) in an attempt to get two state statutes declared unconstitutional on grounds of violation of the Establishment Clause. One state statute authorized a one-minute period of silence for meditation or voluntary prayer, and the second authorized teachers to lead "willing students in a prescribed prayer to Almighty God...the Creator and Supreme Judge of the world." The federal district court ruled that the two statutes were constitutional because "Alabama has the power to establish a state religion if it chooses to do so." However, the U.S. Court of Appeals, Eleventh Circuit, held the two statutes to be unconstitutional, and the U.S. Supreme Court agreed, stating that "the individual freedom of conscience protected by the First Amendment embraces the right to select any religious faith or none at all" (*Wallace* v. *Jaffree*, 1985).

Thus, vocal prayers in the classroom as well as moments of silence for the specified purpose of prayer have been ruled unconstitutional. The focus then turned to prayers and other religious exercises at school-related activities. In the early 1990s, the issue of prayer at public school graduation ceremonies arose when Daniel Weisman went to court to get a permanent injunction to prevent prayers at his daughter Deborah's middle-school graduation. The court did not act quickly enough to stop the school from inviting a rabbi to offer a prayer that was in accordance with the guidelines in a school pamphlet. Eventually, the U.S. Supreme Court in *Lee* v. *Weisman* (1991) ruled that clergy-led prayers at public school graduation ceremonies do violate the Establishment Clause of the First Amendment even though attendance at graduation is voluntary and even though the prayers are short and nonsectarian.

Religion will continue to be a divisive issue for the schools. Prayers before athletic contests or graduation, students reading the Bible, students or teachers wearing religious jewelry, students depicting religious topics in artwork, and school music or drama programs at Christmas with a religious focus have all been challenged in lower courts. In 2000, the U.S. Supreme Court rule in *Good News Club* v. *Milford Central School* that allowing religious organizations to meet on school grounds was not a violation of the Establishment Clause nor did it interfere with a parent's right to guide a child's upbringing. As our nation becomes more diverse, the number of challenges to the curriculum and extracurricular activities based on religious arguments will increase.

> ### Reflection...
>
> Your school has always had a Christmas concert with choruses, orchestras, and bands performing a variety of songs of the season, including some traditional Christmas carols. A Muslim family has recently moved in and has requested that no Christian music be performed in the school. One of the children is in the orchestra. What is your response? Other families join the dispute, citing tradition and community values as reasons to continue the concert. How will you handle this issue?

Another first amendment issue that has involved parents, schools, and the courts is book censorship. The Free Speech clause of the First Amendment of the U.S. Constitution generally rules against any type of book banning. In the 1980s, the number of challenges to textbooks and curriculum materials increased rapidly as several organizations began sponsoring conferences about and publishing lists of books that the organizers claimed should not be found in schools. A New York school board took action to remove several of these books from the school library, and a group of students, parents, and teachers went to court, claiming censorship. Asserting that "the State may not, consistent with the spirit of the First Amendment, contract the spectrum of available knowledge," the U.S. Supreme Court in *Board of Education, Island Trees Union Free School District* v. *Pico* (1982) settled the question about school library books. Once books are on the shelf, they may not be removed.

Two well-publicized cases related to textbook censorship were heard in 1987 by the circuit courts of appeal. A Tennessee case involved several parents who argued that the Holt, Rinehart and Winston reading series contained stories that violated the religious beliefs of the parents. Because the reading series was required of all students, the parents claimed that their Free Exercise rights and those of their children were being violated. In an Alabama case, parents wanted forty-four textbooks banned because of their secular humanism teachings. In both cases, the parents prevailed at the federal district court level. However, the U.S. Courts of Appeal, Sixth and Eleventh Circuits, overturned the lower court decisions. The Sixth Circuit Court decision noted that the parents "testified that reading the Holt series 'could' or 'might' lead the students to come to conclusions that were contrary to teachings of their and their parents' religious beliefs. This is not sufficient to establish an unconstitutional burden..." (*Mozert* v. *Hawkins County Board of Education*, 1987). The Eleventh Circuit Court stated the following:

> There simply is nothing in this record to indicate that omission of certain facts regarding religion from these textbooks of itself constituted an advancement of secular humanism or an active hostility towards theistic religion prohibited by the establishment clause. (*Smith* v. *Board of School Commissioners of Mobile County*, 1987)

School personnel must have policies in place to deal with requests for banning books. Every year school boards, teachers, administrators, and librarians face a community organization that wants such books as *Huckleberry Finn, Lord of the Flies,* or the Harry Potter series banned. Anticipating these requests and having policies in place will often defuse an emotional outburst.

Reflection...

What are your school policies for handling requests to remove a book from a reading list, a course curriculum, or a library?

Parents are going to continue to challenge the school curriculum. Instead of such challenges becoming a threat to the autonomy of the schools or the academic freedom of the teachers, parents should be welcomed as part of the curriculum development and textbook selection processes, especially as members of textbook selection and curriculum improvement and evaluation committees. Their suggestions and criticisms should be taken seriously, but school administrators must ensure that representatives of all segments of the community are heard, not just the loudest, most organized, or most articulate. Parental input must be balanced against the professional expertise of teachers and administrators. Schools should have a coherent curriculum revision process to ensure that all textbooks, activities, and instructional methods are meeting educational objectives. Teachers must be sure that their textbooks, supplemental materials, lessons, and activities are based on sound educational principles and are meeting district and state educational objectives and standards. Processes for handling challenges to textbooks, methods, and materials should be developed and followed. Reasonable exceptions should be allowed, but policies defining exceptions to the standard required curriculum should be established before the first request is made. Welcoming parents as partners in the teaching–learning process, even in the building of the curriculum, may encourage parents to view the schools as their allies in guiding the upbringing of their children.

Reflection...

Kenneth and Grace are becoming concerned about how African Americans are portrayed in the literature taught in their children's English classes. They know *Huckleberry Finn* and *Gone with the Wind* are required reading, but students are not required to read anything that portrays African Americans in anything other than slave roles, nor are they required to read anything written by African American authors. They do not want any books removed from the curriculum, but they would like to request that books such as the *Autobiography of Malcolm X* and *I Know Why the Caged Bird Sings* be added to the required reading.

- What legal questions should Kenneth and Grace ask?

- What does your state law and case precedent state about textbook selection?
- What questions should Kenneth and Grace ask of the school district? Of the English teachers?
- Who selects textbooks and makes curriculum decisions in your school district?

Special Education.   When the writers of state constitutions provided for systems of public schools that were to be open to all children, they did not consider children with disabilities. Most children with disabilities were not in public schools at the time state constitutions were written, and few persons would have thought that they ever would be. The history of most states in regard to the education of children with various mental and physical disabilities is shameful. Either the children were excluded from any type of education at all or were in settings where they received few, if any, educational benefits. Many states felt they had met the needs of children with disabilities by providing residential state schools for the deaf, blind, and "trainable," and quasi-hospital settings for those with severe or multiple mental and physical disabilities.

By the early 1970s, advocacy groups for veterans and other handicapped persons organized their efforts to secure the civil rights of a formerly silent minority group—the disabled. The result was legislation at the federal level that banned discrimination on the basis of disability (the Rehabilitation Act of 1973) and that provided funding for schools which provided an individualized, free, appropriate public education in the least restrictive environment for children with disabilities (the Education for All Handicapped Children Act of 1975 or PL 94-142). Changed to the Individuals with Disabilities Education Act (IDEA) in 1991, this latter special education law impacted the rights of parents in relation to the schools as no previous legislation, at either the state or national level, had done. Because children with disabilities are the least able to serve as their own advocates, the rights of parents as advocates for the rights of their children are safeguarded in this law. In fact, parents are required to be involved in their child's education as they must be active members of the child's Individual Education Plan (IEP) team. The IEP team is the group that determines the special education and related services the child will receive during the school year.

IDEA is a very complex law, but major parental rights which are defined in the law and which impact the relationship between parents and the school include the following:

- The right to be informed of parental rights under IDEA
- The right to be informed in the parents' native language or other appropriate means
- The right to be informed prior to assessment being done if placement in special education may be the outcome of the assessment
- The right to be informed of outside evaluators and no- or low-cost legal services

- The right to be involved in determining educational goals, services, and placement through membership on the IEP team
- The right to be informed prior to any change in placement or services
- The right to see the child's records
- The right to initiate a due process hearing
- The right to receive a transcript of the hearing and the decision
- The right to appeal through the court system

Although the major laws governing special education at the national level have been in effect for a relatively short time, much case law has resulted from them. In fact, special education has become the subject of the most school-related litigation in state courts. The number of children who qualify for special education is increasing each year as medical science improves the survival rate of at-risk babies and accident victims, as assessment measures become more sophisticated and better able to identify children with special needs earlier, and as more physical and mental conditions are categorized as qualifying for some type of special education service. Advocacy groups for children with disabilities are very strong, and both parents and school personnel need to become more aware of the legal rights of these once forgotten children and work together to facilitate their special education. Otherwise, lawsuits will proliferate.

Reflection...

Can all children be educated? Should all children be educated at public expense?

The first special education case that reached the U.S. Supreme Court involved a hearing-impaired child whose parents wanted the school to provide a full-time sign language interpreter in the classroom. Noting that "this very case demonstrates [that] parents and guardians will not lack ardor in seeking to ensure that handicapped children receive all of the benefits to which they are entitled by the Act," the Supreme Court, nevertheless, ruled against the parents in *Board of Education of Hendrick Hudson Central School District Board of Education* v. *Rowley* (1982) because of the efforts the school had made to assist Amy Rowley to benefit from her education. The court said that a school district does not have to "maximize the potential of each handicapped child commensurate with the opportunity provided nonhandicapped children." Amy was advancing at grade level academically and socially, and even the sign language interpreter testified that her services were superfluous.

In 1984 the U.S. Supreme Court was asked to determine the definition of "*related services*" as provided in the law. Amber Tatro needed clean intermittent catheterization every three or four hours, which the school argued was a medical service that should not be required of school personnel. The parents argued that the service was merely a procedure that would enable Amber to benefit from special education and could be performed by a layperson with minimal training. In ruling in favor of the parents in *Irving Independent School District* v. *Tatro* (1984), the Supreme Court impacted the relationship between parents and the school by requiring the school to provide services once provided only by parents or nurses.

Placement of students with disabilities is probably the most controversial topic dividing parents and the schools. Unfortunately, IDEA has never been fully funded by Congress, leaving the states and local districts with much of the cost of compliance. When parents and school personnel disagree over the services or placement of a child with a disability, the issue almost always involves the cost. The parents are interested in getting the best services possible for their child, and the school personnel are interested in containing costs. The result is a growing number of special education lawsuits.

In 1989 a New Hampshire school district attempted to get the courts to rule that some children with very severe disabilities could not benefit from any type of education and so would be excluded from coverage by the law. Timothy W. was multiply and profoundly mentally and physically disabled, but the U.S. Court of Appeals, First Circuit, ruled that a child does not have to demonstrate the ability to benefit from education in order to qualify for services, no matter how minimal:

> The law explicitly recognizes that education for the severely handicapped is to be broadly defined, to include not only traditional academic skills, but also basic functional life skills, and that educational methodologies in these areas are not static, but are constantly evolving and improving. It is the school district's responsibility to avail itself of these new approaches in providing an education program geared to each child's individual needs. The only question for the school district to determine, in conjunction with the child's parents, is what constitutes an appropriate individualized education program (IEP) for the handicapped child. We emphasize that the phrase "appropriate individual education program" cannot be interpreted, as the school district has done, to mean "no educational program." (*Timothy W.* v. *Rochester, New Hampshire School District*, 1989)

The *Timothy W.* decision meant that all children with disabilities are to be served by special education, no matter how severe their disabilities. The U.S. Supreme Court merely confirmed this decision without comment, and so it is used as precedent for lower court cases.

Another case that involved the cost of placement was *Florence County School District Four* v. *Carter* (1993). This case resulted from a dispute between a school district and parents over services for a child with learning disabilities. Frustrated by the school district's lack of attention to their requests, the parents removed their daughter Shannon from the public school and placed her in a private school that specialized in services for children with learning disabilities. After Shannon completed her schooling, the parents sued the school district for reimbursement of the tuition charged by the private school. Ruling in favor of the parents, the U.S. Supreme Court commented on the cost argument of the school district:

> There is no doubt that Congress has imposed a significant financial burden on States and school districts that participate in IDEA. Yet public educational authorities who

want to avoid reimbursing parents for the private education of a disabled child can do one of two things: give the child a free appropriate public education in a public setting, or place the child in an appropriate private setting of the State's choice. This is IDEA's mandate, and school officials who conform to it need not worry about reimbursement claims. (*Florence County School District Four* v. *Carter*, 1993)

Attempting to stay abreast of case law plus the continually changing regulations in Section 504 of the Rehabilitation Act, the Individuals with Disabilities Education Act, and the Americans with Disabilities Act will be a challenge for parents of children with disabilities and the schools that must provide special education and related services. All teachers, not just special education teachers, will have an opportunity to work with children with various disabilities. Teachers must learn about special needs and how to meet them through classroom and curriculum modifications. Because of the involvement of parents in the education of their children with disabilities, many parents are becoming more involved in the education of all children, sometimes to a degree not known by the schools previously. Some parents question why every child's education cannot be individualized and why more services are not available for all children. For school personnel, the increased interest of parents in their children's education can be an opportunity to set a tone of cooperation and partnership in striving to meet the needs of all children. Parents can become the greatest advocates for the schools if they know the schools are working to assist their child in gaining an education. Then the adversarial relationship between parents and the schools will not exist, and costly, time-consuming lawsuits can be avoided.

Reflection...

Joyce has been notified that her daughter, Beth, is going to be assessed for a possible learning disability. Joyce is to sign a card, indicating her approval for the tests, and return it to the school. Because she had no idea that Beth was having any difficulty in school, Joyce is upset and does not want to sign the card.

- What legal questions should Joyce ask? What are her rights as a parent?
- What does your state law and federal law say about assessment and parents' rights?
- What questions should Joyce ask of the school district? Of the classroom teacher or the special education teacher?

Student Rights.   With all the emphasis on special education, sometimes the rights of students in general seem to take second place. Actually, the rights of students with disabilities were recognized only because of the *Brown* (1954) case, which led to the conclusion that all children had a right to an equal education, and because of an historic student rights case in 1969. In *Tinker* v. *Des Moines Independent Community School District* (1969), the United States Supreme Court declared that "it can hardly be argued that...students...shed their constitutional rights to freedom of speech or expression at the schoolhouse gate." Thus, the constitutional rights of students were legally recognized for the first time, and the relationship between the school and parents and their students subtly changed. Although *in loco parentis* still governs that relationship, *Tinker* and successive court decisions determined that students have a legal right to an education. That right cannot be denied without due process. When that right to an education is in jeopardy, parents become involved in working with the school's disciplinary procedures and sometimes taking their child's case to court. In most court cases involving student rights, whether the issue is expulsion of a student because of fighting or a student being sent home to change a T-shirt with a vulgar message, the parents are the plaintiffs in the lawsuits because of the legal status of almost all students as minors.

The question often arises of "what process is due" when a student claims his or her rights have been violated. Unless school officials know about due process, often a student's claim will prevail because the school official will back off in fear of violating a student's rights. Then the rights of other students and school personnel to an orderly, educational atmosphere may be jeopardized. Generally, as long as rules allow a student to tell his or her side of the story, are fairly and consistently enforced, and provide for fair and consistent sanctions, due process is satisfied. Students and teachers must know what the rules are. The role of student handbooks in due process is to serve as notice to students and parents of the rules and the applicable punishments. The more serious the infraction, the more serious the sanction should be.

More student rights cases are going to court for resolution because of the awareness of individual rights by students and their parents and because many school personnel are not sure of the status of student claims to rights. When school personnel fail to follow due process as outlined in the student handbook or, worse, fail to have a process established, a student's rights may be jeopardized and the courts may be willing to hear the student's case. Generally, the courts do not desire to become involved in the disciplinary procedures of the schools; they prefer leaving those decisions to the educational experts. However, when a student's constitutional rights are violated, the courts will step in.

Reflection...

In light of school violence, including the use of weapons, what rights do school personnel have? What constitutes a weapon? Is it the same for the kindergarten as the high school? What rights do victims of violence in the schools have?

One of the areas of student and parent rights that has a long history of violation prior to the passage of a federal law is student records. Before the Family Education Rights and Privacy Act (FERPA) was passed in 1974, school records policies were generally nonexistent. Parents had little or no access to student records; yet, third parties (college recruiters, military recruiters, police officers) had only to make a request, and a student's file was made available. Few processes were in place to ensure accuracy of records, and the result was blatant violation of the privacy of a student and often the family. FERPA specifies that only parents and educators (who have a need to know) should have access to a student's educational file. That file should contain only official transcripts and other official school documents, not anecdotal notes. The parents have the right to question the information in the file and to write responses to what they perceive as inaccurate data. Requests to see files, to get copies, and to get test scores interpreted do not have to be met on demand; the school cannot be expected to produce records, especially archival records, without notice. Only parents can give permission for third parties to see a student's records. Schools cannot keep secondary or secret files that are used for any decision making about the student's education. Teachers should be aware of records policies and follow them, realizing that parents have rights to see the records of their child but not those of other children. Only one official educational file should exist for each student; a teacher's personal notes are not official records so do not have to be shown to parents. However, those notes should not be used for informing decisions about the child nor kept in any permanent file. The school can facilitate good relations with parents by informing them of their rights under FERPA, having good records policies in place, and following them.

To encourage good relations between parents and the school should be the goal of all teachers and administrators. Parents who feel comfortable coming to the school, calling teachers, or visiting with administrators over school-related issues will be less likely to take their child's side without checking the school's side of the story. Communication channels with parents should be open so that parents know of the school rules and expectations; then they will be less likely to argue when the child breaks the rules. Students and their parents have constitutional rights that cannot be arbitrarily or capriciously violated by the schools, as may have happened in the days prior to *Tinker*. Teachers must be prepared to know the rules, enforce the rules fairly and consistently, and follow the due process outlined in handbooks. Focusing on the student's education and the partnership with parents that can enhance that education may preclude legal resolution to problems that may arise over a student's claim to individual rights.

Liability.   This is a litigious age in the United States, and tort law is where much of the litigation is occurring. When a suit is brought under tort law, the plaintiff is looking for monetary awards for damages. Anyone can sue anybody for almost anything under tort law. Schools in states that no longer have the policy of governmental immunity (governmental immunity means one cannot sue the government) can be held liable for injuries to anyone in the school or at school-related activities if the injuries are shown to have been caused by intent to injure or negligence. More and more people are willing to sue government entities such as schools because they believe that nobody is really being hurt by a damage award. However, the cost of litigation is very high, regardless of the outcome. Time spent preparing for the case, emotional energy expended on attempting to settle the issue amicably, and actual money damages or increase in insurance premiums are some of the indirect and direct costs associated with every lawsuit filed against a school. School personnel must take all reasonable precautions to prevent students, employees, and guests from being injured while at school, recognizing that lawsuits claiming negligence are all too frequent.

Parents believe that their children will be safe at school and are becoming more willing to sue for damages when a child is injured. Yet, most injuries are the result of accidents, not willful, malicious, or negligent actions by teachers or administrators. Schools are held to a very high standard of care for students, and when that standard of care is breached, the courts will award damages. Every teacher and administrator must remember that the standard of behavior the courts will use is the ordinary, reasonable, prudent person standard but adapted to allow for the professional training and experience of educators. If a teacher does not do what the ordinary, reasonable, prudent teacher would have done when in the same situation and a student is injured, negligence may have been the cause of the injury and the teacher and school district may be found liable for damages. Similarly, if a teacher or administrator knew or should have known about a potential injury causing event, structure, or person, and an injury occurs, claims of negligence may be upheld. Threats made by students against the safety of others or themselves must be taken seriously and actions must be taken to deter injury. Such threats cannot be ignored, passed off as "kids wanting attention," or "kids just joking or playing around" if liability for injury is to be avoided. Injuries will happen at school, but parents should be immediately informed and every reasonable action taken to care for the child. Guidelines for all school activities should include provisions for preventing injuries and procedures to follow should injuries occur. All educators should know and follow such guidelines in order to prevent claims of negligence or intent to injure.

In the legal relationship between parents and the school, liability can become an issue when parents are in the school as visitors, but a related issue is the parent who is working in the school or at school-related activities as a volunteer or paraprofessional. Teachers and staff are generally covered by liability policies of the school when they are acting in the course of their employment. However, insurance policies may or may not cover persons acting under the supervision of an employee, and school personnel should check their district liability policies before asking parents to drive students to activities, to chaperon field trips or other off-campus activities, to supervise classroom activities such as reading groups or art projects, to work as volunteer coaches, to supervise playgrounds or lunchrooms, or to perform any of the dozens of tasks which many parents welcome as opportunities to become involved in their child's school. Everything goes smoothly when parents are involved in the school's activities until either the parent or a student under the parent's supervision is injured. Then lawsuits may arise if malice, intent, or negligence can be shown.

Teachers and administrators cannot delegate their responsibility, which means that if a child or the parent is injured when the teacher or administrator is the person in the supervisory role, the ultimate responsibility for the injury will rest with the employee, not with the volunteer. Therefore, it becomes critical for teachers and administrators to train parent volunteers adequately for their roles, whatever they may be. The professional teaching certificate indicates that the teacher or administrator is experienced in the supervision of large numbers of children and should be able to foretell what types of behavior may occur. The parent volunteer may have no such experience in the school setting and cannot be held liable for being unable to foretell that an action may lead to an injury. Schools should develop guidelines for the use of parent volunteers and follow the guidelines in the selection, training, and supervision of such volunteers. There is some irony in the fact that just at a time when the schools need all the help they can get and want to encourage involvement of parents in the schools, the threat of litigation might deter involving parents. The standard to use always is to do what the reasonable, prudent teacher or administrator would do in similar circumstances.

Reflection...

Susan has begun volunteering at her daughter Jenny's school one afternoon per week. She helps with reading groups, assists the classroom teacher with supervising the playground during afternoon recess, and tutors individual children with spelling, writing, and reading. During one afternoon recess, the classroom teacher was called to the office for an emergency phone call, leaving Susan as the only adult on the playground. The teacher had been gone only a couple of minutes when a small girl fell out of a swing and broke her arm. When running over to the swingset, Susan tripped over a rolling basketball and fell, spraining her ankle badly. Angry at the teacher for leaving her alone, Susan is also worried because she is not sure her health insurance will cover her injury.

- What legal questions should Susan ask?
- Generally, do school insurance policies cover volunteers and children?
- What questions should Susan ask of the school district?

One of the areas of liability where the relationship between parents and schools can become most strained is in the reporting of suspected child abuse. The role of educators in reporting suspected child abuse is mandated by law; teachers and administrators must report abuse to the state social services agency or other designated authority. Schools should have guidelines in place about identifying child abuse, verifying reports of abuse, and the actual reporting process. Failure to report can lead to civil or possibly criminal recriminations against the teacher or administrator.

Reporting a parent for suspected child abuse sets up the potential for a very bad relationship with the parents, but the welfare of the child must be the top priority in all cases. This situation is where *in loco parentis* is probably most critical; the school is acting in place of the parent when the parent has abdicated his or her rights by violating the rights of the child. State laws always provide a good faith clause so that teachers who follow the mandate to report suspected abuse are protected should the report turn out to be false but was made in good faith.

One of the worst situations that may arise to destroy good school–parent relationships is when a school employee is suspected of sexually molesting or abusing students and parents learn that other school personnel knew and did nothing about the actions of the abuser. In *Franklin* v. *Gwinnett County Public Schools* (1992), parents reported to school officials that a teacher was having sexual contact with their daughter, and the school officials did not take the report seriously. Only minimal investigation was conducted, and nothing was done to stop the abuse or remove the teacher from the school. The U.S. Supreme Court ruled that Title IX could be applied to this case, setting the stage for federal court involvement in the violation of student civil rights in these cases when educators, in their official role as government employees, are guilty of abusing students and administrators reasonably knew or should have known the abuse was occurring and did nothing to stop it.

Schools are liable for injuries that occur on the school grounds, whether those injuries are physical or emotional. Developing good relationships with parents so that school personnel and parents can work together when injuries to students occur can prevent the bitterness that sometimes leads to punitive lawsuits. Schools must work to prevent injuries to students and parents when they are on school property or at school-sponsored events. Teachers must realize how vulnerable they are to being held liable for student injuries and take every precaution to prevent injuries. Even though parents can not sign away their own or their child's rights, permission slips for out-of-school activities are necessary to give parents notice about an event and an opportunity to give or deny permission for their child to participate. No one can prevent a lawsuit from being filed, but doing what the reasonable, prudent educator would do in similar circumstances may prevent a lawsuit from going to trial or large damage awards being made.

Discrimination and Harassment. With our nation becoming more diverse, claims of discrimination by members of various minority groups are on the rise as well as claims of reverse discrimination by members of majority groups. Not all claims are valid because not all minority groups are protected under federal and state laws. Discrimination against protected classes of people is illegal. Members of religious minority groups are protected by the First Amendment. Members of racial and ethnic minority groups are protected by the Fourteenth Amendment and various federal civil rights laws, such as Title VI and Title VII of the Civil Rights Act of 1964. Women (and sometimes men, depending on which gender has historically been the majority group in a setting) are protected by various federal laws, including Title IX of the Education Amendments of 1978. Persons with disabilities are protected by the Rehabilitation Act of 1973 and the Americans with Disabilities Act of 1991. The claims of these and other groups also may be protected by state or municipal laws. In addition, all children are to receive an equal opportunity for an education under various federal and state statutes.

For educators, students, and parents, these anti-discrimination laws mean that all children are entitled to an equal opportunity for an education in the nation's public schools. Policies separating students because of race, color, ethnicity, religion, gender, and disability are almost impossible to justify. School districts that are found to discriminate on the basis of these generally unchangeable characteristics risk losing their federal funding.

One area related to discrimination that has received much publicity is athletics. Title IX is very definite in specifying equal opportunity for girls and boys in athletics, and school districts found not to be in compliance with Title IX risk losing all their federal funding, not just funding for athletics. However, Title IX applies much more broadly than just to athletics. School districts must provide equal opportunities for girls and boys in all areas, including curriculum, the extracurriculum, and facilities.

Official discrimination by school districts or school employees is usually brought to public notice quickly and handled through formal channels. More difficult to handle are claims of harassment, which has been defined by the courts as a form of discrimination. Claims of sexual and racial harassment are increasing, whether because of awareness of the problem, media attention to the problem, or intolerant attitudes toward growing diversity in our population. Harassment is difficult to define because every person's tolerance for jokes, comments, teasing, touching, graffiti, and threats differs. However, the relative position of the perpetrator and the victim often determines if harassment has occurred. Persons in higher positions (employers, supervisors, administrators, teachers) should be very careful that persons in subordinate positions (employees, trainees, students) will not be able to interpret the superordinate's words or actions as harassment.

Teachers and other school personnel must never be involved in any type of harassment of students and should not allow students under their supervision to harass other students. One of the latest issues to come before the courts involves sexual and racial harassment of students by students. In several leading Minnesota cases, parents informed school officials that their children were being harassed by other children, and the school officials did little, if anything, to stop the harassment. When the courts have become involved in harassment cases, whether teacher-to-student or student-to-student, generally the rulings have been in favor of the victims and their parents, especially when documentation exists that the parents complained to the school officials but the harassment continued.

Reflection...

Kathy and Robbie are becoming very concerned about stories Amy and Fred are bringing home from school. On the playground at noon, several boys in the fifth grade have started "picking on" some of the younger boys in the first and second grades. The older boys taunt the younger ones, steal their frisbees, balls, and other toys, and sometimes even pull down the jeans of the younger boys. Fred has become afraid to go outside at noon, but the school rules allow students to stay inside only during bad weather.

- What legal questions should Kathy and Robbie ask?
- What does your state law and case precedent state about harassment?
- What questions should Kathy and Robbie ask of the school district? Of the principal?

As our nation's complex diversity increases so will the potential for discrimination and harassment. Schools will help solve this national problem when discrimination and harassment are not tolerated in schools and students are educated about tolerance for persons who are not like them in every way. Most parents will protect their children from the mental and physical harm of discrimination and harassment, even if they have to go to court. Therefore, teachers and administrators must do all they can to stop discrimination and harassment in schools.

Summary

The legal relationship between parents and the schools is becoming more complex every day as more federal and state laws are passed and more court decisions are handed down. Yet, the courts do not want to become involved in school issues; they would prefer if parents and school personnel would work out their differences outside of the courtroom. School personnel set the tone for parental involvement in schools. If schools refuse to recognize the fundamental right of parents to guide the upbringing of their children, the relationships between parents and the schools may become adversarial. If school personnel fear lawsuits and are always looking for an attorney behind the parent who wants to be involved in his or her child's education, they probably will find one because they will always be on the defensive. If teachers fail to respect the rights of students and parents and fail to maintain an orderly, educational atmosphere in their classrooms, all students suffer and parents will be disillusioned about the value of public schools. If schools genuinely welcome parents' involvement in their child's education because it will further the teaching and learning process, then schools and parents can become partners in educating children, not parties to lawsuits where no one wins.

RECOMMENDED ACTIVITIES

1. Read the sections in your state constitution that deal with education. How are they similar to or different from the sample North Dakota Constitution?

2. After the next legislative session in your state, get a copy of all the new laws dealing with schools. How will these laws affect your local schools? The parents in your district?

3. How do the schools in your district "accommodate" religion? Do you agree or disagree with these practices?

4. Interview teachers who were teaching prior to 1969 about their perceptions of student rights. What changes did they observe in schools and students from the early 1960s to the 1980s? What changes did they observe in parents' rights and involvement in schools during that time?

5. How would you answer parents' arguments that sex education is a family or religious issue that has no place in schools?

6. What student fees are charged in your school district? Why are fees charged?

7. What do regular education teachers need to know about special education? What related services are provided students with disabilities in your school district? Why has special education become such a litigious issue in many schools?

8. What rules govern student behavior in the schools in your district? Where are these rules printed?

9. How can school personnel control drugs, alcohol, gangs, and weapons in the schools and not violate student rights?

10. What textbooks or other education materials have been challenged in your school district? By whom? For what reasons?

11. Follow a teacher for a day and note how many potential lawsuits occur. Did you see any negligence? Were any students injured? What could be done to prevent liability in these instances?

12. What do you think will be the role of the courts in parent–school conflicts in the future?

ADDITIONAL RESOURCES

Educational Law and Parental Rights

Websites:

American Bar Association
www.abalawinfo.org

American Civil Liberties Union
www.aclu.org

Children's Defense Fund
www.childrensdefense.org

Children Now
www.childrennow.org

Gender Equity in Sports
www.bailiwick.lib.uiowa.edu/ge
www.schillerlawfirm.com

National Child Rights Alliance
www.ai.mit.edu/people/ellens/NCRA/ncra.html

Native American Bar Association
www.nativeamericanbar.org

REFERENCES

Abington School District v. Schemmp and Murray v. Curlett, 374 U.S. 203, 83 S. Ct. 1560 (1963).

Board of Education, Island Trees Union Free School District No. 26 v. Pico, 457 U.S. 853, 102 S. Ct. 2799 (1982).

Board of Education of Hendrick Hudson Central School District Board of Education v. Rowley, 458 U.S. 176, 102 S. Ct. 3034 (1982).

Board of Education of Mountain Lakes v. Maas, 152 A.2d 394 (App. Div. 1959).

Brown v. Board of Education of Topeka, Kansas, 347 U.S. 483, 74 S. Ct. 686 (1954).

Cardiff v. Bismarck Public School District, 263 N.W.2d 105 (ND 1978).

Cornwell v. State Board of Education, 314 F. Supp. 340 (D. Md. 1969), affirmed 428 F.2d 417 (4th Cir. 1970), cert. denied 400 U.S. 942, 91 S. Ct. 240 (1970).

Cude v. Arkansas, 377 S.W. 2d 816 (Ark. 1964).

Florence County School District Four v. Carter, 114 S. Ct. 361 (1993).

Flory v. Smith, 134 S.E. 360 (Ct. of Appeals, Vir. 1926).

Franklin v. Gwinnett County Public Schools, 112 S. Ct. 1028 (1992).

Good News Club v. Milford Central School, 121 S. Ct. 2093 (2000).

Hartzell v. Connell, 679 P.2d 35 (Cal. 1984).

Irving Independent School District v. Tatro, 468 U.S. 883, 104 S. Ct. 3371 (1984).

Lander v. Seaver, 32 Vt. 114 (Vermont, 1859).

Lee v. Weisman, 112 S. Ct. 2649 (1992).

Medeiros v. Kiyosaki, 478 P.2d 314 (1970).

Mozert v. Hawkins County Board of Education, 827 F.2d 1058 (6th Cir. 1987).

People v. Ekerold, 105 N.E. 670 (1914).

People of State of Illinois ex rel. McCollum v. Board of Education of School District No. 71, Champaign County, Illinois, 333 U.S. 203, 68 S. Ct. 461 (1948).

Pierce v. Society of the Sisters of the Holy Names of Jesus and Mary, 268 U.S. 510, 45 S. Ct. 571 (1925).

Smith v. Board of School Commissioners of Mobile County, 827 F.2d 684 (11th Cir. 1987).

Smith v. Ricci, 446 A.2d 501 (1982).

State ex rel. Andrews v. Webber, 8 N.E. 708 (Ind. 1886).

State ex rel. Kelley v. Ferguson, 144 N.W. 1030 (Neb. 1914).

Timothy W. v. Rochester, New Hampshire School District, 875 F.2d 954 (1st Cir., 1989).

Tinker v. Des Moines Independent Community School District, 393 U.S. 503, 89 S. Ct. 733 (1969).

Veimeister v. White, 72 N.E. 97 (New York, 1904).

Wallace v. Jaffree, 472 U.S. 38, 105 S. Ct. 2479 (1985).

West Virginia State Board of Education v. Barnette, 319 U.S. 624, 63 S. Ct. 1178 (1943).

Wisconsin v. Yoder, 406 U.S. 205, 92 S. Ct. 1526 (1972).

Zorach v. Clauson, 343 U.S. 306 (1952).

11

Family Violence

The Effect on Teachers, Parents, and Children

TARA LEA MUHLHAUSER
University of North Dakota

DOUGLAS D. KNOWLTON
University of Minnesota, Crookston

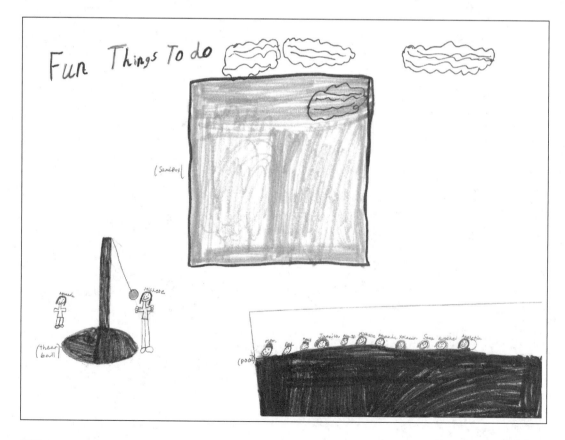

To understand the impact of family violence it is important to be aware of the dynamics of child abuse, neglect, and domestic violence. This chapter will prepare teachers by providing general information about the characteristics of child victims, abusive and neglectful parents, and the impact of violence in the home on children. Specific recommendations for action and decision making are found throughout the chapter. The purpose of this chapter is to help readers:

- Understand the educational and developmental implications of child abuse, neglect, and domestic violence
- Grasp the severity of the problem of family violence
- Gain applicable skills for communicating with children and parents when high risk indicators for violence are present
- Understand the role of teachers in reporting and identifying high risk situations
- Have access to information on resources available at the county, state, and national level
- Understand the family dynamics of, and nexus between, child abuse and domestic violence

Every teacher envisions a classroom of energetic, enthusiastic, and responsive students—students who come to school nurtured, nourished, and without worries that might intrude on their ability to engage in the learning process. This vision is now tempered by our growing realization of the fact that "it is not always happy at our house". Students are instead coming to school encumbered by the anxieties, fears, and diminished self-esteem typical of children who have been victims of abusive and neglectful situations (Becker et al., 1995; Perrin & Perrin, 1999). The following statistics regarding these children are presented to alert us to the magnitude of this problem:

- In 1999, there were an estimated 826,000 child victims of maltreatment in this country.
- Nationwide approximately 1.5 million children received preventative services.
- Over two million reports of alleged child abuse and neglect were received by child protective service agencies.
- An estimated 1,100 children died as a result of abuse or neglect.
- More than half of all reports of maltreatment (54.7 percent) came from professionals, including educators, law enforcement officials, medical professionals, and child care providers (Child Maltreatment, 2001).

Although these data on children as direct victims of violence are sobering, it is clear that just being in the presence of one family member perpetrating violence against another member, such as spouse abuse, also has a significant negative impact. In the past, domestic abuse and child abuse had traditionally been treated as separate issues with interruptions offered by different agencies in the community. More recently, agency personnel recognize the need for collaboration to effectively and efficiently address the multiplicity of issues presented by violent families (Effective Interruptions, 1999). As the research clearly points out, violence between partners frequently occurs in the same homes where violence is perpetrated against children (The Future of Children: Domestic Violence on Children, 1999).

Any child who is living in a home situation that is threatening or assaultive will expend energy coping with that probability. Whether it is devising plans for avoiding the threat or obsessively thinking about what might happen after school, the student will not have their full resources available for functioning in the classroom.

Studies estimate that anywhere from 45 to 70 percent of men who batter their female partners also abuse the children in the home. In an early study, Stark and Flitcraft (1988) found that as many as two-thirds of abused children had mothers who were being beaten. Other studies, including move recent research, have confirmed this premise (The Future of Children, 1999). This abuse might be from direct physical aggression or by being "in the wrong place at the wrong time"; for example, the children may try to protect the parent or they simply get in the way. Given that these child witnesses are also victims due to the exposure to violence, it becomes important to have an appreciation of the level of domestic violence occurring in our homes. It is estimated that four million women are battered every year—one every nine seconds. Two million are beaten severely, and the FBI estimates that between 1,400 and 1,500 women are murdered every year by former husbands or boyfriends. The U.S. Department of Justice estimates that 95 percent of assaults on spouses/partners or ex-partners are committed by men against women (Alsop, 1995).

In addition, we cannot overlook our national concern about the increase of violent and antisocial behaviors on the part of our children. If we are to understand the root causes of this antisocial behavior and particularly the increase in adolescents' school and community violence, the need for information regarding possible explanations becomes a high priority. Over the span of two decades a significant body of information has pointed to child maltreatment as a causative factor for this aggression (Hoffman-Plotkin & Twentyman, 1984; Wodarski, Kurtz, Gaudin, & Howing, 1990). While our national attention has been on this aggressive behavior, other very important developmental consequences for children have also been found: increased anxiety (Wolfe & Mosk, 1983), depression (Kaufman & Cicchetti, 1989), attachment and social interaction deficits (Crittenden, 1992), academic difficulties (Salinger, Kaplan, Pelcovitz, Samet, & Kreiger, 1984), and decreased self-esteem (Fantuzzo, 1990). Any one of these consequences has implications for a child's school performance, and all of them have been tied to school success or failure.

From this data we know that children are arriving for their busy school day having experienced traumas that clearly influence their responsiveness in the classroom. If we are to serve these children well, we will need to understand some of the theories about family violence, as well as the characteristics of children who are victims, characteristics of parents who are victims, and the characteristics of parents who may engage in this violent behavior. In addition, there are societal issues that have frequently been cited for creating an environment that is conducive to child maltreatment. Economic factors such as high unemployment and poverty are associated with increased incidents of abuse. More recently we have seen an increase in homeless families and the children in these families are vulnerable to a variety of maltreatment issues. One prominent researcher has recently begun to link child abuse and domestic violence with animal abuse (Ascione & Arkow, 1999).

- What has led to an environment in which children are routinely maltreated in our society?
- What attitudes and beliefs support this type of interaction with children?
- When does appropriate discipline become abuse?

All of these questions are relevant to the relationships between families and teachers because the answers may have an impact on a child's capacity to learn. Once we understand some of these dynamics and can recognize their impact on our students, we then need to know what we can do to support and, if necessary, intervene with these families. It is clear that children who are physically and emotionally maltreated are going to present significant challenges for our schools and communities. Although some educators might find it tempting to try and ignore this problem or perceive it as just a family issue, our students' needs and their cries for help will continue to push us toward a more active approach.

Child Abuse and Neglect

Child abuse and neglect is a very widespread social phenomenon. The dynamics of abuse and neglect can be found in all settings within the community. Income, race, gender, and family structure aside, the dynamics of adult-to-child violence and the effects of such violence cut across many strata in our classrooms. While the risk factors may be more obvious with certain groups of children, all children remain at risk from abuse and neglect in every home represented in our classrooms.

Child abuse is widely defined as an act of power and control over a child by use of corporal punishment, exploitation (sexual and physical), or emotional or psychological maltreatment. Abuse is often categorized as physical, emotional, or sexual maltreatment (Tower, 1999). *Neglect* is often defined as the deprivation of the child's needs that in turn leaves the child vulnerable to a variety of conditions, harm, or emotional strain. Neglect is categorized as physical, emotional, or medical neglect and includes "lack of supervision" (Dubowitz, 1999; Tower, 1999). Psychological maltreatment is often found within other forms of abuse and neglect and is a very devastating by-product of abuse and neglect (Tower, 1999).

Although defining the terms is not difficult, identifying individual acts or situations as abusive or neglectful can be problematic. Many times the categorization or identification of an act as abusive or neglectful depends on factors such as severity, frequency, and pervasiveness of the action as well as the age and vulnerability of the child.

Generally we hold those in caretaking positions responsible for meeting the child's needs and protecting the child from exploitation; those caretakers may not always be the child's parents. A diverse group of adult caretakers (e.g., child care providers, relatives, live-in partners, grandparents) and the abusive or neglectful caretakers' access to the child can complicate the child abuse and neglect dimension.

Characterizing of the home life of abused and neglected children requires the examination of three separate areas: the caretakers, the child, and the environment where abuse and neglect is found. The dynamics are often described as either *conduct*—what the parent/caretaker does (e.g., striking the child), or *conditions*—the issues a parent/caretaker may be faced with (e.g., mental illness).

Parental Factors in Child Abuse and Neglect

Caretakers who resort to violence in their interactions with children frequently are described as making poor decisions in a time of stress, that is, using corporal punishment out of anger and to exert control over a difficult situation. Their reaction is often intensified by the lingering presence of drugs or alcohol (or the effects of an addiction), the effects of mental illness, the presence of physical illness or depression, or unhappiness about their life situation. All of these factors can trigger a stress response. In addition, research has identified two other very important variables in predicting the risk of child maltreatment: caretakers for whom violence is a learned response (often because of violent family histories and relationships) and caretakers who lack basic parenting skills. In this latter group, the lack of skills can mean a deficit in understanding a child's developmental needs and vulnerabilities as well as a lack of skills to respond to a child's misbehavior.

> ## Reflection...
>
> Corporal punishment in schools and spanking as a form of discipline are much debated issues. The Swedish government has banned all spanking. Should the U.S. government take similar steps to ban spanking or corporal punishment? Should there be specific limitations on types of physical discipline? Are there social supports of use of physical discipline in our communities?

For example, an unskilled and stressed parent may resort to shaking a baby because the parent is frustrated and thinks the act will provide a signal to the baby that it is time to quit crying and resume sleep. In doing so, the parent exposes the infant to a developmental vulnerability (head injury by shaking the baby) and misjudges the child's developmental readiness to understand both act and consequence. Frequently, abusive parents simply don't understand how damaging certain attempts to discipline or punish younger children can be. Lack of skills also plays a part in the abuse of older children. With younger children, parents frequently reach a threshold of frustration and strike out. These parents think that the child will then heed their request or understand and learn their point of view.

Children who are sexually exploited by family members (often called intrafamilial child sexual abuse) also have caretakers who fall into the above dynamic, but in a slightly different way. In these families it is common to see a blur of boundaries among the generations (for example, between parent and child). The expectations of family members follow that pattern, and the children are expected to step into the shoes of an adult member for some of the family functions (i.e., sexual partner). This creates great chaos and confusion in the family which compounds the secret being kept between the adult and child in regard to the sexual relationship (Faller, 1990; Perrin & Perrin, 1999).

The caretaker's available cognitive and emotional skills have a significant impact on the choices they make, particularly when stressed. The lack of such skills or compromised skills can contribute to a condition which makes children in their care more vulnerable to abuse.

Many of the same characteristics are seen in neglectful situations. Often the scenario of a child's life includes both neglect and abuse. Neglect dynamics are also inextricably bound to environmental characteristics. These conditions frequently set the stage for a situation of child neglect to occur.

Chronic neglect can be one of the most difficult situations for us to work with in the classroom. It is not uncommon to find conditions of physical neglect creating a dynamic of emotional neglect for a child in class. For example, a child who has poor hygiene creates a social situation that impacts his or her ability to build or sustain peer relationships. Even with intervention, sometimes the parental condition and conduct are so pervasive and deeply ingrained in the family structure and history that successes are small and take time. In these situations, it is important not to underestimate the impact a positive school relationship can have on a child. We may be meeting, or have an opportunity to meet, some very basic self-esteem, emotional, and developmental needs that are not being met in the home.

As we work to build relationships with parents or caretakers who may arouse our concerns, remember that they often are very isolated physically, emotionally, or psychologically from the needs of their children because they are frequently overwhelmed with other issues in life. Isolation, in combination with a lack of parenting or social/emotional skills and any conditioning factors (such as alcohol abuse, mental illness), can be very difficult to work with, and you may benefit from working with others as a team to build and maintain personal relationships.

Environmental Factors in Abuse and Neglect

Although child abuse and neglect are widespread in all communities, we must be aware of the important environmental indicators of risk. Poverty and the surrounding conditions (unemployment, poor housing and diet, etc.), social isolation, and the stress of single-parenting, or a combination of these factors, are widely accepted as environmental risk factors. Certainly the lack of income contributes in direct and indirect ways to the child abuse and neglect dimension (Tower, 1999). For instance, a parent may not have the ability to afford after-school child care, this places the child in an unsupervised situation everyday for several hours. This may not be a true reflection of the parent's decision-making capability; it may instead reflect the financial reality the parent faces and how the parent may have to balance and weigh risk factors (e.g., a job that will bring in money versus supervising their eight-year-old child after school). If a parent is not socially isolated in this scenario, they may have the ability to leverage available resources to provide care for their child in the form of a neighbor or a play/recreation group with revolving parental supervision. If the parent is socially isolated, their choices and alternatives narrow and this may create undue stress on the parent–child relationship, leaving the child more vulnerable to risk.

This scenario creates a good opportunity for home–school partnerships with an emphasis on a win–win outcome. If the school or community provides alternatives for working parents in these situations, the child stays in a safe after-school environment where he or she is supervised. In this setting, the child is given the chance to build peer relationships or enhance a variety of skills. The parent can then complete a full day of work with assurance that their child is safe. This can provide that layer of support that can make tremendous difference in the parent–child relationship.

Characteristics of Child Victims

It is clear that all of us will at some time be involved with a child who has been a victim of physical or emotional abuse, sexual abuse, neglect, or a witness to violent behavior. Therefore, it is important that we are familiar with the characteristics and behaviors of these children. Although each child is an individual and will have a different configuration of symptoms or classroom problems, there are some commonalities to their psychological and behavioral status. Sometimes children will give us very simple clues that indicate they are uncomfortable in certain situations or appear to be different than other children in the classroom. At other times, they may be very hostile and angry and may tend to alienate other children as well as alienating teachers or other adults in the school setting. Perhaps one of the most striking symptoms is a dramatic change in a child's demeanor or personality. These changes are often very sudden; for example, a child who has been very outgoing and involved with other children may suddenly become isolated and avoidant. These changes are often reflected in a student's performance, grades, or social situations. A sudden drop in responsiveness or accomplishment in the classroom can be a cue that something significant is going on in the child's life. Listed below are some of the typical distressful emotions that a child victim may experience and explanations of how they might affect children at different developmental points.

Anxiety. One of the child's very early developmental needs is for security and safety. A young child who does not feel safe may have significantly elevated anxiety.

This might show up in simple nervous behaviors (habits such as twirling hair or biting nails) or actually be seen in the development of phobias, panic disorders, obsessive/compulsive disorders, and so forth. At times this anxiety may be associated with a particular person or environment, or it may be more generalized with the child constantly feeling on edge or irritable. Young children often use avoidance to cope with this kind of anxiety or develop other symptoms such as nightmares, bed wetting, or physiological symptoms such as headaches or stomach distress.

As the child gets older, the anxiety may take on other behavioral manifestations. In adolescence these young people may cope with their anxieties by becoming aggressive or resorting to the use of alcohol and drugs to numb some of the agitation or irritability they may experience.

Depression.   Depression can be seen in children through classical symptoms (i.e., change in appetite, change in sleep patterns, overall mood problems). It is important to note that in young people, depression can also look like an agitated state with increased activity and inattention. There have even been children diagnosed with Attention Deficit Disorder (ADD) or Attention Deficit Hyperactivity Disorder (ADHD) who may very well have been depressed, but their activity levels were significantly increased due to agitation. Although the diagnosis of depression is not often made for very young children, these symptoms could clearly be manifestations of a child who is in an abusive situation.

In the area of adolescent development, depression may take on a more serious note, particularly as it is paired with an increase in adolescent impulsive behavior. This impulsiveness can add to the potential for drug and alcohol abuse and the risk of adolescent suicide.

Anger.   It is important to note that anger, when expressed by a young child, may simply be increased irritability or uncontrollable behavior; it may be a result of their difficulty understanding and/or expressing feelings of anger. Sometimes this anger can become self-directed and contributes to depression or high-risk behavior. At other times, these children may display behavioral difficulties and become more aggressive, particularly toward other children. This behavior is often difficult to manage in the classroom and if we don't see this behavior as a cry for help, we may take a very destructive or punitive approach with the child. Anger expressed by adolescents tends to be more hostile and can be seen in aggressive behaviors with the increased possibility of sexually aggressive behavior.

Self-Concept.   It is becoming increasingly clear that a child's sense of self is negatively impacted by involvement in any abusive situation. Levels of self-esteem (a child's positive view of him- or herself) and appropriate self-concept (a child's realistic view of their capabilities) are crucial to the on-going psychological development and well-being of children. An assault on this self-esteem can negatively impact the child's developmental progress. When children have an impaired sense of self or a reduced sense of self-esteem, they are often unable to control their own emotions. They may not be able to calm or soothe themselves when they are in a situation in which there is a lot of stress. This can also have an impact when children need to separate or become independent from others; a diagnosis of separation anxiety disorder may be associated with these particular times. Later in the child's development, there may be difficulties defining one's own boundaries or appreciating the needs and desires of others in their environments. In addition, there are reports of increased suggestibility or gullibility, inadequate self-protectiveness and a greater likelihood of being victimized or exploited by others.

Post-Traumatic Stress Disorder (PTSD).   Highly distressing or threatening environmental situations can cause a reaction that has been called post-traumatic stress and diagnosed as post-traumatic stress disorder (PTSD). This disorder is evidenced by: (a) a numbing of emotions or responsiveness to events; (b) frequent reexperiencing of events sometimes through intrusive thoughts or nightmares; and (c) increased irritability, sleep disturbance, and poor concentration. Children who have been abused tend to exhibit more post-traumatic fear, concentration problems, and anxiety than do children who have not been abused.

Although these symptoms are most common in children who have been exposed to high levels of violent or abusive behavior, there are other symptoms that are sometimes problematic and indicative of this type of exposure. These include the potential for suicide, high-risk sexual behavior, and a higher incidence of suicidal thinking and behavior in children. Some children, particularly adolescents, might engage in indiscriminate sexual behavior as an expression of the need for acceptance and self-worth. It is also not uncommon to see eating disorders such as anorexia or bulimia. Bulimia is evidenced primarily by binging and purging behaviors and these symptoms have been associated with higher incidents of abuse, particularly sexual abuse.

One of the most obvious characteristics of these children is their difficulty negotiating within their personal relationships. A sudden change in the child's relationship with other children can be a clue that there is a source of additional stress in their life. These children may engage in avoidance behaviors (withdrawal, isolation) which create problems with their interpersonal activities. These children may actually perceive themselves as less worthy of appropriate relationships. In general, abused children have been found to be socially less competent, more aggressive, and more withdrawn than their non-abused counterparts. In later life, it becomes very difficult for these children to develop intimate relationships, and if they do develop, the relationships often center on some type of ambivalence or fear about becoming vulnerable.

Reflection...

Consider the characteristics of abused children and how each would appear in a classroom environment. How will you be able to recognize these behaviors? How will you address the undersirable behaviors?

Intervention and Treatment

Obviously, the intervention and treatment process cannot begin until the children and families at risk of further abuse and neglect have been identified. That is why it is so crucial for us to identify and report abusive and neglectful situations and incidents to the local child protection agency. Once identified, an assessment process is conducted by social workers to determine the safety of the child in their present environment, to identify risks, and to recommend a treatment service. Usually this process will include some determination, by the child protection services agency or multi-disciplinary child protection team, of whether the reported act or situation is recognized as abusive or neglectful.

If the child is in need of immediate protection from further abuse or harm, the child protection agency will seek the authority of the court to remove the child from this harmful environment. Taking temporary or emergency custody of a child generally means that the child will be placed with a nurturing relative or in a foster home or facility until the agency personnel and court determine it is safe for the child to return home. If it is found that the abuse or neglect did occur, the court will usually mandate parents/caretakers to participate in some kind of recommended treatment before the child will be returned home. In child sexual abuse cases, the child protection agency may require that the abusive adult leave the home and cease to have contact with the child. In this situation, sometimes the child can remain at home with the supervision of a supportive parent while the abusive adult is monitored and allowed to return home after completing a sex offender treatment program or is released from a secured facility.

Treatment recommended by the child protection agency is generally part of a plan for the child and/or family. Many different treatment options are available and can vary greatly depending on the resources available in each community. Often the family is involved in some educational process to assist the parents/caretakers with developing or enhancing parenting skills. Support groups, individual therapy, family therapy, and in-home, family-based services (with a specific set of goals and a case worker in the home) are used. If there are conditions such as mental illness or alcoholism, the parent/caretaker is referred to the appropriate treatment facility or agency prior to participating in the aforementioned treatment services. Also, social workers frequently work with families to provide or suggest resources in the community to assist with financial issues, feelings of isolation, and domestic violence. In some cases, we may be asked to be involved in a team process to monitor, recommend, and assist agency treatment providers with assessment, development, or implementation of a treatment plan for a child and/or family.

Long-Term Effects of Abuse on Children

Significant research and pages of popular media have been devoted to the long-term effects of abuse and neglect on children. There are so many possible effects that it is difficult to predict an outcome. Some individuals even claim to gain a sense of strength from the early maltreatment. Much of the current research on resiliency indicates that positive forces in a child's life may be able to mitigate some or most of the harm of abuse and neglect, although nothing will completely obliterate the abuse or neglect harm from a child victim's life or memory (Wolin & Wolin, 1993). It is clear that the maltreatment does have a diminishing effect on a child's abilities, although which abilities and to what degree seem to vary on a case-by-case basis.

Research has documented neurological, cognitive, behavioral, psychological, emotional, and intellectual effects. Educationally, effects of child abuse and neglect have been linked to academic outcomes and lower test scores, indicating that maltreatment may diminish a child's ability to fully participate and advance (Tower, 1992).

Domestic Violence

Domestic violence is defined as a pattern of assaultive and controlling behaviors in the context of an intimate adult relationship. While domestic violence is often referred to as spouse abuse, that term is not inclusive enough to apply to the violence that happens between adult intimates outside of marriage or in the context of a familial environment. The pattern of assaults and control frequently takes the form of coercion, terrorism, degradation, exploitation, and actual violence in the form of physical assault (Peled, Jaffe, & Edelson, 1995; Renzetti, Edelson, & Burgen, 2001). One author (Ganley, 1993) describes domestic violence as "hands-on" (meaning the physical assaults) and "hands-off" (meaning the psychological pattern of terrorism that leaves no visible scars). According to the FBI in their 1990 Uniform Crime Report, battering is the establishment of control and fear in a relationship through violence and other forms of abuse. The batterer uses acts of violence and a series of behaviors, including intimidation, threats, psychological abuse, isolation, and privilege, to coerce and control the other person. The violence may not happen often, but it remains as a hidden (and constant) terrorizing factor.

When research tells us that 30 percent of all women will suffer from some form of abuse in an adult relationship (Peled, Jaffe, & Edelson, 1995), it is clear that the effects of domestic violence are far reaching in any community setting, including the classroom. The pattern of adult violence usually has ebbs and flows; there are periods of chaos and immediate fear interrupted by periods of controlled calm, apology, and remorse. The violence often escalates with each new onset and in the latter stages often involves weapons. As domestic survivors will tell you, they must spend tremendous energy "keeping a lid" on everything so that an episode of violence does not erupt. It is frequently asked why they stay in such situations. Aside from the obvious issue of parenting, there are financial concerns, family issues, and practical issues of where to live (many battered women who leave abusive relationships find themselves and their children homeless), how to provide for children if one leaves a relationship, and danger (LaViolette & Barnett, 2000). Also, research confirms that women who leave their batterers are at a 75 percent greater risk of being killed by the batterer than those who stay (Hart, 1990). Casey Gwin, a prominent prosecutor who led a legal reform in this area through his work with the City of San Diego, reminds us that the better question to ask is "Why does he hit her?"

Characteristics of Violent Households

While the great majority of reported incidents of battering involve male batterers, there is a small percentage of reported battering by women. Because domestic violence is a crime, the report of an incident can be a very difficult time for a family and a confusing time for the children. While many once thought that the effects on children living in a violent home were minimal, research is strongly confirming that the effects are clearly damaging, both because children are caught, literally, in the crossfire and because they are passive witnesses to violent and abusive acts (Holden, Geffner, & Jouriles, 1999; Jaffe et al., 1990; Peled, et al., 1995; Roy, 1988).

Reflection...

Isn't it difficult to understand why someone who is being battered or exploited doesn't leave the relationship? Why might it be very difficult or dangerous for someone to leave a violent relationship? What are the risks of leaving? What are the risks of staying? What might be some of the early characteristics or signals in our own relationships that might include the potential for violent interactions?

Often we hear of violent incidents that children disclose in the classroom long before the incidents are reported to any authority. As classroom teachers, we must be prepared to listen to the children and let them talk about what they have observed and heard at home and give them an opportunity to talk about what they are feeling. How, and if, you then approach the issue with a parent will be a very crucial decision. Consideration must be given to issues of safety, shame and guilt of the victim, the stigma of being battered, and fear on the part of both the child and the battered parent. The patterns of control in violent families is so pervasive that it may take a battered parent years before she is ready to take the risk of leaving the violent relationship.

As indicated in Table 11.1, the characteristics of the batterer are similar across the categories of family violence we've discussed in this chapter. This violent interaction between intimate partners creates the same kind of reoccurring crisis and chaos that we see in families where there is abuse and neglect. Although conditions such as alcohol use and abuse and mental illness may aggravate the pattern of power and control in a family, the use of power and control to dominate family members is a learned behavior, not a result of the use or misuse of chemical substances, biological factors, or a chemical imbalance. According to researchers and therapists in the field, men who batter minimize or deny the seriousness of their behavior; externalize responsibility for the violence to other situations and people; have a need to control and dominate people, most specifically their partners; and

TABLE 11.1   Commonalities in Family Operations across Violent Families

	Child Maltreatment	Sexual Abuse	Conjugal Violence	Elder Mistreatment
(1) Confused and distorted attachments	X	X	X	X
(2) Unequal power and status distributions	X	X	X	X
(3) Frustration	X	X	X	X
(4) Distorted cognitions and attributions	X	X	X	X
(5) Role incompetence in the face of stress	X	X	X	X

From: Bolton, *Working with Violent Families,* 163. Copyright © 1987. Reprinted by permission of Sage Publications, Inc.

isolate their victims to keep the abuse inside the family (Cardarelli, 1997; Stordeur & Stille, 1989).

From the other perspective, battered women can be so compromised by fear that their ability to respond to a situation of violence can be diminished. Psychologically, research shows that battered women can be characterized by the following:

> learned helplessness (i.e., the belief that their best efforts to be effective will produce random results); a diminished perception of alternatives (to the violence, especially); a heightened tolerance for ideas that do not belong together (e.g., I love him and I fear him); and knowledge of the abuser's potential for violence and the range of violent acts which they can perform. (Blackman, 1996)

These characteristics may also diminish these women's ability to nurture children and provide the necessary encouragements and supports for their children's emotional growth and development and sense of security. Susan Schechter, an expert in the field of domestic violence, is frequently quoted as saying "the best way to protect the children is to protect their mother." Because of the battered woman's response to the violence, they may not be able to fully protect their children while they continue to live in a violent environment (Roy, 1988).

Intervention and Treatment

Because domestic violence is a crime, intervention is available through law enforcement agencies. Most states have a protocol used for domestic violence cases that determines how arrests will be made and how the case will proceed in the criminal justice system. Arrest has been shown to be an effective intervention in domestic violence situations. It is important for the intervention process to include a comprehensive treatment component to assist batterers with "unlearning" the learned behavior. During treatment, the batterer learns new skills and ideas to help replace old behavior with acceptable and appropriate ways of expressing anger and managing power and control in relationships. Many treatment programs are available in community settings; the best programs combine elements of education, therapy, self-awareness, and crisis management in a group therapy setting. Most comprehensive programs include weekly sessions for at least twenty-four weeks.

Battered women are provided treatment consisting of support through formal support group sessions and individual therapy, generally available through a community domestic violence agency. Many programs also provide treatment services for children by using a support group/education process or play therapy to help the child identify, express, and understand feelings.

Many communities currently have efforts of ongoing collaboration to provide a team approach for delivery of services and to enhance the array of services and intervention available to assist families and children living in violence (Shepard & Pence, 1999). Because the effects of violence are so far reaching in our communities, it is important for us to be involved with collaborative efforts and understand the issues from the perspectives of domestic violence advocates, child abuse and neglect agencies, and law enforcement (Klein, Campbell, Soler, & Ghez, 1997). Involvement at this level can also assist us in building confidence in how we can respond when one of our students discloses a violent incident at home, when a colleague discloses a violent incident, or when a parent confides in us about a situation. The potential for lethality in these incidents is great, and we must be prepared to use community resources in assisting families and children in finding a safe haven and a way out of the cycle of violence.

Long-Term Effects of Domestic Violence on Family Members

The effects of domestic violence on children, as stated earlier, correlates with the child's developmental stage and the severity and frequency of the abuse. The effects must always be assessed on a case-by-case basis—some children may experience a very traumatic result from witnessing or being exposed to only one act. Generally, research shows that boys who witness violence are three times more likely to grow up to use violence in their intimate relationships than those boys not exposed to family violence (Stark & Flitcraft, 1996). This same research shows that violence is quite a legacy; sons of violent fathers have an estimated rate of woman abuse 1,000 times higher than the sons of nonviolent fathers. Conversely, girls who witness their mothers being abused may have a greater rate of tolerance for abuse in a relationship (Hotaling & Sugarman, 1986).

According to Jaffe in some early research in the field, one third of the children witnessing violence show behavioral and emotional disruptions, anxiety, sleep disruption, and school problems. Approximately 20 to 40 percent of the families of chronically violent delinquent adolescents had family histories of domestic violence (Jaffe, Wolfe, & Wilson, 1990). Other research indicates that depression and reduced verbal, cognitive, and motor abilities are predictable results of witnessing adult violence (Holden, et.al, 1998; The Future of Children, 1999; Effective Intervention, 1999). Significant volumes of research consistently show that witnessing violence as a youth promotes the use of violence in adulthood to solve problems and as a means of gaining control. Research on the long-term effects on adults show that depression, low self-esteem, emotional trauma and post-traumatic stress, and revictimization are often experienced by survivors of violence (Bolton & Bolton, 1987). All of these factors must be considered before examining a specific situation and creating a plan or opportunity to work on building a relationship with a parent who is living with violence.

The Link between Child Abuse and Domestic Violence

As educators we have been sensitized to the issues of child abuse. We have been given information on the reporting procedures to employ when we suspect abuse, but few of us have been aware of the significant problems caused when children witness or are exposed to adult violent behavior in their homes. There is a growing awareness of the link between domestic violence and child abuse in children's lives. The American Humane Association (AHA) was one of the first national organizations to highlight this link in their publication *Protecting Children* (1995).

One of the articles in the AHA publication, written by Schecter and Edleson (1995), cited studies that indicate the link among patterns of response between children who are witnesses and those who are actually abused themselves. Many other authors and researchers (see references in previous sections) continue to reconfirm this link in the area of family violence. Increased aggression and antisocial behaviors, lowered social competence, higher anxiety and depression, and lowered verbal, cognitive, and motor abilities were found to exist when children are exposed to the range of family violence (Holden, et al., 1998). The cognitive and emotional implication for the educational setting is obvious. If we, as teachers, are to promote and facilitate learning, we must be aware of the negative impact family violence has on our students.

Because of the interrelatedness of child abuse and domestic violence, there has been some tension between the Child Protective Services and those services directed at helping victims of domestic violence. For example, child protection social workers might determine that if a woman is not able to protect herself, then she might not be able to protect her children. The domestic violence advocates feel that the battered woman is the best way to judge the level of safety and fear; If she continues to stay in the situation, they respect her decision and provide her support. These different perspectives can lead to differences in the recommended intervention. Thus, cross-agency collaboration is crucial in arriving at a resolution that will protect both mom and child(ren).

Our vision of a classroom of children who are completely free from violence in their homes may not be realistic. However, the first step in creating change in our communities is to recognize, identify, and acknowledge the presence of family violence. The problem can be overwhelming and lead to a feeling that nothing can be done to protect our students. The information presented in this chapter is best used as a knowledge base to increase our confidence and empower us to make a difference in our students' lives. The following recommendations provide positive courses of action.

Recommendations for Action

Be Alert to Behavioral Cues

By educating ourselves we can be aware of the kinds of behavioral manifestations that we may see in our classrooms. These are most clearly seen in academic and social clues, with the primary indicator being sudden changes in academic performance, social isolation, or aggression. There may also be indications in achievement test score problems, truancies, suspensions, and infractions of disciplinary codes.

Emotional and psychological cues are also very evident and may include the change from one particular demeanor to another; for example, a child who has been cooperative becoming more hostile, angry, and alienating.

Be Alert to the Cues That Parents May Provide

Your contacts with family members, such as conversations with parents during parent conference time or other contacts, may very well provide some clues as to what may be going on in the family. Be especially alert for the following parental behaviors that may be an indication of potential problems:

- Blames or belittles child
- Sees the child as very different from his or her siblings (in a negative way)
- Sees the child as bad, evil, or a "monster"
- Finds nothing good or attractive in the child
- Seems unconcerned about the child
- Fails to keep appointments or refuses to discuss problems the child may be having in school
- Misuses alcohol or drugs
- Behaves in bizarre or irrational ways

By being in contact with the family, we may be able to tell whether there are situations arising that are potentially dangerous to both the child and the family members.

Interacting with the Child

When having a conversation with a child in which issues arise that lead to concern, there are some guidelines that can be helpful in responding to the child. Remember that there is no benefit in conducting an investigation yourself—that is the role of the child protective services staff. When it is necessary to talk to the child about a situation, remember that the child may be very fearful, apprehensive, or actually in pain. It is, therefore, important to make the child as comfortable as possible. The person who talks with the child should be someone who the child trusts and with whom he or she feels safe. There may be an individual in the school who has been trained and is more capable of performing these interviews, such as the school social worker or psychologist. Remember to conduct these kinds of conversations in a very private and non-threatening place to reinforce to the child that they have not done anything wrong. The following suggestions will prove helpful in the interviewing process:

- Children need to be assured and reassured that they are not in trouble and they have not done anything wrong. Children in these situations often feel responsible and blame themselves for the abuse, neglect, or family dynamics and there is some potential that a conversation about these issues could increase those feelings. Children need to know very clearly and directly that they are *not* at fault.
- It is important to assure the child that information they provide will not be shared with other teachers or classmates, but may have to be shared with a social worker or law enforcement officer.
- If we feel that we will have to report the information, we should inform the child while continuing to let the child know that we will be their support and that they can come to us at any time.
- When talking with a child, make sure the language used is at an appropriate developmental level. If the child says something that is confusing or not understandable, ask for clarification.
- Do not press for answers or details if a child seems unwilling to give them. Again, this should not be an investigation; the child needs to feel that they can protect themselves in terms of the information they might give. Initial and repeated interviews in cases like this have sometimes led to the dismissal of criminal charges because of legal problems with the interview process.
- Don't ever insist on seeing a child's injuries; if they want to show the injuries, don't hesitate to let them do so using good professional judgment. Be sure pieces of clothing are never removed; if for some reason we must remove clothing to view an injury, we must be sure a school nurse or an appropriate school official is present.

Guidelines for Talking with Parents

Sometimes a conversation during a parent conference leads to concerns about abuse or violent behavior. A decision should be made as to whether the teacher is the most appropriate person to meet with the parent or whether a principal or some other staff member would be in a better position to speak with the parent. Often, parents will be apprehensive and may be very angry when first confronted about the existence of violent behavior. It is important to make the parents feel as comfortable as possible. Again, conversations should be in private and parents should be informed immediately as to what action might be taken. Try to be empathetic and do not display any kind of anger, repugnance, or shock. It is usually best not to give advice but to allow the parent to make some determination of their own course of action. This is particularly true for cases in which there has been some domestic violence and the mother has disclosed information; it will be up to her to make some decisions regarding future action. To force her into some kind of position or to give strong advice may very well be disempowering to her and create more problems for the family.

Reporting

Educators are mandated, by both state laws and federal standards and regulations, to report concerns or suspicions about child abuse and neglect, and sometimes about domestic violence. These regulations often tell us what is required and expected of us. Many state statutes specifically name educators as mandated reporters; other statutes indicate that any citizen must report. It is necessary for teachers to have copies of their state's guidelines, laws, and the local regulations regarding this reporting and to be prepared by reviewing this information. When reporting incidents or suspicions, most states will require some basic information. This may include:

1. Child's name, age, and address; parent's name and address
2. Nature and extent of the injury or condition observed
3. Prior injuries and when they were observed
4. Reporter's name and location (sometimes this is not required but it is often helpful to child protective services staff)

The National Education Association offers a publication entitled *How Schools Can Help Combat Child Abuse and Neglect*. As cited in Tower (1992), it provides an outline to aid schools in preparing appropriate school policy. Such a policy should include answers to the following questions:

1. At what point should the teacher report child abuse? Suspicion? Reasonable cause to believe? (This may be based not only on school policy but also state law.)
2. Who does the teacher notify? Nurse? Principal? School social worker?
3. What specific information does the teacher need to know to report?
4. What other school personnel should be involved?
5. Who makes the report to the appropriate authorities? How?
6. What information should be included in the report? (This may be dictated by state law and protective service agency protocol.)
7. What follow-up is expected on reported cases?
8. What role will the school play in possible community/child protection teams?
9. What commitment does the school have to in-service training or community programs? (pp. 36–37)

Reporting is often a very difficult and anxiety-provoking process for us. Often personal feelings about parents or a particular child may have an impact on our decisions. It is difficult for people to make decisions that cause others to become angry. Because of this, we sometimes fear for our own safety. At times, we may also feel that we are not appropriately supported by administrators or other school officials and this may have some impact on our decisions. In other cases, previous difficulties or bad experiences with child protective services or law enforcement may make us hesitant about reporting. This hesitancy may involve thoughts that "nothing can be done." Often we feel left out of the "information loop" with regard to what happens to the child after child protective services has become involved. Confidentiality laws and policies at times reduce the ability to share information with all individuals involved with the child and family. However, some state laws do allow a release of information from child protective services to other professionals when the individual is the member of a multi-disciplinary team. This is another area in which you must read your state law and policy to discover what role and what information you will be allowed in the case.

Awareness of Community, State, and National Resources

It is important for us to be aware of the various programs in our community which offer services to children and families, particularly those intervening in and providing treatment for violent families. Locate your child protection agency for more information regarding child abuse and neglect issues in your community and contact either the domestic violence program or a law enforcement agency for more information on domestic violence issues. These programs can provide a profile of the needs of families in the community as well as educational resources to assist you and your students, colleagues, and parents in learning more about the issues and the available services.

Several national resources exist that provide information on family violence. The National Resource Center on Domestic Violence (800-537-2238) is an excellent resources that has many fine materials available at no cost. The National Clearinghouse on Child Abuse and Neglect Information (800-394-3366) also has excellent materials and provides technical assistance. There may be similar state entities or affiliates that provide information specific to your state; the local programs you contact in your community should have names and addresses of those resources.

Our Role As Educators

The most important role we can play in family violence situations is to identify and recognize the presence of violence. If the violence involves or impacts a child, we need to report and support the child and parent in the best possible way. This is the first step in breaking the cycle of family violence.

RECOMMENDED ACTIVITIES

1. Invite Child Protective Services or domestic violence staff to provide a staff development in-service on reporting and identifying high risk situations.

2. Participate in child abuse and neglect prevention activities such as wearing a blue ribbon during the month of April to bring attention to the issues.

3. Investigate whether a specific curriculum has been adopted by the school to address family violence or child abuse and neglect issues.

4. Have students design a poster and theme for the class on child abuse/neglect or domestic violence to speak to children living with daily violence in their home.

5. Gather and distribute a list of community resources of agencies/groups that respond to and help families who are violent.

6. Role play a parent conference in which you suspect your student has witnessed significant violence in the home. Identify your feelings as you struggle with the idea of reporting or identifying the violence.

7. Get involved as a community or agency volunteers.

ADDITIONAL RESOURCES

Child Abuse and Neglect, Domestic Violence, and Family Violence

Books:

Cardelli, A. (1997). *Violence between intimate partners: Patterns, causes, and effects.* Boston, MA: Allyn & Bacon.

Dubowitz, H. (Ed.). (1999). *Neglected children: Research, practice, and policy.* Thousand Oaks, CA: Sage.

Kempe, C. H., & Helfer, R. E. (Eds.). (1987). *The battered child (4th ed.).* Denver, CO: Kempe National Center Division of University Health Science Center.

Jasinski, J., & Williams, L. (Eds.). (1998). *Partner violence: A comprehensive review of 20 years of research.* Thousand Oaks, CA: Sage.

Kantor, G., & Jasinski, J. (Eds.). (1997). *Out of the darkness: Contemporary perspectives on family violence.* Thousand Oaks, CA: Sage.

Myers, J., Berliner, L., Briere, J., Hendrix, C., Jenny, C., & Redi, T. (Eds.). (2001). *The APSAC handbook on child maltreatment* (2nd ed.). Thousand Oaks, CA: Sage.

Nelson, M., & Clark, K. (Eds.). (1986). *The educators guide to preventing child sexual abuse.*

This may be the best single source on the topic of child sexual abuse. It is an important part of every educator's professional library. 208 pp. ISBN: 0-941816-17-6.

Network Publications
1700 Mission Street, Suite 203
P.O. Box 1830
Santa Cruz, CA 95061-1830
Phone: 408-438-4060

Violence and the Family: Report of the American Psychological Association Presidential Task Force on Violence and the Family. (1996). Washington, DC: American Psychological Association.

Tower, C. (1999). *Understanding child abuse and neglect* (4th ed.). Boston: Allyn & Bacon.

Peled, E., Jaffe, P., & Edelson, J. (1995). *Ending the cycle of violence: Community responses to children of battered women.* Thousand Oaks, CA: Sage.

Videos:

Breaking the Silence: Journeys of Hope

> Contact www.marykay.com for a copy.

Child Abuse

This video deals with the subject of physical and emotional abuse. It identifies common characteristics of the offender, examines therapy for young victims of physical and sexual abuse, and offers tips in selecting day-care settings for young children. (19 minutes, color)

> Films for the Humanities & Sciences
> P.O. Box 2053
> Princeton, NJ 08543
> Phone: 800-257-5126

Child Abuse: It Shouldn't Hurt to Be a Kid

Educators and other school personnel are required by law to report suspected child abuse. This video advises these mandated reporters of their responsibilities under the law. It defines child abuse and explains how to recognize it. 1987. (27 minutes, color)

> Insights Media
> 2162 Broadway
> New York, NY 10024
> Phone: 212-721-6316

I Wish the Hitting Would Stop

> Red Flag, Green Flag Resources 1-800-627-3675

Scared Silent

> Harpo Productions

You're Hurting Me Too: Children and Domestic Violence

> Intermedia 1-800-553-8336.

Websites:

> American Bar Association Domestic Violence Commission
> www.abanet.org/domviol/home.html

> American Humane Association
> www.americanhumane.org

American Professional Society on the Abuse of Children (APSAC)
www.apsac.org

CAVNET (Access to a network of experts and advocates in the area
of family violence)
www.cavent.org

Child Abuse and Prevention Network
www.child-abuse.com

Children's Defense Fund (CDF)
www.childrensdefense.org

Family Violence Prevention Fund
www.fvpf.org

International Society for Prevention of Child Abuse and Neglect (IPSCAN)
www.ispcan.org

National Clearinghouse on Child Abuse and Neglect
www.calib.com/nccanch

National Coalition Against Domestic Violence
www.ncadv.org

National Data Archive on Child Abuse and Neglect
www.ndacan.cornell.edu

National Institutes of Health (NIH)
www.nih.gov

National Institute of Mental Health (NIMH)
www.nimh.nih.gov

National Resource Center on Child Maltreatment
www.gocwi.org/nrccm

Prevent Child Abuse American
www.preventchildabuse.org

REFERENCES

Alsop, R. (1995). Domestic violence and child abuse: Double jeopardy for families. *Protecting Children, 11*(3), 2.

Ascione, F., & Arkow, P. (Eds.). (1999). *Child abuse, domestic violence and animal abuse.* West Lafayette, IN: Purdue University Press.

Becker, J., Alpert, J., Subia Big Foot, D., Bonner, B., Geddie, L., Henggeler, S., Kaufman, K., & Walker, C. (1995). Empirical research on child abuse treatment: Report by the child abuse and neglect treatment working group, American Psychological Association. *Journal of Clinical Child Psychology, 24,* 23–46.

Blackman, J. (1996). "Battered women": What does this phrase really mean? *Domestic Violence Report, 1*(2), pp. 5, 11.

Bolton, F. G., & Bolton, S. R. (1987). *Working with violent families: A guide for clinical and legal practitioners.* Newbury Park, CA: Sage.

Cardarelli, A. (Ed.). (1997). *Violence between intimate partners.* Boston: Allyn & Bacon.

Child maltreatment 1999: Reports from the states to the national center on child abuse and neglect. (2001). U.S. Department of Health and Human Services. National Center on Child Abuse and Neglect. Washington, DC: Government Printing Office.

Crittenden, P. (1992). Children's strategies for coping with adverse home environments: An interpretation using attachment theory. *Child Abuse and Neglect, 16,* 329–343.

DePanfilis, D., & Salus, M. K. (1992). *A coordinated response to child abuse and neglect: A basic manual.* U.S. Department of Health and Human Services. NCCAN.

Dubowitz, H. (Ed.). (1999). *Neglected children: Research, practice, and policy.* Thousand Oaks, CA: Sage.

Effective Intervention in Domestic Violence and Child Maltreatment Cases: Guidelines for Policy and Practice. (1999). National Council of Juvenile and Family Court Judges.

Faller, K. C. (1990). *Understanding child sexual maltreatment.* Newbury Park, CA: Sage.

Fantuzzo, J. (1990). Behavioral treatment of the victims of child abuse and neglect. *Behavior Modification, 14,* 316–339.

Federal Bureau of Investigation (1990). *Uniform Crime Report.* Washington DC: U.S. Printing Office.

The Future of Children: Domestic Violence and Children. (1999). Packard Foundation, Vol. 9 (3).

Ganley, A. L. (1993). Workshop Notes, "Domestic violence in civil cases," North Dakota Judicial Conference, Bismarck, ND, November, 22, 1993.

Hart, B. (1990). Gentle jeopardy: The further endangerment of battered women and children in custody mediation. *Mediation Quarterly, 7,* 317–330.

Hoffman-Plotkin, D., & Twentyman, C. (1984). A multimodel assessment of behavioral and cognitive deficits in abused and neglected preschoolers. *Child Development, 55,* 794–802.

Holden, G., Geffner, R., & Jouriles, E. (Eds.). (1998). *Children exposed to marital violence.* Washington, DC: American Psychological Association.

Hotaling, G. T., & Sugarman, D. B. (1986). An analysis of risk markers in husband and wife violence: The current state of knowledge. *Violence and Victims, 1*(2), 101–124.

Jaffe, P., Wolfe, D., & Wilson, S. (1990). *Children of battered women.* Newbury Park, CA: Sage.

Kaufman, J., & Cicchetti, D. (1989). Effects of maltreatment on school age children's socioemotional development: Assessment in a day camp setting. *Developmental Psychology, 25,* 516–524.

Klein, E., Campbell, J., Soler, E., & Ghez, M. (1997). *Ending domestic violence: Changing public perceptions/Halting the epidemic.* Thousand Oaks, CA: Sage.

LaViolette, A., & Barnett, O. (2000). *It could happen to anyone: Why battered women stay.* Thousand Oaks, CA: Sage.

McKay, M. (1994). The link between domestic violence and child abuse: Assessment and treatment considerations. *Child Welfare, 73,* 29.

Peled, G., Jaffe, P. G., & Edelson, J. L. (1995). *Ending the cycle of violence.* Newbury Park, CA: Sage.

Miller-Perrin, C. L., & Perrin, R. (1999). *Child maltreatment: An introduction.* Thousand Oaks, CA: Sage.

Renzetti, C., Edelson, J., & Bergen, R. (2001). *Sourcebook on violence against women.* Thousand Oaks, CA: Sage.

Roy, M. (1988). *Children in the crossfire.* Deerfield Beach, FL: Health Communications.

Salinger, S., Kaplan, S., Pelcovitz, D., Samit, C., & Kreiger, R. (1984). Parent and teacher assessment of children's behavior in child maltreating families. *Journal of the American Academy of Child Psychiatry, 23,* 458–464.

Schlecter, S., & Edleson, J. (1995). In the best interest of women and children: A call for collaboration between child welfare and domestic violence constituencies. *Protecting Children, 11*(3), 6–11.

Shepard, M., & Pence, E. (Eds.). (1999). *Coordinating community responses to domestic violence.* Thousand Oaks, CA: Sage.

Stark, E., & Flitcraft, A. (1988). Women and children: A feminist perspective on child abuse. *International Journal of Health Services, 18,* 97–118.

Stark, E., & Flitcraft, A. (1996). *Women at risk: Domestic violence and women's health.* Thousand Oaks, CA: Sage.

Stordeur, R. A., & Stille, R. (1989). *Ending men's violence against their partners: One road to peace.* Newbury Park, CA: Sage.

Straus, M., & Gelles, R. (Eds.). (1990). *Physical violence in American families.* New Brunswick, NJ: Transaction Publishers.

Tower, C. (1992). The role of educators in the protection and treatment of child abuse and neglect. U.S. Department of Health and Human Services. DHHS Publication No. (ACF) 92-30172.

Tower, C. (1999). *Understanding child abuse and neglect* (4th ed.). Boston: Allyn & Bacon.

Violence and the Family: Report of the American Psychological Association Presidential Task Force on Violence and the Family. (1996). Washington, DC: American Psychological Association.

Wodarski, J., Kurtz, P., Gaudin, J., & Howing, P. (1990). Maltreatment and the school age child: Major academic, socioemotional, and adaptive outcomes. *Social Work, 35,* 506–513.

Wolfe, D., & Mosk, M. (1983). Behavioral comparison of children from abusive and distressed families. *Journal of Consulting and Clinical Psychology, 51,* 702–708.

Wolin, S. J., & Wolin, S. (1993). *The resilient self: How survivors of troubled families rise above adversity.* New York: Villard Books.

CHAPTER

12 Poverty

The Enemy of Children and Families

MARY LOU FULLER
University of North Dakota

The number of children in poverty is growing, and educators must understand the complexities of poverty in the lives of these children and their families. Schools have traditionally been designed for the Euro-American, middle-class student, in order to make the schools a positive learning environment for these children. The purpose of this chapter is to help the reader:

- Understand the demographics of poverty
- Examine some of the myths about poverty
- Understand the effects of poverty on the lives of children and their families
- Explore the school's relationship with these children and their families

Societies must be judged by the way they treat their children, and while an equal chance at life has long been a United States policy goal, that goal is not being met. (Rainwater & Smeeding, 1995)

This chapter examines the influence of poverty on the families of school children. There are obvious differences between the families of those that have, and those that do not, but there are also more subtle differences—both damaging to families generally and children specifically. If, as educators, we are to engage in an effective partnership with families of a lower-income status, we must understand the effects and dynamics of poverty and families.

As an educator, it is imperative that you understand the structures of families and how they function, but it is equally as important to understand how financial resources affect the way families function. The consequences of limited financial resources can be obvious as well as subtle.

Clearly children living below the poverty line may lack adequate diet, sufficient health care, adequate housing, and child care. But poverty also affects the less obvious needs that influence a child's ability to do well academically. Furthermore, as school children get older, clothes become more important for acceptance. The "in crowd" generally wears more expensive, designer clothes that are often out of the reach of low-income families. Who are these victims of poverty?

What Is Poverty?

The government officially determines what constitutes poverty. The standards are determined by the size of the family, total family income, and an annual adjustment for inflation (e.g., the rising cost of rent, food, utilities, clothing, transportation). When we talk about the national poverty level, what are we actually talking about?

Currently, the poverty level for a family of four is $15,150 (*Federal Register*, 1995). This figure does not mean that a family of four can provide for all of their basic needs with this sum, but the figure represents that on which a family can marginally exist. It often doesn't even mean basic medical and dental care—much less "extras" such as visits to the orthodontist, trips to Disneyland, special lessons, or sports. Parents in poverty lack options. The average poor family with children in 1992 had a total income of $7,541—$5.40 per person per day, $37.80 per person per week. "Every day you face impossible choices about cutting back on food, housing quality and your children's other needs," and to make matters even worse nearly one in two poor live in extreme poverty, with incomes below one-half of the poverty line (Sherman, 1994, p. 3).

Reflection...

Consider the ways that the life of a child living in poverty is different from the life of a middle-class child. Consider not only the major areas such as nutrition but also the small pleasures and experiences of childhood. What are some of your favorite childhood memories? Do children of poverty have access to these experiences?

To put these numbers into perspective, the cost of rearing a child born in 1990 to age 18 is approximately $150,000 (Outtz, 1993), and this doesn't include the costs of post-secondary education. For a family with three children, the cost would be $450,000 dollars—close to half a million dollars. Compare the resources of families and you can begin to understand the inequality of the experiences between the children of poverty and their middle-class counterparts.

Middle-class families simply have more choices as to how they'll meet the cost of raising their children. Families living in poverty are less able to purchase goods and services that allow them to share in a way of life that is characteristically American (Lichter & Eggebeen, 1993). Currently, the gap between the haves and the have-nots is widening. In addition, the economic gap between minority and majority groups continues to increase as well, with a disproportionate number of minority families living in poverty (Chavkin, 1993).

It is important to note that there is a difference between being "broke" and living in poverty. Being broke is a temporary state, while living in poverty is usually seen as a hopeless condition. As college students, many educators have been broke; they barely survived from month to month, but they knew that their financial situation would at some point in time improve. People in poverty generally can't see their situations changing.

In addition, while it is easier to discuss people living below the poverty line (the demographics are more readily available), we must also remember that there are a sizeable number of families who live just above the poverty line and who also struggle to meet the basic needs of their children. The observations in this chapter are also pertinent to this very large population.

Who Lives in Poverty and Why?

Approximately 16.2 percent of all U.S. children live in poverty. To make matters worse, these figures are even higher for children under the age of six (the most important years developmentally) (Dalakar, 2001). The United States ranks eighteenth out of twenty industrialized countries of the world for childhood poverty, and a child is nine times more apt to live in poverty in the United States than in countries such as Britain, France, Italy, Australia, and Finland (Children's Defense Fund, 1996).

One reason for the rise in child poverty in recent years is the failure of hourly wages to keep pace with inflation, particularly for young workers and those with less than a college education. Another reason is the increase in the number of families headed by a single parent—usually the mother. Mother-only families are at high risk for poverty due to the absence of a second adult wage earner and the historically lower earning power of women.

The 1995 guidelines for poverty (see Table 12.1) are not planned to provide enough money to support a family but only to assist in survival. It means that families living below the poverty line must sacrifice, and often these sacrifices are in the area of necessities—medical care, adequate food and housing, and so forth.

Reflection...

Make a list of the costs for a middle-class family of four. Include the obvious (e.g., food, shelter, utilities, clothing, medical care, recreation, transportation) as well as those less obvious items (e.g., car, health, life insurance, funds for emergencies, the dentist/orthodontist, lessons, computer, vacations). Add up these costs and note the discrepancy between those living in poverty and those in the middle class.

Myths about Poverty

Myth: We have all heard the stereotypes concerning poor people: They are people of color who are too lazy to work. This stereotype is not only inaccurate and un-

TABLE 12.1 2000 Poverty Guidelines for the Forty-Eight Contiguous States

| One Person | $8,959 | Family of three | $13,470 |
| Family of two | $11,531 | Family of four | $17,761 |

From: U.S. Census Bureau, 2000.

fair, but it makes understanding the dynamics of poverty more difficult and, consequently, harder to consider appropriate interventions.

Reality: The reality is that the percentage of people of color in poverty may not be greater than that of white children. In fact, there are more poor white children than children of color.

Myth: Poor people live in the inner city.
Reality: More children in rural settings (27 percent) are poor than children in the inner city (11 percent) (Sherman, 1994).

Myth: Families are poor because they are lazy and don't work.
Reality: The reality is that most of the children of poor families have at least one parent who is working; these children receive twice as much support from the paid work their parents do than from welfare programs (Children's Defense Fund, 1996).

Myth: If they just worked harder, they wouldn't be poor.
Reality: The reality is that a person can work forty hours a week at minimum wage and the salary earned won't raise a family above the poverty line. And, contrary to popular opinion, welfare is not a way of life for most poor people. The majority of families who receive welfare benefits receive them for less than two years (Sherman, 1994).

The Effects of Poverty

Poverty dims the future and creates stress and anxiety in the present. It limits opportunities and prospects. Although poor children can and often do succeed despite their poverty, researchers have documented a host of ways in which basic economic security helps children and poverty hurts them. Arloc Sherman (1994) has identified areas where money makes a big difference.

Money Buys Good Food

Money buys good food and good food results in healthy children. Lack of good food may result in iron deficiency, hunger, stunted growth, clinical malnutrition, and under-nutrition among low-income pregnant women.

Money Buys Safe and Decent Shelter

With poverty comes a lack of safe and decent shelter, homelessness, inadequate housing, moving from house to house and consequently from school to school. In addition, other problems include heating and electricity problems, utility shut-offs, cold and dampness, mold and allergies, cockroaches and rats, peeling paint and falling plaster, lead poisoning, crowded housing, and fire-prone mobile homes.

Money Buys Opportunities to Learn

Coming from a family in poverty means that the child(ren) probably will attend an inferior school, with inadequate supplies, which often is unable to retain the most skilled teachers and administrators. There will be fewer educational materials in the home, fewer stimulating activities (trips, lessons, museums, concerts, etc.), and less exposure to computers. While children from more affluent families often enter school with a strong educational background and degree of familiarity with computers, few children of poverty do. Also, children of poverty have greater home responsibilities that compete with school.

Money Reduces Family Stress and Conflict

As economic hardships increase so do the parents' level of stress and depression. Low incomes have an effect on mental health both for the parent and for the child. Their lives are unpredictable—the loss of a job may result in homelessness. The inability to pay the heating bill may result in illness. Because of their poverty, they often feel shame, fear, and anger. There is apt to be conflict about how best to use the limited resources that are available. Furthermore, stress increases the chances of child abuse and neglect.

Money Buys a Decent Neighborhood

The lack of resources increases the chance that children will live in noisy, crime-ridden neighborhoods, or be more likely to live in neighborhoods that pose a threat from chemicals and pollution. The neighborhood is less likely to have libraries, organized recreational opportunities, and parks, and more likely to have gangs.

Money Buys Health Care, Health Supplies, and Safety Devices

Even with Medicaid, the families of poor children have trouble affording medical care—particularly preventive medicine, and their children receive lower quality medical care and less dental care. Due to the lack of funds, they are more apt to delay seeing health care providers and consequently are more apt to need the services of a hospital emergency room. The dollars available may not stretch far enough to cover basic health care supplies and safety devices such as vitamins, sterile bandages, antiseptics, safety locks for doors and windows, smoke detectors, child car-safety seats, and more.

Money Buys Healthy Recreation

Low-income families are less able to afford the expense of extracurricular school activities (sports equipment, fees, uniforms). There are fewer recreational facilities available and those that are available usually charge a fee (swimming pools, etc.).

Money Buys Transportation, Communication, and Economic Opportunity

People in poverty lack cars (only 42 percent have cars). If there is public transportation, it may be too expensive (the cost of a Sunday family outing to a city park may be prohibitive) or the public transportation may not provide needed routes. This lack of transportation may limit access to child care, health services, recreation, jobs, job-training programs, post-secondary education, and low-cost stores (grocery stores in an inner city are often more expensive than in other neighborhoods). A major communication problem is the lack of a telephone in many poor homes. This again limits access to opportunities, emergency services, contact with the school, and a means of reducing the feeling of isolation.

Having read the above list you can now begin to comprehend the effects of poverty on the lives of these families. Figure 12.1 is a valuable aid in furthering that understanding.

> ## Reflection...
> Select a name and grade level for a student. Now walk your student through Figure 12.1 and then predict what that child's school experience is going to be. Most importantly, how can you best help this student?

The victims of poverty are our students and their families. Their lives are different from children with greater resources, but their needs are not. Without knowledge of, and concern for, the limitations imposed by poverty, educators will not be able to understand the functioning of these families. Consequently, we will be less effective as educators.

Schools and Families of Poverty

Poverty is a serious issue, both because the children it touches risk unsatisfied biological and safety needs (Reed & Sautter, 1990) and because the public schools are not designed to serve impoverished children.

Because the students bring the effects of poverty with them to school, teachers must understand and deal with poverty and its consequences. This study provides insights into how teachers understand poverty and how they relate to children of poverty and their families. Hopefully, these insights will provide some

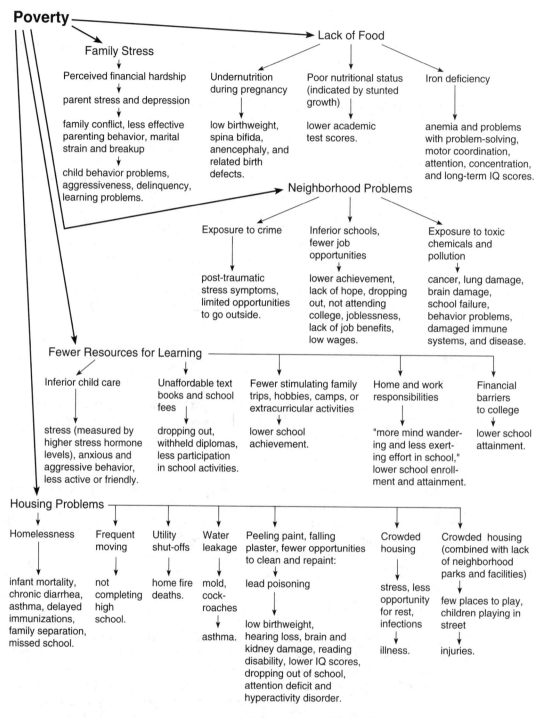

FIGURE 12.1   Examples of "pathways" from poverty to adverse child outcomes.

From: Writing America's Future by Children's Defense Fund. © 1994 by Children's Defense Fund. Used by permission of Beacon Press, Boston.

direction in how to prepare pre-service teachers to better understand and teach children of poverty.

Children

Unlike their middle-class peers, children living in poverty often experience discontinuity between schooling and other areas of their lives (Banks, 1993). Studies focusing on the relationship between socioeconomic status and academic success equates standards that are based on middle-class experiences and opportunities. This includes middle-class social and language behaviors. Students from middle-class families generally acquire these behaviors prior to entering school, while students with limited resources may not have had these advantages and, consequently, enter schools that were designed for someone else.

The children frequently live with parents or a parent who may not have had positive school experiences. Substantial numbers of these parents dropped out of school before completing high school. Still other students live in homes with language-minority parents who did not attend school in the United States.

The home environment is often cited as the reason for lack of academic achievement among low-income students. These parents are apt to be criticized for not being sufficiently involved. However, survival issues (e.g., money for food, clothing, affordable housing, adequate health care) command the time and energy of low-income parents, and they are often described as too distracted to attend to the educational needs of their children (Ascher, 1988). A list constructed by Ornstein and Levine (1989) outlines ten reasons for low achievement among low-income students, none of which refers to home environment. Ornstein and Levine (1989) suggest a need to transform the ways that teachers think about low-income students and their families.

With all their problems, these children must not be underestimated—they have impressive potential. A Kentucky science teacher describes how students in her highly impoverished school district won a statewide academic competition.

> Some of them get up with the problem every morning: How do you wake up without an alarm clock or a parent there to wake you? How do you get up and go to school when you probably didn't have a bed to sleep in the night before? These kids could beat anybody. They solve problems all day. (Sherman, 1994, p. 78)

Parents

Low-income parents are often thought to have little interest in the education of their children. The limited school involvement of low-income parents can be attributed, in part, to their lack of trust in the school personnel, as well as a lack of understanding of the way schools function. Often, differences in economic backgrounds between teachers and parents lead to discomfort on the part of parents when interacting with schools. This psychosocial distance between parents and teachers also leads to a lack of understanding of the dynamics operating within low-income families among teachers. Haberman (1995), in his book *Star Teachers of Children in Poverty,* discusses the difference between "star" teachers' perceptions of parents of poverty and those of other teachers.

Most teachers define "support from home" as parents helping children with assigned homework or supporting some action of school discipline. Star teachers, on the other hand, described parental support in terms of parents showing interest in what their children do in school and providing them with basics such as privacy, safety, sleep, nutrition, and health (Sherman, 1994, pp. 10–11).

Parents in poverty, like parents of all other socioeconomic groups, love their children, but may feel uncomfortable in their children's schools. They frequently feel helpless in their relationships with schools and teachers. In some cases, they may feel denigrated by the way in which schools and teachers communicate. Haberman says, "'Star' teachers do not blame parents. As much as they may find out about the child and the family, they see the information as a basis for helping children learn or want to learn more" (Haberman, 1995, pp. 11–12).

Poverty wears people down and defeats them, leaving little energy to deal with the problems within the family outside of fulfilling basic, daily needs (Webb & Sherman, 1989). They feel inadequate to participate in their children's learning, and their experience has been that the school assumes the responsibility to educate. Lack of information, skill, and transportation further isolates the parent from the school.

Working with Low-Income Families

In establishing a working partnership with low-income parents, you must remember that lack of resources doesn't indicate a lack of love or dreams for their children. Furthermore, although they may not be pedagogical experts, they are experts as far as their children are concerned and we need that expertise.

Teachers from middle- and lower-middle-class families have been enculturated into a middle-class world. Unless educators have had exposure to poverty and an understanding of the dynamics of poverty, they will subconsciously take middle-class expectations of parent–school relationships into their classrooms with them. Since most teachers are products of middle-class or lower-middle-class families, it is important that they not have inappropriate expectations for parents (Fuller, 1994).

The prolonged burdens and pressures of low-income families are considerable and not normally within the experience of most educators. Consequently, it is important to be well informed and sensitive when working with low-income families. The educator and the parent(s) have a strong common bond—all want the best for the child, and this can be the basis for a good working relationship.

Suggestions for Working with Low-Income Parents

Check Your Attitude

What is your attitude toward families who live in poverty? Do you blame the victim? Example: "If they just tried harder, they could significantly improve their financial situation." Do you deny the problems of poverty? Example: "If they can afford to have a television and VCR, they can't be doing too badly." Do you feel that people of poverty are intellectually inferior to those of the middle class? Example: "If they were more intelligent, they wouldn't be poor."

Educators are sensitive people who want the best for their students, but they still may have some unexamined attitudes toward poverty. How did you formulate your attitudes toward poverty? Have you checked the validity of your attitudes?

Know the Environment in Which Your Low-Income Children Live

If your students come from an urban/suburban area or a small town, walk around the neighborhood. See where your students play and investigate the quality and quantity of the recreational facilities that are available to them. Where do families shop for groceries? Walk through the stores and observe the selections available and the cost. In many such stores in these settings, the items are more expensive and the choices more limited than those in some middle-class neighborhoods. Is there a library in the neighborhood? Are there churches? A disproportionate number of bars? What is the cultural make-up of the area? If you feel that this is not a safe environment to explore (although this is not usually the case), ask an appropriate person to join you in this adventure.

If your students live in a more rural environment, drive around the area until you know it well. Again, familiarize yourself with the stores in the area as well as identifying the churches, recreational facilities, bars, and so on. Who lives there? Ride the school bus on each of the routes of your students and see where they get off. How long a ride do they have to and from school? How long is their walk from the bus stop to their home? What is the nature of the housing in that area? It is important to remember not to criticize your low-income students' physical environment. The area is a part of the child, and, as a result, they will feel demeaned by negative comments. An objective discussion of a community problem (e.g., drugs, garbage collection) should not be negative. After exploring your low-income students' environment, identify the strengths and weaknesses of the area and determine how each will affect your teaching strategies.

Gathering Basic Information about Low-Income Families

The school office is a good place to start becoming acquainted with families. There you will find a record that can act as an introduction, and you will discover information that will help you understand some of the dynamics of the family. How many children are there in the household? What are their ages? Are any preschool age? How many parents are in the home? Do one or both work? Is the place of employment listed? What is the address of the family? Do they have a telephone? Is there a work number listed?

Communicate with the Low-Income Parents

The best communication model is two-way communication—parents and educators talking and listening to one another, and this should be every teacher's ultimate communication goal. Unfortunately, this is not always possible, for some parents are unable, unwilling, or uncomfortable in communicating with the schools. Nevertheless, it is important to actively endeavor to inform parents. Contacting parents about positive matters will make it easier and more productive if you need to work with them on a problem at a later date. Writing notes, assuming parents can read in your language, to a parent about their child's positive behaviors will demonstrate that you care about their child and that you recognize and appreciate their desirable behaviors. Phone calls can be particularly helpful in establishing positive parent–teacher communication. Also, brief calls to make a positive comment about a student encourages parents to become more actively involved in communicating with the school; after all, if a parent starts to believe, "That teacher likes my child," parental enthusiasm in school affairs will more likely result. Unfortunately, not all low-income families have phones, which means a letter or visit will be your options.

Getting Low-Income Families Actively Involved: Creating a Partnership

The view of parent involvement has changed over the last twenty-five years. In the past, high profile, low participation was the norm. This involvement often took the form of large meetings held in the evenings when parents listened to what educators had to say. The schedules of contemporary families no longer make this a viable activity. More importantly, these meetings no longer fit the contemporary goals of parental involvement—they were monologues rather than dialogues. The nature of parent involvement has changed, and true parent involvement is now seen as a partnership between the school and the home.

Low-income families have many demands on their time, as mentioned earlier in the chapter, and lack the economic resources necessary to reduce some of the stress caused by these demands. In addition, they may have had a negative school experience and not feel comfortable in the school environment. Flexibility, practicality, and creativity can help you mitigate some of these problems. For example, meetings with parents needn't always be held in the classroom. You can meet for a cup of coffee, make a home visit, and so forth. Moreover, although it is usually more productive to meet face to face with a parent, a phone call can also provide you with an opportunity for two-way communication. If there isn't a telephone available, you could provide your home phone number and the times you will be available.

Partnerships are based on respect, and it is imperative that parents are shown the same respect we show our colleagues. Also, in partnerships with low-income parents, it is important to remember that the stresses of life may be such that there will be times when parents do not have the emotional or physical energy to be full partners. A single father who has a minimum-wage job, a sick child, no day care, and is being evicted may have to expend his energies elsewhere.

Become Involved in the Community

To understand families, you must understand them as a part of a community as well as individual units. The following recommendations are suggestions of ways to become involved in a community. While understanding teachers are very busy people who work hard emotionally, intellectually, and even physically, at the end of the school day, or week, they need time to rejuvenate. However, the opportunities to learn about students and families continues beyond the classroom. You may not be able to participate in all of the suggested activities, but select those that interest you the most. In addition, your friends or family might want to join you in some of these activities.

If there is a community celebration, such as street fairs, ethnic holidays, and events such as pow-wows, attend. Accept as many invitations as you can: Bas- or Bar-Mitzvahs, confirmations, first communions, quinceneroes, and so forth. If you have a student singing a solo with a church choir, playing in the little league finals, or being honored for their talents in any way, attend.

Be Sensitive to the Financial Limitations of Low-Income Families

Low-income families may find it very difficult to send money for field trips, school projects, or special materials. Even requests for cookies for a party may be beyond some families. Also, some children are not able to participate in school sports due to the cost of the registration fee, equipment, or clothing. Imagine how demeaning and disappointing these situations are to the children and their parents.

Summary

In conclusion, as educators we have a wonderful opportunity, as well as a responsibility, to help the children and families of poverty. We must respect these families for a variety of reasons—their perseverance, hard work, and, of course, strong desire for success and a good life for their children. Not all educators are making positive contributions for a variety of reasons. Webb and Sherman (1989) take a rather dim view of educators' attitudes toward their students in poverty. They state, "The stigma of poverty is a powerful force in American classrooms. It manipulates teacher behavior in ways that educators themselves seldom realize. It can lower a teacher's expectations for a child, and can initiate a self-fulfilling prophecy of failure" (p. 487).

Lastly, well-informed teachers will not be influenced by the stereotypes of poor children. Educators that are knowledgeable and skillful can add to the quality of life for these children and their families and grow professionally themselves.

RECOMMENDED ACTIVITIES

1. Volunteer at a homeless shelter and keep a journal of your experience.

2. Interview a social worker about the lives of children and families living in poverty.

3. Volunteer in a thrift shop. Write a description of three of the regular customers.

4. Ask a social worker, Head Start teacher, and a nutritionist from WIC to speak to your class about the problems of children and families in poverty, either individually or as a panel.

5. Volunteer in a Head Start classroom and keep a journal of your experience.

6. Collect demographics about the resources of the poor as opposed to the middle class. Then use those figures to predict the kind of childhood experience each will have.

7. Determine the income and expenses of a single parent making minimum wage and raising three children. Use your community to determine expenses: housing, food, transportation, health care, and so forth.

ADDITIONAL RESOURCES

Poverty and Students

Books:

Haberman, M. (1995). *Star teachers of children in poverty.*

Haberman is recognized as an expert in teacher education for urban schools—primarily schools that serve children of poverty. In this book he describes how those who have been recognized as "star" teachers work with children of poverty. It is practical and yet sensitive and makes specific suggestions. ISBN: 0-912099-08-9.

Director of Publications
Kappa Delta Pi
P.O. Box A
West Lafayette, IN 47906
Phone: 800-284-3167

Kozol, J. (1995). *Amazing grace: The lives of children and the conscience of a nation.*

Amazing Grace is a book about the hearts of children who grow up in the South Bronx—the poorest congressional district in our nation. Kozol takes the reader into the lives of these children and their families and introduces them to a world they don't know. Kozol uses the words of his participants to help us understand the kindness of their hearts and the difficulty of their lives. This is a book that should be on every educator's bookshelf. ISBN: 0-517-79999-5.

Crown Publishers
201 East 50th Street
New York, NY 10022
Phone: 212-751-2600

Nunez, R. (1996). *The new poverty: Homeless families in America.* New York: Insight Books.

This book explores the issues surrounding homelessness and suggests solutions for stemming homelessness, poverty, and welfare dependence, describing a model for a family-based system of comprehensive residential, educational, and employment training centers. Includes black-and-white photos and excerpts from interviews with homeless people. Of interest to general readers, policymakers, and professionals in sociology and education.

Sherman, Arloc. (1994). *Wasting America's future: The children's defense fund report on the costs of child poverty.*

For the first time in one place, there is sweeping evidence on the human, social, and economic costs of child poverty in the Unites States. This book gives surprising evidence that even a brief episode of poverty can do lasting damage to children and families. Also, we learn that low-income family background is a devastatingly powerful predictor of negative outcomes for children. For many readers, the essence of this book will lie in the stories of children and their families, many of whom endure unfair and damaging lives with grace, and who remind us that good things—whole and healthy lives—are worth paying for. ISBN: 0-8070-4107-6.

> Beacon Press
> 25 Beacon Street
> Boston, MA 02108
> Phone: 617-742-2110

Chapters:

Moles, O. C. (1993). Collaboration between schools and disadvantaged parents: Obstacles and opening. In N. F. Chavkin (Ed.), *Families and schools in a pluralistic society* (pp. 21–52). Albany, NY: State University Press.

Articles:

Children's Defense Fund. (1993). Child poverty hits record level. *CDF Reports, 14*(12), 11.

Children's Defense Fund. (1987). *Declining earnings of young men: Their relation to teenage pregnancy and family formation.* Washington, DC: Children's Defense Fund.

Children's Defense Fund. *Adolescent pregnancy and family formation.* Washington, DC: Children's Defense Fund, Adolescent Pregnancy Prevention Clearing House.

Videos:

America's Children: Poorest in a Land of Plenty
A narration by Maya Angelou of the tragic neglect of children in the United States and a call for change. NTC Resource Center.

Children of Poverty

This video examines some of the effects of poverty and the prognosis of children in poverty growing up to be healthy, both emotionally and physically. 1987.

Films for the Humanities & Sciences
P.O. Box 2053
Princeton, NJ 08543
Phone: 800-257-5126

Faces of Poverty

A correction of a number of misconceptions about the poor and reveals them not as objects of compassion, but as our neighbors.

NTC Resource Center
Phone: 972-490-3438
Fax: 972-490-7216
Email: sgordon@ntcumc.org

The Homeless Home Movie

Produced in collaboration with homeless people and shown on PBS. This thought provoking homeless video is recommended by the National Coalition for the Homeless. The video is widely considered to be the best and most broadly applicable case study available on the scope and diversity of homelessness in America.

Media Visions, Inc.
108 8th Avenue South
South Saint Paul, Minnesota 55075
www.2.bitstream.net/~mvisions/purchase.htm

Organizations:

Children's Defense Fund
122 C Street, NW
Washington, DC 20001
Phone: 202-628-8787
Email: info@childwelfare.com
www.childrensdefense.org

Websites:

Center on Budget and Policy Priorities
www.cbpp.org

Child Welfare Home Page
www.childwelfare.com

Child Welfare Library
www.childwelfare.com/kids/library.htm

Human Resource Policy Center
www.urban.org/ar95/resource.html

Institute for Children and Poverty
www.opendoor.com/hfh/icp.html

Institute for Research on Poverty
www.ssc.wisc.edu/irp

National Center for Children in Poverty
www.cait.cpmc.columbia/edu/dept/nccp

Politics of Poverty
www.americanradioworks.org/features/14_million

REFERENCES

Ascher, C. (1988). Improving the school–home connection for poor and minority urban students. *The Urban Review, 20*(2), 109–123.

Baca Zinn, M. (1987). Structural transformation and minority families. In L. Beanery & C. Stimpson (Eds.), *Women, households, and the economy* (pp. 155–171). New Brunswick, NJ: Rutgers University Press.

Banks, C. R. (1993). Restructuring schools for equity: What have we learned in two decades. *Phi Delta Kappan, 75*, 42–44, 46–48.

Chavkin, N. F. (Ed.). (1993). *Families and schools in a pluralistic society.* Albany, NY: State University of New York Press.

Children's Defense Fund. (1996). Key facts about children. *Children's Defense Fund Reports, (17)*2, p. 5.

Coontz, S. (1995). The American family and the nostalgia trap. *Phi Delta Kappan, 76*(7), pp. K1–K20.

Dalaker, J. (2001). Poverty in the United States: 2000. Current Population Reports: Series P60-214. Washington, DC: U.S. Government Printing Office.

Federal Register. (1995). 60(27), pp. 7772–7774.

Fuller, M. L. (1994). The monocultural graduate in the multicultural environment: A challenge for teacher educators. *Journal of Teacher Education, 45*(4), 269–278.

Haberman, M. (1995). *Star teachers of children in poverty.* West Lafayette, IN: Kappa Delta Pi International Educational Honor Society.

Katz, M. (1986). *In the shadow of the poorhouse: A social history of welfare in America.* New York: Praeger Publishers, Inc.

Lasch, C. (1977). *Haven in a heartless world.* New York: Basic Books.

Lichter, D., & Eggebeen, D. (1993). Rich kids, poor kids: Changing income inequality among American children. *Social Forces, 71*(3), 761–780.

Ornstein, A., & Levine, D. (1989). Social class, race, and school achievement: Problems and prospects. *Journal of Teacher Education, 40*(5), 17–23.

Outtz, J. H. (1993). *The demographics of American families.* Santa Monica, CA: Milken Institute for Job and Capital Formation. (ERIC Document Reproduction Service No. ED367 726)

Polakow, V. (1993). *Lives on the edge: Single mothers and their children in the other America.* Chicago: The University of Chicago Press.

Rainwater, L., & Smeeding, T. M. (1995). U.S. doing poorly—compared to others—policy points of view. *Child Poverty News, 5*(3), 4–5.

Reed, S., & Sautter, R. C. (1990). Children of poverty: The status of twelve million young Americans. *Phi Delta Kappan, 71*(10), K1–K12.

Sherman, A. (1994). *Wasting America's future: The children's defense fund report on the cost of child poverty.* Boston: Beacon Press.

U.S. Census Bureau. (2000). Poverty in the United States. In *Current Population Research Series.* Washington, DC: U.S. Government Printing Office.

Webb, R. B., & Sherman, R. R. (1989). *Schooling and society* (2nd ed.). New York: MacMillan Publishing Company.

CHAPTER

13 Fatherhood, Society, and School

CHARLES B. HENNON
Miami University

GLENN OLSEN
University of North Dakota

GLEN PALM
St. Cloud State University

This chapter will enable the reader to recognize the role of the father in a child's life in the context of family, school, and society. The father's role in school will be discussed, and change relating to that role will be presented. The purpose of this chapter is to help the reader to:

- Describe the culture of fatherhood
- Compare fathers of today to fathers of previous generations
- Identify fathering in the context of family systems
- Describe the relationships between fathers and school achievement
- Identify ways of involving fathers in schools and their children's education
- Identify ways of making the community and school environment more father friendly

A new movement for reviving the faded image of the strong male parent ignited a debate in the mid 1990s. "Tonight, about 40 percent of American children will go to sleep in homes in which their fathers don't live." Are fathers really disappearing from the lives of children, as Blankenhorn (1995, p. 1) asserts? "Father hunger, or awareness of it, is especially acute in the United States. Some observers believe that the United States is in danger of becoming, in effect, a fatherless society, shorn of its male parents not by war or disease, but by choice." Is the United States becoming "fatherless" as lamented by Louv (1994, p. 2)?

The advantages of families being more in partnership with schools is recognized by educators (e.g., Epstein, 1995; National Center for Education Statistics, 1997; Riley, 1994; U.S. Department of Education, 2000). Both schools and families benefit and techniques for building such partnerships are being disseminated. One aspect often overlooked, however, is the role fathers play in forming these partnerships as well as in the academic achievement of their children. The examination of fathers' roles is imperative to the understanding of family dynamics and how they influence children. It is widely believed that divorce and fatherless homes have dire consequences for school achievement (Amato, 1994; 1998). Perhaps less recognized is the influence of fathers in all types of family systems on school attendance, schoolwork, and school and personal success (Amato, 1998; Marsiglio, Amato, Day, & Lamb, 2000). These influences are explored in this chapter.

In some people's view, the role of gender in parenting is swinging from clearly defined difference in roles and complement of functions of the 1950s (Parsons, 1955) to an ideal of androgynous parenting (Rotundo, 1985) in which gender differences grow smaller if socialization changes. The latest fatherhood movement, however, appears to emphasize gender differences. Gender as a concept is mired in a complex of social and political issues (Thompson & Walker, 1995) and often is discussed in emotionally charged atmospheres. Some writers express ambivalence about delineating parenting roles based on gender while understanding that the changing roles of fathers represent both threats to the status quo and opportunities (Louv, 1993).

The authors of this chapter are advocating for more father involvement in all aspects of children's lives. Society in general, and families and schools in particular, benefit from supporting men in their roles as fathers. We believe that fathering is qualitatively different from mothering and that while some men and women desire less gender-specific parenting practices, others support more conventional approaches to parenting. Here we highlight some of the advantages of more androgynous approaches while articulating unique differences and strengths that fathers bring to parenting. We respect individual values and approaches to fathering and cultural differences in conceptions of what a father is and how fathering is done.

Our approach is not value free. We believe that more involvement by fathers with their children is valuable for the child, the father, the mother, the schools, and the society. We believe that fathers can be more involved regardless of their marital status and living arrangement relative to the child. Recognizing diversity in family forms and functioning, we believe that certain principles and practices can be more universally applied, whereas in other cases more selected interventions may be appropriate. For example, married fathers living with their children, divorced fathers living elsewhere, remarried fathers living with stepchildren while their own children are living with stepfathers, fathers in prison, and fathers in intimate same-sex relationships who are living with their children, all face unique issues and may benefit from different resources, supports, and services.

Exploring fatherhood and father involvement, especially involvement with education and schooling, we first examine how the culture of fatherhood both pressures and reinforces fathers. Secondly, we discuss the conduct of fathering. Understanding fathers, social change, and how fathers can be part of negotiated social change allows a better appreciation of fathers' activities relative to their children's education and schooling. Next, we discuss how family systems influence fathering and thus how interventions must be sensitive to systemic rather than merely individualistic characteristics. Finally, we turn to a discussion on involving fathers in schools and education.

Basic Premises

Five premises underlie the focus on the unique characteristics of men as parents. These underline the importance of fathers and fathering and are the guiding principles and rationale for making specific efforts to increase and support father involvement in families, schooling, and schools.

- *Fathers and mothers are different.* Not as clear-cut as they used to be, gender boundaries for individuals have been stretched so that men can be nurturers and women providers. Individual differences aside, there are generic gender differences based on the interaction of biology and gender socialization (Biller, 1993; Roberts, 1996). Men and women tend to approach parenting with different goals, values, and styles (Amato, 1998; Gottman, 1998). These differences are more subtle than the instrumental and expressive functions described by Parsons (1955).

- *Fathers are essential and not easily replaceable* by other male role models (Blankenhorn, 1995). Children benefit from the unique style and investment of male energy in their well-being (Roberts, 1996). The real importance of fathers may hinge more on their being different from mothers than being a clone of a good mother.

- *Standards for fatherhood must be revised to reflect a higher common ground* (Jackson, 1994). Fatherhood standards have eroded as family diversity and self-gratification are accepted as predominant values, changing the focus from clear expectations to fuzzy criteria for good fathering (Samuelson, 1996). It seems critical to create a set of high standards that respects diversity of family forms and cultural practices. At the same time, fathers must meet their own needs without diluting their commitment to their children. There is some consensus that caring, commitment, and leadership is areas where standards need to be emphasized (Palm, 1994).

- *Fathers and mothers often contribute different human, financial, and social capital resources.* Children's development is related to the quality and quantity of resources provided by parents. Human capital is the skills, knowledge, and traits that promote achievement. Numeric and verbal ability, effective work habits, and knowledge of correct forms of dress and speech are among the human capital resources that parents can possess. Parents with high levels of human capital can foster their children's cognitive and scholastic abilities through providing stimulating home environments, modeling behavior, and encouraging high academic and occupational aspirations. Financial capital includes income as well as the goods and experiences purchased. Parents with financial capital can provide children good food and shelter, safe environments, access to high-quality schools, support for attending college, and commodities facilitating academic success such as computers, Internet access, books, tutoring, and travel. Social capital is a resource related to the relationships between people. This includes family and community relations benefiting the cognitive and social development of children. An important aspect of social capital is a coparental relationship in which parents are able to present a unified authority structure. Such structures, even if parents are divorced, can show children that there is agreement on rules and discipline, support for each other's decisions, and that parental authority is not arbitrary. Such hierarchical authority learned in the family helps children adjust to other institutions so organized, such as the schools. Supportive coparenting also influences the parent–child relationship, as mothers become more effective and fathers improve the quality of their parenting (Amato, 1998).

- *Differences between mothers and fathers should be reframed from deficits to strengths* (Doherty, 1991). Men have unique characteristics based on their socialization that can be beneficial to the parent role (Gottman, 1998). Some examples are problem solving, sense of humor, playfulness, and risk-taking (Johnson & Palm, 1992). How men interact with their children forces youth to "stretch" both emotionally and physically. Fathers push children to deal with the world outside the mother–child bond. Children, consequently, develop a complex set of interactive and emotional communications skills. Fathers also encourage differentiation from the family and help adolescents, in particular, develop individual autonomy (Dudley & Stone, 2001; Roberts, 1996). Men can benefit from learning more about empathy and expressing feelings and sensitivity but are more likely to focus on these when feeling respected for some of the strengths they bring to parenting.

Differences must be acknowledged by schools to involve more men in the education process and to support their unique contributions to children as learners as well as to schools as institutions. The premises identified can be used by educators to develop a clearer understanding of how to facilitate fathers encouraging children to achieve their best, to take risks, and to solve problems.

Reflection...

What are the differences, from your experience and reading, between fathers and mothers? Are the differences based on biology or gender socialization? Because there are differences, how do we as a society deal with the differences? Do we change men, change women, or change society? Do we want androgynous males and females?

Fatherhood in Context

Culture of Fatherhood

Some authors suggest that a popular culture of fatherhood exists in the United States. This popular culture is fueled by the mass media and supported by many parenting experts (LaRossa, 1988; LaRossa & Reitzes, 1993) and can influence how fathers parent. Consumers of this culture are those attentive to the mass media's presentations about the fathering role and how fathers ought to parent. This popular culture includes ideals about the appropriate amount and type of father–child interactions, responsibilities of fathers, and such things as how fathers ought to be involved in their children's schooling. This culture exalts androgynous, new, or modern fatherhood.

Some media, educators, and social scientists are portraying and advocating more nurturing fathering. Men should place less emphasis on being a distant and stern father who is a good provider, it is argued, and place more emphasis on playing, talking, caring, and nurturing. Some see this as new, better, and more responsive fathering. Others see it as feminizing the role of the father or, at least, making it more androgynous. In any case, the roles of fathers may be becoming more complex and confused. Traditional measures for being a good father may no longer prevail (Amato, 1998). This focusing on new fatherhood is not confined to the United States. Similar questioning of fathers' roles is found in many societies worldwide. (Bruce, Lloyd, & Leonard, 1995; Hennon, in press; Lamb, 1987, 1998; Louv, 1994).

Reading about parenting is not likely to have a great influence on a father's behavior if there are other, more pressing desires and needs (LaRossa & Reitzes, 1993). These other desires and needs might include worries about unemployment, job security, career advancement, perpetual overworking, and so on. Attention to social and economic achievement and providing for one's family appears to be a major focus of men (Amato, 1998; Bruce et al., 1995; Hennon, in press). This is apparent even in the face of data suggesting that "family comes first" or that men are now more involved with and attuned to their families (Cohen, 1987).

LaRossa (1988) argues there has been more change in the culture of fatherhood than there has been in the conduct of fathering.

> The idea that fathers have radically changed—that they now are intimately involved in raising their children—qualifies…as a folk belief, and it…is having an impact on our lives and that of our children. On the positive side, people are saying that at least we have made a start. Sure men are not as involved with their children as some of us would like them to be, but…the fact we are talking about change represents a step in the right direction. (p. 454)

Discourse may be an important preliminary step and may lead to action. It can also be seen as more pressure on men to change and be something else, perhaps something they do not want to be. Whereas some men relish involved fatherhood and appreciate information on and support for better nurturing and involvement, others do not. Some do not because fathering is a private affair, and some do not because they are already fulfilling the role in the way they think is best. It is their mode of fathering, perhaps the same as their fathers, and it works. "Best" may or may not include a lot of direct care giving and responsibility.

Modern Father

Given the popular parental culture and the sense of egalitarianism prevailing today in many segments of society, it is likely that fathering will continue to evolve (Cherlin, 1998; Draper, 1998; Lamb, 1998). This is especially likely in the white middle class (LaRossa, 1988). The middle class is the driving force behind the changes, at least attitudinally, in the culture of fatherhood.[1] Thus men socialized to be fathers in a more conventional mode may feel pressure and tension to accept and change to a more modern mode.

Some modern fathers may be feeling pressured by more traditional wives to change their fathering activities. Research (LaRossa & LaRossa, 1981; Roberts,

1996) points to certain women protecting their turf and monitoring and evaluating men's household and child-care activities in ways men find uncomfortable. Or at least women do not expect men to be very involved (Marsiglio, 1991; Thompson & Walker, 1989).[2] Men and women tend to develop parenting and household management strategies along lines of believed competencies. Both parents assess their own abilities and preferences relative to those of the partner and their expectations of their partners (Kaplan & Hennon, 1992). Likely, each then assumes responsibility for tasks within the areas where they hold competencies and expertise (Anderson & Sabatelli, 1999).

Both parents can learn and master many tasks. However, earlier socialization and cultural and reference group expectations influence the perceptions of competencies as well as "what ought to be." Fathers tend to become involved when their wives expect them to be highly involved in household management and child care (Simons, Whitbeck, Conger, & Melby, 1990). Nevertheless, the distribution of household and child-care tasks may be more a function of power and its use than strict cultural norms about parenting. Women continue to do most of the work (Arendell, 2000; Hennon, in press; Hennon & Loker, 2000; Marsiglio et al., 2000).

Reflection...

Who did most of the household and child-care tasks in your home when you were growing up? Will it be the same in your household? Does power have a role in their decisions?

Radoslav and Maria

Radoslav and Maria Popescu immigrated twenty-five years ago from Eastern Europe and are living in an ethnic neighborhood in a large midwestern city. They both grew up in a cultural context emphasizing more formal but loving relationships between fathers and children, especially sons. Fathers were stern and worked to care for and protect their families. In fact, Radoslov and Maria's fathers worked hard to get them to the United States where they could experience a better life. In the United States, their families wanted to acculturate and be like the rest. Radoslav and Maria grew up speaking English, listening to rock music, watching portrayals of family life on television and in movies, and made friends with American kids in their schools. In their neighborhood, some things remained more traditional and yet there was pressure to "be American."

After high school, Radoslav (Rad as he is called) got work with a construction firm owned by his dad's brother. Maria pursued a nursing degree part-time at a community college, while working part-time. Being in love, they got married and soon had two children. Now, the older child is in fifth grade and the younger one is in third. Maria is back in school part-time, attending day classes so she can be home evenings with her family. A problem is arising with the older child. In school, she seems distracted and is falling behind the other students. The school psychologist wants to meet with the parents. A question thus arises: does Radoslav take time off work to go?

The macrocultures (society) of the United States and that of the original homeland may be in conflict in this case. Perhaps not, Rad goes only if there is a behavioral problem and he needs to "straighten his daughter out," or perhaps if he perceives the school is at fault and he wants to straighten out the school. He remembers that his dad wanted him to do well in school, but Rad's father always respected and deferred to the school as the authority. His mother attended meetings; his dad never set foot inside a U.S. school. Rad's work buddies and the uncle who owns the company depend on him. Taking time off work would be a problem, and he would have to explain this to his uncle and workmates. Besides, even though Rad supports and loves his daughter, this is "women stuff," not an issue for men (at least according to his friends).

But the mesoculture (community) may also offer some different and conflicting norms. Some neighbors seem to be involved in PTO, field trips, parent–teacher conferences, and the like. Some fathers help their children with homework. And the microculture (family) also influences thinking about what is right. Maria is working and going to school, and she is "modern." She expects and even demands that Rad get involved with his children, reminding him of how much he disliked the distant relationship he had with his dad. She would have to miss either work or class to go to the meeting. She thinks, "Why should I be the one to always make the sacrifices?" Besides, she remembers how Rad used to be so considerate in helping with housework and watching the children. What has happened? Why do their expectations about Rad's role as father seem to be at odds, and why is this creating conflict in their marriage?

Conduct of Fathering

On Time Activities

Although some research indicates that today there is more male involvement in household and child-rearing activities, it is not clear exactly how widespread this change in family organization may be (Anderson & Sabatelli, 1999; Arendell, 2000; Canary, Emmers-Sommer, & Faulkner, 1997; Coltrane, 2000; Gottman, 1998; Lamb, 1998; LaRossa, 1988; Marsiglio et al., 2000; Mintz, 1998; Robinson, 1990). While women have reduced and men have increased, slightly, their time contributed to housework, in the 1990s, women still did at least twice as much routine housework as did men (Coltrane, 2000). But, when both paid and unpaid work is considered, both men and women average about 60 hours per week with men's greater involvement in paid employment and women's in unpaid housework (Canary et al., 1997). A commonly cited statistic is that men in dual-earner households do about 30 percent of the housework. In some studies, child care is included in housework.

Empirical data are confusing and inconsistent concerning the amount of father involvement with their children and how much change, if any, there has been in this involvement. Sanik (1990) found that in 1986 fathers were spending an average of 1.7 hours per day in child care, compared to 0.5 hours in 1967. Other data (Bruce et al., 1995) show that in 1986 men were spending an average of 0.8 hours per week in direct child care whereas women were spending 2.0 hours. Other research indicates the following:

> Even as the concepts of shared parenting and shared bread winning gain currency in Western media, the reality of emotional and physical fatherlessness grows.... A study of four-year-olds in 10 countries discovered that the average daily time that fathers spent alone with their children was less than one hour, ranging from 6 minutes per day in Hong Kong and 12 minutes in Thailand to 54 minutes in China and 48 minutes in Finland. When the average time spent by both parents with their children was added to these amounts, the number of hours that fathers were present with their children ranged from 1 hour and 36 minutes per day in the United States to 3 hours and 43 minutes in Belgium. These findings suggest that even when fathers are present as an active member of a family, their direct involvement in childcare can be very limited (Louv, 1994, p. 2).

Robinson (1990) reports that U.S. men increased their average hours per week in housework from five hours in 1965 to twenty hours in 1985.[3] A *Parents* 1993 fatherhood poll finds that men are moving closer to child-care parity with women, especially in households with mothers employed full-time outside the home (Louv, 1994). Lamb (1987) reports that fathers shoulder about one-tenth of the responsibility for children, regardless of the employment status of the mother in two-parent households. A study in the 1980s showed that fathers in dual-career households spent twice the time (5.3 hours per day) as did fathers in single-career households. (2.1 hours) in solo child care (Canary et al., 1997). Research documents a "slow increase in the level of father involvement in two-parent households since the 1970s, both in proportionate and absolute terms, although levels of fathers' engagement and accessibility remained significantly lower than those for mothers" (Marsiglio et al., 2000, p. 1182). Fathers' involvement in child care appears to be best explained by mothers' work hours and the fathers' adherence to nontraditional sex role. Men, in general, participate in child care because of necessity. "Daddy fills in when Mommy's work schedule leaves her unavailable for infant care" (Canary et al., 1997, p. 111). Thompson and Walker (1995) register that "women and girls do more than their share of housework in families" (p. 852) and note that feminist research does not forget that "overall mothers, not fathers, are responsible for children" (p. 858). James LeVine, director of the Fatherhood Project, is quoted in *American Health* (Schroepfer, 1991) as saying society is in the midst of an evolution, not a revolution, concerning fathers' involvement in child-related chores.

Research indicates that fathers are less likely than mothers to provide most of the continuous care for children and are less likely to sacrifice their own time to do so (LaRossa, 1988). Fathers are less involved in providing care, attending to, responding to, holding, soothing, and comforting their children (Arendell, 2000; Darling-Fisher & Tiedje, 1990; LaRossa, 1988; Marsiglio, 1991; Thompson & Walker,

1989). Even fathers completing specially designed parent education programs are not especially involved in parent–child interaction. This is possibly due to work responsibilities, social obligations, and other factors (McBride, 1990).

There are contradictions in the evidence about fathering. Although they do less "on time" activities with their children than mothers, men still report parenting to be an important role for them (Cohen, 1987). Other studies suggest that fathers consider their primary responsibility as being a good provider (Bruce et al., 1995; Hennon, in press; Lamb, 1987; Thompson & Walker, 1989). Many studies report increased involvement in parenting, especially among younger men in dual-earner families. However, statements such as "men appear to be more conscientious parents than some might expect" (Canary et al., 1997, p. 110) and "men's greater involvement…in parenting likely is the hallmark of the 1990s" (Gilbert, 1993, p. 43) can be contrasted with "although people are moving toward the idea that fathers should be more involved with children, demographic and social changes have resulted in fathers being less involved with children than perhaps at anytime in U.S. history" (Amato & Booth, 1997, p. 228). In a 1992 National Center for Fathering Gallup Poll, 96 percent agreed that fathers needed to be more involved in their children's education, 54 percent agreed that fathers spent *less* time with their children than their fathers did with them, and only 42 percent agreed that most fathers knew what was going on in their children's lives (U.S. Department of Education, 2000). Given the available data, the involved father may be more apparent than real.

While the concern about fatherless families has driven much of the debate about fatherhood during the 1990s, our understanding of the contributions of nonresidential fathers has also increased (Reichart, 1999). The focus on levels of father involvement has detracted from our understanding of the contributions made by the 40 percent of fathers who are nonresident fathers. This group is composed of divorced fathers who do not have or share custody of their children, fathers who are unmarried and may have cohabited for a period of time. Many of these fathers are young and their families are often described as fragile (Maclanahan & Garfinkel, 1999). There is also a growing number of fathers who are absent through incarceration (Mumola, 2000). Nonresident fathers are not a homogeneous group of deadbeat, absent fathers. The paths to nonresident fatherhood are diverse and involve varying levels of commitment and father involvement.

In the real lives of men, fathers may not perceive the necessity or appropriateness of being involved with their children in other than playful or providing ways. Those wishing to negotiate a change in this social reality may find more profit from working directly with men and their families. These agents of change may want to pay special attention to what fathers say is important about what they do and what they see as shortcomings. Learning the meanings that real men attach to parenting and to how they may wish to change may be more constructive in negotiating social change. It will also be important to construct services and create policies that are sensitive to the diverse family settings that have evolved for nonresident fathers (Sorensen & Zibman, 2001).

Conceptual Framework

Lamb (1987) provides a conceptualization for considering father involvement. He discriminates among *engagement* (time spent in one-on-one interaction with a child, in nurturing, playing, or disciplining), *accessibility* (less intense interaction, in which the father is engaged in another task but is available to respond to the child if needed), and *responsibility* (being accountable for the child's welfare and care, such as making and tracking appointments and being sure the child's needs are being met). Being responsible does not always require direct interaction with the child. A father can be anxious, worried, satisfied, or planning for contingencies while otherwise engaged (such as in driving a car, in employment, or playing a round of golf). This typology indicates the wide range of possibilities, some of which could include quality interactions, whereas others might include being accessible when necessary and taking responsibility either directly or indirectly for the welfare of his children. This typology also "supports a culturally varied explanation of involvement" as ethnic and religious minorities can have a different sense of what it means to be a good father (Dudley & Stone, 2001, p. 61). For example, Puerto Rican fathers might place more emphases on disciplining children, and less on direct caregiving. Asian American fathers might place their greatest emphasis on being economic providers. At the same time, these fathers can reinforce academic achievement, emotional maturity, self-control, and social courtesies. Hispanic American families tend to emphasize a close mother–child relationship, with fathers helping instill values of interpersonal responsiveness including understanding the importance of interacting and relating to others with respect and dignity. Mormon American fathers might have less frequent individual contact with each child due to larger family size, thus helping less with homework, for example, while still influencing positive social values (Anderson & Sabatelli, 1999; DeGenova, 1997; Dudley & Stone, 2001). Whatever the differences, these fathers can still be considered good fathers who are engaged, accessible, and responsible within the parameters of particular cultural contexts.

The relative distribution of their saliency and the time and energy directed to the engagement, accessibility, and responsibility components of fathering may vary widely (1) across cultural and socioeconomic groups, (2) by phase of the life cycle, (3) from family to family, (4) from child to child within a family, and (5) from day to day, not to mention from minute to minute. However, we argue here that each family establishes rules about the relative distribution of the various but interrelated components of parenting among the members of the parenting subsystem. These parenting strategies reflect each family's themes and thus exhibit some stability. However, these rules and strategies can be renegotiated and may change over time given different circumstances and needs (Anderson & Sabatelli, 1999).

Our reflection of family system dynamics and themes is the *traditionalization of gender roles* (LaRossa, 1988). In general, regardless of how egalitarian their marriages are before the arrival of children, men do less household work after, relative to the increased total workload. On becoming parents, fathers and mothers experience a growing separation of roles (Belsky & Pensky, 1988; LaRossa, 1988). There is thus regression to more familiar cultural expectations. Others suggest that often men maintain "role distance" from parenting whereas women embrace the parenting role (LaRossa & LaRossa, 1981). Women engage parenting as "maternal practice" and "motherwork" in ways distinctive from how men connect with parenting practices (Arendell, 2000).

One explanation for the traditionalization phenomenon suggest that spouses have biographic and socialization experiences giving them competencies in what are considered traditional domains (Amato, 1998; Arendell, 2000; Canary et al., 1997; Hennon, in press; Marsiglio et al., 2000). Gender socialization, cultural values, and expectations appear to play a part in how and how much fathers parent. Families can negotiate more or less egalitarian divisions of childcare and other labor.

Understanding Fathering

Sometimes fathering might be perplexing, confusing, or frustrating for men. Sometimes it is forgotten or not in one's immediate stream of consciousness. But often fathering is joyful, involving, easy, unquestioned, and taken for granted. In the United States there is a *folk psychology* about fathering. It is distilled from living in and experiencing the culture. This folk psychology includes the readily understood, experiential meaning of being a father, without attention to issues of race, ethnicity, and so on. It is what fathering is. This folk psychology is one of the taken-for-granted, generally unquestioned, aspects of the natural world. It is the way things are. Although being a father is complex and not easily understood, it is perhaps even harder for outsiders to grasp in a scientific way than it is for insiders who are experiencing it and understanding it in their natural, taken-for-granted, way. Outsiders, that is, researchers and other professional experts, may also create and use "fictions"[4] to describe parenting that are not real to the lived experiences of fathers. That is, as fathers perceive how they are socially situated and act in their families, jobs, friendship groups, communities, and society in general.

To better understand fathering, one must include in the consideration the ethnoculture (or stock of knowledge) of fathers (in contrast to either the popular parental culture, or culture as known to the social scientist or educator). This ethnoculture consists of the values, norms, beliefs, attitudes, and material times as known to specific fathers. This stock of knowledge is the reality within which individual fathers operate. It is their reference world, with images of "who I am as a father" based at least partially on expectations held by significant others and reference groups. It is the personal meaning of fatherhood. Fathers' transactions with this culture (or life-world as it is also known), as they understand and attend to it, influence their cognitive and behavioral actions. Other men, as well as children and women, help in shaping a father's life-world and stock of knowledge. Aspects of the popular parental culture may be a part of this lived culture. Although it might be assumed that the predominate culture is hegemonic, in the contemporary United States, with all its diversity, one cannot assume that it is prevalent and directive everywhere and for everyone. That is, while there is some general, society-wide (macro) sharing of values and basic understandings concerning fatherhood, ethnic and other subculture enclaves (meso) may provide stronger context for behavior. And within these subtexts, idiosyncratic individual and family systems (micro) behavior will be found.

To reiterate, although there is more hegemonic macrocultural context for fathering in the United States, there are also important distinctions of a more meso- and microcultural level, for example, the environmental context differences that might be found within an Indian reservation in Wisconsin versus suburban Connecticut, or between a Jewish enclave in New York City and African American Mennonites in North Carolina, or a divorced architect with one child both living in New Mexico and a married father of nine children all living in southern Idaho. To understand fathering in these various contexts, and to design better ways of increasing and enhancing involvement in schooling, it is important to (1) recognize difference, (2) be open to cultural definitions varying from one's own, (3) appreciate cultural context, (4) accept that a carefully constructed program may be culturally irreverent and culturally specific, (5) understand family system influences, and (6) consider fathering as part of the larger tapestry of men's lives.

Fathering and School Achievement

Some research indicates that fathers experience the same parental joys, worries, and frustrations as mothers (Entwisle, 1985; Thompson & Walker, 1989). There are, however, qualitative differences between mothers and fathers in how parenting is conducted. There are, as well, differences within groups of fathers. Fathers bring certain strengths to parenting. In some cases, fathers would like to change the way they father, perhaps becoming more involved, nurturing, skillful, close, and so forth. Some fathers want involvement in their children's schooling whereas others do not know how, feel alienated from school systems in general (especially if their own school experiences were not positive), or do not feel comfortable within a particular school setting. Some fathers may not realize that active school involvement is appropriate or useful.

Irrespective of other factors such as social class, family structure, or developmental characteristics and stage of the child, positive outcomes for children appear to be related to certain parenting styles. Various publications report positive developmental outcomes for children associated with parenting styles characterized by logical reasoning, clear communication, appropriate monitoring, support, involvement in the role and with the children, and love (Anderson & Sabatelli, 1999). Children raised with this style of parenting are observed to be successful in school, altruistic, cooperative, trusting, having good self-esteem, and better able to enter into and maintain intimate relationships. Likewise, a style characterized by being sensitive to the children's developmental needs, nurturing without being overly restricting, acting responsive without being overly controlling, and stimulating without being overly directive is related to positive academic and other outcomes for children (Belsky & Vondra, 1985; Marsiglio et al., 2000). This is a style referred to as authoritative parenting, and research indicates that it is this style that best predicts more desirable outcomes among children, including academic success.

Research on school attendance, achievement, and adjustment indicates that various aspects of family and household environments appear to influence educational outcomes of youth.[5] Some characteristics identified include socioeconomic status (SES), parents' employment status and educational backgrounds, family structure, and the role of the father (DuBois, Eitel, & Felner, 1994; Dudley & Stone, 2001; Marsiglo et al., 2000; U.S. Department of Education, 2000). For example, several studies, even when controlling for SES, demonstrate a relationship between father absence and poor academic performance and dropping out of school. (Cooksey & Fondell, 1996; Dudley & Stone, 2001; Horn, 1998; Krantz, 1988; Marsiglio et al., 2000; Samuelson, 1996). Father absence is associated with poor academic attainment and school dropout, perhaps more so than the effect of poverty alone (McLanahan, 1997; McLanahan & Sandefur, 1994). One important aspect of father absence is the payment or nonpayment of child support. The amount of child support is positively associated with children's school grades and less behavioral problems at school. Reading and math scores and years of school attainment are also positively associated with the amount of child support paid. These associations do not appear to differ by the gender or race of the child. Overviews of research in the 1990s confirm "that nonresident fathers' child support payments are positively associated with children's educational success" (Marsiglio et al., 2000, p. 1182).

Among teens, noncustodial fathers are less likely than are married fathers to be the primary source for discussions about school and careers (Dudley & Stone, 2001). Teens also describe their dads as being more distant than their mothers. Daughters particularly often describe their fathers as uninvolved. Possibly, fathers are viewed as more often showing intimacy toward their teenage children through sharing an activity or helping out in some way, such as fixing something. That is, "doing" rather than verbally expressing their love and concern.

Given the relationship between school adjustment and aspects of the family environment, including fathers' support, it would appear that a better understanding of fathering and fathers' involvement with schools might provide better foundations for enhancing children's school adjustment and success. Bronfenbrenner (1986), for one, emphasizes transactions between families and schools. Factors such as the quantity and quality of contact between parents and the child's school could be consequential for academic outcomes. Although we realize that promoting this idea can create more pressure and higher expectations for father involvement, we believe that fathers' involvement in the schooling of their children is important and should be encouraged.

Reflection...

Given that many children are living in female-headed households and have little or no contact with their fathers, what can teachers and schools do for these children? Are they "doomed" because their fathers are not involved in their lives? Or given current norms of gender equality and inclusion, is it appropriate to design interventions specifically for fathers only?

Benefits of Involving Fathers in Schools

We believe there are several reasons for attempting to increase and support the involvement of fathers in schools and schooling. Included among these are:

- *Fathers* deserve, and some need, involvement support and services. Many men are interested in and open to this type of involvement, and others can be. The new father image has created a cultural expectation for more involvement in parenting, schooling, and schools. This expectation requires buttressing with new strategies by schools and other institutions to invite and engage fathers. An example would be the security dads at Arlington High in Indianapolis. Fathers, instead of security guards, ride buses on field trips and to sporting events (Louv, 1994).

- There are many positive effects on *children* related to father involvement. Roberts (1996) reviews the many strengths that fathers confer on children's development and how these differ from the important contributions of mothers. Fathers can assist in a variety of ways with their school-age children's intellectual and social development. Empathy development is one area. Children who have fathers spending time along with them doing routine child care at least twice weekly are more likely to grow up to be compassionate. Fathers also play an important role in the development of prosocial behavior, especially for boys (Dudley & Stone, 2001). A study among Ojibwa families in Michigan shows that children, boys especially, when their fathers spend a greater amount of time as their primary caregiver, had higher academic achievement (Williams, Radin, & Coggins, 1996). It can be concluded from a variety of research that children with a positive father influence benefit, being better able to deal with the many challenges presented by schools, peers, and other adults (Dudley & Stone, 2001).

- *Families* benefit by increased participation of fathers in their children's schooling. Such attention and interest can strengthen and reinforce family interactions and ties in many important areas, including marriage and transgenerational relationships. A greater involvement by fathers also reinforces the importance placed on education by the family. (Gottman, 1998; Marsiglio et al., 2000).

- *Schools* benefit from more father involvement. This involvement enriches the resources to draw on. That is, fathers' knowledge and skills can be tapped. Teachers' reports of children having few problems at school, such as poor attendance or failing a grade, are associated with children's reports of positive paternal behavior (Marsiglio et al., 2000).

- Increased involvement in schools by fathers would also have positive influences on *society*. The style of male parenting in U.S. culture offers a number of importance strengths that support school success. These include the encouragement to be independent, the fostering of competition that raises levels of achievement, and the high expectations that fathers often hold for their children that fosters competence. Social life can be more stable, with less violence, addictions, crime, and other pathologies. A more informed and involved citizen strengthens society. Father involvement can also strengthen society through strengthening the labor force and helping the economy remain productive and growing (Briar-Lawson, Lawson, Hennon, & Jones, 2001; Hennon, in press; Hennon, Jones, Hooper-Briar, & Kopcanová, 1996).

Strategies for Involving Fathers in Schools

Efforts to enhance and support father involvement in schools and schooling should be sensitive to three levels of intervention: the macro-, meso-, and micro-cultures of fathers. In some cases, efforts to involve fathers more can be considered primary in nature. That is, efforts to change culture and social systems that provide the framework, guiding and shaping what men believe to be appropriate fathering. These primary interventions are attempts at negotiated social change that leads to new male socialization practices and values. They include expectations held by the military, religion, economy, education, or other institutions concerning appropriate male behavior toward children. These types of interventions are investments for the future of society by encouraging fathers supporting and investing in the human capital development of their children.

Other interventions are secondary in nature in the sense that they are intended to overcome preexisting conditions and patterns. Such efforts are likely aimed at individual employers, churches, families, or men. These include attempts to convince fathers that, contrary to what they have learned and believe, other ways of acting are better. That is, fathers are to be nurturing, caring, and involved, bringing the strengths and perspectives of men to parenting. Other interventions of this genre include those for fathers who are believers in more involvement, but are looking for more resources, support, and services to further this involvement.

Educators can design good interventions including appropriate resources, support, and services. Schools can assist in the provision of, or help in identifying, the resources available to fathers (such as family resource centers in schools that are father friendly, or parental leave policies and other employment benefits). Schools can also involve themselves in providing or assisting fathers in locating the support they deem necessary (such as a wife's words of encouragement or a network of other fathers in similar situations who can provide information and encouragement). Likewise, schools can offer empowering services (such as parenting classes for divorced fathers) that are useful tools for enhancing fathers' involvement with their children's schooling. However, this is not to discount the necessity of considering family- or relationship-level interventions.

Parenting is a relationship, and it is conducted under the influence of the relationships. "Fatherizing" a program or practice does not necessarily mean reducing interventions to individual characteristics or psychological terms. The support necessary may include information about how to talk with ones' wife or ex-wife about the concerns the father has about parenting. Resources may include skills training on how fathers can achieve more involvement without trespassing on the mothers' turf. Other relationship-oriented practices could include school lessons to children about fathers in diverse families and working directly with fathers and children in ways that reinforce positive mutual interactions. Parenting or school involvement programs that authentically involve all parents may prove to be of more benefit than a program targeted only to fathers or mothers.

What efforts are needed to provide more resources, support, and services at the macro-, meso-, and microlevels for families and fathers so that men can be more involved with schools? Some ideas for such efforts to create and reinforce social change follow.

Reflection...

Why has there been this sudden change in how fathers want to be involved in schools? Why didn't this change take place in the 1960s and 1970s? Are the changes that are taking place an overreaction to fathers' current and perhaps less involved roles? Do you think this discussion will be taking place twenty years from now?

Society-Level Interventions

People interested in negotiating social change that values father involvement in schooling should consider more primary interventions that are oriented to helping families and men develop values, themes, strategies, and rules that support and encourage father involvement with their children. These might include:

- Working for peace, social justice, equitable wealth distribution, safe neighborhoods, and sustainable development that considers the equitable distribution of the consequences of economic development (Briar-Lawson et al., 2001; Hennon & Jones, 2000)
- Advocating policies of full employment in meaningful work at a living wage (Bruce et al., 1995)
- Supporting and encouraging the use of parental leaves, flex time, working at home, and other practices allowing fathers to be able to get time away from work to be engaged with their families (Bruce et al., 1995; Hennon, in press; Hennon & Loker, 2000; U.S. Department of Education, 2000)
- Ensuring equal opportunities for quality schooling that allows all people to achieve and maintain at least an adequate standard of living
- Writing, preparing, or encouraging mass media portrayals of men in diverse positive family roles, including the unique strengths those fathers bring to parenting
- Widely sharing the positive outcomes of efforts to have fathers be more involved, as well as sharing stories of how fathers are involved
- Advocating for fathers' rights; fair child support and visitation guidelines, and strong enforcement of such; encouraging cooperative coparenting (per-

haps with joint custody); and other measures to keep fathers in contact, involved, and supportive of their children after divorce (or if unwed). (Dudley & Stone, 2001; Marsiglio et al., 2000).

Community-Level Interventions

Fathers often are challenged in their efforts at achieving a reasonable balance of home and work life. This challenge can create additional stress, influencing their parenting. However, success at achieving an acceptable balance can be a source of support, and environmental factors, such as regular work hours, vacations, job security, being able to attend school conferences in the early morning or late evening, communication with school via email, and so on, might be resources for helping fathers maintain a lower level of stress. Attitudes toward employment and specific work are also important. For example, research notes an elevated incidence of child abuse among unemployed fathers who would rather be working, compared to working fathers (Anderson & Sabatelli, 1999). Absorption in work is related to fathers being more irritable and impatient with their children (Volling & Belsky, 1991).

School systems can work to encourage community development and economic growth. Holistic paradigms, rather than education-centered ones, can encourage viewing schools, employers, and families as all part of the same mesoculture. Working for what is good for the community as a whole appears to be an important strategy (Briar-Lawson et al., 2001; U.S. Department of Education, 2000).

Proactive steps must be taken if fathers are to be involved in more appropriate and active ways in schools and schooling. Waiting for fathers to "show up at the door" may not prove strategic; other factors are required. We present here some ideas for resources, supports, and services that may prove essential in enhancing father involvement. These tips are offered for teachers, administrators, and school support staff (social workers, family educators, school psychologists, etc.) as well as parents and others concerned about schools and families. Staff and administration must:

- Help create family-friendly communities (Briar-Lawson et al., 2001).
- Structure schools that are accessible and family- (especially father-) friendly, including flexibility in scheduling meetings with parents (Hooper-Briar & Lawson, 1994).
- Guarantee that schools are accountable and responsive to families.
- Commit to the importance of involving fathers. School personnel must understand the benefits and show courage and resiliency in facing difficult questions arising with this kind of change.
- Focus on the uniqueness of fathers and the strengths they bring to parenting and in supporting children's education. Schools should capitalize on fathers' encouragement of students to solve problems and to excel. Many fathers like

taking on the role of teacher/mentor. This role reinforces feelings of competence, and fathers feel they are doing something important. Inviting fathers to share skills or knowledge in schools is a way of taking advantage of these feelings. As a parent, one of the authors of this chapter was invited to share his expertise on future problem solving with a sixth-grade class and felt honored to be asked.

- Create environments that are father-friendly and portray fathers positively. The most obvious examples would be male teachers. Other ways to enhance the school environment are posters in the school and classroom of men at work, play, or with families. Videos, music, and other multimedia material about men in their varied roles can be used. Invite men to visit the classroom, not only on Father's Day or Career Day, to share something about themselves (work, hobbies, or special interests).

- Provide opportunities geared for fathers' interests. For example, building and setting up playground equipment, helping to coach a basketball team, or judging a science fair. These may be stereotypical opportunities, but they can help fathers feel welcome and comfortable. They also encourage male openness to less stereotypical activities, perhaps directing a play or teaching a lesson.

- Sponsor more naturally occurring positive fathering activities involving fathers in clubs, scouts, outings, projects (including building and repairing), games, camping, fishing, and the like. More fun and active events can be opportunities for fathers to observe parenting and share information, as well as for "experts" to provide parenting information and model behavior.

- Include fathers in invitations. A generic invitation to "parents" can still be a code name for mothers. Fathers need explicit invitations to know that they are both expected and welcome.

- Offer father-only or father–child events and make special invitations to fathers. Be inclusive in invitations so that male father figure (e.g, uncles, grandfathers, and mother's boyfriend) feels welcome.

- Sensitize to male communication styles. Fathers may want to get right to business and have relationship building as a secondary priority.

- Establish family resources centers in the schools that are father-friendly, and that are as accessible as necessary in helping individuals and couples build capacity for better quality parenting. Such centers can help families in meeting the totality of their needs (such as health, financial management, stress management, leisure) (Hooper-Briar & Lawson, 1994; Strom, 1985).

Achieving more school involvement by fathers goes beyond the important step of making schools more father-friendly. Perhaps more primary interventions or comprehensive programs are necessary. These more comprehensive interventions can assist fathers in acquiring or enhancing their capacity for engaging with children and the other parent. Consequently, the importance of school involvement can be more readily understood, appreciated, and desired.

Parent Education

Palm (1995) identifies some specific gender differences that are pertinent to effective parent education. These differences include:

- Goals of mothers and fathers differ in parent education. Mothers appear more interested in getting support from other parents whereas fathers seem most interested in building a close relationship with their children and learning about discipline techniques.
- A second important area to acknowledge is the difference between mothers and fathers in relation to a knowledge and experience base (Palm & Palkovitz, 1988). Girls play more at being parents as part of their childhood experience whereas boys more often practice other roles. Girls and young women take classes on child development and family relations much more frequently than boys. These differences suggest that educational opportunities for boys and men are critical if fathers are to be more competent in skills and knowledge related to childrearing.
- Differences in interaction style are another area identified. Many earlier studies were based on research with infants. Fathers' interactions are described as being more physical, tactile, and arousing, whereas mothers are more verbal, soothing, and calming (Arendell, 2000; Dudley & Stone, 2001). Androgynous fathers appear to engage in the typical male styles of interactions (i.e., rough-and-tumble play) but are able to express affection (Palkovitz, 1984).
- Discipline is another area of perceived differences. Being strict and harsh is characteristic of fathers (Bigner, 1994). Fathers seem able to be firmer, uphold limits, and be authoritative because of hierarchical views (Thevenin, 1993). Perhaps fathers focus more on the immediate outcomes (obedience and compliance) and less on longer-term implications of relationships. This style difference may be changing as more men try to avoid the role epitomized by the phrase "wait till your father gets home."
- Solving parent problems also appears to differ by gender according to some research (Amato, 1998: Arendell, 2000; Dudley & Stone, 2001; Holden, 1988). Mothers appear more effective at solving infants' crying problems, for example. The differences are explained by mothers' greater exposure to and experience with this type of problem.

Fathers' Involvement with Schools

Fathers are getting more involved in schools for a variety of reasons:

- Fathers are being specifically asked to be involved. This involvement includes PTO, riding buses in place of security guards, giving presentations to students, and inclusion in home–school communication and conferences.

- Fathers are creating work schedules, or their companies have family-friendly policies allowing personal time off to engage in school activities. Some fathers are working at or from their homes (including in their own or family businesses), which can allow more flexibility for involving themselves in their children's schools. Some men would like more flexibility in employment responsibilities but face resistance from employers. Some men refuse promotions, some change jobs, some do not have this luxury or determination.
- Fathers are finding schools creating more father-friendly environments, including the curriculum. These environments result in more fathers participating in schools as speakers, volunteer aides, or on the PTO or PTA board. Some school districts in Minnesota have young dad programs. These programs include young fathers talking to elementary children about the responsibilities and problems associated with being a teen father. Some school districts, in conjunction with other organizations, identify teen dads who want older fathers for a mentor. Pruett (1987) and Cunnighman (1994) suggest ways of portraying fathers and other men in the curriculum. The U.S. Department of Education (2000) offers many suggestions for creating a father-friendly environment.

There may be some negative reactions to these activities. Educators must listen to the needs of single mothers and others who may feel excluded when schools attempt to reach out to fathers. Providing opportunities for all parents, especially single parents or parents who may be left out when fathers are specifically invited, is encouraged.

Reflection...

Schools want to involve parents more, but if fathers don't get involved, how can schools reach out to fathers? Is this a gender equity issue? Would you anticipate a backlash, and if so, what would it be?

Barriers to Fathers' Involvement in Schools

Fathers can offer various accounts and disclaimers for why they do, or do not, engage in certain behaviors (Kaplan & Hennon, 1992; LaRossa, 1988). These vocabularies of motive help presenting to themselves and others the images of "father" they wish to offer. Self-image can be thought of as a retelling of a narrative (Schafer, 1983): "This is my story; this is who I am." Perhaps the telling of the fathering story is more often to self than to others. Fathers need to know who they are and give it justification so that they can be comfortable and secure. Father inclusion programs based primarily or exclusively on outsider expert knowledge and delivered in a prescription mode are likely to be ineffective (Hennon & Arcus, 1993).

The real needs, desires, and wishes of men must be considered in order to overcome barriers to father involvement in schools. Likewise, those wishing to negotiate social change must understand the lived realities of the men they are targeting, as perceived by those men. This does not mean accepting at face value the excuses, justifications, and disclaimers offered by men. Fathers should be held accountable for their actions. But realizing that these actions and justifications are part of the self as constructed by each father is important. These narratives are aspects of the fathers' stock of knowledge and form part of the material that must be used for enhancing father involvement.

Palm (1985) examines types of father involvement in schools serving young children with disabilities. The results show that fathers tend to be most involved in events such as holiday parties, concerts and conferences, but only 40 percent of fathers participate. In Palm's study, 20 percent of fathers observe a program, help with therapy at home, or attend parent meetings. Fathers are least likely to volunteer in the classroom, serve on a parent bard, or help to make or repair classroom materials (less than 5 percent). These low percentages are surprising because early education, especially with children with disabilities, includes parent involvement as an integral part. What keeps fathers away from schools?

- The main barrier appears to be time and schedule conflicts (Johnson & Palm, 1992). Most fathers work full-time, and many work during typical business and school hours. In comparison to fathers, mothers are involved more often in part-time employment.
- One barrier is the fathers' perceptions that the tasks are not part of their role. (U.S. Department of Education, 2000). For example, one of the authors was meeting with a group of Even Start fathers and talking about the importance of reading to young children. The response from the men was that their wives did the reading; it was not their job.
- Another barrier is fathers' not feeling invited to a program. If a father walks into a program and looks around and sees adult females and children, he gets the message that this place is for women and children. Mothers may also play a gatekeeper role and either decide to push for fathers going to an event or class, or discourage them from going. Often fathers do not know about opportunities for involvement because they are not in the direct line of communication. If the children come home to mother, they are likely to pass on information from the school directly to mother who then takes responsibility for requests from school.
- Programs may be hesitant to make specific efforts to reach out to fathers. With a large portion of children not living with their dads on a regular basis (Blankenhorn, 1995), events and outreach targeted toward dads may seem offensive and disrespectful of family diversity. We know of a school that invited fathers to a school dance with elementary-aged daughters. This was upsetting to a colleague who had a daughter whose father had died. She was upset for two reasons; first, her daughter was excluded, but perhaps more importantly, the event represented inappropriate gender role and age stereotypes.

The fear of offending parents, especially single-female parents, makes it difficult to make specific overtures toward fathers.

The barriers listed suggest special efforts need to be made to capitalize on the benefits of father involvement. Understanding subtle barriers that can be addressed by schools is an important step in involving more fathers. Suggestions for overcoming barriers to fathers' involvement and best practices can be located in many publications and on the Web. *A Call to Commitments: Father's Involvement in Children's Learning* (U.S. Department of Education, 2000) is a good place to start. Good information is available at North Central Regional Educational Laboratory (www.ncrel.org) and the National Head Start Association (www.nhsa.org/parents/parents_father_assess.htm) offers the *Father Friendly Assessment and Planning Tool* with checklists for programs to assess their readiness to serve fathers and to develop a father-friendly action plan.

Family-Level Interventions

Marital stress influences the quality of parenting. In some cases, parents attempt to compensate for a poor marriage by using their children as a source of support and gratification. This might translate into more involvement with school activities. In other cases, parents blame children for the marital strife, or scapegoat the children to focus the problem elsewhere. Children will also keep the marital and family systems balanced by acting out or being compliant. Doing well or poorly in school, for example, can be a child's device to divert attention away from marital strife and toward the child and his or her needs. The outcome, as seen by school personnel, may be less or more father involvement in schools. In any situation, fathers will likely be less attentive to their children in appropriate ways when there are marital problems, or in the adjustment phase of divorce (Krantz, 1988; Stewart, Copeland, Chester, Malley, & Barenbaum, 1997).

Earlier in this chapter we documented some of the gender dynamics and turf issues involved with parents. The mothers (especially divorced ones or others estranged from their children's fathers) can be nonsupportive and resistant to changes in father involvement. Even in good marriages there can be resistance to change. A way for counteracting this tendency is for mothers to learn to expect such territorial feelings and to talk about them with the fathers. Fathers should not rise to the competition (Schroepfer, 1991). However, fathers should not be "junior mothers" playing secondary roles, or be "competing mothers" for their children's attention and love. Children benefit from having parents who cooperate together as the parenting team, supporting each other while playing complementary roles (Anderson & Sabatelli, 1999; Louv, 1994).[6] One caution offered to fathers by Levine (Latham, 1992) is to protect against trying so hard to connect with their children to be superfathers that their wives are neglected. Keeping marriages strong is one of the best ways to facilitate being a better father (Anderson & Sabatelli, 1999; Gottman, 1998). As Gottman (1998) argues:

There is no question...that those husbands who have a fondness and admiration system for their wives, who actively build a cognitive map of their wife's world and of the relationship, who turn toward their wives on an everyday basis, and who can accept influence from their wives, are clearly way ahead of the game. As long as they are wedded to women who soften their startup of the conflict and do not reciprocate low-intensity negative affect...these men also tend to sail through the transition to parenthood,...[and] become emotionally involved fathers. Not only are their marriages more stable and more satisfying, but their children are on entirely different development trajectory, one that affects their cognitive, affective, social, and physical development. (p. 188)

Here are some ways in which schools can facilitate family-level intervention:

- Schools can include in their curricula value-based family life education from the primary school years through adulthood (Hennon & Arcus, 1993).
- School systems and individual school personnel, such as social workers or trained lay leaders, can encourage, support, advertise, and offer marital enrichment programs as well as interventions of a more therapeutic nature. Program possibilities include stress management, positive discipline techniques, parenting after divorce, couples' communication techniques, conflict management strategies, and exercises to help fathers and mothers become more self-aware and self-reflective about their behavior. Such resources can help parents realize how they respond to others' behavior and their influence on how others respond to them. Reflexivity is a critical process of increasing self-awareness and sensitivity to the experiences of both self and others. Reflexivity is a crucial component of any efforts directed toward change in the fathering role. Enrichment and education can be offered in conjunction with businesses, agencies, or religious institutions (Hennon & Arcus, 1993; Hooper-Briar & Lawson, 1994).
- Educators can help people in understanding that family interaction, interpersonal competency, and love for family, as well as spending engrossing time with family, are as important as occupational achievement.
- School personnel can establish their own quality marriages and other interpersonal relationships.

Familial behavior is context sensitive, conditioned by where they occur (Gubrium & Holstein, 1993). Men experience what is termed *organizational embeddedness* (Gubrium, 1987); that is, the social systems men are involved in are not discrete, but rather men carry the meanings of one into others. Whereas analytically one can separate family from work, fathering from truck driving, in the wholeness of life as known to fathers, this may not be meaningful. To do so may be creating differences without distinction. But scholars and laypersons alike do discuss how one role impacts another. For example, how driving a long-haul truck interferes with or shapes fathering, due to time, energy, stress, and so on. (McCall, 1988). Interventionists need to take this embeddedness and wholeness into account. In this way, they can become more empathetic with fathers in how they concurrently perceive themselves as situated in family, employment, and community. Simple, one-factor or single-sector (such as education) interventions will miss the richness and interdependency of a father's total life. More family-centric (or if necessary, father-centric) paradigms and practices might prove more effective (Hennon et al., 1996).[7] In all, more holistic "fatherized" strategies for negotiated change in parenting and involvement in schools and schooling are called for.

Summary

In this chapter, we presented background information and conceptualizations helpful to educators in understanding men as a socially constructed gender and fathering as diverse social roles. We stressed that father involvement in families, schooling, and schools is valuable and should be further encouraged by educators. Men bring diverse strengths and capabilities to fathering, and no single model or mode is argued as being the best. Fathers are important; and although attempts to encourage more quality involvement with children are beneficial for families, schools, communities, and society, attempts to create androgynous fathers or to feminize the role may not be appropriate. Educators who appreciate the benefit of father involvement while respecting gender and individual differences are more likely to enjoy successful efforts at increasing father involvement. Negotiating social change is difficult; trying to do so without engaging and being empathetic with those most effected (fathers especially, but also wives, lovers, ex-wives, and children) is extremely problematic. This chapter focused on fathers and their understanding of their roles, including their ethnocultures and self-narratives about being fathers. Understanding flesh-and-blood fathers in one's own community, rather than generalities gained from the mass media and popular culture of disengaged or modern fathers, appears more profitable in creating the types of communities, schools, and families conducive to best educating and serving all children. The educator should thus focus on "real" culture as known to real men.

We offer a multitude of examples and general strategic ideas for making fathers more appreciated and respected for their strengths and abilities. These can be capitalized on to make schools more father-friendly and to have fathers involved in meaningful ways with their families, schooling, and schools. Although we believe that these ideas are solid, they only scratch the surface of the fertile soil of ideas. We are confident that the reader will generate and utilize other, equally good if not better, strategies. We hope that these ideas will also be shared.

What can we say in closing? Examine all ideas for parent involvement to check for gender bias. Provide for the needs of both mothers and fathers. Measure success of father involvement not by the number, but by the quality, of the experience for men and children. Schools often must build programs slowly and expect some trial and error in learning what the men in their communities will respond to. For some communities it may mean bringing out a sports figure to draw men to an event, for others special invitations from the children to their fathers may work. There are many barriers in men themselves, their families, and in schools that make father involvement a real challenge.

Just inviting fathers into schools, or engaging in a discourse conducted in academic texts, magazines, and on PBS may not be enough. Reaching beyond the white, suburban middle class is necessary if widespread change in fathering culture and conduct is desired. There are many ways of getting men involved. In addition to those already discussed, Arcus (1995) provides some parent education examples. Levine, Murphy, and Wilson (1993) suggest involvement strategies for early childhood education settings: (1) expect men to be involved—send notes; (2) put out the welcome mat and meet them at the door, recognizing the men's contributions; (3) find out what men want, ask questions, do surveys, establish focus groups; and (4) display images of men in brochures, posters, and other areas of education settings.

Engaging fathers to learn their strengths, hearing their stories, taking advantage of their stocks of knowledge, participating in their lives, and appreciating their family themes and parenting strategies are important. This allows educators better recognition of rationalizations versus role conflicts, desires to change without knowing how versus not wanting to change, technically present fathers as well as functionally present fathers, and perhaps new ways to appreciate traditional fathering for what it offers to children and society, as well as the promise of new fathering.

One aspect of promoting good fathering and school involvement consists of efforts to support, strengthen, and enrich marriages (Gottman, 1998). This argument is advanced by those in the marriage and family enrichment fields (L'Abate & Weinstein, 1987; Lewis, 1979). School personnel demonstrate interest in promoting quality marriages because children are observed to have negative developmental outcomes when raised with family systems that include marital conflict and parenting styles characterized by lack of supervision, hostility, rejection, or coercion. These outcomes include academic failure, substance abuse, aggressiveness, delinquency, and psychopathology (Anderson & Sabatelli, 1999). Divorced and other fatherless homes appear especially problematic.

Educators concern themselves with community and society change. Making communities more family-friendly and working to create a culture respectful and supportive of fathers' myriad roles in the nurturing of children can be useful efforts. In some cases, educators can work to change culture in primary ways; in other cases, the efforts are secondary in that they are directed to change culture as a whole. Thinking holistically, acting assertively, listening to and respecting real fathers, and being committed to father involvement and resilient to criticism can allow educators to provide resources, services, and supports that men deserve and need. Ultimately, it is children and society that benefit.

RECOMMENDED ACTIVITIES

1. Interview fathers from different generations, from the 1930s on. Discuss with the fathers their roles in the family regarding child care, work, nurturing children, activities with children, amount of time spent with children, responsibility for discipline, and gender issues relating to their children.

2. Interview fathers who had their first children when they were teenagers, in their 20s, in their 30s, and in their 40s. Ask them to address the following issues: their

age in respect to raising children, responsibility of child rearing, types of interaction with their children, and their ability to father.

3. Observe a parent education class predominantly made up of males. What types of interaction do you observe between the fathers and their children? What types of interaction do you observe between the fathers and the parent educator?

4. Invite a panel of fathers into the class to describe parenting from their perceptive. Is it different from mothering? Has the role of fathers changed over the years?

5. Locate a listerv group on the Web or email that is designed to be a fathers' discussion group. Monitor or speak through this medium to identify issues that fathers may be discussing.

6. Describe the role your father played or did not play in your life. If this is too difficult, describe the role any significant male played in your life prior to age 18.

NOTES

1. LaRossa (1988) notes that middle-class men have authored most books and other texts about the "new" fatherhood.

2. Additionally, researchers such as LaRossa (1988) show how couples socially construct gender relationships by offering accounts, justifications, and excuses for why fathers are not more involved in parenting.

3. In some studies, housework includes aspects of child care. Also, some families' strategies allocated the division of labor such that men do some housework tasks as a tradeoff, in terms of egalitarianism, as women do some child-care tasks. For example, see Barry (1993).

4. Deutscher (1973) and others (e.g., Hennon, 1992) note that social scientists create fictional concepts, or constructs known only to scientists, to explain everyday behavior. These concepts, such as personality and social structure, have no relevance for the average person, and do not explain their actions in the same way as "ethnoconcepts," or terms and stories that people give to account for their actions.

5. Due to the research designs, the direction causality or whether there is mutual influencing (school achievement influences in family life, and vise versa) cannot be determined. From a systems viewpoint, the argument appears to be that they are mutually influencing and reinforcing of one another.

6. An article by Barry (1993) refers to complementary but not similar contributions to the division of parenting labor as the *Jack Sprat approach*.

7. That is, social policy and program from the inside out; practices that put families (rather than schools or other systems) center stage with their needs and strengths as the foundation for policy and practice agendas that are accountable to the end-users, that is, accountable to families (Briar-Lawson et al., 2001).

ADDITIONAL RESOURCES

Involvement of Fathers in Schools

Agencies and Programs:

The Center on Fathers, Families & Public Policy
Family Resource Center
200 South Michigan Avenue
Chicago, IL 60601
Phone: 312-341-0902
www.cffpp.org

DAD to DAD
3771 Admiral Drive
Atlanta, GA 30341
Phone: 404-457-1595
www.slowlane.com/d2d

The Fatherhood Project
c/o Families & Work Institute
330 Seventh Ave., 14th Floor
New York, NY 10001
Phone: 212-465-2044
www.fatherhoodproject.org

Father-to-Father
Children, Youth & Family Consortium
12 McNeal Hall 1985 Buford Avenue
University of Minnesota
St. Paul, MN 55108
Phone: 612-626-1312
www.cyfc.umn.edu/FatherNet

MELD for Young Dads
123 North Third Street, Suite 507
Minneapolis, MN 55401
Phone: 612-332-7563

National Center for Fathering
10200 West 75th Street, Suite 267
Shawnee Mission, KS 66204-2223
Phone: 913-384-4661
www.fathers.com

National Center on Fathers & Families
Graduate School of Education
University of Pennsylvania
Philadelphia, PA 19104
Phone: 215-686-3910
www.ncoff.gse.upenn.edu

National Fatherhood Initiative
600 Eden Road, Bldg. E
Lancaster, PA 17601
Phone: 717-581-8860
www.fatherhood.org

National Head Start Association
www.nhsa.org

Videos:

Being A Single Parent. (1987). Films for the Humanities & Sciences. (19 minutes)

Fatherhood USA-Dedicated not Deadbeat, Juggling Work & Family, Fatherhood. (1998). Families & Work Institute.

Fathers Matter. (1998). Active Parenting Publishers. (19 minutes)

For Dads Only: The #1 Children Survival Guide for Dads. (1990). Luxor Films/ Aylmer Press. (39 minutes)

Importance of Fatherhood. (1996). Concept Media. (28 minutes)

On Being a Father with T. Berry Brazelton. (1985). Family Home Entertainment. (70 minutes)

The Expectant Father. (1992). Conmar Publishing. (45 minutes)

Fathering Issues and Concerns

Websites:

American Coalition for Fathers and Children
www.acfc.org

Center for Successful Fathering
www.fathering.org

Center on Fathers, Families, and Public Policy
www.cffpp.org

Child Trends (includes reports and papers on fathers & related family issues)
www.childtrends.org

Divorce Home Page
www.divorcesupport.com

Fatherhood Project at Work and Families Institute
www.fatherhoodproject.org

Fathers' Network (serves fathers of children with special needs)
fathersnetwork.org

Fathers' Forum Online
www.familyeducation.com

Fathers Rights and Equality Exchange
www.vix.com/free/

FatherWork.
fatherwork.byu.edu

Institute for Responsible Fatherhood and Family Revitalization
www.responsiblefatherhood.org

M.E.N. Magazine
www.vix.com/menmag/

Men's Issue Page
www.vix.com/pub/men/index.html

National Center for Fathering (conducts research on fathering)
www.fathers.com

National Center on Fathers and Families
www.ncoff.gse.upenn.edu

National Fathers Network
www.fathersnetwork.org

National Latino Fatherhood and Family Institute
www.nlffi.org

National Practitioners Network for Fathers and Families
www.npnff.org

Single Dad's Index
www.vix.com/pub/men/single-dad.html

Slowlane—The Online Resource for Stay at Home Fathers
www.slowlane.com

Family Issues

Websites:

CyberParent
www.cyberparent.com

Families and Work Institute
www.familiesandwork.org

Family Education
www.familyeducation.com

Family Planet
www.familyplanet.com

The Family Web
www.familyweb.com

Family Fun
www.family.com

Middle Web
www.middleweb.com

The National Parenting Center
www.tnpc.com

Parents Helping Parents
www.portal.com:80/~cbntmkr/php.html

Parents Place
www.parentsplace.com

Parent Soup
www.parentsoup.com

Positive Parenting Home Page
www.fishnet.net/~pparents

Save the Children
www.winternet.com/~jannmart/nkcindex.html

Single Parent Project
www.alaska.net/~rwarner/spphtml.htm

REFERENCES

Amato, P. R. (1994). Life-span adjustment of children to their parents' divorce. In E. N. Junn & C. J. Boyatzis (Eds.), *Child growth and development* (pp. 149–169). Guiford, CT: Dushkin/McGraw Hill.

Amato, P. R. (1998). More than money? Men's contribution to their children's lives. In A. Booth & A. C. Crouter (Eds.), *Men in families* (pp. 241–278). Mahwah, NJ: Lawrence Erlbaum.

Amato, P. R., & Booth, A. (1997). *A generation at risk: Growing up in an era of family upheavel.* Cambridge, MA: Harvard University Press.

Anderson, S. A., & Sabatelli, R. M. (1999). *Family interaction: A multigenerational development perspective.* (2nd ed.). Boston: Allyn & Bacon.

Arcus, M. E. (1995). Advances in family life education: Past, present and future. *Family Relations, 44,* 336–344.

Arendell, T. (2000). Conceiving and investigating motherhood: The decade's scholarship. *Journal of Marriage and the Family, 62,* 1192–1207.

Barry, J. B. (1993, May/June). Daddytrack. *Utne Reader,* pp. 70–73.

Belsky, J., & Pensky, E. (1988). Martial change across the transition to parenthood. *Marriage and Family Review, 12,* 133–156.

Belsky, J., & Vondra, J. (1985). Characteristics, consequences, and determinants of parenting: In L. L'Abate (Ed.), *The handbook of family psychology and therapy* (pp. 523–556). Homewood, IL: Dorsey.

Bigner, J. (1994). *Parent–child relations: An introduction to parenting.* New York: Macmillan.

Biller, H. B. (1993). *Fathers and families: Parental factors in child development.* Westport, CT: Auburn.

Blankenhorn, D. (1995). *Fatherless America: Confronting our most urgent social problem.* Dallas, TX: Harper, Collins.

Briar-Lawson, K., Lawson, H. A., Hennon, C. B., & Jones, A. R. (2001). *Family centered policies & practices: International implications.* New York: Columbia University Press.

Bronfenbrenner, U. (1986). Ecology of the family as a context for human development: Research perspectives. *Development Psychology, 22,* 723–742.

Bruce, J., Lloyd, C. B., & Leonard, A. (1995). *Families in focus: New perspectives on mothers, fathers, and children.* New York: Population Council.

Canary, D. J., Emmers-Sommer, T. M., & Faulkner, S. (1997). *Sex and gender differences in personal relationships.* New York: Guilford.

Cherlin, A. J. (1998). On the flexibility of fatherhood. In A. Booth & A. C. Crouter (Eds.), *Men in families* (pp. 41–46). Mahwah, NJ: Lawrence Erlbaum.

Cohen, T. (1987). Remaking men. *Journal of Family Issues, 8,* 57–77.

Coltrane, S. (2000). Research on household labor: Modeling and measuring the social embeddedness of routine family work. *Journal of Marriage and the Family, 62,* 1208–1233.

Cooksey, E., & Fondell, M. (1996). Spending time with the kids: Effects of family structure on fathers' and children's lives. *Journal of Marriage and the Family, 58,* 693–707.

Cunnighman, B. (1994, September). Portraying fathers and other men in the curriculum. *Young Children, 4*–13.

Darling-Fisher, C., & Tiedje, L. B. (1990). The impact of maternal employment characteristics on fathers' participation in child care. *Family Relations, 39,* 20–26.

DeGenova, M. K. (1997). *Families in cultural context: Strengths and challenges in diversity.* Mountain View, CA: Mayfield.

Deutscher, I. (1973). *What we say/what we do: Sentiment & acts.* Glenview, IL: Scott, Foresman.

Doherty, W. J. (1991). Beyond reactivity and the deficit model of manhood: A commentary on articles by Napier, Pittman and Gottman. *Journal of Marriage and Family Therapy, 17,* 19–32.

Draper, P. (1998). Why should fathers father? In A. Booth & A. C. Crouter (Eds.), *Men in families* (pp. 111–121). Mahwah, NJ: Lawrence Erlbaum.

DuBois, D. L., Eitel, S. K., & Felner, R. D. (1994). Effects of family environment and parent–child relationships on school adjustment during the transition to early adolescence. *Journal of Marriage and the Family, 56,* 405–414.

Dudley, J. R., & Stone, G. (2001). *Fathering at risk: Helping nonresidential fathers.* New York: Springer.

Entwisle, D. R. (1985). Becoming a parent. In L. L'Abate (Ed.), *The handbook of family psychology and therapy* (pp. 557–585). Homewood, IL: Dorsey.

Epstein, J. L. (1995, May). School/family/community partnerships: Caring for the children we share. *Phi Delta Kappan,* 701–712.

Gilbert, L. A. (1993). *Two careers, one family: The promise of gender equality.* Newbury Park: CA: Sage.

Gottman, J. M. (1998). Toward a process model of men in marriages and families. In A. Booth & A. C. Crouter (Eds.), *Men in families* (pp. 149–192). Mahwah, NJ: Lawrence Erlbaum.

Gubrium, J. F. (1987). Organizational embeddedness and family life. In T. H. Brubaker (Ed.), *Aging, health and family: Long term care* (pp. 23–41). Newbury Park, CA: Sage.

Gubrium, J. F., & Holstein, J. A. (1993). Phenomenology, ethnomethodology, and family discourse. In P. G. Boss, W. J. Doherty, R. LaRossa, W. R. Schumm, & S. K. Steinmetz (Eds.), *Sourcebook of family theories and methods: A contextual approach* (pp. 651–672). New York: Plennum.

Hennon, C. B. (1992). Toward the turn of the century. *Journal of Family and Economic Issues, 13,* 355–372.

Hennon, C. B. (Ed.). (in press). *Diversity in families. A global perspective.* Belmont, CA: Wadsworth.

Hennon, C. B., & Arcus, M. (1993). Life-span family life education. In T. H. Brubaker (Ed.), *Family relations: Challenges for the future* (pp. 181–210). Newbury Park, CA: Sage.

Hennon, C. B., & Jones, A. R. (2000). Family related economic and employment policies and program, in central and eastern European countries. In D. S. Iatridis (Ed.), *Social justice and the welfare state in central and eastern Europe: The impact of privatization* (pp. 132–150). Westport, CT: Praeger.

Hennon, C. B., Jones, A., Hooper-Briar, K., & Kopcanová, D. (1996). A snapshot in time. Family policy and the United Nations International Year of the Family. *Journal of Family and Economic Issues, 17,* 9–46.

Hennon, C. B., & Loker, S. (2000). Gender and home-based employment in a global economy. In C. B. Hennon, S. Loker, & R. Walker (Eds.), *Gender and home-based employment* (pp. 17–43). Westport, CT: Auburn House.

Holden, G. (1988). Adult's thinking about a child-rearing problem: Effects of experience, parental status, and gender. *Child Development, 59,* 1623–1632.

Hooper-Briar, K., & Lawson, H. A. (1994). *Serving children, youth and families through interprofessional collaboration and service integration: A framework for action.* Oxford, OH: Danforth Foundation and the Institute for Educational Renewal at Miami University.

Horn, W. (1998). *Father facts* (3rd ed.). Gaithersburg, MD: National Fatherhood Initiative.

Jackson, J. (1994, June). *The role of men in children's lives.* Luncheon address to Family Re-Union III, Nashville, TN.

Johnson, L., & Palm, G. (1992). Planning programs: What do fathers want? In L. Johnson & G. Palm (Eds.), *Working with fathers: Methods and perspectives* (pp. 59–77), Stillwater, MN: nu ink unlimited.

Kaplan, L., & Hennon, C. B. (1992). Remarriage education: The Personal Reflections Program. *Family Relations, 41,* 127–143.

Krantz, S. E. (1988). Divorce and children. In S. M. Dornbusch & M. H. Strober (Eds.), *Feminism, children, and the new families* (pp. 249–273). New York: Guilford.

L'Abate, L., & Weinstein, S. E. (1987). *Structured enrichment programs for couples and families.* New York: Brunner/Mazel.

Lamb, M. E. (1987). Introduction: The emergent American father. In M. E. Lamb (Ed.), *The father's role: Cross-cultural perspectives* (pp. 3–25). Hillsdale, NJ: Lawrence Erlbaum.

Lamb, M. E. (1998). Fatherhood then and now. In A. Booth & A. C. Crouter (Eds.), *Men in families* (pp. 47–52). Mahwah, NJ: Lawrence Erlbaum.

LaRossa, R. (1988). Fatherhood and social change. *Family Relations, 37,* 451–457.

LaRossa, R., & LaRossa, M. M. (1981). *Transition to parenthood: How infants change families.* Beverly Hills, CA: Sage.

LaRossa, R., & Reitzes, D. C. (1993). Continuity and change in middle class fatherhood. 1925–1939: The culture-conduct connection. *Journal of Marriage and the Family, 55,* 455–468.

Latham, A. (1992, May). Fathering the nest. M., pp. 66–75.

Levine, J., Murphy, D., & Wilson, S. (1993). *Getting men involved: Strategies for early childhood programs.* New York: Scholastic.

Lewis, J. M. (1979). *How's your family?* New York: Brunner/Mazel.

Louv, R. (1993). *Fatherlove: What we need; what we seek; what we must create.* New York: Pocket Books.

Louv, R. (1994). *Reinventing fatherhood.* (Occasional Papers Series. No.14). Vienna: United Nations, International Year of the Family.

Maclanahan, S., & Garfinkel, I. (1999). *Fragile families and child well-being studies.* New York: Columbia University.

Marsiglio, W. (1991). Parental engagement activities with minor children. *Journal of Marriage and the Family, 53,* 973–986.

Marsiglio, W., Amato, P., Day, R. D., & Lamb, M. E. (2000). Scholarship on fatherhood in the 1990s and beyond. *Journal of Marriage and the Family, 62,* 1173–1191.

McBride, B. A. (1990). The effects of a parent education/play group program on father involvement in child rearing. *Family Relations, 39,* 250–256.

McCall, R. B. (1988, September). Real men do change diapers. *Parents,* p. 202.

McLanahan, S. (1997). Parent absence or poverty; which matters more? In G. Duncan & J. Brooks-Gunn (Ed.), *The consequences of growing up poor* (pp. 35–48). New York: Russell Sage Foundation.

McLanahan, S., & Sandefur, G. (1994). *Growing up with a single parent: What hurts, what helps.* Cambridge, MA: Harvard University Press.

Mintz, S. (1998). From patriarchy to androgyny and other myths: Placing men's family roles in historical perspective. In A. Booth & A. C. Crouter (Eds.), *Men in families* (pp. 3–30). Mahwah, NJ: Lawrence Erlbaum.

Mumola, C. (2000). Incarcerated parents and their children. *Bureau of Justice Statistics: Special Report, NCJ 182 335,* pp. 1–12.

National Center for Education Statistics. (1997). *Fathers' involvement in their children's schools.* Washington, DC: Government Printing Office.

Palkovitz, R. (1984). Parental attitudes and father's interaction with their five-month-old infants. *Developmental Psychology, 20,* 1054–1060.

Palm, G. (1985). Creating opportunities for father involvement. *Nurturing News, 7*(4), 12–13.

Palm, G. (1994). Future of fatherhood: A guiding image. *Family information services.* Minneapolis, MN: M&M.

Palm, G. (1995). *Understanding male involvement and promoting healthy male socialization.* Workshop materials for Winter/Spring 1995 Early Childhood Education Regional Inservice Training. Minneapolis, MN: Department of Education.

Palm, G., & Palkovitz, R. (1988). The challenge of working with new fathers: Implications for support providers. In R. Pakovitz & M. Sussman (Eds.), *Transitions to parenthood* (pp. 357–376). New York: Haworth.

Parsons, T. (1955). Family structure and socialization of the child. In T. Parsons & R. F. Bales (Eds.), *Family socialization and interaction processes* (pp. 35–131). Glencoe, IL: Free Press.

Pruett, K. (1987). *The nurturing father: Journey toward the complete man.* New York: Warner.

Reichart, D. (1999). *Broke but not deadbeat: Reconnecting low income fathers and families.* Denver, CO: National Conference of State Legislatures.

Riley, R. (1994, November). Families come first. *Principal,* pp. 30–32.

Roberts, P. (1996, May/June). Fathers' time. *Psychology Today,* pp. 48–56, 81.

Robinson, J. P. (1990, March/April). The hard facts about hard work. *Utne reader,* p. 70.

Rotundo, E. A. (1985). American fatherhood: a historical perspective. *American Behavioral Scientist, 29,* 7–25.

Samuelson, R. J. (1996, April 8). Why men need family values. *Newsweek,* p. 43.

Sanik, M. M. (1990). Parents' time use: A 1967–1986 comparison. *Lifestyles: Family and economic issues, 11,* 299–316.

Schafer, R. (1983) *The analytic attitude.* New York: Basic Books.

Scmidt-Waldherr, H. (1992). From the "Fatherless Society" to the "New Fatherliness." In N. B. Leidenfrost (Ed.), *Families in transition* (pp. 85–90). Vienna: United Nations Office at Vienna, Centre for Social Development and Humanitarian Affairs, IYF Secretariat.

Schroepfer, L. (1991, June). Dad: New and improved. *American Health,* p. 64.

Simons, R., Whitbeck, L., Conger, R., & Melby, J. (1990). Husband and wife differences in determinants of parenting. *Journal of Marriage and the Family, 52,* 375–392.

Sorensen, E., & Zibman, C. (2001). *Poor dads who don't pay child support: Deadbeat or disadvantaged?* Washington, DC: Urban Institute.

Stewart, A. J., Copeland, A. P., Chester, N. L., Malley, J. E., & Barenbaum, N. B. (1997). *Separating together: How divorce transforms families.* New York: Guilford.

Strom, R. D. (1985). Developing a curriculum for parent education. *Family Relation, 34,* 161–167.

Thevenin, T. (1993). *Mothering and fathering: The gender differences in child rearing.* Garden City Park, NY: Avery.

Thompson, L., & Walker, A. (1989). Gender in families: Women and men in marriage, work, and parenthood. *Journal of Marriage and the Family, 51,* 845–871.

Thompson, L., & Walker, A. J. (1995). The place of feminism in family studies. *Journal of Marriage and the Family, 57,* 847–865.

U.S. Department of Education. (2000). *A call to commitment: Fathers' involvement in children's learning.* Retrieved January 15, 2001, from http://npin.org/library/2000/n00490/n00490.html

Volling, B. L., & Belsky, J. (1991). Multiple determinants of father involvement during infancy in dual-earner and single-earner families. *Journal of Marriage and the Family, 53,* 461–474.

Williams, E., Radin, N., & Coggins, K. (1996). Parental involvement in child rearing and the school performance of Objibwa children: An exploratory study. *Merrill-Palmer Quarterly, 42,* 578–595.

14 School Choices in Education

JOE NATHAN
University of Minnesota

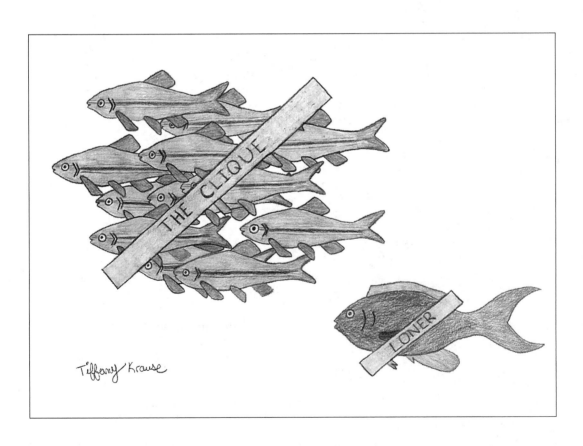

In a nation founded on the promise of freedom, many people believe that families should be able to select among various schools as they do among cars, religions, homes, and so on. The purpose of this chapter is to help readers understand that there are many forms of school choice. This chapter will:

- Discuss the rationale for various school choice plans
- Help readers understand various forms of school choice
- Describe some of the controversy about various kinds of school choice
- Show how school choice has evolved over the last twenty years
- Help readers form their own opinions about various school choice programs

Four Features of School Choice Programs

Schools

A choice program might involve public schools, independent non-sectarian schools, or religious schools. Some choice programs permit high school students to take courses either at their high school or at a post-secondary institution (a college or university).

Scope

A choice program might involve only the school's building. Families may be able to chose among several different schools, all located within one building. Families may also be able to select among different schools located within a town or city. Children may be able to attend school in the community in which they live or in a neighboring community. In some cases, families may be able to select among schools anywhere in a state, or across state lines.

Students

Will choices be available only for the most talented students? For example, magnet schools have admissions tests that are difficult to pass. Will choices be available for students who have not succeeded in other schools? (These are sometimes known as alternative schools.) Will choices be available only for students whose movement helps promote increased racial integration? Will we have the bizarre situation created in some desegregation programs in which white students from affluent suburbs are able to attend well-funded inner-city magnet schools that are closed to many Hispanic and African American students who live near (or even across the street from) the magnet school?

Standards

There are an almost infinite variety of standards that can be applied to choice programs. Are all schools expected to meet certain standards? Are some schools allowed to have admissions tests, while other schools must accept anyone who wants to attend? Is transportation provided to attend various schools, or are students on their own if they want to attend a school other than the closest one in their district? Must participating schools meet racial balance standards? Must teachers working in the schools be certified? These are only a few of the standards that might be applied to various choice programs.

Rationale

A number of reasons have been offered for allowing families and educators to choose among schools. These reasons include educational and philosophical ideas.

1. Some believe that there is no single best kind of school for all students. Some students do best in a more traditional school, others in a more progressive school. Some students thrive in a Montessori school, while others prefer a continuous-progress or language-immersion program.

2. Some choice proponents believe that choice among schools is more consistent with a democratic form of government that promotes freedom. These advocates say that choosing a school for a child is just as important as being able to vote for elected officials, being able to chose a religion, and being able to select among various consumer goods.

3. Some believe that choice among schools can help promote competition, thus improving all kinds of schools.

Brief Historical Background

It is important to understand that wealthy people have always been able to choose among various schools for their children. Even in the earliest days of the nation, the wealthy established schools that charged tuition, thus screening out certain students.

As educational historian Colin Greer explained, despite the "common school" idea that suggested all youngsters attend school together, wealthy families have always had the option not to attend the public schools. Many wealthy people have used that option. Furthermore, the public school was not primarily designed to free the lower-class family from its low self-esteem and advance its members in society. It was an apparatus designed to control most of them and to safeguard society (Greer, 1972).

After World War II, suburbs developed around most U.S. cities. A new form of school choice developed for those who could afford to move to the suburbs. Today the single largest government-supported school choice program is that offered by suburbs. Most suburban families own their homes and therefore pay real estate taxes. Because these taxes are often high in suburban areas, and because they are used to help support suburban public schools, these schools are frequently more affluent than inner-city schools.

Greer (1972) quotes Horace Mann, who is well known as the founder of the common school idea, in a speech to business people. Mann encouraged them to pay taxes to support common schools. He argued

> Finally, in regard to those who possess the largest shares in the stock of worldly goods, could there, in your opinion, be any police so vigilant and effective, for the protection of all rights of person, property and character, as such a sound and comprehensive education and training as our system of common schools could be made to impart; and would not the payment of a sufficient tax to make such education and training universal, be the cheapest means of self-protection and insurance? (p. 75)

From Mann's remarks we see that part of the way the common school idea was promoted to wealthy people was by saying it would offer them cheap insurance.

The real question is not whether families should have options among different kinds of schools, because wealthy people have them. They can choose to move to suburbs that have better school environments than the inner cities do. The real question is what form of school choice low- and moderate-income should families have. The remaining pages of this chapter provide responses to that question.

Vouchers

One of the nation's earliest debates was about whether public funding would be available for schools affiliated with religious institutions. Some argue that the Bill of Rights' prohibition on establishment of religion prevents government support for religious schools. Others insist that the nation's founders were not opposed to government support for religious schools. These people interpret the Bill of Rights as saying that there shall be no *one* established religion, not that there should not *be* established religion.

It is clear that the common schools established in the 1800s by Horace Mann and others in Massachusetts promoted a Protestant view of religion. Historian Joel Spring (1986) concluded, "The Catholic rebellion against public school reformers gave proof to the argument that the common school reflected a primarily Protestant ideology. Beginning in the nineteenth century and continuing into the twentieth, many Catholics would refer to public schools as Protestant schools" (p. 107).

In 1971, Justice Burger, writing for the majority of the U.S. Supreme Court, agreed with this interpretation. Burger wrote

> Early in the 19th century the Protestants obtained control of the New York school system and used it to promote reading and teaching of the Scriptures as revealed in the King James Version of the Bible. The contests between Protestants and Catholics, often erupting into violence, including the burning of Catholic churches, are a twice-told tale.... Parochial schools grew, but not Catholic schools alone. Other dissenting sects established their own schools—Lutherans, Methodists, Presbyterians and others. (Goldstein, 1974, p. 888)

In the early 1800s, funding for schools came primarily from parents through tuition or local taxes. States played a modest role, and the federal government had no role. In this period, some communities and states did help support both the Protestant-oriented common or public schools and the schools Catholics created. James Blaine, New York governor, strongly opposed the idea of tax support for Catholic schools. In the 1830s, he convinced the New York legislature to adopt what became known as the Blaine Amendment, which prohibited state tax support for schools established by Catholics. This was during a period in which there was great prejudice against Catholics, and fear that immigration of Catholics into the United States would threaten the nation. Blaine pushed his view throughout the nation, and a number of state legislatures included some form of the Blaine Amendment in their state constitutions.

This is not the place for an in-depth review of arguments for and against public funding for religious schools because this has been one of the most passionate and long-running controversies in U.S. education.

Briefly, proponents of public funding for religious schools argue that:

1. It is a matter of justice. Parents should have the right to select among various schools for their children, including religious schools. If parents have to pay tuition, some will not be able to afford to send their children to religious schools.
2. The Constitution does allow public funds to go to religious institutions. Proponents point out that such funds have gone for many years to colleges and universities that are affiliated with some form of religion.
3. Competition among schools will help improve all schools.
4. Funding tuition at religious schools would not be a direct support of religion, but support of a family's right to choose a school.

Voucher opponents insist that:

1. The Bill of Rights prohibits funding for religious schools.
2. Allowing public funding of religious schools would create dangerous divisions within the United States because students would not learn about diversity nor would they learn common lessons about the nation.
3. Competition would harm, rather than help public schools.
4. Using tax funds to pay religious school tuition would be a subsidy of religion.

The issue has gone to the U.S. Supreme Court a number of times. In the early 1900s, Oregon passed a law prohibiting students from attending religiously affiliated schools. This did not involve public support for religious schools. The only issue was whether students could attend such schools. In its 1915 decision on the case *Pierce* v. *Society of Sisters,* the Supreme Court decided that families did have the right to send their children to church-related schools (Goldstein, 1974, p. 510).

In 1971, the Supreme Court differentiated between public support for higher education, and for elementary and secondary education. The Court ruled that "there are generally significant differences between the religious aspects of church-related institutions of higher learning and parochial elementary and secondary schools" (Goldstein, 1974). The Supreme Court authorized the use of federal funds to help pay for the construction of church-related higher education institutions, while rejecting support for church-related K–12 schools.

Some states adopted laws permitting tuition tax deductions or tuition tax credits. Somewhat incongruously, the U.S. Supreme Court has rejected tax credits and permitted tax deductions, so long as these are available for all kinds of educational expenses, including those paid by families whose children attend public as well as religious schools.

As this chapter is being written, the U.S. Supreme Court is preparing to rule on a case involving public support for religious schools. In this case, an Ohio state law permits families in Cleveland to attend public, private, or parochial schools with tax funds paying the costs of the schools. Whatever the Supreme Court rules will be important. But it's clear that this issue, having been debated for more than 200 years, will not be resolved by any single Supreme Court decision.

Reflection...

How do you feel about tax support for elementary and secondary schools? Do you feel that some support is justified (such as providing transportation)? Do you believe that funds should be provided to pay tuition costs at private and parochial schools? If independent or religious schools receive tax funds, do you believe that these schools should have to follow the same rules as other publicly-supported schools (in areas like admissions, testing, and serving special education students)? Do you believe that there should be no tax support for schools affiliated with some form of religion?

Home-Schooling

Another form of school choice allows families to educate their children at home. Generally such programs do not receive any tax support. However, the practice of home schooling appears to be growing.

No one is quite sure how many U.S. children are being home schooled. The widely respected publication *Education Week* ("Home-Schooling," 1999) says that the consensus of the people who have studied home schooling is that "at least one million students were being home schooled in 1999." But *Education Week* also notes that "reliable numbers are hard to come by" because some parents of home-schooled children do not report numbers to state officials.

The Home School Legal Defense Association, a group strongly supporting home-schooling, commissioned a 1998 study about the demographics and achievement of home-schooled students. This study was done by Lawrence Rudner of the University of Maryland, who was able to identify more than 20,000 students involved in home schooling. This limited sample yielded the following information:

- The median income of home-schooling families in 1997 was $52,000, whereas the median income of public school families in 1995 was $36,000.
- About 6 percent of home-schooled students are members of minority groups, compared to 32 percent of public school students.
- About 24 percent of students who are being taught at home have at least one parent who is a certified teacher.
- Students in this sample of home-schooled students scored well above their public- and private-school counterparts on standardized tests. The gap appeared to be about a year in grades one through four and increased after that (Rudner, 1998).

Magnet Schools

In the late 1960s and early 1970s, the United States was faced with how to carry out the integration called for in the landmark 1954 U.S. Supreme Court case *Brown* v. *Board of Education*. In the years following *Brown*, various efforts had been made to promote racial integration by allowing African American families to send their children to previously all-white schools, or by telling both white and African American families they had to send their children to previously segregated schools. Not surprisingly, these efforts had mixed results, and often were extremely controversial. Once again, this chapter will not attempt to trace the intense history of desegregation efforts.

However, in the late 60s and early 70s, a new approach was suggested as a way to bring children of different races together. The idea was that additional funds would be provided to create schools offering special, more attractive programs that would attract families of different races. Thus, they would be *magnet schools*. Millions of dollars have been allocated to help create, and in some cases maintain, magnet schools. Magnets have been very popular in many communities.

Magnets can generally be divided into several groups. Some focused on a particular area, such as a school designed to help students prepare for a career in medicine or computers. Some magnets featured a particular philosophy, such as schools using the Montessori idea. And some were focused on students with particular characteristics, such as very high academic talent or strong artistic talent.

A large national study in the 1990s found that 56 percent of the nation's magnet schools have some form of admission test, and 24 percent of elementary magnet schools have admissions tests. Generally these were tests that students had to pass in order to get into the magnet schools (Steel & Levine, 1994).

Not surprisingly, this feature of magnets has been very controversial. Some educators and families have argued that it is not fair or appropriate to allow some publicly supported schools to be able to pick and choose among students, while other publicly funded schools must accept all kinds of students. Some studies have pointed out that magnet schools enroll a higher percentage of wealthy students than neighborhood schools. These critics argue that the magnets are not serving many of the low-income students who could benefit from their programs.

Another controversial aspect of many magnet programs and schools has been the extra money they receive. The *St. Louis Post Dispatch* found that in the 1986–1987 school year, elementary magnet schools received 42 percent more per pupil than neighborhood elementary schools. Magnet middle schools received 25 percent more than neighborhood schools and magnet high schools received 27 percent more than other city high schools (Hughes, 1998). Another study found that magnet schools in New York, Philadelphia, and Chicago had substantially higher per-pupil budgets than neighborhood schools. This study disdainfully called these magnets "The New Improved Sorting Machine" (Davenport & Moore, 1988).

Some research supports magnet schools. For example, a large national study compared the achievement of 24,000 eighth- and tenth-grade students in urban high schools. It compared the achievement of students in large comprehensive high schools, Catholic schools, private schools, and public magnet schools. The author concluded that students who attended urban magnet schools learned more and outperformed those in the other schools. Among the reasons for better performance by magnet students were parental choice, students feeling a sense of membership and belonging, and a focused curriculum (Gamoran, 1996).

Reflection…

If you were a member of Congress or a school board member, would you permit magnet schools to have admissions tests? To receive additional operational funding beyond what is available for neighborhood schools? Or would you insist that magnet schools receive the same per pupil funding, and have to accept all kinds of students, as do other publicly funded schools?

Schools within Schools

In a growing number of school districts educators, parents, and community members are applying the value of small schools to large school buildings. They are creating distinctive schools from which families may choose, right in the same building.

These efforts start with an understanding of small school size. The federal government recently commissioned Dr. Mary Anne Raywid, one of the nation's leading authorities on small schools, to summarize research on small schools. Raywid (1999) examined hundreds of studies, comparing what happened when similar groups of students attended large versus small schools. She noted that in general, students attending small schools had higher achievement, better discipline and attendance, along with higher graduation rates. Students, families, and teachers reported more satisfaction in small schools. Raywid concluded that these findings have been "confirmed with a clarity and a level of confidence rare in the annals of education research" (1999, p. 1).

One widely cited urban example shows what can be done with an existing large high school. Eight years ago Wyandotte High School in Kansas City, Kansas, was an extremely troubled place. Graduation rates were awful, as were attendance and achievement. A new principal, Walter Thompson, came in to help make improvements. After a year of listening and learning, he worked with the faculty to create eight small schools in the building, which serves about 1,500 students.

One of those small schools, Opportunity Center, serves only ninth graders who are repeating the ninth grade. The seven other small schools were created on themes such as business or creative arts. Students from grades 9–12 are allowed to choose among these small schools, and take most of their course work in them.

The results are heartening. People come from all over the country to see this school where attendance, achievement, graduation rates, and behavior have improved dramatically. And what about the faculty, by and large the same folks who were there in the troubled times? They made it clear to me on two recent visits that Wyandotte is a far more satisfying, rewarding place to work than it used to be (G. Thompson, personal communication, October 15, 2000).

Although it had nothing like Wyandotte's problems, a Texas suburban community used some of the same ideas to make improvements. Seven years ago South Grand Prairie High School, outside Dallas, enrolled more than 2,000 students in a typical, above-the-national-average suburban high school.

The faculty and administration were not satisfied. Today the building has been divided into five smaller schools from which students select. Each school has a theme: communications, creative and performing arts, health sciences and human services, math science and engineering, and business and computer technology.

The changes have produced progress. Many more students are taking advanced placement courses than were before, and the already above-average graduation rate has improved. South Grand Prairie is a marvelous example of a faculty that did not face heavy pressure to change because of low student performance, but did so anyway because they wanted all students to move closer to their potential (R. Garcia, personal communication, October 10, 2000).

The same idea can apply to elementary and middle schools. The St. Paul, Minnesota, school district has a large building that hosts three distinctive schools. One, called Museum Magnet, was recently named as a "Blue Ribbon School of Excellence" by the U.S. Department of Education. This school cooperates with the Science Museum of Minnesota, located just a few blocks away. A second school, called Capitol Hill, is a magnet for gifted students. It attracts both urban and suburban students. A third school, Benjamin Mays, is named for a famous African American educator.

New York City has turned a large, failing high school named Julia Richman into eight smaller schools. They include elementary, middle, and high schools, along with a child-care center and health clinic. Each school is available to families as a choice.

The idea that a building can contain more than one school owes its roots, in part, to the extraordinary success of East Harlem schools, which serve some of the most low-income areas in the nation. Over a decade, East Harlem transformed about twenty school buildings into more than fifty small schools. In the process, the district moved from last among New York City's thirty-two community districts, to the middle. Academic achievement and behavior improved dramatically. Vandalism and absenteeism declined (Fliegel, 1998).

Part of the reason for creating small schools or schools within schools is to improve achievement. Another reason is to give teachers a chance to create the kind of schools they think may make sense. There is no one best kind of school for all students, or all faculty. Deborah Meier, who won a McArthur "genius" grant because of her outstanding work in East Harlem, strongly opposes providing public funds to private or parochial schools. However, she strongly supports giving educators and families options among various public schools. For Meier, public school choice is "an essential tool" in the effort to create good public education. She feels that public education needs schools "with a focus, with staffs brought together free to shape a whole set of school parameters" (Meier, 1991, p. 266).

New Small Schools

Some districts are adopting policies allowing parents and teachers to create new small schools. These policies are based on research, cited previously, about the value of small schools. Furthermore, we're learning that smaller schools need not be more expensive. Researchers recently looked at the cost of schools not just per student, but per graduate. An important study in New York City found that if researchers looked at cost per pupil, larger schools were somewhat less expensive. But if they looked at the cost per graduate, small schools clearly were less expensive (Stiefel, Latarola, Fruchter, & Berne, 1998). University of Chicago researcher Tony Bryk (1994) concluded that:

> While school districts that are currently saddled with large physical plants might productively move toward schools-within-schools, there is little reason to continue to build more buildings like this. In light of the positive consequences for both adults and students associated with working in small schools, the reality is one of dis-economy of scale. (pp. 6–7)

New York City is one of a growing number of districts deciding to authorize creation of small schools. El Puente, a small public school located in a very low-income area of New York City, is a great place to start. El Puente was one of several small schools created by educators and community groups when the district wisely offered this opportunity to people throughout the city. El Puente serves a couple hundred high school students in a building that was formerly a church. The school shares facilities with social service staff who help students and families with a range of issues, including medical concerns, counseling, and literacy programs.

With encouragement and assistance from the school's faculty, El Puente's students constantly combine classroom work with community service and activism. For example, they helped create a coalition of African American, Hispanic, and Chasidic Jewish people to successfully block an incinerator that the city was going to put in their already badly polluted neighborhood. Students are combining a study of advanced mathematics with development of a skateboard park that will be located underneath a nearby bridge. The school's full name is El Puente Academy for Peace and Justice. The faculty strongly believes in helping young people develop skills to work for a better world now, along with traditional academic skills.

The results are encouraging. More than 90 percent of the students who enter El Puente as ninth graders graduate four years later (in an area where large high schools have graduation rates of about 50 percent). Although El Puente's faculty strongly resists the idea that their school should be judged only on test scores, their students are doing very well on the challenging New York State Regents Exams (G. L. Acosta, personal communication, October 25, 2000).

The Boston Public Schools learned from New York's new vision schools. About seven years ago the district agreed to give educators a chance to create pilot schools. This was partly in response to the fact that a charter law had passed, and eighteen of the first sixty-four charter proposals came from educators and community groups in Boston.

One of the first pilot schools, Fenway High School, was initially located at a local community college. In the last few years, Fenway has moved to a building directly across the street from the Boston Red Sox's baseball field. Fenway was one of the original members of Ted Sizer's Coalition of Essential Schools. Despite enrolling significant numbers of low-income students, Fenway retains a strong graduation rate and an excellent record of graduates continuing their education after high school. Fenway has a well-developed advisor–advisee system, and graduation is based on demonstration of skill and knowledge.

Fenway shares its space with two other organizations. One is another pilot school, the Boston Arts Academy. This school works with many nationally recognized arts groups located near the school building, providing internship and apprenticeship opportunities. BAA also has a program in which students can apply for grants because the school's faculty believes it is vital for those considering a career in the arts to develop grant-writing skills.

The third group occupying part of the building is the library of the Boston Symphony Orchestra. Because the orchestra shares the library with Fenway and BAA, the library is open later in the afternoon and on Saturday. Moreover, the library's collection is much richer and broader because it is funded in part by the schools and in part by the orchestra (L. Myatt, personal communication, November 1, 2000).

Starting new small schools isn't just for urban areas. Almost ten years ago teachers and parents in the Minneapolis suburban district of Rosemount-Apple

Valley-Eagan came together to discuss the advantages of small schools. They planned seven small schools, all sharing facilities with a medical complex, businesses, and other institutions.

The first has been open for five years. It's called the Minnesota School for Environmental Studies, and is located on the campus of the Minnesota State Zoo (which donated the land for the building). The "Zoo School," which enrolls several hundred eleventh and twelfth graders, was built for exactly the same per pupil cost as the 2,000 student high school buildings found elsewhere in the district. Zoo students make public presentations about what they are learning and participate in internships in a number of places, including, but not limited to, the Minnesota Zoo. The U.S. Department of Education has named the "Zoo School" as a "New American High School" because of its creativity and outstanding performance.

Unfortunately, a new administration in the district has not proceeded with other small school plans that parents and teachers developed. But the Zoo School's success shows that suburban districts can also benefit from using small schools and shared facility research (D. Bodette, personal communication, November 15, 2000).

> **Reflection...**
>
> What do you think of school districts allowing teachers to create new kinds of public schools? If you were a school board member, what guidelines would you put in a policy allowing people to create such new schools? Would you allocate funds from the district budget to help people create such schools? Where else might you go to get "start-up" funds? As a teacher, what kind of school might you like to start?

The Charter School Movement

In 1991, the charter school movement started in Minnesota. The central ideas of the charter school movement are that:

- Charter schools are public, non-sectarian, and open to all kinds of students. Charters can be new schools or schools converted from existing schools.
- More than one organization can authorize or sponsor a charter school (e.g., local school boards, the state, universities, cities, and other publicly responsible entities).
- Charters are freed from most state rules about how to run schools (other than building safety, non-discrimination, and statewide testing programs).
- Charters are free of local labor-management agreements.
- In exchange for the waiver of rules, charters are expected to improve student achievement (Nathan, 1997).

Between 1991 and 2001, the number of states permitting charters grew from one (Minnesota) to thirty-eight including the District of Columbia. The number of charters increased to more than 2,000. Charter laws vary from strong to weak, with the stronger laws permitting multiple sponsors, having clear accountability measures, and permitting freedom for charters to operate outside state and local labor-management requirements. Charters include new schools and existing schools that have converted to charter status (Center for Education Reform, 2001).

One group of educators drew inspiration for a charter from their experiences in Japan. They created a small charter school for several hundred middle school students that uses some of the best ideas of Asian and American education. The Academy for the Pacific Rim (APR), located in Boston, is housed with several other organizations in a large building that was formerly a carriage factory.

Students and faculty start each day with an assembly, during which at least one student receives a *gambatte* award. This Japanese term translates roughly as "persist" or "keep going." Each student at the Academy, which has no admissions tests and serves a variety of low-income students, must take some form of martial art and study an Asian language. Classes start with students standing and bowing to their teacher. The teacher also stands and bows to the students. Another Asian touch is a longer school day and longer year. Each teacher has a computer with a phone on his or her desk.

APR also uses some of the best active-learning ideas of the United States. For example, when students learn about the Constitution, they participate in a mock Constitutional Convention, portraying a person who attended the convention and dressing roughly the way that person did.

Results are impressive. Although the school enrolls a high percentage of students from low-income families, its attendance and test results are among the very best of public schools in Boston, exceeded only by public schools that have admissions tests (S. Blasdale, personal communication, November 2, 2000).

Charters are not being created just in urban areas. In fact, the charter movement has been employed by a variety of rural small school advocates. One of the nation's most intriguing secondary schools is a charter in the tiny Minnesota community of Henderson, called the Minnesota New Country School (MNCS). This secondary charter school enrolls about 125 students, grades 7–12. It is run as a co-op, with the faculty owning the school, setting their own salaries and working conditions (D. Thomas, personal communication, September 10, 2000).

The Bill and Melinda Gates Foundation has given MNCS $4 million to help replicate the school. Each school year starts with a family/student/advisor conference. The conferences help students develop a plan for how they will make progress toward graduation, which is based entirely on demonstration of skill and knowledge. MNCS uses multiple measures to assess student progress. They show improvements in achievement, as well as strong attendance and a high graduation rate. There are no grades or bells at MNCS. Each student has a work station with a computer and the freedom to decorate the station with pictures of friends and family.

Students work individually or in small groups on projects that help them achieve the required mastery. Faculty see themselves as facilitators, advisors, and coaches, moving from student to student throughout the day. Every six weeks the school has a presentation night, during which students share information they've learned. It's like a big science fair, but on various subjects. Each student is expected to make at least three presentations per year.

The presentations often include computer graphics and PowerPoint. Students have become so sophisticated that some of them have been hired by businesses to create websites. But learning at MNCS is not confined to what's available by computer. Students are constantly out in the community, doing research and performing service projects. One project that attracted national attention involved students discovering frogs that did not have four legs. This led to a presentation at the Minnesota legislature, which allocated hundreds of thousands of dollars to learn what produced the frog deformities.

Two recently created examples show what else can be done with shared facilities. In Phoenix, a group of educators approached South Mountain Community College to see if they would house a small charter high school focusing on agriculture and equine science. The college was delighted to do so. The high school has several classrooms of its own and shares the excellent resources of the college—classrooms, library, extensive computer labs, lounges and physical fitness facilities, along with college faculty. The college uses the high school classrooms late in the afternoon and during the evening. Administrators in both the high school and college are very pleased with their collaborative arrangements. Also, academic achievement of the students has been strong. Most students take some college courses while in high school. Some have received their high school degree and an associate arts degree from the college in the same week (D. Krug, personal communication, October 8, 2000).

An Arizona charter school was created on the campus of the South Mesa Boys and Girls Club. The Mesa Arts Academy serves elementary students in one of the lowest-income areas of Mesa, an area also known for several violent gangs. The collaboration between school faculty and the Boys and Girls Club has helped youngsters and their families. State statistics show that some of the greatest growth in academic achievement of any Arizona public school is taking place at this school (S. Douglas, personal communication, October 9, 2000).

Some research suggests the charter movement is helping stimulate improvement in the existing system, precisely because funds follow students. One study of several districts around the nation noted that:

> District personnel on at least five occasions in this study acknowledged, sometimes begrudgingly, that charters had served to jump start their efforts at reform. While they initially opposed charters and the chartering had been accomplished outside their authority, they felt that the district schools ultimately had benefited from the dynamics introduced by the charter school. (Rofes, 1999)

Charters schools can be criticized because they do not always follow the same format as public schools and this varies from state to state. Charter schools are coming under increased scrutiny because they do take dollars from the public schools. Some charter schools have not handled finances very well. Clearly charters, like other public schools, must work on developing better ways of assessing student achievement. Nevertheless, the charter movement is spreading throughout the nation.

Reflection...

If you were to create an ideal school, what would you include? What research-based ideas would you include in your school? Where in the community would you go to for help in creating and operating such a school?

Post-Secondary Options

In 1985, Minnesota became the first state to create a post-secondary options program. This allows high school juniors or seniors to take all or part of their coursework at colleges and universities, with state funds paying for tuition, books, and other fees. The program gives high schools students the power to decide whether to take these courses. A number of other states have a somewhat similar option. In some states, such as Wisconsin, the laws permit students to take only courses not offered in their high schools. In other states, such as Florida, students may enroll in community colleges only if they have permission from their high schools. But other states have followed Minnesota's lead, believing it important to meet students needs and encourage high schools to reform by empowering families to make this decision.

Sharing Facilities

One of the best ways to make small schools no more expensive than massive ones is to share facilities. Moreover, shared facilities can respond to a constant, says Joy Dryfoos (2000), who has studied shared facilities and calls them community schools. These schools, according to Dryfoos, can have a positive effect on children and families. Several of the schools cited previously, including El Puente, Fenway High School/Boston Arts Academy, the Julia Richman complex, Mesa Arts Academy, and the high school at South Mountain Community College are examples of this growing trend.

Another encouraging example comes from Cincinnati, at the city's Parham School. Seven years ago, Parham students had the worst record of any K–8 school in the city. Attendance, achievement, and discipline all needed major improvement. A new principal, Sharon Johnson, was placed at the school.

She immediately asked for assistance from FamiliesFORWARD, a well-respected local social service agency. Bette Hinton, director of FamiliesFORWARD, agreed to place several of her staff at the school. They met with families, asking what kinds of programs they would like to have for themselves and their children.

Based on these requests, FamiliesFORWARD staff set up classes to teach families such things as how to discipline their children, how to handle finances, and how to read. After-school classes for students included help with homework, dance, and history of Africa.

Attendance, achievement, and discipline have all improved dramatically at Parham. The school has won awards from the district two years in a row for the significant progress that has taken place. Unquestionably, curriculum and instruction changes helped. So did the close collaboration with FamiliesFORWARD (B. Hinton, personal communication, November 18, 2000).

Finally, for a marvelous example of leadership, look at the recently established Northfield, Minnesota Community Center. In this rural community, the city, school district, senior citizens center, and war on poverty agencies came together to produce a 50,000 square foot state of the art facility that serves residents, from birth to death. The facility includes a vast array of services for families, children, teenagers, and seniors, as well as a small public high school option. The high school students interview seniors to supplement history research, and help with the Head Start Center, both of which are close to their classrooms. Charlie Kyte, former Northfield superintendent, now director of the Minnesota Association of School Administrators, calls the community center "one of the most rewarding projects I've ever worked on" (C. Kyte, personal communication, August 30, 2000).

Summary

This chapter explains that there is no single school choice program. Instead, there is an array. Each choice plan has its own advocates and critics. Some people support some forms of school choice, and oppose others.

For this author, school choice is a powerful tool. Like electricity, it can help or harm, depending on how it is used. The author hopes readers will be able to use information in this chapter, together with other readings and experience, to use school choice as a way to help students, families, and educators.

RECOMMENDED ACTIVITIES

1. Check to see what school options are available in your community, county, and state. Check with the local school district and the state Department of Education.

2. Ask your state Department of Education or local school district what methods are being used to get information to families about educational choices students have in the K–12 system.

3. Ask your state Department of Education or local school district what opportunities there are for educators, families, and other concerned people to start new public schools in your community or state.

4. Identify magnet schools, charter schools, or families home schooling their children and invite students, parents, and/or administrators to form a panel to discuss their

education and how their program compares to other programs. You can also survey people in these organizations if you are not able to form a panel.

ADDITIONAL RESOURCES

Books:

Bar, R., & Parrett, W. (1997). *How to create alternative, magnet & charter schools that work.* Indianapolis, IN: National Education Service.

Birkett, F., & Tabin, J. (2000). *Charter schools: Everything you need to know to make the right decision for your child.* Roseville, CA: Prima.

Finn, C., Manno, V., & Vanourek, G. (2001). *Charter schools in action: Renewing public education.* Princeton, NJ: Princeton University Press.

Organizations:

Association of Charter Schools
1295 Bandana Boulevard, Suite 165
St. Paul, MN 55108
Phone: 651-644-6115
Fax: 651-644-0433
Email: info@charterfriends.org

National Home School Association
P.O. Box 327
Webster, NY 14580-0327

Videos:

Charter Schools (1995). National Education Association. (22 minutes)

Alternative & Charter Schools: Educating Outside the Box. (2000). Films for Humanities & Science.

Alternative Education: Choices Beyond the Public School System. Films for Humanities & Science. (2 part series, 30 minutes each)

Websites:

Charter Schools

Center for Education Reform
www.edreform.com/charter_schools

Charter Schools Development Center
www.csus.edu/ier/charter/resources.html

Federal Government Listing
www.uscharterschools.org

Minnesota Charter School Evaluation
www.education.umn.edu/carei/reports/charter/Executive_Sum/Section
_V.html

National Charter School Clearinghouse
www.ncsc.info/cgi-bin/link/first.asp

Status of Charter Schools 2000 (fourth year report)
www.ed.gov/pubs/charter4thyear

Magnet Schools

Magnet Schools of America
www.magnet.edu

Schools of Choice
magnets.dade.k12.fl.us

Yahoo Directory of Magnet Schools
dir.yahoo.com/education/k_12/schools/magnet

Home Schooling (Home Education)

Home School World
www.home-school.com

Virtual Home School
www.homeschool.com

Home School Legal Defense Association
www.hslda.org

REFERENCES

Bryk, A. (1994, Fall). *Issues in Restructuring Schools—Commentary.* Madison: University of Wisconsin School of Education, 6–7.

Center for Education Reform. (2001). *National charter school directory.* Washington, DC: Center for Education Reform.

Davenport, S., & Moore, D. (1988). *The new improved sorting machine.* Chicago: Designs for Learning.

Dryfoos, J. (2000). *Evaluation of community schools: Findings to date.* New York: Carnegie Corporation.

Fliegel, S., with MacGuire, J. (1998). *Miracle in East Harlem.* New York: Times Books.

Gamoran, R. (1996). Student achievement in public, magnet, public comprehensive and private city high schools. *Educational Evaluation and Policy Analysis, 18*(1), 1–18.

Goldstein, S. (1974). *Law and education: Cases and materials.* Indianapolis, IN: Bobbs Merrill.

Greer, C. (1972). *The great school legend.* New York: Basic Books.

Home-schooling. (1999). *Education Week.* Retrieved March 31, 1999, from www.edweek.org

Hughes, T. (1998, February 25). Magnets pull weakens in suburbs. *St. Louis Post Dispatch,* p. 8A.

Meier, D. (1991, March 4). Choice can save public education. *The Nation,* p. 266.

Nathan, J. (1997). *Charter schools: Creating hope and opportunity in American education.* San Francisco: Jossey-Bass.

Raywid, M. (1999). *Current literature on small schools.* Charleston, WV: ERIC Clearinghouse on Rural Education and Small Schools.

Rofes, E. (1999). *How are school districts responding to charter laws and charter schools.* Berkeley: Graduate School of Education Policy Analysis for California Education (PACE).

Rudner, L. (1998). Scholastic achievement and demographic characteristics of home school students in 1998 [Electronic version]. *Educational Policy Analysis Review, 7,* 8.

Spring, J. (1986). *The American school, 1642–1985.* New York: Longman.

Stiefel, L., Latarola, N., Fruchter, J., & Berne, R. (1998). *The costs of size of student body on school costs and performance in New York high schools.* New York: Institute for Education and Social Policy, New York University.

Steel, L., & Levine, R. (1994). *Educational innovation in multiracial contexts: The growth of magnet schools in american education.* Washington, DC: U.S. Department of Education.

15 School Violence and Bullying

Implications for Home School Partnerships

JOHN H. HOOVER
St. Cloud State University

MARY BETH NOLL
St. Cloud State University

GLENN OLSEN
University of North Dakota

In the past ten years there has been an outbreak of school violence that is unprecedented in public and private school education. These severely violent episodes have resulted in deaths of teachers and students and have received global attention. However, as educators, we must keep in mind that school is still a safe place for students to be. We need to deal with issues that affect school climate and that includes bullying and other physical or verbal intimidating behavior by students. Any type of bullying, including verbal harassment, is unacceptable. This chapter looks at how parents and schools can work together to create a climate that deals effectively with bullying and school violence.

The purpose of this chapter is to help the reader explore the:

- Impact of violence on the school climate
- Impact of bullying on the bully, victim, and bystander
- Role of the school and families in preventing and stopping bullying
- Different types of curriculum and other resources available to help with issues of bullying and school violence

School Violence

Statistically speaking, students enjoy more physical safety inside the doors of their schools than they do elsewhere (National Center for Educational Statistics, NCES, 1998). Students may be up to ten times safer in school than anywhere else in our otherwise violent society (Goldstein & Conoley, 1997). After roughly two decades of steady increase, violent crime among youth dropped during the 1990s (NCES, 1998). This reduction in youth violence occurred both inside of and outside of school. Nonetheless, schools are not as safe as we would like them to be (Hoover & Olsen, 2001).

Around three million crimes are committed within school walls most years; this averages out to about 16,000 per school day, or one every 3 seconds while school is in session (Stephens, 1997, p. 74). Stephens (1997) cites the following risk factors, at both the individual and institutional level, for the occurrence of school violence (pp. 75–78):

- *Dropping out, literally and symbolically.* Students experiencing difficulty conforming themselves to the social demands of institutions are at much greater risk for committing violent acts such as bullying and fights (Patterson, DeBaryshe, & Ramsey, 1989).
- *Discipline problems, bullying, and harassment.* Levels of mild violence and bullying probably predict the overall level of risk for more serious violence in a school.

- *Drug and alcohol abuse.* A clear association between substance abuse and violence has been noted. More recently, it has been observed that students who pick on their peers are more likely than other students to abuse mind-altering chemicals, including alcohol. Bullying was found to be a primary predictor of substance abuse (Simanton, Burthwick, & Hoover, 2000).
- *Gang membership.* The violence associated with gang rituals and the aggression perpetrated by gang members on others add to the potential risk of violence within schools.
- *The ready availability of weapons.* Easy access to weapons in U.S. society all too often renders simple fights and minor disputes into bloody ordeals with increased potential for serious injury and death.

We believe that in order to address school violence, future teachers must first understand lower levels of aggression, including bullying.

Bullying and Violence

Many lines of evidence suggest that bullying in school, especially when adults do not intervene, produces risks for more serious forms of violence. For example, a strong correlation exists between minor interpersonal incidents (perhaps eliciting a trip to the principal's office) and more serious offenses in schools (NCES, 1998; Wilson & Petersilia, 1995). As Goldstein and Conoley (1997) put it, "Parallel to (and in many instances also underlying) the very substantial levels of student assault, weaponry, theft, intimidation, and other serious violence is lower-level aggressive behavior" (p. 8). For example, permissiveness for violence within families begets higher rates of acting out (Perry, Hodges, & Egan, 2001). It is highly likely, therefore, that failure of school personnel to intervene in low-level interpersonal violence increases risk for serious disturbances.

Anecdotal evidence demonstrates that many students involved in school shootings suffered bullying at the hands of their peers. The manner whereby peer oppression, which typically results in depression, turns some students in the direction of lethal rage is not well understood. Nonetheless, in certain noteworthy cases it clearly exists. Perhaps some insight is to be gained from a letter penned by a frequently bullied student in response to the 1999 shootings at Columbine High School in Littleton, Colorado.

This young man recalled walking to his middle school each morning dreaming up ways to either kill himself or the students brutalizing him (Fransen, 1999). Such daydreaming about violence often sets the stage for acting out.

Although it is not clear that bullying has increased in either frequency or intensity over the past thirty years, some educators assert that it is a significant problem in North American schools (Hoover, Oliver, & Hazler, 1992; Simanton et al., 2000). It has been conservatively estimated that approximately 10 percent of students in rural, Midwestern schools suffer bullying-related psychological trauma. This may be average or below average for the rest of the country.

Parent–School Partnerships Are Important in Reducing Violence

Partnerships between families and schools lie at the core of nearly every successful risk behavior–reduction program. Certainly this is true of programs dealing with bullying reduction, violence deterrence, and substance abuse prevention (Committee for Children, 1997). As students confront bullies in their schools, educators and parents pick up the pieces and work to avoid future peer harassment. It is essential that family members and educators form strong, healthy, working partnerships. Examples of successful partnerships from around the world and the details of such partnerships will be explored in this chapter.

In fashioning a model for successful parent–school partnerships in bullying reduction, several issues must be addressed. In an initial section, a brief overview of bullying research is undertaken; a second section contains information specifically related to the link between family life and bullying or violence. We dedicated a third section to exploring parent–school partnerships for bullying and violence reductions.

Reflection...

Besides the schools, what other agencies should be helping in the area of bullying and school violence, whether on or off school property? If you were being bullied or harassed in junior high or high school, where would you go for help? Are there places outside of school that you would go to for help—social services, church, a trusted adult, a parent, or others? Did young people in your school systems have places to go for help, both inside and outside the school system? Was this help effective?

Basic Bullying Information

Definition

Bullying is the purposeful infliction of psychological or physical pain on one individual by another or by a group. In bullying, the perpetrators are physically or psychologically more potent than the victims. The analysis of bullying episodes can be made more complex in that the defenselessness portrayed by injured parties may be more a matter of individual perception rather than reality.

Frequency and Severity of Bullying

Between 10 percent and 15 percent of North American school children endure significant peer harassment while at school (Hoover, Oliver, & Hazler, 1992; Hoover, Oliver, & Thomson, 1993; Perry, Kusel, & Perry, 1988). An initial study of bullying

(Hoover et al., 1992) reported that over 80 percent of students in rural Midwestern schools were bullied at some point during their school careers. However, when the figures were adjusted to reflect bullying rated above the mid-point on a "degree of trauma" scale, a more reasonable figure of 14 percent emerged. Perry et al. (1988) reported that roughly 10 percent of students experienced severe peer aggression. The proportion of students experiencing bullying (and those experiencing significant levels of trauma from it) peaks during the middle school years, with slightly lower numbers during the intermediate and secondary grades (Hoover et al., 1992). We estimate that just under half of U.S. students report bullying others, suffering bullying, or both during any given semester, while about 10 percent bear significant levels of peer abuse and about 5 percent regularly bully others.

Bullying affects students' perception of safety at school, with up to 10 percent of all students, most of them chronically bullied, either typically afraid or expressing the wish to stay home from school at least once per semester due to bullying (Simanton et al., 2000). Berthold and Hoover (2000) concluded that three times as many bully victims felt unsafe at school (25 percent), as compared to 8 percent of students not suffering from peer depredations. Chronic victims of peer abuse most likely perform much poorer academically than they otherwise might (Hoover & Oliver, 1996). In addition, bullying places already sad and anxious students at even greater risk for depression (Kaltiala-Heino, Rimpels, Marttunen, Rimpela, & Rantanen, 1999; Rigby & Slee, 1999).

Bullying Behaviors

When young people describe either personally-experienced bullying (Hoover et al., 1992) or the harassment of others that they have observed (Hazler, Hoover, & Oliver, 1991), they describe it as largely verbal. Indirect and subtle bullying, such as social ostracism or friendship interference is the second most common form of bullying experienced by females. Mild physical attacks are the second most common form of bullying reported by males (Hoover & Oliver, 1996).

No statistical relationship is typically observed between the bullying behaviors that students are subjected to and the degree of trauma they experience. In other words, long-term verbal harassment is just as devastating to victims as periodic, mild, physical attacks. Some writers have even concluded that dealing with verbal harassment and teasing are central to anti-bullying campaigns (Hoover & Olsen, 2001). Childhood verbal bullying also appears to be the "testing ground" for later sexual harassment. Results show that school officials who don't deal with sexual teasing and verbal gay bashing set themselves up for greater levels of overtly illegal and life-threatening forms of sexual harassment (Stein, 1995). Of course, the verbal climate at school often reflects the language patterns used at home.

Reflection...

Is teasing a form of bullying? When is teasing okay, or is it ever okay? Why don't students just stand up to bullies as a group and stop their behavior? How do we give bullies the power to bully? If your best friend was being bullied or severely teased, what would you do? Do you know adult bullies? Have you ever heard someone being teased and thought that the teasing had gone beyond appropriate limits (whatever you feel those are)?

Adjustment Problems Associated with Bullying

Currently Accepted Categories of Students Involved in Bullying

Experts currently recognize three categories of students involved with bullying: bullies, passive victims, and provocative victims (Olweus, 1993). Bullies tend to act up to direct their behavioral problems outward. (Olweus, 1993). Passive victims tend to match the personality style that some experts call *over-controlled*. Specifically, these youngsters tend to be sad, shy, and anxious. Chronic victims tend to become even more anxiety-ridden as they suffer peer harassment. Finally, a small group of youngsters tend to pick on others at times and yet suffer bullying at other times. These individuals demonstrate that the rare combination of being alternatively sad and angry (c.f., Kaltiala-Heino et al., 1999; Olweus, 2001).

The childhood experience for bullying produces a slew of negative, long-term adjustment effects. For example, being the target of bullies during their formative years is the most common complaint registered by adults seeking psychiatric care for depression and anxiety (Egan & Perry, 1998).

Not just victims, but also bullies, demonstrate significant relational problems as they age. Basing relationships exclusively on the exercise of power may well be habit forming, setting the stage for a lifetime of maladjustment. Evidence shows that bullies are at a significantly greater risk for dropping out of school, as well as for encountering drug and alcohol abuse problems (Berthold & Hoover, 1999; Simanton et al., 2000). Childhood bullies are four to five times as likely as non-bullies to experience mental health, legal, and job related difficulties as they age (Olweus, 1993). The negative effects of bullying are so strong that, despite the real and significant trauma experienced by chronic victims, a world-renown expert in the field concluded that childhood bullies suffer greater adulthood adjustment problems than victims do (Olweus, 1993).

Bullying is a significant problem in that it affects the lives of students—both bullies and victims. It extends beyond the lives of only the bullies and victims and worsens the learning climate for everyone at school. It is difficult for students to focus on learning while dealing with the fear produced by bullying. Bullying also reigns as a social problem, contributing to the climate of violence that troubles U.S. society (Hoover & Olsen, 2001).

To a significant degree, bullying can be addressed through an understanding of family dynamics, including child-rearing practices. Elements of family life may either contribute to or reduce risks that an individual child will become a bully or a victim of bullying. This, of course, means that partnerships between educators and parental caregivers are essential in reducing the problems associated with bullying and school violence. Finally, partnerships between helping professionals and school personnel play a central role in reducing bullying and victimization among school-aged youngsters (Committee for Children, 1997).

Reflection...

Consider a situation in which a physically robust fifth-grade boy picks on a shy third-grade girl. What do you see as the motivations, experiences, and emotions of members of the following three groups: the bully, the victim, and the bystanders?

Family Interaction Patterns Affecting the Bullying and Victimization of Children

Three patterns or styles of parenting associated with the development of chronic bully or victim status have been identified: intrusive-overprotective parenting, parental psychological over-control, and parental coercion (Perry et al., 2001). Young people with healthy social and emotional adjustment, bullies, passive victims, and provocative victims can all emerge from any of these styles. Other factors, such as individual temperament, results of first experiments with violence, and resilience also affect a child's role in bullying. However, the intrusive-overprotective style and the over-controlled style are generally associated with victimization status, whereas coercion appears to foreshadow bullying behavior (Olweus, 1993; Perry et al., 2001).

The Overprotective Parent or Caregiver

Hoover and Oliver (1996) referred to the "hothouse" family as an analogy to the intrusive-overprotective parenting style. A hothouse can be set up to tightly control all factors leading to health in plants. Yet, when flowers from over-controlled hothouses are transplanted into natural surroundings, they often wither because they cannot tolerate less-than-perfect conditions.

Likewise, young people frequently receive so much protection at home that they grow to be poor at tolerating other children's rough-and-tumble ways. Such youngsters become accustomed to adults' predictability and find the playground's confusion distressing. Overprotective parents may not allow their children the opportunity to enter into the roughhewn negotiations that facilitate acquisition of conflict resolution skills. For example, children often learn the indelicate art of conflict resolution through arguments about the rules of games. These negotiation and related social skills learned informally among peers are often missing in children raised in an overprotective style. This may be particularly problematic if the youngster is born with a tendency toward social anxiety.

Parental Over-Control

Parents may exert more than a healthy degree of psychological control over their offspring. Over-control refers to invalidation of children's feelings via frequently interrupting, and rebuking with children regarding the invalidity of their feelings (Perry et al., 2001, p. 84). Youngsters often, as a result, lose confidence in the validity of their own emotions. Such individuals manifest internalizing (shy and anxious) symptoms.

Coercive Parenting

In summarizing over a decade of research, Olweus (1993) characterized the family lives of bullies as cold emotional environments, punctuated by episodes of physical and verbal violence. Perry et al. described the coercive parenting style in the following terms:

> Coercion encompasses direct verbal attacks, bossiness, sarcasm, and power-assertive discipline and surely undermines the child's feeling of being loved and respected (2001, p. 84).

Young people with the physical and psychological resources to aggress on their peers frequently learn their belligerent response patterns from hostile parents and caregivers. It stands to reason that youngsters approach relationships aggressively if the majority of interpersonal episodes they encounter as children reflect physical or psychological control of the weak by the strong. Generally, students learn to be aggressive via coercive parenting styles, but occasionally a youngster will react to parental hostility by becoming shy and anxious and thus become prone to victimization (Perry et al., 2001).

Perry et al. (2001) pointed out that boys tend to become bullies if parenting styles are hostile and aggressive. Girls on the other hand, tend to manifest the set of behaviors associated with victimization. Boys with oversolicitous, overprotective parents are most at risk for becoming bully victims.

Social Cognitive Schemes: A Way for Educators to Understand the Role of Families in Bullying and Victimization

When educators encounter students who react to actual or perceived conflict with either maladaptive levels of aggression (bullies) or passivity (chronic victims), it is tempting to merely assert that these generalized response patterns somehow "are a product of the child's home environment." Although generally accurate, this statement does not explain how specific response patterns are carried from home to school. At least metaphorically it can be said that behavioral styles are "put in youngsters' heads" by means of the patterns of interpersonal relations and conflict management they encounter.

The best model we have seen for explaining how parenting engenders behavioral styles is social cognitive theory (e.g. Baldwin, 1992) as applied to the development of chronic victimization status (Perry et al., 2001). In order to understand this approach it is important first to define cognitive schemes, because the entire model depends on what Baldwin called *relational schemes.*

Schemes

Schemes may be best comprehended as the structures of long-term memory. Psychologists have long understood that information in the form of concepts, facts, images, and even emotions is not retained randomly. Rather, these are arranged in patterns. Long-term storage is made up of these relational structures and it is these networks that are called schemes. Schemes are the memory formations that develop as children grow and learn. As the structures become firmly established, they also predict how individuals remember, understand, and act in particular situations.

Social schemes are internalized portrayals of the sum of events that have occurred in a child's lifetime of interactions. At least four elements seem to form the structure of thoughts related to social discourse. Cognitive social structures include (1) an understanding of the parents (or "other person") role, (2) the sense or understanding of the self as typically played out in social situations, (3) patterns of responding (to social exchanges) that have been rewarded or have helped avoid punishment in the past, and (4) the emotions typically attached to the outcomes of social events.

If the schematic view is accurate, it is easy to understand why the formation of thought patterns surrounding social situations depends so much on the nature and style of interactions between children and their primary adult caregivers. Perry et al. (2001) suggested that social schemes become "automatic routines that are played out with little reflective thought" (p. 87).

Victim Schemes.   In past social events, victims have discovered they can defuse situations through passivity (passive victims). They are reinforced by the reduction of stress that results from giving in (ending the exchange). Unfortunately, passivity such as giving up a preferred object or place on the playground serves as a signal to bullies. This individual then becomes selected more and more for victimization.

The passive individual tends to lack effective problem-solving strategies. Even if the individaul has such skills, they are typically not used as the exchange unfolds. This occurs because parents have not encouraged the development of such skills (generally via overprotective, overinvolved parenting). Emotional arousal attached to social exchanges (anxiety, shame, depression, and guilt) crowd out more objective situational analyses. Although most passive children can name appropriate social problem-solving strategies, the weight of the evidence supports the latter hypothesis, that emotional arousal embedded in social schemes interferes with the ability to select or act on appropriate strategies.

Bully Schemes.   Much of what individuals believe about interacting with others derives from their observation of the social world around them. This is frequently shown through the actions of bullies. As a result of their relationships with parents or other caregivers, bullies tend to form worldviews in which violence- or control-based relationships are the norm. They may see the strong physically control the weak (e.g., through spousal abuse) (Olweus, 1993).

Parents and other caregivers often directly reward bullies for managing social relationships with power and control. Children on their way to becoming bullies often accrue rewards for violent performance—a preferred seat on the bus, entertainment through the emotional arousal of the victim, or a desired object (lunch money, a pen, a ball). Parenting styles that reward violence, and those in which emotional exchanges tend to be cold or inconsistently waiver between emotional coldness and psychological or physical abuse, are most toxic in terms of bully development.

Not all students who witness spousal abuse or who experience parenting styles that permit violence will become bullies. A final element must be present—the physical and psychological wherewithal to carry off the bullying. This need to succeed at bullying probably explains why male bullies tend to be, on average, stronger than other youngsters (Olweus, 1993) and tend not to show low self-esteem. Perhaps more children would bully others if they could carry it out successfully.

The social schemes of bullies probably include deep-seated beliefs that people manage social relationships with control and, if need be, through the exercise of violence. Bullies may also believe that they, as individuals, have the capability of using psychological or physical violence to successfully manage social situations they encounter. It is little wonder that we frequently see bullies interpreting neutral social cues as aggression and then explaining their own aggression as counter-aggression (Dodge & Frame, 1982).

Reflection...

List three specific mannerisms related to dealing with others that you can trace to the parenting you received. Discuss how each mannerism was passed along to you. Now describe the way that child–caregiver interactions form structures of thought about social situations and styles of interacting in social situations.

Home–School Relations and Bullying: What Educators and Future Educators Should Know

Next we present two brief discussions of solutions to bullying. Initially, the high points of a well-documented, system-wide campaign for dealing with bullying are offered. These are largely based on a model tested first by the Norwegian Ministry of Education, but also shown to be effective in North America. Readers interested in this model can find out more by looking at Olweus's (1993) English-language version of the model. A second section deals with the specific implications of the social schema model for understanding parents' role in bullying.

A System-Wide Approach for Reducing Violence and Bullying

Under the leadership of Daniel Olweus (c.f., 1993; 1996), an anti-bullying program was developed and tested in Norway. The same model has been tested in the United States, where it has been determined that the frequency and intensity of bullying can be reduced by up to 50 percent during the first program year. These gains are sustained over time as long as the program is kept in place.

From this study, Olweus concluded that activities at three levels of involvement were required to reduce bullying and school violence. Measures are proposed at the whole school level, the class level, and the individual level.

School Level. In order to reduce bullying and school violence, data regarding the school climate must first be collected. Data can include surveys (Olweus, 1993; Hoover & Oliver, 1996), observations, and interviews. Sprague, Sugain, Horner, and Walker (1999) argued that incident reports were the most sensitive data that could be collected to track dangerous spots in the school and with which to track the interpersonal climate in the building.

Other core features of a successful program at the school level included school conference days and improved supervision during lunch, hallway time, and recess. School conferences refer to large-scale assemblies scheduled to encourage student and parent enthusiasm for anti-bullying efforts. In addition, peer mediation programs have been used successfully in some schools as another alternative to break the chain of bullying. However, the mediators must make sure that those involved in mediation are perceived to be equals. If the victim does not have the power, nor perceive to have the power as an equal, the mediation is doomed for failure. There are many good mediation programs in the country (Olsen & Hoover, 1997).

Classroom Level. Classroom rules against bullying must be spelled out in the clearest possible terms. These must be clearly communicated to students and their parents. In addition, it is best if teachers instruct the class on the content of classroom rules just as they would any other material. Olweus's (1993) data suggests that mild consequences for violations of rules must be applied if any of the other methods are to work. It is essential that teachers enforce rules calmly, gently, and with a minimum of emotional overlay.

Educators (and parents) are placed in something of a bind as they apply consequences for bullying. If they do not apply mild consequences for bullying, this may relay the subtle message that it is appropriate to pick on fellow students. However, if sanctions are too severe or students' dignity is damaged, bullying-type relationships are actually modeled. This is something to be avoided. A middle ground between overly-permissive and overly-authoritative styles is desirable. The middle ground is referred to as authoritative.

Social skill instruction including role-plays, regular classroom meetings, and the use of instructive readings are other methods at the classroom level. Primary teachers will recognize Anderson's *The Ugly Duckling* (2000) as a wonderful story about bullying and redemption.

The Individual Level.   The systemic model includes counseling and intensive social skills instruction for students who bully others and some students who are at risk for suffering peer harassment. For the former group, anger management is recommended; for the latter, friendship making and assertive skills training are recommended. Olweus (1993) recommends involving the parents or bullies in intensive discussions of the long-term problems associated with bullying.

We have seen that the information about bullying as related to child-rearing styles can be captured and organized most clearly by means of a social learning or cognitive-social schema model. But unless this organizational rubric leads educators to solutions, it is not particularly worthwhile. Several implications are explored below for maximizing the effectiveness of interactions between educators and the parents of bullies, passive victims, and provocative victims.

Knowledge and Skills.   Future teachers must explore the relationship between students' worldviews (schemes) and their behaviors. In addition, educators must recognize that students' angry or timid outlooks are often related to the type or overall tone of parent–child interactions. For example, a student who has been able to avoid conflict by means of ultra-passivity will experience a great deal of difficulty learning to demonstrate assertiveness in the face of mild aggression, which is a recommended intervention (Hoover & Oliver, 1996). Further, this student's difficulty with assertiveness may help the school social worker or counselor see why parents, for example, react strongly to mild-conflict situations at school and why the same elders may insist that their child be protected from the rough-and-tumble of school life rather than receive social skills instruction.

The relationship between a bully's aggressive behavior and the hostility shown to the well-meaning educator will make more sense if the teacher understands the relationship between the student's behaviors, the student's understandings of relationships, and the child-rearing practices used for the student. School officials may also legitimately worry about whether a parental referral for bullying may result in abuse at home—not because the caregiver is opposed to the use of force in relationships but because of the humiliation or bother engendered by a call from the school.

Working with Parents.   An educator armed with information about the relationship between parental attitudes and student behavior is better prepared to work with parents on a strengths-based basis (Hoover & Oliver, 1996; Oliver, Oaks, & Hoover, 1994). An essential starting point is reframing what are seen as problems by educators but are seen by the family as strengths. The assets of the family are acknowledged as a solution is sought, a practice that may be particularly useful in situations in which the educator and the parent experience differing cultural or linguistic backgrounds. For each of the family patterns mentioned previously, some strength-based statements are suggested:

1. The educator could reframe what they see as an overinvolved, overcontrolling family as tight-knit and close. The strength and vitality of that child's relationships with adults, especially parents, should be acknowledged and supported as a solution is sought to the child's passivity.

2. Families seen by educators as violent and coercive could be recast as preparing the child for independence in a tough, no-nonsense world (Oliver et al., 1994).

Without some acknowledgement of family strengths, family members are unlikely to work with educators on problems related to bullying and peer victimization. It is important that educators admit the strengths inherent in certain modes of interactions, prior to initiating interventions.

Reflection...

Relate how you would rephrase the following behaviors as strengths, as you might in discussing a behavior situation with parents:

- A child often verbally threatens others
- A child is extremely shy with other children, but likes to talk one-on-one with adults.
- A student frequently fights with others during unsupervised periods. When asked about the scuffles, the youngster replies that the other child was behaving unfairly.

Avoiding Blame and Secondary Victimization.   It is all too easy to see pathology in struggling families or in situations in which the perspectives of family members differ significantly from the experiences of educators. A parent advocacy group might be helpful in interceding in instances in which an impasse is reached between educators, who feel that the students' troubled or troubling behavior is pathological, and parents, who view the responses as essentially normal.

The Federation of Families for Children's Mental Health is a wonderful advocacy organization operated by and for parents. They are dedicated to putting forth a strength-based model and to working cooperatively with school personnel. The organization publishes an excellent magazine entitled *Claiming Children* (www.ffcmh.org).

Parent Training and Support Models.   A useful mind set is for educators to rethink what they perceive as parenting weaknesses as a lack of knowledge and skill. We see this as the most important piece in the anti-bullying puzzle. Once parents and the educators establish a relationship based on mutual respect and built around problem solving for the child in question, a referral to a parent support and education center could be made.

Parent resource centers should include childcare, flexible hours, and all other types of supports that would allow parents to effectively access the program. If such programs do not exist, educators can become part of a team that advocates for such an approach and develops grant projects to start and support parent education and advocacy centers.

The Full-Service (Wrap-Around) School Model.   Because bullying, both from the victim's and the bully's perspective, ties in with so many other risk factors it is possible that the full-service, or wrap-around school model proposed by Dryfoos (1994) may represent the most fruitful approach for teams of educators and parents. The full-service school is one in which public welfare, health, mental health, dental, child advocacy, and other family- and child-service professionals reduce risk by breaking down the all-too-common divisions and resultant turf fighting between programs.

Many times full-service or wrap-around schools locate health and social service sites on campuses. Another approach is to strengthen the administrative bonds between all agencies and programs dealing with the welfare of at-risk families and children. The Grand Forks Public Schools in Grand Forks, North Dakota participated in such a program, in which social welfare and counseling services were strengthened and administrative ties were forged between programs serving at-risk students and families from pre-K to grade 12. Project leaders approached the problem of violence by forging district- and community-wide family stress- and violence-reduction programs.

Another very effective twist on the full-service schools model is to stress after-school programs for at-risk students. The point is to deliver anger-management, counseling, recreational, academic, and fine arts programs to students between the hours of 3:00 and 7:00. This time period supports parents for two reasons. First, it is a period during which many students experience the most behavioral and risk difficulties, thus placing extra burdens on already-stressed families. Second, these programs serve as respite and child care during times when supervision is difficult for many two-income families. Projects like those described above funded through the Twenty-First Century Schools Initiative have shown success both in reducing risk factors (including violence) and fostering school–family partnerships.

Monitoring Television, Internet, and Media Use.   As Garbarino (2000) and Pipher (1994) argued so persuasively, one manifestation of our culture's toxicity to youth is the huge menu of violence offered to children that are not yet developmentally prepared to manage these images and concepts. Data regarding the media's severe effects on violence are so strong that it is no longer arguable that this does not contribute to social problems (Garbarino, 2000).

> **Reflection...**
>
> What can be done by working with parents and children to help them understand the violence that is in the media (television, music, the Internet, and video games)? How do we protect our children? Are there organizations that are working in the area of violence in the media and its effects on children?

Educators and parents could work together discussing media violence and the subliminal messages of revenge and violent problem solving that are being subtly sold to youth. Educators could foster such partnerships through the use of well-designed media analysis lessons embedded in social studies and language arts curriculum. Frequent letters home to parents that include methods for either avoiding, or at least discussing, media violence with children could be employed. Frequent meetings within the structure of the PTA or PTO may be useful, but it is also possible for teachers and parents to forge partnerships to work specifically on the issue of violence and media's role in fostering conflict. For example, together they could plan and hold informational meetings for the community and lobby advertisers and local television networks.

Programs.   All programs that we have inspected that effectively deal with violence and bullying in schools contain a parent-cooperation component. Three programs deserve particular mention, though many more excellent packages are available for educators. "Second Step" and "Bullying Prevention" (Committee for Children, 1997, 2001) are excellent packages that include parent partnership and involvement components. Likewise, the Johnston Institute's "Respect and Protect" will serve the needs of educators. Finally, a program based on many years of testing by the Norwegian Ministry of Education has found its way to the United States (Olweus, 1993).

Summary

In this chapter we have established that although schools are relatively safe places within the larger context of violent society, they are not as safe as educators would like them to be. In addition, we spelled out the relationship between bullying and violence, noting that low-level violence sets the stage for and increases the risk for more dangerous sorts of behaviors.

We suggested a model for analyzing the relationship between parenting style, bullying, and chronic victimization. This model suggests that social relationships and problem-solving styles are coded in long-term memory schemas, much like other information and skills are organized. Furthermore, we noted that the development of social schemes is largely dependent on children's early experience with social interactions and role modeling.

Because primary caregivers and teachers are so intimately involved in fostering children's problem-solving styles, they also lie at the core of effective intervention programs. A well-documented intervention model at the school or district level was spelled out, as were specific suggestions for involving parents in solving problems with school violence.

RECOMMENDED ACTIVITIES

1. Working with one classmate, describe a bullying episode that each of you has observed. The event could involve either children or adults. Pick one of the stories and attempt to analyze it in terms of (a) what motivated the bullying, (b) what, as an educator, you would do to deal with the bully, and (c) what, as an educator, you would do to deal with the victim. Be as specific as you can about the dynamics of the incident and how you would deal with it. Be prepared to report to the larger group.

2. Debate the following proposition: Verbal teasing should not be allowed in classrooms because it leads to bullying and raises the risk for school violence. Use material in the chapter and from your experience to support or dispute the proposition. Present your arguments in a formal debate.

3. Meet in groups of three to four and propose a model or theory explaining how child-rearing practices affect children's behavioral styles. As you develop your model, you might want to consider the following components of behavior. Your theory should be as specific as possible and should make specific predictions regarding the relationship(s) between parental and child behavior.

   - Sense of humor and the absurd: How is this passed down through generations?
   - Anger and its expression: Why are some children quick to anger and why do children differ in their ability to cope with anger-arousing situations?
   - Verbal interaction style: What is the relationship, if any, between parental and child language style?
   - Beliefs about the world and unstated assumptions: How and why, if at all, do children acquire parents' unstated assumptions?

4. Develop a role-play related to holding a parent conference for a student who consistently bullies others (and/or for a student who is frequently the victim of peer harassment). Role-plays can be based on one or more of the following assumptions:

   - The parents become hostile and angrily state that the child's behavior is the school's fault.
   - The parents become angry with one another, blaming the child's misbehavior on one another.
   - The parents calmly, but assertively, state that fighting and bullying are just part of life and they do not see it as a problem. They say the problem is with the wimpy kids who tattle.
   - The parents passively listen to the educator's issues, but resist or don't respond much when solutions are suggested.

Request feedback from the rest of the class regarding the group's role-play. Then try it again, instituting worthwhile improvements.

5. Watch three episodes of a television situation comedy and evaluate the humor in them for hostile content. It would help to define hostile content ahead of time. For example, you might decide that jokes that require putting one person down for their humor might be defined as hostile. Likewise, jokes featuring insults about appearance or behavioral style might be defined as hostility. Write a report in which you (a) briefly outline the episodes in terms of character and content, (b) define hostile humor, (c) report the number of instances of hostile humor from the three episodes, and (d) use examples of the hostile humor to perform a content or communication analysis of the hidden messages presented in the show.

6. Conduct library research and write a report on the relationship between media and violence. Summarize your report by suggesting specific ways for educators, school administrators, and parents to work together on dealing with violence in the media.

7. Devise a survey regarding school safety and school–parent issues with the help of your instructor. Administer the survey to at least twenty parents. Summarize the information and write a report about your findings. End your report with specific suggestions for working with parents and caregivers to reduce violence in schools.

8. Pretend that you were designing a bullying- or violence-prevention program for an elementary, middle, or high school (whichever best fits your situation). Please describe at least three practices or features you would include in your program. Be specific about how you would work with parents. Compare the features of your programs with the suggestions offered in this chapter.

ADDITIONAL RESOURCES

Books:

Beane, A. (1999). *Bully free classroom*. Minneapolis, MN: Free Spirit.

Garbarino, J. (2000). *Lost boys: Why our sons turn violent and how we can save them*. New York: Anchor.

Goldstein, A. P., & Conoley, J. C. (1997). *School violence intervention: A practical handbook*. New York: Guilford.

Hoover, J. H., & Oliver, R. O. (1996). *The bullying prevention handbook: A guide for principals, teachers and counselors*. Bloomington, IN: National Educational Service (www.nesonline.com).

Hoover, J. H., & Olsen, G. W. (2001). *Teasing and harassment: The frames and scripts approach for teachers and parents*. Bloomington, IN: National Educational Service (www.resonline.com).

Juvonen, J., & Graham, S. (Eds.). (2001). *Peer harassment in school: The plight of the vulnerable and victimized.* New York: Guilford.

Olweus, D. (1993). *Bullying at school: What we know and what we can do.* Cambridge, MA: Blackwell.

Curriculum Guides:

Committee for Children. (1997). *Second step: A violence-prevention curriculum.* Seattle, WA: Author (www.cfchildren.org).

Committee for Children. (2001). *Steps to respect: A bullying prevention program.* Seattle, WA: Author (www.cfchildren.org).

Eggert, L. L., Nicholas, L. J., & Owne, L. M. (1995). *Reconnecting youth: A peer group approach to building life skills.* Bloomington, IN: National Educational Service (www.nesonline.com).

Garrity, C., Jens, K., Porter, W., Sager, N., & Short-Camilli, C. (1995). *Bully proofing your school: A comprehensive approach for elementary schools.* Longmont, CO: Sopris West.

Johnson Institute. (1996). *Respect and protect: Violence prevention and intervention program.* Minneapolis, MN: QVS.

Videos:

Preventing sexual harassment (With Leader's guide, 2000). (1999). Virginia Beach, VA: Coastal Training Technologies (800-695-0756).

School violence: Draw the line (With leader's guide, 1999). Virginia Beach, VA: Coastal Training Technologies (800-695-0756).

Set straight on bullies (With Leader's Guide by J. H. Hoover). Bloomington, IN: National Educational Service (www.nesonline.com).

Web Sites:

Anti-Bullying Network:
www.antibullying.net

Bullying and Sexual Harassment in Schools:
www.cfchildren.org/bully.shtml

Centers for Disease Control (Facts about youth violence):
www.cdc.gov

Early Warning, Timely Responses: A Guide to Safe Schools:
www.ed.gov/offices/OSERS/OSEP/Products/earlywrn.html

Illinois Office of Education Online Safety Assessment:
www.schoolsafetyonline.org

National Association of Elementary School Principals:
www.naesp.org/whatsnew.html

The Safe and Drug Free Schools Program:
www.ed.gov/legislation/ESEA/sec4011.html

REFERENCES

Anderson, H. C. (2000). *The Ugly Duckling*. New York: Morrow/Avon.

Baldwin, M. W. (1992). Relational schemas and the processing of social information. *Psychological Bulletin, 112*, 461–468.

Berthold, K., & Hoover, J. H. (2000). Correlates of bullying and victimization among intermediate students in the Midwestern USA. *School Psychology International, 21*, 65–78.

Committee for Children. (1997). *Second step: A violence prevention curriculum.* Seattle, WA: Author.

Committee for Children. (2001). *Steps to respect: A bullying prevention program.* Seattle, WA: Author.

Dodge, K., & Frame, C. L. (1982). Social cognitive biases and deficits in aggressive boys. *Child Development, 53*, 62–65.

Dryfoos, J. G. (1994). *Full-service schools: A revolution in health and social services for children, youth, and families.* San Francisco: Jossey-Bass.

Egan, S. K., & Perry, D. G. (1998). Does low self-regard invite victimization? *Developmental Psychology, 34*, 299–309.

Fransen, R. (1999, April 27). With enough antagonism, violence in schools can happen anywhere—even in Grand Forks (Letter to the editor). *Dakota Student*, p. 6.

Garbarino, J. (2000). *Lost boys: Why our sons turn violent and how we can save them.* New York: Anchor.

Goldstein, A. P., & Conoley, J. C. (1997). Student aggression: Current status. In A. P. Goldstein & J. C. Conoley (Eds.), *School violence: A practical handbook* (pp. 3–19). New York: Guilford.

Hazler R. J., Hoover, J., & Oliver, R. (1991). Student perceptions of victimization by bullies in school. *Journal of Humanistic Education and Development, 29*, 143–150.

Hoover, J. H., & Oliver, R. O. (1996). *The bullying prevention handbook: A guide for principals, teachers and counselors.* Bloomington, IN: National Educational Service.

Hoover, J. H., Oliver, R., & Hazler, R. J. (1992). Bullying: Perceptions of adolescent victims in the midwestern USA. *School Psychology International, 13*, 5–16.

Hoover, J. H., Oliver, R. L., & Thomson, K. A. (1993). Perceived victimization by school bullies: New research and future directions. *Journal of Humanistic Education and Development, 32*, 76–84.

Hoover, J. H., & Olsen, G. (2001). *Teasing and harassment: The frames and scripts approach for teachers and parents.* Bloomington, IN: National Educational Service.

Kaltiala-Heino, R., Rimpels, M., Marttunen, M., Rimpela, A., & Rantanen, P. (1999). Bullying, depression, and suicidal ideation in Finnish adolescents: School survey. *British Medical Journal, 319*, 348–351.

National Center for Education Statistic. (1998). *Violence and discipline problems in U.S. public schools, 1996–1997: Executive summary.* Retrieved March 20, 2000, from http://nces.ed.gov/pubs98/violence/98030001.html

Oliver, R., Oaks, N., & Hoover, J. H. (1994). Family issues and interventions in bully and and victim relationships. *The School Counselor, 41*, 199–202.

Olsen, G., & Hoover, J. (1997). Conflict resolution in schools: A review. *North Dakota Journal of Human Services, 1*(2), 28–37.

Olweus, D. (1993). Victimization by peers: Antecedents and long-term outcomes. In K. H. Rubin & J. B. Asendorf (Eds.), *Social withdrawal, inhibition, and shyness in childhood* (pp. 315–326). Hillsdale, NJ: Lawrence Erlbaum.

Olweus, D. (1996). Bully/victim problems at school: Facts and effective intervention. *Reclaiming Children and Youth, 5*, 15–22.

Olweus, D. (2001). Peer harassment: A critical analysis and some important issues. In J. Juvonen & S. Graham (Eds.), *Peer harassment in school: The plight of the vulnerable and victimized* (pp. 3–20). New York: Guilford.

Patterson, G. R., DeBaryshe, B. D., & Ramsey, E. (1989). A developmental perspective on antisocial behavior, *American Psychologist, 44,* 329–335.

Perry, D. G., Hodges, E. V. E., & Egan, S. K. (2001). Determinants of chronic victimization by peers: A review of a new model of family influence. In J. Juvonen & S. Graham (Eds.), *Peer harassment in school: The plight of the vulnerable and victimized* (pp. 73–104). New York: Guilford.

Perry, D., Kusel, D., & Perry, L. (1988). Victims of peer aggression. *Developmental Psychology, 24,* 807–814.

Pipher, M. (1994). *Reviving Ophelia: Saving the selves of adolescent girls.* New York: Ballentine.

Rigby, K., & Slee, P. T. (1999). Suicidal ideation among adolescent school children. Involvement in bully-victim problems, and perceived social support. *Suicide and Life Threatening Behavior, 29,* 119–130.

Simanton, E., Burthwick, P., & Hoover, J. H. (2000). Small-town bullying and student-on-student aggression: An initial investigation of risk. *The Journal of At Risk Issues, 6,* 4–9.

Sprague, J. R., Sugai, G., Horner, R., & Walker, H. M. (1999). Using office discipline referral data to evaluate school-wide discipline and violence prevention interventions. *Oregon Center for the Study of Conflict Bulletin, 42*(2), 5–18.

Stein, N. (1995). Sexual harassment in school: The public performance of gender violence. *Harvard Education Review, 65,* 145–162.

Stephens, R. D. (1997). National trends in school violence: Statistics and prevention methods. In A. P. Goldstein & J. C. Conoley (Eds.), *School violence: A practical handbook* (pp. 72–90). New York: Guilford.

Wilson, J. Q., & Petersilia, J. (1995). *Crime.* San Francisco: Institute for Contemporary Studies.

INDEX

Abington School District v. *Schemmp*, 234

Academy of the Pacific Rim (Boston, Massachusetts), 336

Accessibility, of fathers to children, 300

Accommodations, of families of children with disabilities, 169–171

Active listening, 117

Adaptability
   of families of children with disabilities, 169
   in functional families, 33

Affluent parents, 99

African American families
   historic, 18
   nature of, 51–54
   resources on, 62–64, 67

African American Mothers and Urban Schools (Winters), 108

After-school programs, 355

Age of Reason, 16–17

Alliance for Parental Involvement in Education, 108, 156

Alternative Education (video), 340

Amazing Grace (Kozol), 286

American Association for Retarded Citizens (ARC), 163–164

American Association of Family and Consumer Science, 88

American Civil Liberties Union (ACLU), 67

American Humane Association (AHA), 264

American Step Family, An (video), 41

Americans with Disabilities Act (Public Law 101-376, 1990), 166, 240, 245

America's Children (video), 287

Anger
   of child victims of abuse and neglect, 257
   of chronic complainer parents, 129–131

Anxiety
   of child victims of abuse and neglect, 256–257
   of victims of bullying, 347

APSAC Handbook on Child Maltreatment, The (Myers et al.), 269

Asian American families
   nature of, 54–56
   religion in, 59
   resources on, 68

Assimilation/enculturation, 8–9, 49–50
   African American, 53
   Asian American, 54
   Latino, 57
   Native American, 58
   religion and, 59
   as responsibility of family, 3–4, 14

Attachment, of parents to children, 96–97

Authoritarian parents, 75

Authoritative parents, 75

AVANCE Family Support and Education Program, 195, 216

Balanced lifestyle, of families of children with disabilities, 169

Basic Parenting Skills (video), 88

Battered Child, The (Kempe and Helfer), 269

Being a Single Parent (video), 318

Better IEPs (Bateman and Linden), 174–175

Bewildered parents, 100–101

Beyond the Bake Sale (Henderson et al.), 132

Biculturalism, 50, 53

Bill and Melinda Gates Foundation, 336

Birth control, 22

Black families. *See* African American families

Black Families at the Crossroad (Staples and Johnson), 63

Black Fatherhood (Hutchinson), 62

Black History (video), 64

Blended families. *See also* Divorce; Single-parent families; Unmarried mothers
   of children with disabilities, 173
   contemporary, 28–32
   facts about, 29
   historic, 18
   myths about, 30
   parenting in, 82–84, 87, 105
   perspective on schools, 105
   resources on, 41–42, 84
   strengths of, 30–31

Blending Families (Shomberg and Shimberg), 41

Board of Education, Island Trees Union Free School District v. Pico, 235
Board of Education of Hendrick Hudson Central School District Board of Education v. Rowley, 238
Board of Education of Mountain Lakes v. Maas, 227
Body language, as barrier to communication, 115–117
Books
   on African American families, 62–63
   on blended families, 41
   on cultural diversity, 61–62
   on families (general), 36
   on families of children with disabilities, 174–177
   on family violence, 269–270
   on gay and lesbian families, 66
   on Latino families, 64–65
   on military life, 67
   on parenting, 87–88
   on parent involvement, 108, 154–155
   on parent–teacher communication, 132
   on poverty and students, 286–287
   on school choice, 340
   on school violence and bullying, 358–359
   on single-parent families, 39
Boston Arts Academy (Boston, Massachusetts), 334
Brady Bunch (TV show), 30
Breaking the Silence (video), 270
Bridging Early Services for Children with Special Needs and Their Families (Rosenkoetter et al.), 177
Brothers, Sisters, and Special Needs (Lobato), 176
Brothers & Sisters (Powell and Gallagher), 176
Brown v. Board of Education of Topeka, Kansas, 229, 240, 330
Bulletin boards, parent, 127–128
Bully Free Classroom (Beane), 358
Bullying, 344–360. *See also* School violence
   adjustment problems associated with, 347–348
   behaviors associated with, 346
   defined, 345
   family patterns affecting, 348–349
   frequency and severity of, 345–346
   home–school relations and, 351–356
   parent–school partnerships and, 345
   resources on, 358–360

   social cognitive patterns in, 349–351
   system-wide approach to reduce, 352–356
Bullying at School (Olweus), 359
Bullying Prevention Handbook, The (Hoover and Oliver), 358

Call to Commitment, A (U.S. Department of Education), 312
Cardiff v. Bismarck Public School District, 232
Censorship, 235–236
Center for Research on the Education of Students Placed at Risk (CRESPAR), 203, 216
Center for Study of Parental Involvement, 108
Center for the Improvement of Child Caring (CICC), 198–199
Center on Families, Communities, Schools, and Children's Learning, 156, 216
Center on Fathers, Families & Public Policy, 316
Charter schools, 335–338, 340–341
Charter Schools (Birkett and Tabin), 340
Charter Schools (video), 340
Charter Schools in Action (Finn et al.), 340
Child Abuse (video), 270
Child Abuse: It Shouldn't Hurt to Be a Kid (video), 270
Child abuse and neglect, 253–260
   abuse in schools, 244–245
   characteristics of child victims, 256–258
   child abuse, defined, 253
   environmental factors in, 255–256
   intervention and treatment of, 259
   link between domestic violence and, 264
   long-term effects on children, 259–260
   neglect, defined, 253
   parental factors in, 254–255
   recommendations for action, 265–268
   reporting, 267–268
   resources on, 269–271
Child care
   of families of children with disabilities, 170
   by fathers, 295–296, 298–299
Child in the Family, The (video), 36–37
Children of Poverty (video), 288
Children's Defense Fund, 288
Child Who Never Was, The (Buck), 162
Chinese Americans, 54
Choosing Options and Accommodations for Children (COACH), 187

Civil Rights Act (1964), 245
Clans, 14
COACH (Choosing Options and
    Accommodations for Children), 187
Coercive parenting, 349
Cohesion, in functional families, 33
Coinstruction, 187–189
Collaborating with community, 150, 202
*Collaborative Teams for Students with Severe
    Disabilities* (Rainforth et al.), 177
Colonial North American family, 17–18, 221–222,
    223, 224
Common schools, 327
Communicating with Parents of Exceptional Children
    (Kroth), 132, 176
Communication. *See also* Parent–teacher
    communication
    in functional families, 33
    parental involvement and, 140–141
Community
    collaborating with, 150, 202
    of families of children with disabilities,
        173–174
    father involvement and, 297, 302, 305, 307–308
    teacher involvement in, 285
Complainer parents, 129–131
Compulsory attendance, 226, 228–229, 230–232
Computer classes, for parents, 126–127
Conducting Effective Conferences with Parents
    (video), 133
Conferences
    parent–teacher, 122–124, 266–267
    student–parent–teacher, 124–125
Conflict resolution
    in blended families, 31
    family resources versus school
        requirements, 205
Con Respeto (Vades), 65
Cornwell v. *State Board of Education*, 231
Council for Exceptional Children, 177
CRESPAR (Center for Research on the Education
    of Students Placed at Risk), 203, 216
Crisis situations
    model for family involvement and,
        206–207, 212
    parent–teacher communication in, 129
Crossing Cultural Borders (Delgado-Gaitan and
    Trueba), 108
Cuban Americans, 56

Cude v. *Arkansas*, 231
*Cultural Diversity, Families, and the Special
    Education System* (Harry), 175
Cultural pluralism, 49
Culture of fatherhood, 294–295, 301–302
Curriculum, education law and, 227–228, 231,
    233–236

DAD to DAD, 317
Death, blended families and, 28–29
Decision-making, 147–149
    sample activities for, 148–149
    tips for successful, 149
Defensiveness, of parents, 97–98
Delayed parenting, 22
Demographics of families, 8
Depression
    of child victims of abuse and neglect, 257
    of victims of bullying, 347
Difference in the Family, A (Featherstone), 175
Difficult parents, 129–131
Disabilities. *See* Families of children
    with disabilities
Distrust, in dysfunctional families, 34
Diversity among families, 8–9, 44–70
    changing family, 45–46
    ethnic and cultural, 49–59, 61–66
    families of children with disabilities, 172–173
    family structure, 46–49, 66–67
    model for family involvement and, 210–211
    parent involvement and, 152
    religious, 59–60
Diversity in the Classroom (Kendall), 62
Divorce, 9–10, 25–28
    finances, 26
    noncustodial parents and, 81–82, 86–87
    single-parent versus unmarried-mother
        households, 27–28
    stigmatization, 26–27
    time period, 26
Divorce and the Family (video), 41–42
Do Children Also Divorce (video), 40
Domestic violence, 260–264
    household characteristics, 261–262
    intervention and treatment of, 262–263
    link between child abuse and, 264
    long-term effects on family members, 263–264
    recommendations for action, 265–268
    resources on, 269–271

Double consciousness, 53
Dual-employed parents, 76–79, 86
  coping patterns of, 78–79
  life roles of, 77–78
  role of father in, 298–299
  role strain of, 76–77
Dysfunctional families, 34–35

Early childhood education
  family-involvement models, 189–196
  home-based learning in, 146–147
  special education, 170
Early Childhood Family Education (ECFE), 216
Early Head Start, 191–192
East Harlem schools (New York City), 333
Education. *See also* Early childhood education;
    Special education
  in African American families, 51–53
  in Asian American families, 55
  in mainstream families, 51
  in Native American families, 57–58
  parent, 126–127, 309
  of parents, 99
  religious diversity and, 59–60
Educational Amendments (1978), Title IX,
    245–246
Education for All Handicapped Children Act
    (Public Law 94-142, 1975), 163, 164–165,
    183–184, 237
Education law, 220–249
  censorship, 235–236
  compulsory attendance, 226, 228–229, 230–232
  curriculum, 227–228, 231, 233–236
  discrimination and harassment, 245–246
  federal court cases, 225–247
  federal legislation, 163–167
  history of, 221–223
  liability, 242–245
  religion in schools, 227–228, 233–235, 327–329
  resources on, 248
  school fees, 232–233
  sex education, 231
  special education, 163–167, 237–240
  state constitutions, 223–224
  state court cases, 225–247
  state legislation, 224–225
  student rights, 229, 240–242
*Educators Guide to Preventing Child Sexual Abuse,
    The* (Nelson and Clark), 269

Elementary education, family-involvement
    models, 196–201
El Puente (New York City), 333–334
Empowering Hispanic Families (SotoMayor), 64–65
Enculturation/assimilation. *See* Assimilation/
    enculturation
Ending the Cycle of Violence (Peled et al.), 270
Engagement, of fathers with children, 300
Enlightenment, 16–17
Ethnic and cultural diversity. *See also specific
    ethnic and cultural groups*
  resources on, 61–66
  types of, 49–59
Ethnic Families in America (Staples), 63
Even Start, 192, 218
Expectant Father, The (video), 318
Extended kin network
  in African American families, 52
  in blended families, 31
  of families of children with disabilities,
    170–171, 173
  working parents and, 47

Faces of Poverty (video), 288
Families (general), 1–43. *See also* Blended
    families; Home–school relations; Single-
    parent families; Unmarried mothers
  changes in, 4–5, 7–10, 45–46
  contemporary U.S., 22–32
  defined, 3
  dysfunctional, 34–35
  functional, 32–34
  history of, 5–6, 10–11, 13–22
  resources on, 36–38
  responsibilities, 3–4, 21–22, 138–140
  teacher roles and, 4
Families, Professionals, and Exceptionality (Turnbull
    and Turnbull), 155
Families, Schools, and Communities (Barbour and
    Barbour), 154
Families and Schools in a Pluralistic Society (Dauber
    and Epstein), 62
Families and Teachers of Individuals with Disabilities
    (O'Shea et al.), 176
Families First (video), 37
FamiliesFORWARD, 338–339
Families Matter (video), 37
Families of children with disabilities, 159–181. *See
    also* Special education

family systems, 167–174
historical perspective on, 161–163
laws and legislation, 163–167
number of children receiving educational
    services, 163
resources on, 174–178
Family-centered intervention
for families of children with disabilities,
    185–189
father involvement and, 297, 302, 305, 312–314
Family Education Rights and Privacy Act
    (FERPA, 1974), 241–242
Family Influences (video), 37
Family-involvement models, 182–219. *See also*
    Parent involvement
in early childhood education, 189–196
in elementary education, 196–201
in middle schools, 201–215
resources on, 216–218
in special education, 183–189
Family Literacy Branch Department for Adult
    Education and Literacy, 216
Family structure. *See also* Blended families;
    Single-parent families; Unmarried
    mothers
changes in, 9–10
gay- and lesbian-headed families, 48–49, 66–67
grandparents as parents, 24, 48
married-couple families, 46–47
Family systems, 167–174
accommodations in, 169–171
adjustments to disabilities, 168–169
conceptual framework for, 184–185
perspectives of family members, 171–174
Family violence, 250–272
child abuse and neglect, 253–260
domestic violence, 260–264
extent of, 251–253
recommendations for action, 265–268
resources on, 269–271
Father absence, 299, 303
Father(s) and fatherhood, 290–323
basic premises of, 292–294
changes in role of, 9–10
conceptual framework for, 300–301
culture of, 294–295
of families of children with disabilities, 171
gender roles and, 296–297, 300–301
historic role of, 6

modern, 295–296
mothers versus, 292–294
new, 72–74
noncustodial, 81–82, 299, 303
resources on, 316–320
school achievement of children and, 302–303
Fatherhood Project, The, 317
Fatherhood USA-Dedicated not Deadbeat
    (video), 318
Father involvement in schools
barriers to, 310–312
benefits of, 304–306
community-level, 297, 302, 305, 307–308
family-level, 297, 302, 305, 312–314
parent education, 309
reasons for, 309–310
resources for, 316–318
society-level, 297, 301–302, 305, 306–307
Fathers Matter (video), 318
Father's Resource Center, 317
Father-to-Father Children, Youth & Family
    Consortium, 317
Fenway High School (Boston,
    Massachusetts), 334
Flexibility
of African American families, 52
of blended families, 31
Florence County School District Four v. *Carter*,
    239–240
Folk psychology, 301
For Children's Sake (video), 109
For Dads Only (video), 318
Franklin v. *Gwinnett County Public Schools*,
    244–245
Functional families, 32–34

Gay- and lesbian-headed families
nature of, 48–49
resources on, 66–67
Goals 2000, 135–136, 138–139, 199
Good News Club v. *Milford Central School*, 234–235
Grandparents, as parents, 24, 48
Great Depression families, 19–20
Greek period families, 14–15, 161
Groups, communicating with, 129

Happiness, in blended families, 31
Harassment, 246, 359
Hartzell v. *Connell*, 232

Head Start, 21, 74, 164, 189–192, 217
Helping Parents Flourish (video), 155
High-risk behaviors, 202
Hispanic Children and Youth in the United States
    (Carrasuillo), 65
Hispanic families. *See* Latino families
Hispanic Policy Development Project, 156
History of family, 13–22
    Age of Reason, 16–17
    American industrialization, 18–19
    colonial North America, 17–18, 221–222,
        223, 224
    early history, 14–16
    families of children with disabilities, 161–163
    Great Depression, 19–20
    home–school relations, 5–6, 221–223
    Industrial Revolution, 17, 21–22
    legal relationship between parents and schools,
        221–223
    1950s to 1970s, 20–22
    parent involvement, 6, 10–11
    World War II, 19–20
Home, School, and Academic Learning
    (Comer), 108
Home, School, and Community Relations
    (Gestwicki), 154
Home and School Institute, 217
Home-based learning, 146–147, 329–330, 341
    sample activities, 146–147
    tips for, 147
Homeless Home Movie, The (video), 288
Homeschooler Information Network, 217
Home–school relations. *See also* Father
    involvement in schools; Parent involvement;
    Parent–teacher communication
    bullying and, 351–356
    diversity among families, 60–61
    historic, 5–6, 221–223
    parent involvement, 6, 10–11
Homeschool World, 217
Home visits, 128
Homework hot line, 126
Homosexuality. *See* Gay- and lesbian-
    headed families
Honesty, 117–118
Hothouse family, 348
*How Schools Can Help Combat Child Abuse and
    Neglect*, 267

*How to Create Alternative, Magnet, and Charter
    Schools That Work* (Bar and Parrett), 340
Human capital, 293

I'll Fly Away (video), 64
Importance of Fatherhood (video), 318
Inclusion, 167
Income levels of families. *See also* Poverty
    changes in, 7
    divorce and, 26
    single-parent families, 79–80
Indifferent parents, 99–100
Individual education plan (IEP), 165, 237
Individualism, in mainstream families, 51
Individuality of families, 10
Individualized Family Service Plan (IFSP),
    165–166
Individuals with Disabilities Education Act
    (Public Law 105-17, 1997), 164, 165, 183–184,
    237–239, 240
Industrialization
    American, 18–19
    Industrial Revolution, 17, 21–22
Infertility, 22
Informal communication, 119–120
Information for parents, model for family
    involvement and, 207–208, 212–213
In loco parentis (in place of the parent), 222,
    241, 244
Institute for Responsive Education, 62
Intact families, 46–47
Intake interviews, 118–119
Intercultural Development Research
    Association, 62
Intervention
    in child abuse and neglect, 259
    in domestic violence situations,
        262–263
Involving Parents in Education (video), 109
Irving Independent School District v. *Tatro*,
    238–239
I Wish the Hitting Would Stop (video), 270

Jehovah Witnesses, 59–60
Joy
    in functional families, 34
    lack of, in dysfunctional families, 34
Julia Richman (New York City), 333

Kaiser Child Care Centers, 20
Kids in Crisis—Self-Esteem Tips for Kids from Dysfunctional Families (video), 37–38
Knowing and Serving Diverse Families (Hildebrand et al.), 39, 41, 61, 63, 65
Korean Americans, 54

Lander v. *Seaver*, 222
Language, as barrier to communication, 114–115
Latchkey children, 47
Latino families
    nature of, 56–57
    resources on, 64–66, 68
Latino Family, The (video), 65
Learning From Our Lives (Neumann and Peterson), 108
Lee v. *Weisman*, 234
Lesbian and Gay Marriages (Sherman), 66
Lesbians. *See* Gay- and lesbian-headed families
Liability of schools, 242–245
Life-long education, 202
Lost Boys (Garbarino), 358

Macroculture, 297, 301–302, 305, 306–307
Magnet schools, 330–331, 341
Mainstream families, 50–51
Marital satisfaction, of new parents, 72–74, 86
Married-couple families, 46–47
McCollum v. *Board of Education*, 228
Medeiros v. *Kiyosaki*, 231
Medieval families, 15, 21–22, 161
MegaSkills, 198
MELD for Young Dads, 317
Melting pot, 49
Mesa Arts Academy (Arizona), 337
Mesoculture, 297, 302, 305, 307–308
Mexican American Legal Defense and Education Fund, 66
Mexican Americans, 56
Microculture, 297, 302, 305, 312–314
MiddleSchool.com, 217
Middle-school education, 124–127, 201–215
    computer classes for parents, 126–127
    homework hot line, 126
    impediments to family involvement, 203–206
    model for family involvement, 206–213
    outcomes of family involvement, 201–203
    student–parent–teacher conferences, 124–125
    supporting parent involvement, 213–215

Military life, 67
Minnesota Early Childhood Family Education (ECFE), 193–194
Minnesota Early Learning Design, 217
Minnesota New Country School (MNCS), 336–337
Model minority, 55–56
Modern fathers, 295–296, 298
Morale, of teachers, 95
Mothers. *See also* Unmarried mothers
    divorced noncustodial, 81–82
    of families of children with disabilities, 172
    fathers versus, 292–294
    historic role of, 6
    new, 72–74
Mozert v. *Hawkins County Board of Education*, 235
Murray v. *Curlett*, 234
Museum Magnet (St. Paul, Minnesota), 332
My Family, Your Family (video), 88

Narrative reports, 121
National Association for the Advancement of Colored People (NAACP), 229
National Association for the Education of Young Children (NAEYC), 192–193
National Black Child Development Institute, 64
National Center for Fathering, 317
National Center on Fathers & Families, 317
National Clearinghouse on Child Abuse and Neglect Information, 268
National Clearinghouse on Family Support and Children's Mental Health, 178
National Coalition for Parent Involvement in Education, 156
National Committee for Citizens in Education (NCCE), 109
National Committee for Citizens in Education Center for Law and Education, 217
National Congress of Parent Teacher Organizations, 38, 89, 156
National Council on Family Relations, 38, 89
National Education Association (NEA), 267
National Fatherhood Initiative, 317
National Head Start Association, 312, 317
National Information Center for Children and Youth with Disabilities, 178
National Middle School Association, 217
National Network of Partnership Schools, 138, 156, 199–200, 217

National Parent Teacher Association, 156, 217

National Resource Center on Domestic Violence, 268

Native American families
 nature of, 57–58
 religion in, 59
 resources on, 68

Negative feelings, of parents toward school, 103–104

Neglected Children (Dubowitz), 269

New American Schools, 335

New Beginning, A (Dinkmeyer et al.), 39

New parents, 72–74

New Poverty, The (Nunez), 287

New Realities of the American Family (Ahlburg and De Vita), 36

Newsletters, 120–121

New small schools, 333–335

Nonverbal communication, as barrier to communication, 115–117

North Central Regional Educational Laboratory (NCREL), 156

On Being a Father with T. Berry Brazelton (video), 318

On Being an Effective Parent (video), 88

One-Parent Children, The Growing Minority (Gouke and Rollins), 39

On the Home Front (video), 38

Organizational embeddedness, 313–314

Organizations
 on African American families, 64
 on blended families, 42
 on cultural diversity, 62
 on families (general), 38
 on families of children with disabilities, 177–178
 on family involvement, 216–218
 on gay and lesbian families, 67
 on Latino families, 66
 on parenting, 88–89
 on parent involvement, 108–109, 156
 on poverty and students, 288
 on school choice, 340
 on single-parent families, 40–41

Our Families, Our Future (video), 38

Out of the Darkness (Kantor and Jasinski), 269

Over-control, of parents, 349

Parent(s). *See also* Father(s) and fatherhood; Mothers; Parenting; Parent involvement
 in African American families, 51–54
 in Asian American families, 54–56
 attitudes toward school, 103–105
 bewildered, 100–101
 blended families and school, 105
 of bullies, 353–356
 changing role in schools, 95–96
 domestic violence and, 260–264, 265
 educated/affluent, 99
 factors in child abuse and neglect, 254–255, 265
 historic role of, 6
 indifferent, 99–100
 in Latino families, 56–57
 in mainstream families, 51
 in Native American families, 58
 as partners of teachers, 101–102, 106, 113–114, 150–154, 284–285
 perspectives on teachers and schools, 102–106
 poverty and, 281–282
 teachers as, 96–99, 106

Parent and Child Education (PACE), 195–196

Parent bulletin boards, 127–128

Parent–Child Relations (Binger), 87

Parent education
 computer classes, 126–127
 mothers versus fathers, 309

Parenting, 71–91. *See also* Father(s) and fatherhood; Mothers; Parent(s); Single-parent families; Unmarried mothers
 in blended families, 82–84, 87, 105
 after child's first year, 74
 compared to teaching, 94
 of divorced noncustodial parents, 86–87
 in dual-employed parent families, 76–79, 86
 marital satisfaction and, 72–74, 86
 new parents, 72–74
 of noncustodial parents, 81–82, 299, 303
 resources on, 87–89, 108–110
 rewards and satisfactions of, 85
 styles of, 74–75, 86, 302–303, 348–349
 teaching versus, 94–96

Parenting in Contemporary Society (Hamner and Turner), 36

Parenting Special Children (video), 177

Parent involvement, 92–110, 134–158. *See also* Family-involvement models; Father involvement in schools

benefits of, 136–137
defining, 135–136
foundations of meaningful, 150–154
historic, 6, 10–11
parent perspectives on teachers and schools, 102–106
resources on, 108–110, 154–156
teacher perspectives on parents, 96–102
teaching versus parenting, 94–96
types of, 137–150
Parent Involvement (video), 155
Parent Involvement in the Schools (Reitz), 108
Parents and Teachers as Partners (Rockwell et al.), 155
Parents as Teachers National Center, Inc., 109, 218
Parent–school partnerships, school violence and, 345
Parents' Rights Organization, 109
Parents' Views of Living with a Child with Disabilities (video), 177
Parents Without Partners, Inc., 40
Parent–teacher communication, 111–133
    aids to, 117–118
    barriers to, 114–117
    coequal relationship in, 113–114
    computer classes for parents, 126–127
    in crisis situations, 129
    difficult parents, 129–131
    group, 129
    informal, 119–120
    initial, 118–119
    low-income families and, 282–285
    parents of middle-school students, 124–127
    parent–teacher conferences, 122–124, 266–267
    problems with, 203–204
    regular, 119–121, 127–128, 151–152
    resources on, 132–133
    student–parent–teacher conferences, 124–125
    written, 120–121
Parent to Parent Model, 186–187
Parent trainers, 188
Parham School (Cincinnati, Ohio), 338–339
Partnerships with Parents (video), 109, 155
Partner Violence (Jasinski and Williams), 269
Peer Harassment in School (Juvonen and Graham), 359
Pennsylvania Association for Retarded Citizens, 164
People v. *Ekerold*, 227

Permissive parents, 75
Pierce v. *Society of Sisters*, 226, 329
Pilot Parents Program (Ohio), 186–187
Positive feelings, of parents toward school, 104–105
Post-traumatic stress disorder (PTSD), of child victims of abuse and neglect, 258
Poverty, 273–289
    in African American families, 51–52
    divorce and, 26
    effects of, 277–279
    extent of, 276
    in Latino families, 56
    myths about, 276–277
    nature of, 274–276
    resources on, 286–289
    schools and, 279–285
    working with low-income families, 282–285
Power of Their Ideas, The (Meier), 108
Prehistorical families, 14
Preventing Sexual Harassment (video), 359
Pride, in functional families, 33
Process of Parenting, The (Brooks), 88
Protestant denominations, 59
Public Law 94-142 (Education for All Handicapped Children Act, 1975), 163, 164–165, 183–184, 237
Public Law 99-457 (1986), 165–166, 167, 184
Public Law 101-376 (Americans with Disabilities Act, 1990), 166, 240, 245
Public Law 102-119, 173, 184
Public Law 105-17 (Individuals with Disabilities Education Act, 1997), 164, 165, 183–184, 237–239, 240
Puerto Ricans, 56

Racial harassment, 246
Racism, 53
Recognition, of volunteers, 145–146
Recruitment, of volunteers, 143–144
Reformation families, 15–16, 21
Regular communication, 119–121, 127–128, 151–152
Rehabilitation Act (1973), 237, 240, 245
Relational schemes, 349–351
    bully, 351
    victim, 350
Religion in schools, 227–228, 233–235, 327–329
Religious diversity, 59–60

Renaissance families, 15–16, 21
Responsibility, of fathers to children, 300
Role ambiguity, 83
Role models
  in blended families, 31
  male, 293
Role strain, of dual-employed parents, 76–77
Roman period families, 14–15, 161
Rural areas
  function of family, 18–19
  historic function of schools, 5–6
  poverty in, 283

Safety, as responsibility of family, 3
Scared Silent (video), 270
School(s)
  changes in, 5
  parents' perspectives on teachers and, 102–106
School, Family, and Community Partnerships (Epstein), 154
School and Family Partnership (Buzzell), 175
School choice, 324–341
  charter schools, 335–338
  features of choice programs, 325–326
  historical background of, 326–327
  home-schooling, 329–330
  magnet schools, 330–331
  new small schools, 333–335
  post-secondary options, 338
  rationale for, 326
  resources on, 340–341
  schools within schools, 331–333
  sharing facilities, 338–339
  vouchers, 327–329
School climate, 151, 352
School–community collaboration, 150, 202
School Development Program (SPD), 200
School–home journal, 121
Schools within schools, 331–333
School violence, 343–345. *See also* Bullying
  nature of, 343–344
  parent–school partnerships and, 345
  resources on, 358–360
  system-wide approach to reduce, 352–356
School Violence (video), 359
School Violence Intervention (Goldstein and Conoley), 358
Search Institute, The, 203, 218

Self-concept, of child victims of abuse and neglect, 257–258
Self-esteem, in dysfunctional families, 34
Self-reliant family, as myth, 20
Sensitivity, of parents, 97–98
Set Straight on Bullies (video), 359
Sex education, 231
Sexual abuse, 255
Sexual harassment, 246, 359
Shame, in dysfunctional families, 34–35
Shared Decision Making (video), 155
Sharing facilities, 338–339
Siblings, of families of children with disabilities, 172
Sibships (Meyer and Vadasy), 176
Single-parent families, 79–81, 86. *See also* Blended families; Divorce; Unmarried mothers
  African American, 52
  contemporary, 23
  financial issues of, 79–80
  historic, 18, 21
  increased number of, 23
  perspective on schools, 104–105
  resources on, 39–41
  stress of parents, 80–81
Single Parenting (video), 40
Single Parents Association Online, 40–41
Six Stages of Parenthood, The (Galinsky), 88
Skip generation parenting, 24, 48
Smith v. Board of School Commissioners of Mobile County, 235
Smith v. Ricci, 231
Socialization, as responsibility of family, 3–4, 14
Social support, in functional families, 33
Society-level interventions, father involvement and, 297, 301–302, 305, 306–307
South Grand Prairie High School (Dallas, Texas), 332
South Mountain Community College (Arizona), 337
Special education
  in early childhood education, 170
  family-involvement models, 183–189
  federal and state laws, 163–167, 237–240
Standard of living, in blended families, 31
Star Teachers of Children in Poverty (Haberman), 281, 286
Status of the Latina Women, The (video), 66
Stepfamilies. *See* Blended families

Stepfamilies (Visher and Visher), 41
Stepfamily Association of America, 42, 84
Stepfamily Foundation, 42
Stereotypes, 9
    divorce and, 27
    poverty and, 276–277
Stigmatization, divorce and, 26–27
*Strategies for Communicating with Parents of
    Exceptional Children* (Kroth and Edge), 176
Stress
    of dual-employed parents, 76–79
    as factor in child abuse and neglect, 255
    of families of children with disabilities,
        168–169
    marital, 312
    poverty and, 278
    of single parents, 80–81
Student rights, 229, 240–242
Student's Guide to African American Genealogy, A
    (Johnson and Cooper), 63
Student's Guide to Mexican American Genealogy, A
    (Ryskamp and Ryskamp), 64
Supervision, of volunteers, 144–145
Support, in functional families, 33
Support groups, of families of children with
    disabilities, 171
Support Networks for Inclusive Schooling (Stainback
    and Stainback), 177

Teachers. *See also* Parenting; Parent–
    teacher communication
    home–school relations, 11
    morale of, 95
    as parents, 96–99, 106
    parents as partners of, 101–102, 106, 113–114,
        150–154, 284–285
    pedagogical knowledge of, 95
    perspectives on parents, 96–102
    responsibilities of, 4
    working with low-income families, 282–285
Teachers Involve Parents in Schoolwork
    (TIPS), 197
Teacher TV (video), 109
Teaching, compared to parenting, 94
Teasing and Harassment (Hoover and Olsen), 358
Teenage Pregnancy (video), 67
Teen Indian Parents Program, 317
Teen Mothers (video), 40
Television, 355–356

They Stole It But You Must Return It (Williams), 63
Time pressures, on parents, 98–99
*Timothy W. v. Rochester, New Hampshire School
    District*, 239
*Tinker v. Des Moines Independent Community School
    District*, 240–241, 242
Title I/Even Start, 192, 218
Traditional culture, 50
Training
    for educators, in parent involvement, 153
    for parents, in parent involvement, 153
    of volunteers, 144–145
Treatment
    of child abuse and neglect, 259
    of domestic violence, 262–263
Tribes, 14

Understanding Child Abuse and Neglect
    (Tower), 270
Understanding Families (Dickenson and
    Leming), 61
U.S. Department of Education, 203, 312
    Goals 2000, 135–136, 138–139, 199
U.S. Department of Justice, 252
U.S. Hispanics (Valdivieso and Davis), 65
Unmarried mothers. *See also* Single-
    parent families
    age 20 and over, 23–24
    contemporary, 23–25
    grandparents as parents, 24, 48
    teenage, 24–25

Values
    of families of children with disabilities, 170
    in functional families, 33–34
Very Young Children with Special Needs (Howard et
    al.), 175–176
Victims
    of bullying, 347, 350
    of child abuse and neglect, 256–258
Victor, "Wild Boy of Aveyron," 161–162
Videos
    on African American families, 64
    on blended families, 41–42
    on families (general), 36–37
    on families of children with disabilities, 177
    on family violence, 270
    on fathers and fatherhood, 318
    on gay and lesbian families, 66

Videos (*continued*)
    on Latino families, 65–66
    on parenting, 88
    on parent involvement, 109, 155
    on parent–teacher communication, 133
    on poverty and students, 287–288
    on school choice, 340
    on school violence and bullying, 359
    on single-parent families, 40
    on teenage pregnancy, 67
Viemeister v. *White*, 227
Vietnamese Americans, 54
Vietnam War, 21
Violence. *See* Bullying; Family violence;
    School violence
Violence and the Family (American Psychological
    Association), 270
Violence Between Intimate Partners (Cardelli), 269
Volunteering, 142–146
    sample activities, 142–143
    tips for programs, 143–146
Voucher programs, 327–329
Vulnerability, of parents, 97–98

Wallace v. *Jaffree*, 234
War Nurseries, 19–20
War on Poverty, 21
Wasting America's Future (Sherman), 287
Way We Never Were, The (Coontz), 36, 46
We Are Family (video), 66
Websites
    on African Americans, 67
    on Asian Americans, 68
    education law and parental rights, 248
    on families of children with disabilities, 178
    on family issues, 320
    on family violence, 270–271
    on fathering, 318–319
    on Hispanics/Latinos, 68
    on Native Americans, 68
    on parenting, 89
    on parent involvement, 109–110
    on parent–teacher communication, 132
    on poverty and students, 288–289
    on school choice, 340–341
    on school violence and bullying, 359–360
West Virginia State Board of Education v.
    Barnette, 228
*What Children Need to Know When Parents Get
    Divorced* (Coleman), 39
Wisconsin v. *Yoder*, 230–231
Working mothers, 6, 21
    latchkey children and, 47
    role of father and, 298–299
Working with Parents (Curran), 175
Working with Parents (video), 109, 133, 155
Works Progress Administration (WPA), 19
World War II families, 19–20
Wrap-around school model, 355
Written communication, 120–121
    narrative reports, 121
    newsletters, 120–121
    school–home journal, 121
Wyandotte High School (Kansas City,
    Kansas), 332

Yale University Child Study Center, 200
You, Your Child, and "Special Education"
    (Cutler), 175
Young Children with Special Needs (Davis et
    al.), 175
You're Hurting Me Too (video), 270

Zoo School (Minneapolis, Minnesota), 335
Zorach v. *Clauson*, 228